Theories for Direct Social Work Practice

SECOND EDITION

JOSEPH WALSH
Virginia Commonwealth University

WADSWORTH
CENGAGE Learning™

Australia • Brazil • Japan • Korea • Mexico • Singapore • Spain • United Kingdom • United States

WADSWORTH
CENGAGE Learning

Theories for Direct Social Work Practice, Second Edition

Joseph Walsh, Virginia Commonwealth University

Publisher: Marcus Boggs

Acquisitions Editor: Seth Dobrin

Assistant Editor: Diane Mars

Editorial Assistant: Rachel McDonald

Media Editor: Andrew Keay

Senior Marketing Manager: Trent Whatcott

Marketing Assistant/Associate: Darlene Macanan

Marketing Communications Manager: Tami Strang

Content Project Management: Pre-PressPMG

Art Director: Caryl Gorska

Print Buyer: Paula Vang

Permissions Editor: Mardell Glinski Schultz

Production Service: Pre-Press PMG

Copy Editor: Janet Gokay

Cover Designer: Irene Morris

Compositor: Pre-Press PMG

For product information and technology assistance, contact us at **Cengage Learning Academic Resource Center, 1-800-423-0563**

For permission to use material from this text or product, submit all requests online at **www.cengage.com/permissions**. Further permissions questions can be e-mailed to **permissionrequest@cengage.com**.

Library of Congress Control Number: 2008943379

Student Edition:
ISBN-13: 978-0-495-60120-3
ISBN-10: 0-495-60120-9

Wadsworth Cengage Learning
10 Davis Drive
Belmont, CA 94002-3098
USA

Cengage Learning products are represented in Canada by Nelson Education, Ltd.

For your course and learning solutions, visit **academic.cengage.com**.

Purchase any of our products at your local college store or at our preferred online store **www.ichapters.com**.

Printed in the United States of America
3 4 5 6 7 13 12 11 10

For my older brother Mike
I always wanted to be like you. I couldn't make it in sports, but then you led me
into academia. Thanks for your good modeling!

Brief Contents

Contents

Preface

*T*heories for Direct Social Work Practice includes concise but comprehensive coverage of eleven major clinical practice theories that social workers commonly use in their assessment, planning, and intervention tasks with individuals, families, and groups. The purpose of this book is to provide Master of Social Work course instructors and students (as well as practicing professionals) with a single volume that incorporates the major theories and intervention strategies used in a variety of clinical settings. The *Theories* book is a resource that students will be able to use long after they finish school.

APPROPRIATE COURSES FOR USE

Most of the Master of Social Work programs operating in this country include a Clinical Practice concentration and require students to take at least one, and more often several, courses on topics related to direct practice. Textbooks that cover practice theories, most of which have been developed outside the social work profession, must be faithful to their sources, but also true to social work's values and its appreciation of the environmental context of client systems. A challenge to instructors is selecting a reasonable number of theories to include in those courses: not so many as to allow for little more than an overview, and not so few that students acquire a limited repertoire of practice skills. The scope of theories covered in *Theories for Direct Social Work Practice* is intended to provide a fairly broad view of the practice field while allowing students to learn the material in depth.

This book may be appropriate for foundation *and* second-year courses in MSW programs. It provides current, practical information about social work practice theories and techniques that can be used at both the beginning and advanced levels of practice. The *Theories* book may also be suitable for a variety of clinical electives (such as community mental health practice, crisis intervention, and health care social work) because the material is not setting specific. The relatively small number of included theories should appeal to instructors, as the entire book can be covered in one or two semesters.

COVERAGE AND ORGANIZATION OF THE BOOK

As noted earlier, *Theories for Direct Social Work Practice* covers eleven major theories; more specifically, it covers nine *theories* and two practice *models*. A model, described more thoroughly in Chapter 11, is a set of techniques for working with certain types of clients. I have included one model (interpersonal therapy) as an example of how a theory (or two) can be concretely adapted to a specific client population, and another (motivational interviewing) because of its tremendous popularity and influence in clinical practice today, as well as its applicability across many practice theories.

The book begins with two chapters that are intended to orient readers to the importance of theory-based clinical practice and the elements of theory that are central to the mission of the social work profession. These elements include values, attention to strengths, client empowerment, spirituality, and the ability to evaluate one's practice. The following 11 chapters are organized with a historical perspective, presenting the theories *roughly* in the order they were developed. Chapters 3–5 are devoted to psychodynamic theories, including ego psychology, object relations theory, and Bowen's family systems theory (which, while not analytic, derives from an analytic base). Chapters 6–9 are devoted to the cognitive-behavior theories, including behavior theory, cognitive theory, interpersonal theory (a model), and structural family theory (which I argue is consistent with cognitive-behavioral methods). Chapters 10–12 focus on several "newer" theories or approaches, including solution-focused therapy, motivational interviewing, and narrative theory. The final chapter of the book, devoted to crisis intervention, is integrative in that it draws on techniques from other chapters in the book for organizing a rapid response to clients in crisis.

Each chapter is organized according to the following outline:

- The focus of the theory
- Its major proponents (past and present)
- Its origins, including the social context
- Perspective on the nature of the individual
- Intrapersonal or interpersonal structural concepts (if applicable) and other major concepts
- Human development concepts (if applicable)
- Nature of problems
- Nature of change

- Intervention goals
- Assessment and intervention strategies (including the nature of the worker/ client relationship)
- How the client's spirituality can be addressed
- Attention to social justice issues
- Case illustrations
- Evidence of effectiveness and utility
- Criticisms
- Questions for discussion and class activities
- Appendices (including an outline of each theory)

The theory outlines that conclude each chapter may be particularly useful to instructors and students for systematically comparing the theories.

To bridge the human behavior in the social environment–clinical practice connection, each chapter focuses on how the theory addresses issues of human development within a context of human and cultural diversity. In addition to this organizing theme, there is an exploration of how the theories address issues of spirituality and social justice. A summary of the research on each theory's effectiveness and utility concludes each chapter.

Graduate students are almost always highly motivated to learn practice methods. They have made significant time and monetary investments in their professional development, and have only a few years to develop some mastery of the complex material. They are also involved in field placements in which they are expected to competently provide direct practice interventions. As a long-time instructor of such students I know that they are invariably excited at the prospect of acquiring a broad repertoire of practical intervention techniques. My hope is that this book will be a resource that satisfactorily meets their needs and that its format brings the material to life.

I am a long-time clinical practitioner who has always enjoyed reading about and experimenting with various approaches to direct intervention. I like to think that as I try to master theories and models, and select methods that seem to work well with different client populations, I am developing a personal approach to practice, but one that is nonetheless based in the traditions of our profession. My hope is that this book will help social work students to undertake the same developmental journey.

Changes to the Second Edition

This new edition of *Theories for Direct Social Work Practice* includes many updates. Most generally, the book contains updated references, new research reports on the effectiveness of each theory or model, more references to social work authors associated with the development of each theory or model, some new topics for discussion, and an improved narrative flow throughout the book. More specifically, the book includes a lengthier discussion of evidence-based practice and common curative factors across theories (Chapter 1), additional material on the strengths perspective, risk and resilience framework, and empowerment theory (Chapter 2), new sections on contemporary psychodynamic theory, attachment theory, and ethno-cultural transference (Chapters 3 and 4), material on the influence of the social worker's own family of origin when providing family therapy (Chapter 5), a discussion of ecobehaviorism and eco-maps (Chapter 6), a discussion of dialectical behavior therapy and the "structured session approach" of cognitive theory (Chapter 7), a major reorganization of the material on interpersonal therapy (Chapter 8), inclusion of material relative to family therapy issues with gay and lesbian clients (Chapter 9), an expanded section on the worker/client relationship (Chapter 10), a new case example on adolescent sex offenders in Chapter 12, and material on suicide assessment and trauma de-briefing in Chapter 13. The author is indebted to his students, colleagues, and the text reviewers for help in identifying these areas for enhancement.

AUTHOR'S ACKNOWLEDGMENTS

I want to thank Lisa Gebo at Brooks/Cole for encouraging me to undertake this project, and editors Shelley Gesicki and Monica Arvin for seeing it through. I also appreciate the work of project manager Karol Jurado, production coordinator Aaron Downey, and copy editor Anna Reynolds Trabucco for their assistance during production. I would like to thank the following individuals at Cengage Learning for their work on the second edition: Publisher Marcus Boggs, editors Seth Dobrin, Diane Mars and Allison Bowie, and editorial assistant Rachel McDonald. I also appreciate the work of project managers Angelique Amig and Mary Stone, and copy editor Janet Gokay for their assistance during the production of the second edition. The following professionals read drafts of the book and offered excellent suggestions for improvement: Gerald Matthews, Ferris State University; Gary Paquin, University of Cincinnati; Jody Gottlieb, Marshall University; Charles Joiner, Arkansas State University, Jonesboro; and Deborah Rougas, University of West Florida. In addition, I wish to acknowledge the following reviewers of the second edition: Shelly Cohen Konrad, University of New England; Daniel Coleman, Portland State University; and Gary L. Villareal, Western Kentucky University.

Closer to home, I owe a great debt of gratitude to Jacqui Corcoran, a colleague and friend who co-authored one chapter and helped me significantly with one other. Another colleague, Leticia Flores, reviewed a draft of one chapter for the second edition. My outstanding former students R. J. Arey, Erica Escalante, Linda Fowler, Valerie Holton, and Cynthia Lucas provided material for five of the case illustrations. Amy Waldbillig served patiently and reliably as my research assistant for the first edition. I am grateful to them all.

About the Author

Joseph Walsh is a professor of social work at Virginia Commonwealth University. He has been a direct service practitioner in the field of mental health for many years, first in a psychiatric hospital, and later in community mental health center settings. He has provided services to older adult and general outpatient populations, but has mostly specialized in services to persons with serious mental illness and their families. Since 1993 Joe has been at VCU, teaching courses in generalist practice, clinical practice, human behavior, research, and social theory. He continues to provide direct services to clients at the university's Center for Psychological Services, and has worked in area shelters, clubhouses, and group homes. He has published widely in social work and other human services journals on topics related to clinical practice, and is the author of seven other books, three of them published by Brooks/Cole. These include *Generalist Social Work Practice: Intervention Methods* (2008), *Clinical Case Management with Persons Having Mental Illness: A Relationship-Based Perspective* (2000), and *The Social Worker and Psychotropic Medication: Toward Effective Collaboration with Mental Health Clients, Families, and Providers* (third edition 2006; co-authored with Kia J. Bentley).

1

Thinking about Theory

I dwell in Possibility –
A fairer House than Prose –
More numerous of Windows –
Superior – for Doors –

Of Chambers as the Cedars –
Impregnable of Eye –
And for an Everlasting Roof
The Gambrels of the Sky –*

E ach August, as my second-year graduate students begin another year of study
in the classroom and field, I give an assignment to help them become oriented to their field agencies. "Ask the clinical staff in your agencies about the
theoretical basis of their practice. In other words, what theory or theories do
they use in working with clients?" I also ask my students to inquire whether
their agency has an "official" theory, or if staff work from a variety of perspectives. I am always curious to learn from students what is going on in the field,
and whether social workers who serve different types of clients (such as hospice
clients, persons with mental illnesses, children with behavioral problems, and
legal offenders) gravitate toward certain practice theories.

Students bring a variety of responses to the classroom. Some students are
placed in agencies that subscribe to a particular theory such as object relations
or dialectical behavior theory, but this is unusual. Most agencies support a range
of theoretical perspectives for their staff as long as practitioners can produce positive outcomes (and outputs—numbers of clients seen, intakes, terminations, and

---

contact hours). What concerns me, however, are the not-infrequent remarks that "They don't operate with any theory. They just do what they have to do to get results." I understand that clinical practitioners may not actively dwell on issues of theory after they leave graduate school, and that this may have no bearing on their effectiveness. I once worked at a mental health agency for four years with little clinical supervision, and would have been hard pressed to articulate how I worked with clients. What upsets me, though, is the occasional response from a student that his or her supervisor "has no use for academic types who waste time talking about abstractions rather than getting things done," or that theoreticians "have no idea what goes on in the real world."

It may be that universities include a fair number of faculty members who seem to function in a realm apart from the "real world." But I have always been a practitioner as well as a professor, and am convinced that all clinical social workers operate from a theoretical basis. They may not always be able to articulate their perspectives, but they have "automatically" learned, absorbed, and revised ideas about how to work with clients. They orient themselves with assumptions and presumed knowledge about human behavior, including beliefs about the nature of problems and the nature of change. From this they develop strategies for how to help various types of clients resolve their difficulties. So I worry about practitioners who actually feel hostile toward the idea of theory. It seems to me that a practitioner's methods of working with clients, if left unexamined, will become overly influenced by his or her moods, attitudes, and personal reactions. At the least, adherence to one or several theoretical perspectives encourages the practitioner to be systematic in approaching clients. A practitioner who is more reactive than proactive with clients may behave in ways that are less effective, less efficient, and perhaps even dangerous to the client's welfare.

Of course, the social work profession's recent push toward evidence-based practice does promote a process of systematically choosing interventions without adherence to a particular theoretical base. We will consider this issue more fully later in the chapter.

The purpose of this chapter is to introduce several definitions of a practice theory, describe its functions, consider elements common to all theories, and consider how practitioners may evaluate the worth of a practice theory. We will then be in a position to review the many practice theories described in the coming chapters.

WHAT IS A THEORY?

I have taught a doctoral seminar in social science theory in which I used a different opening exercise. I challenged students to, between the first and second class sessions, find one or several definitions of theory that were both comprehensible and not boring. This was always a daunting task, and students inevitably failed, at least with regard to the second criterion. I have always felt that the idea of theory in social work practice should be rather simple, but apparently I am wrong. It is often defined in ways that are alienating and overly abstract and impractical for social workers, who must be able to operationalize theory in practice. Perhaps it is no wonder that some practitioners become hostile to the idea. Listed below is a sample of definitions that my students have produced, from least to most complicated. A theory is:

- An attempt to explain something

- An orderly explanation of confusing experiences

- A systematic but speculative explanation for an event or behavior

- A set of propositions linked by a logical argument that is advanced to explain or predict an area of reality or type of phenomenon

- A set of variables or characteristics that have been hypothesized, presumed, or demonstrated to bear a relationship with one another

- A set of statements about relationships among variables that presents a systematic understanding of a behavior, event, or circumstance, and offers an explanation for why it occurred

Later in this chapter we will examine the components of social work practice theories. But with regard to the above definitions, it is helpful to recall that there are several types of theories (Bisman & Hardcastle, 1999). *Case theories* explain the behavior of one person (for example, an individual spouse abuser). Social workers routinely develop theories about the causes of the behavior of their individual clients. *Mid-range theories* explain a set of cases or events (for example, the behavior of unemployed alcoholic men who abuse their spouses). Clinical social workers also develop these theories as they develop expertise with certain types of clients over time. *Grand theories* attempt to explain all sets of events and cases (such as Freud's theory of psychosexual development or Piaget's theory of the stages of cognitive development). With regard to their explanatory power, grand theories have fallen out of favor in the social sciences in the past 25 years or so. The universal theories of human behavior developed by Freud, Erikson, Gilligan, Kohlberg, Piaget, Skinner, and others are still taught in schools of social work, and they are still useful to a practitioner's understanding of what accounts for human behavior over the life span. Still, there is a greater appreciation nowadays for human nature's infinite diversity and the idea that no principle of human development can be applied to everyone.

WHAT IS A PRACTICE THEORY?

Practice theories represent a subset of theories as defined above and are limited to perspectives on clinical intervention with individuals, families, and groups. One useful definition of a practice theory is a coherent set of ideas about human nature, including concepts of health, illness, normalcy, and deviance, which provide verifiable or established explanations for behavior and rationales for intervention (Frank & Frank, 1993). Many other definitions are available, but this one is suitable as a basis for reflecting on theories and their relevance to clinical intervention. There are, of course, many theories that may be used in clinical practice, and social workers should feel challenged to decide which one or several will serve their clients well. The value of utilizing any theory (with conviction) in clinical practice is that it provides the social worker with a framework to (a) predict and explain client behavior, (b) generalize among clients and problem areas, (c) bring order to intervention activities, and (d) identify knowledge gaps about clinical situations.

Despite its uses, there is also potential harm in rigid adherence to a practice theory. Because all theories necessarily simplify human behavior (they all select a limited number of variables from a seemingly infinite number that can possibly affect a client's life), they are reductionist and can become dehumanizing. Adherence to a theory may create self-fulfilling prophecies (the practitioner will tend to see what he or she is looking for) and blind the practitioner to alternative understandings of behavior.

How does a social worker choose a theory to use in practice? One's choice may be influenced by a variety of rational and irrational factors, including (Turner, 1996):

- The theory's research support
- A belief that the theory produces positive results (perhaps with the least expenditure of time and money)
- Its provision of useful intervention techniques
- Its consistency with the practitioner's values, knowledge, skills, and worldview
- Personal habit
- Its use by co-workers or supervisors

It was mentioned earlier that some clinical practitioners cannot articulate their theory base. They may be effective practitioners (what was once a deliberative process may have become automatic), but all practitioners benefit from thinking critically about their work.

The Relationship between Theory and Intervention Techniques

It is important to emphasize that theories and intervention techniques are not the same thing. Theories are abstract, and include concepts that suggest to the social worker which intervention strategies may be effective with clients. Intervention strategies are the concrete actions taken by social workers to help clients achieve their goals. There should be consistency, however, between a practitioner's working theory and interventions. For example, the theory of ego psychology purports that it is often useful for clients' goal achievement that they develop insight into their manner of addressing life challenges. One intervention strategy that derives from this concept is "person-situation reflection," a process by which the social worker asks questions to stimulate the client's self-reflection. In contrast,

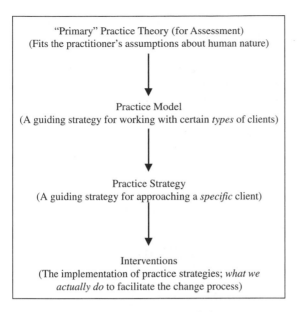

FIGURE 1.1 The Relationship of Theory to Practice

behavior theory suggests that client change occurs when the person's behavioral reinforcers are adjusted. An intervention strategy might include designing an environmental plan (in a classroom or household, for example) to reward (encourage) some behaviors and punish (extinguish) others.

The relationship between theory and intervention becomes complicated, however, because there is overlap among the intervention strategies suggested by different theories. That is, not every theoretical perspective includes a unique set of intervention strategies. This point is often confusing to students (so please read this paragraph twice). An ego psychologist and a behaviorist might both use relaxation skill training with a client, although their rationales for using this technique would be different. The ego psychologist may hope to enhance the client's ability to reflect, while the behaviorist may be helping the client manage task-related anxiety. The reader will readily see this overlap among intervention strategies throughout this book. How the same technique can have a different purpose will be discussed in each chapter.

The point above can be clarified in another way (see Figure 1.1). In my view, most social workers tend to adopt a primary theory for purposes of assessment. That is, if ego psychology, cognitive theory, or some other theory "fits" a practitioner's assumptions about human nature, he or she will tend to assess clients from that perspective. For example, if I believe that unconscious processes influence mental functioning, it will be hard for me to completely ignore that assumption even if I set out to practice from a behavioral perspective. My practice model (or guiding strategy for working with certain types of clients), however, may rely heavily on behavioral methods when I work with substance abuse clients. I may believe that these clients are not capable of effectively responding to "reflective" interventions due to their denial and need for strict limits, and thus I put my "preferred" theoretical perspective aside. My model may include the teaching of behavioral techniques for abstinence. I may hope to undertake reflective interventions with those clients following their termination of substance use, but I may not assume that this is necessary for their recovery. My practice strategy for an individual client will be based on my model but individualized as I take into account that person's particular personal and environmental characteristics. One client may be receptive to self-help interventions while another is not. Finally, my specific intervention will consist of activities undertaken by the client and myself to achieve his or her goals.

To summarize, the nature of our clients and agency settings may guide our practice strategies and interventions as much as our theoretical preferences, even though we can never put those preferences completely aside.

THE FUNCTIONS OF THEORY

Theory is important because it has a direct influence on how the social worker approaches clinical practice. It serves the functions of (Nugent, 1987; Polansky, 1986; Tzeng & Jackson, 1991):

- Simplifying complex phenomena, and focusing the practitioner's attention on thoughts, feelings, behaviors, and events in a client's life that are relevant to explore

- Helping the social worker to establish causal relationships and thus predict a client's future behavior

- Simplifying the task of selecting outcomes of intervention

- Guiding the social worker's choices about potentially effective intervention

- Protecting against irrational procedures, because the commitment to a body of thought "greater than oneself" bolsters professional self-discipline

- Mobilizing social energy, as the ability to effectively coordinate the work of several service providers depends on understanding one's own theoretical base and that of other providers

- Making the social worker's development of knowledge cumulative from one clinical situation to the next, and promoting some level of generalization among clients

One of my former students developed a useful illustration of the functions of theory with reference to music. She wrote that the elements of music theory include notes, keys, intervals, chords, and time. The musician uses this knowledge to select notes and put them together in chords with different rhythms to explore musical ideas including harmonies, dissonance, and improvisations. Yet, music theory is not the music. The theory is a way to describe the music and gain an understanding of how it can be performed. It explains why some combinations of notes and chords seem to work well while others do not, and gives the music student ideas for writing new songs. So, too, in social work, theories provide lenses through which the practitioner can describe and understand the world, facilitating insights into what might happen next and how the practitioner might enter into the client's world to assist in the process of positively changing that world.

CURATIVE FACTORS IN ALL PRACTICE THEORIES

Twelve theories or models are described in this book, and many others are used by clinical social workers. Why are there so many? Are they all fundamentally different? Several authors have attempted to identify the "curative" factors that are common to all effective interventions. Their starting point is the assumption that because there are so many practice theories, and all of them seem to be helpful with at least some clients, effectiveness may be less dependent on particular theories and techniques than the practitioner's personal qualities and approach to the clinical work. In one worldwide study of professional helpers, the following common characteristics of effective interventions were found (Frank & Frank, 1993):

- The client enters into an emotionally charged, confiding relationship with the practitioner, and perceives that the practitioner is competent and caring. This relationship is an antidote to alienation, enhances the client's morale, and promotes the client's determination to persist in the face of difficulties.

- The formal or otherwise "special" setting of the intervention helps the client feel safe and arouses the expectation of help.

- Interventions are based on an understandable (to the client) rationale and procedures that include an optimistic view of human nature. The practitioner's explanations are compatible with the client's view of the world and thus help the client make sense of his or her problems.

- Interventions require the active participation of the practitioner and client, both of whom believe them to be a valid means of restoring health or improving functioning. The client is given new opportunities for learning and successful experiences so as to enhance his or her sense of mastery.

These authors conclude that a practitioner's ability to be effective with clients is largely due to having confidence in whatever theories and interventions he or she uses. They also emphasize that a client's emotional arousal (experiencing a moderate amount of anxiety) is a prerequisite for all behavioral and attitudinal change.

The more recent work of Miller, Duncan, and Hubble (2005) is consistent with the above assertions about common elements of effective practice. These researchers conclude from their studies of clinical practice that the two elements of (a) the therapeutic alliance and (b) the practitioner's ongoing attention to the client's frame of reference about the intervention account for positive outcomes more than anything else. They write that client characteristics (the nature of problems, motivation, and participation) account for 40% of the clinical outcome, and the quality of the therapeutic alliance accounts for an additional 30%. The practitioner's guiding theory or model accounts for 15%, and the remaining 15%

is a placebo effect. These researchers state that the presence of shared goals, a consensus on methods used, and the emotional bond are most predictive of positive clinical outcomes. As a part of this process the practitioner should regularly solicit feedback and input from the client about the intervention process. Further, the practitioner's allegiance to *some* model of practice, but not any *particular* model, is associated with positive outcomes. This last finding supports the social worker's use of a theoretical perspective or intervention model toward which he or she feels comfortable and committed.

SELECTING THEORIES FOR PRACTICE

If a particular theory does not determine clinical outcomes, how do social workers—or, how should social workers—select theories for use in their practices? There is no single answer to this question, no uniformly accepted criteria to apply. I do not propose a particular set of criteria for theory selection or evaluation in this book, because any criteria are biased toward the assumptions inherent in some theories and not others. Some social workers feel that a theory needs only to be useful for organizing their work with clients, while others feel that it should provide intervention strategies with empirically demonstrated effectiveness for a range of clients. It is widely accepted, however, that a "good theory" for practice should be (Goldstein, 1990; Payne, 2005; Polansky, 1986; Witkin & Gottschalk, 1988):

- Coherent (internally consistent)
- Useful with the practitioner's current clients
- Comprehensive (able to direct practice activities across a range of clients)
- Parsimonious (relatively uncomplicated for use)
- Testable, and able to withstand scrutiny (there are a variety of methods for doing this)

Another important criterion for social workers is that the theories they use should facilitate the pursuit of social justice activities with clients. This issue will be discussed in detail in Chapter 2.

Eclecticism: Pro and Con

Some social workers use one theory to guide their practice. Others rely on several theories, finding through experience that one is not sufficient to help all clients they encounter. Still other social workers describe themselves as "eclectic," which means that they draw on a variety of theories, depending on the client's presenting situation. This idea is somewhat controversial. Although flexibility is a positive aspect of one's practice, it may be difficult to achieve real mastery in the use of more than three or four theories (Turner, 1996). Further, some theories contain assumptions that are incompatible with one other (object relations and narrative theory, for example).

Payne (2005) has summarized arguments for and against eclecticism in theory selection. Its positive aspects are that clients stand to benefit from a range of ideas about managing a clinical issue; effectiveness is not directly related to theory selection; several theories may contain common elements; and some theories do not apply to all situations. The negative aspects of eclecticism are that a practitioner who attempts to use many theories may lack mastery of any of them. The process may result in the practitioner's loss of a common core of practice and his or her clients may suffer.

The Effect of Agency Culture on Theory Selection

All practitioners live in professional "cultures" represented by their schools, agencies, and professional associations. Following graduation from a professional program and employment in an agency, a social worker's ideas about theory and practice are likely to change to resemble those of immediate colleagues. Research in the field of health administration has shown that the intervention behavior of professionals is significantly accounted for by their conformity to prevailing practices in their employing agencies (Westert & Groenewegen, 1999). That is, they tend to act in ways that gain or maintain positive peer reinforcement. For example, at one point in my career I went from being a cognitive practitioner to an object relations devotee after taking a new job.

In some settings the practitioner may be encouraged to seek new knowledge about theory and practice, but in others he or she will lack incentives to look beyond the status quo. Agency characteristics that have an effect on a social worker's choices about theory include the supervisor's preferences, exposure to some theories but not others, the level of administrative support for professional development, the extent to which risk-taking by clinical staff is encouraged, and the agency's emphasis on program evaluation and client outcome research.

Faced with the choices of many possible perspectives, and being subject to agency cultural factors, social workers should ideally rely on critical thinking skills to guide their use of theory.

CRITICAL THINKING

Critical thinking can be defined as thinking that is purposeful, reasonable, goal-directed, and evaluative of its outcomes (Gambrill, 2006). The ability to engage in critical thinking is essential for clinical social workers, because the use of theory and intervention strategies includes a reliance on many assertions that cannot be "proven" to be true or false. A practitioner must have confidence in the validity of his or her theories, because hard facts are difficult to come by in social work practice.

Critical thinking qualities are important for clinical social workers to develop because they are immersed in unstructured problem areas every day in which goals, the relevance of information, and the effects of decisions they make are unclear. The social worker must reflect on the assumptions that underlie a theory and be open to contemplating alternative ways of thinking and working. He or she must be flexible, persistent when solutions are not obvious, and willing to self-correct when conclusions run contrary to usual practice. Other characteristics of the critical thinker include (Rogers & McDonald, 1993; Smith, 1990):

- A willingness to question basic assumptions

- Making an effort to work toward (an elusive) objectivity (looks for opposing as well as supporting evidence for procedures)

- An ability to imagine and explore alternatives

- An understanding of the importance of social and cultural contexts to human behavior

- An ability to distinguish between questions of fact and questions of value (facts can be resolved with testing; values are based on beliefs and cannot be tested)

- Cautiousness when inferring causality or making generalizations

Critical thinking may seem self-evidently beneficial, but it has costs as well. Its benefits include a means of clarifying the assumptions underlying one's work, increased accuracy in decision making, shared understanding among practitioners, colleagues, and clients, and guidance in clarifying the influences of one's values on practice. Its costs are that it takes time (rarely a resource in the practice world) and effort, requires a tolerance for doubt, and may negatively affect one's self-worth when acknowledging mistakes. Critical thinking requires courage, too, as it may result in disagreements with peers and agency practice guidelines.

The principles of critical thinking suggest that a clinical social worker should always be open to examining his or her use of theory and intervention strategies. If a social worker feels somewhat limited by agency culture from engaging in this process, he or she may use other resources such as books and research-based journals (for self-development), external supervision, informal support systems with practitioners from other agencies, contact with former professors, and involvement with professional associations.

SOCIAL WORK RESEARCH ON THEORY AND PRACTICE EVALUATION

We now consider more formally what is known about the effectiveness of social work practice. These findings do not always directly pertain to theory but to intervention methods that may not be specific to one theory. In each chapter of this book we will review the efforts of clinical practitioners and researchers to demonstrate the effectiveness of particular theoretical perspectives.

The methods by which clinical social work interventions, as well as those offered by other professionals, are tested for effectiveness have evolved during the past 50 years (Conte, 1997). During the 1950s and 1960s, non-specific theories and strategies were applied to heterogeneous client populations and examined for evidence of impact. Case studies were common in the professional literature. Though informative, they were rarely based on structured research designs.

So what is known about effective clinical social work? Thirty years ago, two literature reviews by Fischer (1973, 1976) created a stir within the profession by concluding that there was no evidence for the effectiveness of casework. A later analysis of 44 studies concluded that effectiveness was difficult to determine because of a lack of rigor in research methods (Reid & Hanrahan, 1982). The researchers recommended that social workers increase the structure of their interventions (that is, better specify the components and steps) so that effectiveness studies could be better developed.

Thomlinson (1984) made a contribution to this issue with a broad review of the social work literature. He did not set out to determine whether any general intervention strategies were effective, but to identify particular components of effective practice. He found that effective social workers were able to adjust their theories and practice to fit with the client's presenting problem, properly orient the client to intervention, specify the purposes of selected interventions, and attend to time limits (not necessarily short term).

Corcoran and Videka-Sherman (1992) noted that in outpatient mental health settings effective social workers tended to provide active interventions focused on exploration, modeling, advice, reinforcement, and task assignments. They concluded that adherence to a particular theory did not seem to be related to effectiveness; what mattered was the social worker's intervention, not the theory behind the action. They admitted that much remained to be learned about practice effectiveness and called for more studies using comparison groups, unbiased samples, and long-term clients.

Another meta-analysis of outcome research in social work included 45 studies conducted between 1990 and 1994 (Gorey, Thyer, & Pawluck, 1998). The researchers attempted to compare the effectiveness of practice by the social workers' theoretical orientation. The researchers found no overall differences in outcomes by theoretical orientation, which were primarily cognitive/behavioral but also included psychosocial, psychoanalytic, problem-solving, task-centered, systems, and radical-structural approaches. They did find, however (rather obviously), that theoretical frameworks focusing on individual client change were most effective at changing client behaviors, and that systems and structural frameworks were most effective at changing target systems beyond the individual client. The authors echoed sentiments voiced by many practice researchers— that greater specificity in social workers' intervention procedures was needed to facilitate useful future studies of outcome effectiveness.

The field of psychology has specified rigorous practice effectiveness criteria. A task force of the American Psychological Association (APA) put forth a list of recommendations for evaluating clinical practice (Crits-Cristoph, 1998). The goal of this project was not to endorse certain interventions, but to facilitate the education of practitioners by identifying interventions with empirical support. The criteria for "well-established" treatments include: (a) at least two group comparison experiments that demonstrate efficacy in terms of superiority to pill, placebo, or other treatment, or that are experimentally equivalent to another established treatment; or (b) a series of at least nine single-subject experiments demonstrating efficacy in comparison with a pill, placebo, or other treatment. Additional criteria are (c) the use of treatment manuals (structured protocols that direct the practitioner's actions and the duration of intervention) to maximize specificity; (d) clearly described sample characteristics; and (e) the demonstration of effects by at least two different investigators.

The APA criteria for determining *best practices* include two experiments that show an intervention to be more effective than waiting-list control group outcomes, one or more experiments that meet all of the above criteria except for that of replication, or at least three single-subject designs using manuals and clear sampling procedures. Somewhat less rigorously, an intervention is considered *probably efficacious* when there is only one study meeting the criteria for "well-established"; all investigations have been conducted by one researcher or team; or the only comparisons have been to no-treatment control groups (this requires two studies by independent investigators).

Evidence-Based Practice

In the past decade it has become imperative for clinical social workers to demonstrate their practice effectiveness. This movement toward *evidence-based practice* (EBP) is related to social work's increased emphasis on accountability to clients and third-party payers and its desire to further the knowledge base of the profession. EBP means that treatment outcome studies justify a certain treatment approach for a particular disorder (Cournoyer & Powers, 2003; Roberts & Yeager, 2004). Thyer and Wodarski (2007) feel so strongly about this issue that they advocate for the Code of Ethics to emphasize social workers' responsibility to use only empirically validated interventions.

In social work, evidence-based practice refers to the process of using a variety of databases to guide interventions that foster client change (Vandiver, 2002). Put simply, the social worker is faced with the question of "What evidence do you have that your proposed intervention will be effective with your client?" There are three approaches to operationalizing EBP in practice, including (in order of preference) the social worker's use of formal practice guidelines, expert consensus guidelines, and, when appropriate guidelines are not available for certain client problems, a self-directed approach. Practice guidelines have the purpose of providing social workers with organized knowledge based on some degree of evidence as to its effectiveness in reaching relevant outcomes (Rosen & Proctor, 2002).

The following hierarchical model in EBP includes six "levels" of knowledge (Rosenthal, 2004):

- Systematic reviews or meta-analyses (summaries and critiques of all available research on a topic) of well-designed controlled studies
- Well-designed individual experimental studies

- Well-defined quasi-experimental studies
- Well-designed non-experimental studies
- Series of case reports or expert committee reports with critical appraisal
- Opinions of respected authorities based on clinical experiences

For social workers intent on using EBP, the steps involved in using practice guidelines include assessment, diagnosis, and the selection of diagnostic-specific practice guidelines for goal development, intervention planning, outcome measure establishment, and evaluation.

All social workers want to use interventions that have been shown to be effective, but efforts to identify evidence-based practice models have been controversial for a number of reasons (Beutler & Baker, 1998; Chambless, 1998; Rosenthal, 2004). Most research methodologies have not been able to examine relationship factors in clinical intervention, and these are considered fundamental in many theories (Miller, Duncan, & Hubble, 2005). Likewise, personal characteristics of social workers are often overlooked, such as their experience with particular problem areas and overall competence in carrying out particular interventions. With regard to research methods there is a bias toward cognitive and behavioral strategies. Chambless (1998) states that whereas a majority of the demonstrably effective interventions to date are cognitive or behavioral, this is due in part to an under-representation of other interventions in research studies, rather than an inherent superiority of the featured approaches. Qualitative researchers are distrustful of efforts to generalize intervention outcomes because of the complexities involved in every instance of clinical intervention (O'Connor, 2002).

Further, the use of intervention manuals (written directives used in many research studies) may limit the natural responsiveness of practitioners to clinical situations. In fact, it is not always clear how closely practitioners follow these procedures, as they may respond differentially to challenges that emerge in the course of intervention. In a related criticism, it is not always practical to replicate research protocols in agency environments. Perhaps most importantly, diagnostic categories are rarely precise in capturing the essence of a clinical condition. Evidence-based practice has been adapted from the medical model of care, but in the social sciences practitioners must be very cautious in assuming that two clients are "alike," even if they share the same diagnosis. Variables such as a client's social support, socioeconomic status, distress level, motivation, and intelligence may be more important predictors of response than diagnosis.

So what is the relationship between evidence-based and theory-based practice? Some proponents of EBP argue that theory is superfluous, as the social worker needs to be concerned only with what interventions are most likely to provide desired outcomes. Others emphasize that EBP is reductionistic, simplifying the personality of the client, nature of diagnosis, skill level of the practitioner, the range of interventions that a practitioner actually provides, and the role of theoretical orientation in determining outcomes (Miller, Duncan, & Hubble, 2005). Issues related to incorporating EBP into mental health practice (Institute for the Advancement of Social Work Research, 2008) do point to its limitations, and to the importance of theory:

- Social workers must be skilled in assessment and diagnosis so the interventions they select appropriately match the identified problem. (Assessment is always theory-based.)

- EBP must be adapted and personalized for clients based on their culture, interests, and circumstances. (Clients are not merely "diagnoses.")

- The perspectives of both consumers and professionals must be taken into account in developing research agendas so that real-world issues of resources, service access, and consumer and organizational culture are all considered.

- The prevalence of co-occurring disorders, and the array of settings in which intervention may be provided, indicate that EBP must take these multiple disorders and setting into account. (EBP does not address co-occurring disorders as much as "single" disorders, and theory is needed to sort out the many issues that these kinds of clients face.)

- Knowledge of interventions must be broader than being able to implement specific evidence-based interventions. (This "knowledge" must be based at least in part on practitioner judgment, which may be formed by adherence to a theoretical orientation).

Ways to Improve Theory and Practice Research

With the above factors in mind, there are practical ways for clinical social workers to participate in research regarding their practice effectiveness. Most of these opportunities derive from a principle of collaboration between researchers and clinical social workers (Bloom, Fischer, & Orme, 1995). Such strategies might include developing university/agency relationships in which social workers are given control of the intervention being provided and the researcher functions as the design expert. Further, disentangling the "practitioner versus intervention strategy" conundrum may be achieved by assessing the personal characteristics of the social worker as well as what that person does. Many social workers have had the experience of being told, "You have the perfect personality to work with X type of client!" or "Perhaps you shouldn't work with X type of client, given your temperament." We all have gifts and limitations that we bring to our practice. Monitoring the social worker/client relationship might be a productive way to take this variable into account. Horvath's (1994) Working Alliance Inventory provides one example of doing so. The client and the social worker complete this 36-item instrument at various intervals to provide comparison data on their perceptions of bonding, goal orientation, and task focus. Finally, in evaluation research, strategy (a general approach to a type of client) may be a more relevant variable to study than theory or specific intervention technique (Beutler & Baker, 1998). Characteristics dictating a practitioner's therapeutic strategy include such factors as the client's set of strengths and limitations, levels of social support, and problem severity. These variables might be important to include in research studies when client homogeneity is sought.

Regarding self-directed practice, evaluating one's own interventions through the application of single-system or pre-experimental designs can be implemented in most agency settings. All that is required is a social worker with a background in basic research methods as taught in all undergraduate and graduate programs. Any theoretical perspective, strategy, or intervention can be evaluated through these methods. Doing so can help the social worker go a long way toward establishing the quality of his or her intervention practice with clients, supervisors, and administrators.

SUMMARY

The purposes of this chapter have been to define theory, discuss its relevance to social work practice, consider how social workers select theories for practice, and review current thinking in the profession about theory and practice evaluation. We close with some thoughts about who is best suited to develop theory for social work practice.

Practice-relevant theory can best be developed and advanced by agency social workers, especially those directly engaged with clients (Polansky, 1986). Direct service workers are immersed in the raw material of the profession every day. Trying to bring about change always prods one to question and improve ideas and practices that do not seem adequate to meet clinical challenges. Once the social worker achieves a certain level of expertise, then the main source of useful new ideas becomes one's clientele. Universities are better equipped repositories of knowledge in professions like social work than its creators. Partnerships between practitioners and researchers for testing theory in the field can be a constructive means of developing knowledge for clinical social workers who are committed to theory and the advance of its applications.

Our "thinking about theory" in a general sense is not quite complete. In the next chapter we will consider several issues that are specifically important to theory as used by social workers, distinctly from members of other professions.

TOPICS FOR DISCUSSION

1. Think of a time in your own life that a friend or other acquaintance has helped you with a personal problem. What was it about that person's approach that was helpful to you (validation, confrontation, active listening, concrete advice, or something else)? What does that tell you about your own problem-solving process? Compare what is helpful to you with what is helpful to your classmates.

2. Social workers tend to emphasize the importance of the worker/client relationship in clinical practice, but not all practice theories give this factor equal

emphasis. What elements of a helping relationship do you think are universally important?

3.   Social workers often work in agency settings that are quite modest, or even drab. Some practitioners do not have offices at all, but work out of cubicles or even their cars. Given this, what do you think about the assertion in this chapter that the nature of the intervention "setting" is a curative factor for clients?

4.   Should clinical intervention be evaluated beyond asking clients to state whether they achieved their goals, and to what degree? Can intervention outcomes ever be generalized across clients and client populations?

5.   Material in this chapter suggests that not all social workers engage in critical thinking. Assuming that critical thinking is a good thing to do, how can it be supported in agencies, both formally and informally?

IDEA FOR CLASS ACTIVITY

As described on the first page of this chapter, ask a variety of clinical staff in your field agencies about the theoretical basis of their practice. What theory or theories do they use in working with clients? Why? Has it changed over time? Does the agency have an "official" theory, or do the staff work from a variety of perspectives?

2

A Social Work Perspective on Clinical Theory and Practice

> Hope is the thing with feathers
> That perches on the soul –
> And sings the tune without the words –
> And never stops – at all –
> And sweetest – in the Gale – is heard –
> And sore must be the storm –
> That could abash the little Bird
> That kept so many warm –*

Most of the practice theories described in this book have been developed outside of the social work profession. They are used as much by practitioners from other professions as they are by social workers. The *manner* in which these theories are used may be somewhat different among professional groups, however, depending on the client population served, the practice setting, and, most important, the *value perspective* of the profession. In fact, it is sometimes said that professions are distinguished more by their value bases than by any other defining characteristics (Dolgoff, Loewenberg, & Harrington, 2005).

This is a book for social workers, of course, so it is important for us to consider how the material presented in the upcoming chapters is, or should be, used by social workers in ways that are true to their professional mission and values. In this chapter we will review several defining characteristics of the social work

---

* Reprinted by permission of the publishers and the Trustees of Amherst College from *The Poems of Emily Dickinson*, Thomas H. Johnson, ed., Cambridge, Mass.: The Belknap Press of Harvard University Press, Copyright © 1951, 1955, 1979, 1983 by the President and Fellows of Harvard College.

profession, including its value base, respect for multiculturalism, emphasis on *strengths* and *empowerment* perspectives, attention to *risk and resilience* mechanisms in client's lives, and attention to the *spiritual concerns* of clients. Throughout the book each theory will be considered (and, in part, evaluated) for the ways in which it promotes or detracts from these professional concerns.

DEFINING CLINICAL SOCIAL WORK PRACTICE

Clinical social work practice can be defined in a variety of ways. The definition presented here, developed by the author and other faculty from Virginia Commonwealth University's School of Social Work, represents an effort to capture the profession's broad scope. Clinical social work practice is the application of social work *theory* and *methods* to the *resolution* and *prevention* of psychosocial problems experienced by individuals, families, and groups. These problems may include challenges, disabilities, or impairments, including mental, emotional, and behavioral disorders. Clinical practice is grounded in the *values* of the social work profession and, as such, promotes social and economic justice by *empowering* clients who experience oppression or vulnerability to problem situations. Clinical practice is based on an application of human development theories within a psychosocial context and is focused on issues of human diversity and multiculturalism. Clinical social workers help clients to enact psychological and interpersonal change, increase their access to social and economic resources, and maintain their achieved capacities and strengths. Assessment always incorporates the impact of social and political systems on client functioning. Interventions may include therapeutic, supportive, educational, and advocacy activities.

With this working definition we can now consider the concepts of values, strengths, risk and resilience, multiculturalism, and empowerment more fully.

THE VALUE BASE OF SOCIAL WORK PRACTICE

All professions espouse distinct value bases that are intended to define their purposes and guide the actions of their members. *Values* are principles concerning what is right and *good*, while *ethics* are principles concerning what is right and *correct*, or rules of conduct to which social workers should adhere in order to uphold their values (Dolgoff, Loewenberg, & Harrington, 2005).

People may adhere to several sets of values in their different life roles, which may be generally consistent with each other, or sometimes in conflict. *Personal* values reflect our beliefs and preferences about what is right and good for people. *Societal* values reflect a consensus among members of a group about what is right and good that has been reached through negotiation, often politically. *Professional* values specifically guide the work of a person in his or her professional life. Professional ethics are the obligations of social workers in relationships with other persons encountered in the course of their work, including clients, other professionals, and the general public. Social work's values and ethics are intended to help practitioners recognize the morally correct way to practice, and to decide how to act correctly in specific professional situations. Social workers routinely experience ethical dilemmas—for example, around issues of confidentiality and participating in mandated interventions.

The National Association of Social Workers (NASW) Code of Ethics (1996) is "intended to serve as a guide to the everyday professional conduct of social workers." The primary mission of the social work profession, according to the Code, is "to enhance the human well-being and help meet the basic human needs of all people, with particular attention to the needs and empowerment of those who are vulnerable, oppressed, and living in poverty" (p. 1). The six core values of the profession relate to *service, social justice, dignity and worth of the person,* the *importance of human relationships, integrity,* and *competence.* The Code of Ethics further states that social workers should challenge social injustice; that they should "pursue social change, particularly with and on behalf of vulnerable and oppressed individuals and groups of people" (p. 6). This can be done through social change activities, particularly with vulnerable and oppressed individuals and groups, around such issues as poverty, unemployment, and discrimination. Social workers can help their clients develop the external resources required for a fulfilling life. They should strive to ensure clients' access to needed information, services, and resources, equality of opportunity, and meaningful participation in decision making.

The social work profession's first great advocate for social justice activities among direct service providers was Bertha Reynolds (1885–1978), one of the pioneers of the profession (Reynolds, 1963). While a direct practitioner, she developed a conviction that social workers should advocate for the working class and other oppressed groups which went beyond the young profession's concern with individuals and families. She suffered for her convictions, losing a prestigious job at Smith College in 1938 when she advocated for social work unionization, political activity, and more overt concern with civil rights. Her perspective is now commonplace in the profession.

The major implication of the social worker's obligation to uphold professional values with regard to theory selection is that the practitioner's activities should promote the mission of the profession. We will refer to these core values in that context throughout the book.

STRENGTHS-ORIENTED CLINICAL PRACTICE

Strengths-oriented practice implies that social workers should assess all clients in light of their capacities, talents, competencies, possibilities, visions, values, and hopes (Saleebey, 2002). This perspective emphasizes human resilience, or the skills, abilities, knowledge, and insight that people accumulate over time as they struggle to surmount adversity and meet life challenges. It refers to the ability of clients to persist in spite of their difficulties.

Dennis Saleebey (2002), the profession's foremost writer on this topic, asserts that social workers (and other helping professionals) have been historically guided by a deficits perspective, one that exists in opposition to humanistic values. This "problem orientation" encourages individual rather than ecological accounts of psychosocial functioning, which is contrary to social work's person-in-environment perspective. Saleebey adds that several negative assumptions need to be adjusted toward the development of a more "balanced" strengths perspective, including notions that:

- The person is the problem (rather than person-in-environment interactions).
- There are fixed, inevitable, critical, and universal stages of development.
- Childhood trauma invariably leads to adult psychopathology.
- There are social conditions, interpersonal relationships, and institutional relationships so toxic that they invariably lead to problems in functioning for people, families, groups, and communities.
- The disease model and its linear view of causes and solution should be followed.

In this writer's view, Saleebey is overly harsh in his statements about how clinical social work practitioners approach their clients. Further, social work's (and other professions') problem-driven focus is perpetuated in part by managed care and insurance company reimbursement criteria. Still, his work is constructive in offering positive concepts for social workers to use that will more adequately identify client strengths. The major principles of strengths practice include the following:

- All people have strengths.
- Problems can be a source of challenge and opportunity.
- Practitioners can never know the "upper levels" of clients' growth potentials.
- There should be greater collaboration between practitioners and clients, to replace the traditional worker/client hierarchy.
- Every environment includes resources (many of them informal) that can be mobilized to help clients change.

By the time some clients seek help from a social worker, the problem may have preoccupied them to an extent that they have lost sight of their resources. When working from the strengths perspective, the social worker, regardless of theoretical orientation, develops an awareness of strengths and openly conveys them to clients. For example, if a client seems to have a solid social support system, he or she needs to be told this is a strength critical to adjustment. One could take this intervention a step further and ask about the resources clients have used to develop these strengths. The client could be asked, "What would your husband say makes you a good partner?" or "Why do your friends like to be around you?"

The social worker must further be alert to the strengths clients bring to other contexts, such as work settings, their hobbies, and pastimes. The social worker can also ask directly about strengths: "What do you do well?" "What are your best qualities?" "What would other people say you do well, or that is good in you?"

When clients talk about the challenges and problems they face, their full range of thoughts and feelings need to be validated. Only then should they be asked about the resilient qualities they may possess. The social worker can inquire about the aspects of the client's life that are still intact despite the problem, and explore for resources that were drawn upon in these areas. Questions can further center on personal or family qualities or strengths that have developed as a result of dealing with the presenting problem. A recent research review found that when people are able to find benefits after a major stressor, they experience less depression and a greater sense of well-being (Helgeson, Reynolds, & Tomich, 2006). In summary, strengths-oriented social work practice mandates that social workers give attention to the protective influences in a client's life, and any practice theory can accommodate this perspective.

A RISK AND RESILIENCE FRAMEWORK FOR CLINICAL PRACTICE

The *risk and resilience* framework provides a basis for social workers to identify and bolster client strengths and reduce risk influences. This framework, first developed in other disciplines (such as psychology and education), considers the balance of risk and protective mechanisms that interact to determine a client's ability to function adaptively despite stressful life events (Fraser, 2004). *Risks* can be understood as hazards in the individual or the environment that increase the likelihood of a problem occurring. The presence of a risk influence does not guarantee a negative developmental outcome, but it increases the odds of one occurring. *Protective* influences involve the personal, social, and institutional resources that foster competence and promote successful development. They decrease the likelihood of engaging in problem behavior and increase the likelihood of a client's rebounding from trauma and stress (Dekovic, 1999). *Resilience* refers to the absence of significant developmental delays or serious learning and behavior problems, and the mastery of developmental tasks that are appropriate for a person's age and culture, in spite of exposure to adversity (Werner & Altman, 2000).

Social work researchers have expanded the risk and resilience framework, organizing it into a "risk and resilience biopsychosocial framework" (Fraser, 1997). Relevant influences are considered with regard to the client's biological constitution, psychological status, and social environment. This framework fits well with social work's emphasis on empowerment and the strengths-based perspective. The strengths perspective underlies the concepts of protective influences and resilience, in that people are not only able to survive and endure but can also triumph over difficult life circumstances.

In the risk and resilience conceptualization, the presence of a certain risk or protective influence may increase the likelihood of other risk and protective influences. For example, an aversive parenting style with poor monitoring increases the risk of children socializing with deviant peers (Smokowski, Mann, Reynolds, & Fraser, 2004). If parents are overwhelmed by environmental stresses, such as unemployment, a lack of transportation and medical care, or living in an unsafe neighborhood, their ability to provide consistent warmth and nurturing may be compromised. This phenomenon also operates for protective influences. Adolescents whose parents provide emotional support and structure the environment with consistent rules and monitoring tend to associate with peers who share similar family backgrounds. Supportive parenting, in turn, affects the characteristics of the child in that he or she learns to regulate emotions and develop cognitive and social competence. Systems interactions also play themselves out from the perspective of a child's characteristics. If a child has resilient qualities, such as social skills, effective coping strategies, intelligence, and self-esteem, he or she is more likely to attract quality caregiving. Another example of this process is seen in the attachment patterns formed with early caregivers in infancy. The attachment pattern persists into other relationships—for example, with preschool teachers.

Although the exact nature of how risk and protective mechanisms work together is unknown, different mechanisms are hypothesized. Two primary models are the additive and the interactive models (Pollard, Hawkins, & Arthur, 1999). In an *additive* model, protective influences exert a positive effect to counterbalance the negative influences of risk. In an *interactive* model, protective influences enact a buffering function against risk. At times, risk and protective mechanisms are the converse of each other. For instance, at the individual level, difficult temperament is a risk influence and easy temperament is a protective influence for problems in social functioning. Even though it is not easy to use knowledge of risk and protective mechanisms with specificity in assessment and intervention, the social work practitioner's attention to these balancing factors can sustain an orientation to strengths and possibilities for client change.

Some instruments have been developed to assist in the measurement of risk, one of which is the *North Carolina Assessment of Risk* scale for juvenile offenders (Schwalbe, Fraser, & Day, 2004). While precise mechanisms of action are difficult to specify, data has begun to accumulate that four or more risk influences may overwhelm an individual and represent a threat to adaptation (Epps & Jackson, 2000). Further, risk seems to have a stronger relationship to problem behavior than does protection (Dekovic, 1999). While some have found that the more risks, the worse the outcome (Appleyard, Egeland, van Dulmen, & Sroufe, 2005), others have argued that risk does not proceed in a linear, additive fashion (Greenberg, Speltz, DeKlyen, & Jones, 2001). Neither are all risk factors equal in weight. The association between risk and protection and outcomes are complex and involve changing conditions across stages of human development (Walsh, 2008).

MULTICULTURALISM

A hallmark of the social work profession is its commitment to working with diverse, underserved, and marginalized populations. In the early 1900s both Mary Richmond and Jane Addams developed principles for working with impoverished, inner-city populations, although with different methods (Specht & Courtney,

1994). It was only in the 1960s and 1970s, however, that the social work literature featured an increase in the numbers of articles about practice with clients from minority cultures (Harper & Lantz, 2007). This literature was prompted by two social developments. Population changes in the United States indicated that people of color, including African Americans, Native Americans, Latinos, and Asians and Pacific Islanders, would eventually comprise a larger segment of the population than Caucasian Americans. Social globalism also brought attention to the international nature of professional practice. Many of these articles reflected the profession's growing awareness that some traditional practice methods were not helpful for minority clients, and might in fact be damaging to them.

Multiculturalism, or a social worker's ability to understand and work from the perspective of a variety of client cultures, represents an advance from the more generic "self-awareness" that has always been a feature of the profession. The development of culturally competent perspectives is based on the principle that minority clients (including persons of different racial and ethnic groups, gender, age, immigrant status, geographic background, sexual orientation, and disability) have their own ways of seeking and receiving assistance, and these should be respected (Fong & Furuto, 2001).

Cultural competence demands an approach to client in which "assumptions are few and are held only until the truth becomes known" (Dorfman, 1996, p. 33). In Lee's (2002) model of social work education, two dimensions of competence, including cultural knowledge and cultural sensitivity, are the primary factors involved in providing effective transcultural intervention. *Cultural knowledge* refers to the practitioner's ability to acquire specific knowledge about his or her clients' cultural background, racial experiences, historical experiences, values, spiritual beliefs, world view beliefs, resources, customs, educational experiences, communication patterns, thinking patterns, coping practices, and previous help-seeking experiences. *Cultural sensitivity* refers to a social worker's attitudes and values about cross-cultural direct service practice.

Members of some cultures experience barriers to treatment due to providers' "lack of awareness of cultural issues, bias, or inability to speak the client's language, and the client's fear and mistrust of treatment" (U.S. Department of Health & Human Services, 2001). In addition, although there has been a movement in the helping professions toward evidence-based practice, there is a shortage of research on treatment outcome for mental disorders for people from different ethnic groups. Few models of culturally sensitive services have been tested, so we know little about the key ingredients needed and their effect on treatment outcome for ethnic minorities.

Social workers must realize that it is impossible to "know" another culture. A social worker's competent responses to transcultural helping situations, however, include high levels of cultural knowledge and sensitivity. In addition to acquiring considerable culture-specific knowledge about minority culture clients, the competent practitioner must also demonstrate openness, empathy, and care with minority cultural clients, and be able to maintain an informed and empathic response to them. When a helping professional has developed a competent response to the transcultural helping situation, he or she can make sound clinical judgments from an informed point of view, be open and sensitive in the cross-cultural helping situation, not be bounded by conceptual knowledge, connect with clients at an individual empathic level, and maintain awareness of his or her own personal experiences which might distort judgment.

We now turn to a discussion of client empowerment in social work practice, a process by which clients can be helped to utilize their existing strengths toward the achievement of their goals.

CLIENT EMPOWERMENT

In keeping with the profession's values and mission, social work practitioners at all levels desire to enhance the capacity, or *power*, of clients to address their life concerns. Power can be understood as including (Lee, 2001):

- A positive sense of self-worth and competence
- The ability to influence the course of one's life
- The capacity to work with others to control aspects of public life
- An ability to access the mechanisms of public decision making

Many clients do not, or perceive that they do not, have power, either over themselves, their significant others, or the agencies and communities in which they reside. This sense of powerlessness underlies many problems in living. It can be internalized and lead to learned helplessness and alienation from one's community. An empowerment orientation to practice represents the social worker's efforts to combat the alienation, isolation, and poverty of substantive content in clients' lives by positively influencing their sense of worth, sense of membership in a community, and ability to create change in their surroundings (Rose, 1990).

Clients may be empowered at a *personal* level (changing patterns of thinking, feeling, and behaving), an *interpersonal* level (managing their relationships more effectively), or perhaps a *political* level (changing their manner of interacting with larger systems) (Lee, 2001). Clinical social workers are generally more inclined to address a client's personal and interpersonal concerns. Empowerment at the individual level is a process by which clients gain mastery and control over their lives and a critical understanding of their environment (Zimmerman, Israel, Schulz, & Checkoway, 1992). *Psychological* empowerment includes a client's beliefs about his or her competence, efforts to exert control, and understanding of the social environment (Zimmerman, 2000).

Empowerment incorporates three themes (Parsons, 1991). It is a *developmental process* that can be experienced along a continuum from individual growth to social change. Second, it is at least in part a *psychological state* characterized by feelings of self-esteem, efficacy, and control over one's life. Third, it may involve a client's *liberation from oppression*, a process that begins with education and politicization of his or her presenting problems. In a sense, empowerment is a political concept, though the extent to which this is apparent to clients and practitioners depends on their approach to intervention (Adams, 1996).

In every case of empowerment practice, the social worker helps clients become aware of the conflicts and tensions within themselves and their surroundings that oppress or limit them, and also helps them become better able to free themselves from those constraints. Clinical social workers may perceive this concept to be more relevant to practice with large systems (organizations and communities), but in fact it has implications for intervention at *all* levels. From the person-in-environment perspective, even the most "individual" of problems, such as physical and mental illness, have intervention implications that may include helping the client to create an environment conducive to recovery.

With their person-in-environment perspective on human functioning, social workers are well-positioned to promote client empowerment. A key to empowerment practice is the social worker's awareness of the complex interactions between the broad implications of a client's problem situation and the client's capacity to interpret and act on the problem (Leonardsen, 2007). For this process to be effective, social workers must possess theoretical knowledge about how organizations function, and they must be empowered themselves in ways that give them the competence to act with clients in these ways. The sources of power over social workers in an agency (administrative or interprofessional) may create client/worker power disparities that undermine the goals of empowerment practice.

In clinical practice, the social worker's specific actions toward empowerment ends are less important than the general orientation toward helping clients become more involved in their communities (however defined) and feeling more capable of exerting control there. The concept of *perceived control* has been found to be related to reduction in psychological stress and increased social action (Zimmerman, 2000). Empowerment can, in fact, be achieved through the use of *any* of the practice theories described in this book, although some may be more conducive to the process than others. Empowerment involves helping clients learn decision-making skills, manage resources, and work productively with others. Appropriate outcomes may include the client's increased sense of control, critical awareness, and participatory behaviors.

Clinical practice is empowering to the extent that it helps people develop skills to become independent problem solvers and decision makers. Toward this end, the practitioner must establish a positive relationship with the client and help him or her to manage the presenting problem. The social worker should strive for collegiality, which means abandoning the expert role and developing a more egalitarian relationship with clients so that they have the "final say" in decisions that affect their lives. The practitioner must be willing to teach clients the knowledge and skills necessary to enact interventions for themselves. The practitioner must also be willing to help clients learn skills to secure external resources and participate in social change activities if they so desire. Not all clients should receive interventions targeted toward all of these areas, but the social worker should have the capacity to initiate these change activities if so requested.

Empowerment has become a popular concept and a politically correct buzzword in the social work profession, but it may be misunderstood and difficult to operationalize in clinical practice. Social workers may be uncomfortable with its call for client/worker partnerships and the education of clients in change activities that go beyond their presenting problems. Some practitioners may believe that it is unethical to suggest goals and activities for clients that do not directly relate to their presenting problems (Clark, 2000). Others emphasize that social workers cannot empower their clients unless they themselves also have power (respect and influence) among their peers in the service professions. The status of the profession with respect to furthering the interests of clients has historically been a topic of concern among academic scholars (Ehrenreich, 1985).

Empowerment and Research

Clinical research from the empowerment perspective is conducted differently from traditional methods in which the professional is the "expert" and in control of the process. Empowerment research involves doing "with" rather than doing "to" and emphasizes social worker/client collaboration (Boog, Coenen, & Keune, 2001). From this perspective, clinical research uses clients as participants rather than "subjects" in the areas of research design, accountability, implementation, and utilization. An example of empowerment research might be a social worker's meeting with members of a drop-in center for persons with mental illness to discuss possible ways of evaluating the center's effectiveness. Members would be invited to participate in the design of the project, data-gathering activities, and decisions about how the results are used. At present, empowerment research is not often done in social work except in the context of narrative therapy (see Chapter 12), which is openly collaborative in nature. There are no other examples of empowerment research included in this book, which suggests that social work researchers who wish to operationalize the concept have their work cut out for them!

Several qualitative research studies illustrate the challenges social workers face in using empowerment practice. In a study of 28 clients and social workers (including administrators) in a community-based service setting, frontline workers were interviewed about their perceptions of the empowerment process (Everett, Homstead, & Drisko, 2007). The researchers found that social workers sometimes experienced role conflicts in the process of helping clients become more involved in their own problem-solving activities, moving back and forth from the roles of "expert authority" to "collaborator" to "outreach worker." They were often challenged by the apparent powerlessness of their clients to make changes in their lives, and they felt the same sense of powerlessness at times in dealing with organizational barriers and limited job roles. The authors concluded that for empowerment practice to be effective, the process must be formally valued and articulated at all levels of an organization. In another study of 145 clients and professionals it was found that the two parties sometimes had different perspectives on empowerment practice (Boehm & Staples, 2002). Clients were more interested in the practical, tangible outcomes of empowerment activities, while social workers were more interested in the process of empowering clients, with less focus on specific outcomes.

The difficulty of implementing empowerment-based practice was demonstrated in another qualitative study of practitioner perceptions of empowerment

(Ackerson & Harrison, 2000). The eight practitioners in the study, who worked with highly impaired clients at a mental health clinic, noted empowerment dilemmas related to the *practical limits of their roles* in practice, necessary *issues of control* in the clinical relationship, and *interprofessional conflicts*. The practitioners felt that empowerment was a sometimes-impractical goal; they perceived a need to exert control over clients at times when the clients' judgment appeared to be poor or their behavior dangerous. Balancing occasional directives with empowerment values was difficult for them. The participants also noted that it was difficult to support client empowerment activities among other members of a treatment team who did not observe this value. For example, the social workers supporting a client's active participation in considering what medications he or she should take may be met with strong resistance by a prescribing physician. The researchers concluded that many social workers seem to define the term at a personal level that does not capture the breadth of some formal definitions, and that there is tension between promoting client self-direction and acting on behalf of clients. The practitioners in this study did reach consensus on one component of empowerment: There should always be mutually agreed-on roles in which the client and social worker share some responsibility and power.

Limitations to Empowerment Practice

The possible *risks* of the empowerment perspective have been considered by other authors (Adams, 1996). These include:

Empowering without "doing for." Some clients prefer the social worker to be an "expert," and rely on his or her guidance in seeking solutions for their problems.

Empowerment may draw attention away from the individual client. The client may not get his or her primary needs met if clinical attention shifts to larger-scale issues.

The values on which empowerment is based may at times be conflicting. Self-determination, distributive justice, and collaborative and democratic participation may be operationalized in ways that are in conflict with each other (Carroll, 1994). For example, one interest group's sense of self-determination (disabled students at a university) may result in initiatives that are non-democratic (attempting to usurp power from university administrators). This point relates to the one noted earlier, that empowerment is not necessarily a win-win proposition for members of different social groups.

To summarize, empowerment is a relatively new concept in social work that is useful for guiding practice at all levels. Over time it will likely become more clearly operationalized for use with diverse client populations and situations. Despite its limitations, it has the potential to help client groups develop more secure lives through substantive interpersonal and community connections. The actions of social workers can *always* be productively driven by a concern with clients' capacities to take control of their lives.

SPIRITUALITY IN CLINICAL PRACTICE

The term *spirituality* has many definitions, but can be generally understood as a person's search for, and adherence to, meanings, purposes, and commitments that lie outside the self (adapted from Krill, 1996). There are two contrasting perspectives on this idea (Frankl, 1988). One is that we may *create* what is meaningful in our lives. That is, there are no "objective" or external sources of meaning that we must observe. Meanings emerge within us and reflect our interests and values. An example is the person who chooses to devote her life to working with abused children, having realized that doing so fulfils a personal preference that is also important to society. The second perspective holds that at least some meanings reflect a reality that exists independently of us. It becomes our challenge to *discover* meanings that exist objectively. Some religious groups believe that there is a divine plan and a correct set of beliefs about a Supreme Being and codes of conduct, and that persons should live in accordance with this plan. It is possible to hold both views simultaneously, as we may consider some purposes objective and others based on our preferences.

Spiritual (or existential) meanings can be summarized in four categories, which may overlap (Frankl, 1988). *Belief systems* may be religious or secular. One can believe in the teachings of the Baptist faith because of its divine origins, or in the Golden Rule (act toward others as you want them to act toward you) because of purely humanitarian concerns. *Social concerns* include commitments to social causes. One can demonstrate such a commitment, for example, in volunteer service of various types, commitments to bettering the quality of life for certain oppressed groups, or environmental concerns. *Creative pursuits* include art, music, and literature, but may also include approaches to one's work (for example, the development of innovative agency programs). Also included in this category is the experience of creative pursuits that bring meaning to one's life. Some persons feel most alive, for example, when responding to a piece of music. *Hope* includes the defiance of suffering. This comes to the forefront of existence at times when one experiences great self-doubt or despair, but recognizes that he or she values life enough to persist in overcoming the adversity.

Spiritual concerns help people manage anxieties produced by confrontations with death, isolation (or being alienated from others), and freedom (and the responsibilities involved in making choices), as well as concerns about their place in the world (Yalom, 1980). Coming to terms with these issues is a challenge for all people. Although we may not deal with these concerns daily, they influence how we organize our lives.

Some emotions provide signals that we are struggling with existential concerns (Lazarus & Lazarus, 1994). Most prominently, *anxiety* results from uncertain threats to one's identity, future well-being, or life-and-death concerns. Anxiety is fueled by the struggle to maintain a sense of connection to others, and we often feel threatened by the fragile nature of life. The emotion of *guilt* results from thoughts or actions that we perceive as violations of important social standards of conduct. Guilt results from a perceived "moral flaw" when we have not behaved in accordance with an important value. A religious person who sins may feel guilt, and a social worker who provides poor service to a client may feel guilt. The emotion of *shame* is similar to that of guilt, but refers more specifically to the failure to live up to a personal (rather than social) ideal. A Caucasian person who believes in equality of opportunity may feel shame when he reacts negatively to an African-American family moving into his neighborhood. It is also important to emphasize that persons experience positive emotions such as *happiness* and *joy* when they behave in ways that affirm the spiritual self. A client who performs well as a Habitat for Humanity volunteer may experience great joy from making a contribution to the community.

Incorporating Spirituality into Direct Practice

Spiritual issues are not appropriate to address with clients in all practice situations (May & Yalom, 2000). In general, such concerns may not be appropriate to raise with clients who are absorbed in immediate problem situations for which they are seeking practical assistance. On the other hand, purpose-in-life issues may be appropriate for intervention when the client is troubled by anxiety, guilt, and shame, or demonstrates inclinations to look beyond the self and immediate situation in understanding personal dilemmas. Spiritual issues should be included as part of a multidimensional assessment with *all* clients, as it is always possible that a person's present problems and needs may contribute to, or result from, struggles with a broad life concern.

With regard to utilizing spiritual themes in clinical practice, challenges to social workers are fourfold:

- To understand his or her own existential issues and their impact on practice
- To consider client functioning within a broad context of meaning (that is, to bring consistency to the client's present and ultimate concerns)
- To encourage client disclosure of existential concerns, when appropriate
- To help clients identify meanings and purposes that can guide them in making growth-enhancing decisions

Spiritual, theory-guided interventions can increase the client's attention to three issues. They can encourage the client's *investment in constructive life activity* (rather than passivity), encourage the client to *look externally* for solutions to problems (rather than be preoccupied with internal emotions), and encourage the client to *care about something outside the self*.

Interestingly, mental health practitioners have tended to feel uncomfortable or unqualified to address issues of spirituality with clients. This may be due in part to a reluctance to risk imposing one's values on clients. Fortunately, this reluctance is less prevalent today than in the recent past. In a 1992 random survey of Virginia social workers, psychologists, and counselors, it was found that respondents valued religious or existential dimensions in their own lives (Sheridan, Bullis, Adcock, Berlin, & Miller, 1992). Though they addressed these issues to varying extents in their practices, many expressed reservations about the potential abuse of doing so, particularly with regard to imposing their beliefs.

Sheridan and Bullis (1991) presented additional data from this sample, indicating that professionals struggle with these issues, with no consensus about pursuing them in practice. The same interventions were viewed by some clinicians as appropriate, and by others as unethical. A recent national study, however, examined social workers' attitudes and behaviors about religion and spirituality in practice with children and adolescents (Kvarfordt & Sheridan, 2007). The majority of respondents regarded religion and spirituality as relevant to this population and used a wide variety of spiritually-based interventions. However, the vast majority reported that religious or spiritual issues were rarely addressed in their social work education.

Spirituality, as defined here, is a natural part of every person's life. Although it is not overtly addressed in all practice theories, it can be incorporated into the processes of assessment and intervention. The feasibility of the social worker addressing issues of spirituality with clients will be discussed throughout the text in the context of each theory (or group of similar theories).

SUMMARY

This chapter has highlighted aspects of clinical practice that are central to the perspective of the social work profession, including attention to professional values, a strengths orientation, risk and resilience influences, multiculturalism, client empowerment, and spirituality. We will see that all of the practice theories presented in the coming chapters can potentially be used in ways that are consistent with the social work perspective, but each practitioner must discover for him- or herself how well they seem to work in particular settings. These theories were largely developed outside the social work profession, so one of our tasks will be to consider how they can be implemented to fit with the values and priorities of clinical social work practice.

TOPICS FOR DISCUSSION

1. Compare the characteristics of clinical social work practice to clinical practice as carried out by several other professions, such as psychology, psychiatry, rehabilitation, and nursing. How is social work similar to, and different from, these other professions? What do the differences suggest about the values of the social work profession (and those of the other professions)?

2. Discuss a variety of ways in which a social worker might, accidentally or purposely, address a client's spiritual or religious life that are not ethically appropriate. How can these pitfalls be avoided? Conversely, describe situations in which a social worker might constructively engage these aspects of a client's life.

3. What are some specific areas of a client's life that a social worker can investigate to assess his or her strengths? What are some questions you might ask, or observations you might make, toward that end?

4. Consider a variety of types of clients who may come to an agency for clinical intervention. Speculate about the risk and resilience factors that may be operating in the clients' (or families' or group's) lives, at the biological, psychological, social, and perhaps spiritual levels. How might you incorporate these into an intervention plan?

5. Toward the goal of client empowerment, some social workers believe that the worker and client should be equal partners in the intervention process. What does this mean to you? Do you agree? Are there circumstances in which the notion of partnership might not apply?

IDEAS FOR ASSIGNMENTS

(Students can write papers or prepare discussion points on the following topics.)

1. Consider an adolescent client who is referred for counseling because of oppositional behavior in school, characterized by a failure to do homework or even attend class on a regular basis. The client lives in low-income housing with a single unemployed mother and aging grandmother. What kinds of social justice activities *might* the social worker incorporate into the intervention plan? What portion of the intervention would be devoted to individual and family counseling, compared to any possible social interventions?

2. Many Asian-American clients strictly observe traditional family norms in which the mother is in charge of raising the children and the father is responsible for earning money to support the family. Further, wives generally defer to the opinions and decisions made by the husband. Even though an Asian-American client may not likely seek formal counseling services, how might you use cultural sensitivity and cultural awareness in working with this woman and her family?

3

Psychodynamic Theories I:
Ego Psychology

Tell all the Truth but tell it slant —
Success in Circuit lies
Too bright for our infirm delight
The Truth's superb surprise
As lightning to the Children eased
With explanation kind
The Truth must dazzle gradually
Or every man be blind —*

Ego psychology is the oldest practice theory discussed in this book, having emerged in the United States by the 1940s. It is one of the *psychodynamic* theories, along with psychoanalysis, object relations theory (which is the subject of Chapter 4), and self psychology. All of the psychodynamic theories emphasize the importance of stages of psychosocial (or psychosexual) development and unconscious mental processes on human behavior. The psychodynamic theories were dominant in the social work profession between the 1920s and the 1970s. They have increasingly come under attack in the past 50 years by proponents of newer theories, however, for allegedly being overly abstract, unstructured, and impractical in today's practice environment that encourages more specific problem-solving processes (Hale, 1995). Proponents of psychodynamic practice argue, in turn, that many newer theories are relatively superficial and fail to

---

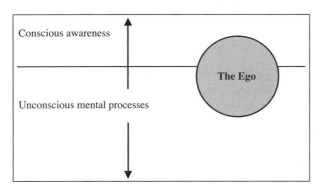

FIGURE 3.1 The Ego

appreciate the complexity of human behavior. Proponents also assert that ego psychology has demonstrated flexibility in its adaptability to short-term interventions (Wallerstein, 2002).

Both ego psychology and object relations theory are commonly used as a basis for psychodynamic interventions. Ego psychology, the focus on this chap ter, is concerned with individuals in the context of their psychosocial environments, and object relations, covered in the next chapter, has a stronger focus on interpersonal relationships and their effects on individual functioning.

Psychodynamic theorists initially described the mind as consisting of three components: id, ego, and superego (Fenichel, 1994). Put simply, the id represented innate drives; the ego was the part of the mind that adapted the drives to socially acceptable outlets; and the superego represented the conscience, or internalized value system. Ego psychology developed as a theory of human behavior that focuses on the role of the ego rather than the mind's other two components. Your "ego" is largely (but not completely) your conception of "who you are." It is the "you" who thinks, feels, and acts in a reasonably consistent manner. It is everything you do to reflect, plan, and act in ways that allow you to "fit in" more or less adequately with the environments in which you live. More formally, the ego is the part of one's personality that is responsible for negotiating between internal needs and the demands of social living (see Figure 3.1). It is where cognition occurs, but unconscious mental processes also influence conscious thinking. *Defense* (or coping) mechanisms, which are unconscious distortions of reality, frequently come into play as we attempt to manage our interpersonal and other conflicts. A client's potential for personal growth or problem resolution does not always require attention to unconscious processes, but doing so often maximizes his or her potential for change.

ORIGINS AND SOCIAL CONTEXT

Social work emerged as an occupation in the United States during the late nineteenth century as Charity Organization Societies and "friendly visitors" attempted to resolve the problems of poverty, illness, and crime that were becoming prominent in the cities of the northeast (Lubove, 1965). This was the Progressive Era, characterized by a broad interest in the negative effects of urbanization and industrialization on some citizens. As the new occupation of social work grew in importance, many (although not all) of its members began to seek its legitimacy as a profession. Toward that end, its pioneers tried to formulate a knowledge base that would make it distinctive. The most famous early product of this effort was Mary Richmond's *Social Diagnosis* (1917), which detailed a systems approach to working with clients, with attention to both their personal and environmental circumstances. It should be emphasized that other notable social workers of the time, such as Jane Addams (1910), were not interested in the move to professionalization.

Social developments in the United States eventually led to the young profession's adoption of psychoanalytic theory in the 1920s as its basis for assessment and intervention with individuals and families (Ehrenreich, 1985). Freud's landmark work, *The Interpretation of Dreams*, published in 1899, signaled the arrival of psychoanalytic theory. Freud's ideas, which he continued to develop until his death in 1939, were revolutionary in their description of the importance of unconscious thought processes and defense mechanisms in determining human behavior. His theory of childhood sexuality (defined broadly) was both scandalous and intriguing in his repressed European society. Analytic ideas were relatively little known in America until after World War I. By then the country had become more politically conservative. The pre-war Progressive faith in the possibilities of broad social engineering dissipated as the country experienced dramatic economic growth. There was less interest in collective social movements and greater interest in individuals and their emotions and pleasure-seeking activities. The nation was opening up to Freud's ideas.

During the post-war years the "occupation" of social work was still trying to professionalize in order to legitimize itself with clients and state legislatures, foundations, and other sources of funding and institutional power. It has already been noted that social work had been searching for an identified body of knowledge around which to focus its activities. Analytic theory seemed ideally suited to the task. It offered a comprehensive system of client assessment and was attractive to middle-class persons (social workers and their funders). Its focus on relationship dynamics helped social workers to understand their roles in the intervention process more clearly. Analytic theory also narrowed social work's interest in environmental conditions to issues within the family (though ego psychology later expanded this), which was consistent with the broader retreat of society from reform activities.

Psychoanalytic practice in the United States evolved to reflect changing social conditions and social work's developing value base. The theory of ego psychology emerged from psychoanalysis, beginning in the 1930s (Goldstein, 1995; Fenichel, 1994). Its development was related to the desire of some theorists to build a psychology of normal development, the influence of new humanistic ideas in the social sciences that emphasized adaptive capacities rather than pathology, and the American social value of pragmatism (or practicality).

Ego psychology was initially developed outside the profession (Hartmann, 1958), but reflected changes within the social work profession. "Pure" psychoanalysis was represented in the *diagnostic school* of social work, in which assessment and treatment planning, independent of the client's preferences and environmental constraints, was considered most appropriate. The newer *functional school* recognized that intervention should be client-driven (collaborative) and that social workers needed to mold their techniques to the realities (and limitations) of the service environment, including the time factor (Furman, 2002). With ego psychology, the social work profession shifted its thinking away from the role of the unconscious in psychological activity toward a greater emphasis on client strengths and adaptability. This was in part a reaction against Freud's heavy emphasis on drives, and highlighted the ego's role in promoting healthy social functioning.

Gordon Hamilton (1940) was the first social work scholar to incorporate elements of psychoanalytic theory (including transference, defense, and interpretation) into casework practice. She eventually asserted that ego psychology was more consistent with social work values than psychoanalysis because of its emphasis on the healthy functioning of individuals (Hamilton, 1951). She also reaffirmed social work's traditional concern with the environment, demonstrating a commitment not only to understanding the structure and dynamics of personality but also to environmental or social therapy. Hamilton was the first to make use of the phrase "person and situation" to define the distinguishing feature of social work as a human services profession. Hamilton used the concept to highlight the interaction between the "intrapsychic" and the "objective," with the point of interaction being the primary domain of the social worker.

Florence Hollis (1964) later helped to expand social work's understanding of the interaction between the individual and the environment. While she limited her understanding of the "situation" to an interaction between the client and client's significant others (families and friends), rather than broader socio-political concerns, she did articulate some ways in which social workers could intervene in the client's environment. These included referring to other professional experts, suggesting resources, preparing the client to make use of resources, enlisting social supports, influencing others on behalf of the client, and directly accessing resources on the client's behalf.

MAJOR CONCEPTS

The following four major assumptions underlie the concepts of ego psychology (Hauser & Safyer, 1995):

- People are born with an innate capacity to adapt to their environments, and this capacity further develops through learning and psychosocial maturation.

- Social influences on psychological functioning are significant, and many of these are transmitted through the family unit.

- The innate drives of mastery and competence are important motivators of human behavior.
- Problems in social functioning can occur at any stage of development, due to person–environment, as well as internal, conflicts.

All of these points will be elaborated below.

The Drives

Ego psychology recognizes three innate human drives. These include drives toward *pleasure* and *aggression* (when one's well-being is threatened), from psychoanalytic theory, and a drive toward *mastery and competence* (White, 1963). *Mastery* refers to a person's ability to influence his or her environment, and *competence* is one's subjective feeling about that ability. The drives toward pleasure and aggression bring people into conflict with social norms. They must be channeled into appropriate outlets for their fulfillment and thus may be frustrated at times. The drive to mastery and competence, however, is considered conflict-free, representing an innate inclination to exist harmoniously in one's environment. It evolves throughout life from one's talents, mastery of developmental tasks, motivations that derive from personal goals, and innate relationship-seeking orientation. Acknowledging this drive is consistent with the strengths perspective of social work, because it assumes that all people have talents that can be utilized as they seek functional competence.

The Significance of Emotional Life

The psychodynamic theories recognize the importance of emotional life and focus on its conscious and unconscious aspects. In ego psychology, some conscious thinking is a product of the drives, from which emotions also spring. We are pleasure seekers and "feelers" by nature, and thoughts are our means of deciding how to gratify the drives. Defense mechanisms result from the need to manage drives when we become frustrated, as we frequently do in the social world, where impulses must always be converted into acceptable behaviors. Further, personal growth is not always feasible when attending only to our conscious processes. We need to explore our thoughts and feelings to understand our essential drives. Our capacity for change may be facilitated by uncovering ideas and feelings that we typically keep out of consciousness. In that way, we can better understand our impulses and direct them toward appropriate sources for gratification.

Several theorists have elaborated on the processes of emotional life. Magai (1996) asserts that emotional traits form the core of human personality, and that all people possess five primary human emotions, originating in their neurophysiology. Personalities are organized around these "affective biases," which include happiness, sadness, fear, anger, and interest/excitement. These emotions are instinctual and activate thinking and behavior in ways that are adaptive. Thus, emotions influence cognition.

Two examples may help to illustrate these ideas. A person's propensity toward sadness is elicited by the experience of a personal or material loss. This leads to the person's temporary physical slowing down, decrease in general effort, and withdrawal in situations where efforts to recover the loss would likely be ineffective. The sadness allows time for the person to reflect on her needs and priorities, and regain energy for a more focused use of energy to achievable goals. Her expressions of sadness are also a signal within her social network for others to provide more support. As a contrasting example, a person's anger tends to increase energy and motivate behavior that is intended to overcome frustration. Its expression is a signal to others to respond to the person with avoidance or compliance so that she may resolve the problem confronting her.

Social theories of emotion assert that many other emotions are socially constructed to promote social cohesion. Mead (1934), the originator of symbolic interaction theory, wrote that emotions develop as symbols for communication. He believed that we are by nature more sensitive to visual cues than verbal ones. Emotional expressions are particularly powerful in that they are apprehended visually rather than verbally. Emotional expression is a signal to others about how we are inclined to act in a situation, and others can adjust their own behavior in response to our perceived inclinations. A young college student's lack of eye contact, tendency to look down, and physical distancing from others may be manifestations of her sadness. Other persons, in response, might choose to offer support or avoid her, if they interpret her expressions as a desire for distance. All of us must interpret the emotional expressions of others, and this process often takes place outside our conscious awareness. Practice theories focused on emotional experience, such as ego psychology, help clients to become more aware of how they both express themselves and perceive others.

The Ego and Its Functions

The ego is not a physical structure, but a concept describing the part of personality that negotiates between our internal needs and the outside world. It is present from birth and is our source of attention, concentration, learning, memory, will, and perception. The functioning of the ego is partly unconscious, or out of our awareness. In ego psychology, both past and present experiences are relevant in influencing our social functioning. The influence of the drives (toward pleasure and aggression) on emotions and thoughts is not dismissed, but conscious thought processes receive greater emphasis. The ego mediates internal conflicts, which might result from drive frustration, but it also mediates the interactions of a person with stressful environmental conditions. If a client experiences sadness, he or she may be having conflicts related to internal ambivalence or, on the other hand, may be experiencing conflicts with other people. Ego psychology is a developmental theory, so its principles support attention to ego development throughout the life cycle.

What follows is a description of the major ego functions (Schammes, 1996; Goldstein, 1995; Bellak & Goldsmith, 1984):

- *Awareness of the external environment* refers to an accurate perception of the external world. This includes orientation to time, place, and person, and the absence of hallucinations, delusions, and loose associations.

- *Judgment* is our capacity to choose behaviors that are likely to promote our movement toward goals. The quality of our judgment may change in different circumstances.

- The *sense of identity* is a reasonably coherent physical and psychological sense of self. This includes our ability to maintain appropriate psychological boundaries (balancing involvement and distance) from others.

- *Impulse control* refers to our ability to distinguish between primary (drives or impulses) and secondary (planned) mental processes; to control actions in accordance with social norms; and to maintain control of behavior or emotions to a degree that creates significant problems in functioning.

- *Thought process regulation*, related to the above function, is our ability to remember, concentrate, and assess situations so as to initiate appropriate action. These reflect a shift to secondary-process thinking, which is goal-oriented but also rational and reality-focused.

- *Interpersonal (object) relations* refers to two related functions: (a) the ability to manage relationships appropriately toward personal goal attainment, and (b) the ability to see other people as unique rather than replications of significant others from our past. People often manage some types of relationships (such as work or social relationships) more successfully than others (family or other intimate ties). This concept is primary in object relations theory, which is discussed in the next chapter, but is also of interest to ego psychology practitioners.

- *Defense mechanisms* are distortions of reality that enable us to minimize anxiety. They are experienced by all people and may or may not promote productive social functioning. These will be discussed in more detail below.

- *Stimulus regulation* is our ability to screen and select external stimuli to maintain a focus on relevant life concerns. When ineffective, we may become either overwhelmed or underwhelmed in situations.

- *Autonomous functions* are the capacity to maintain attention, concentration, memory, or learning. Any impairment of these functions must be assessed for possible organic origin.

It should be evident that some ego functions are within our conscious awareness and others are not.

The Defense Mechanisms

Ego psychology practitioners are sensitive to a client's use of defense mechanisms, because the manner in which these are employed have a great influence on one's ability to manage challenges. Defenses are unconscious, automatic responses that enable us to minimize perceived threats or keep them out of awareness entirely (Gray, 1994; Vaillant, 1992). They are *coping* mechanisms used by all people to protect themselves against becoming overwhelmed by anxiety. Defenses distort reality to varying degrees, because they provide us with a conscious perspective on a particular situation that is biased toward preserving a sense of security.

People can use defenses in healthy (adaptive) and unhealthy (maladaptive) ways. Defenses are used appropriately when they promote our adaptive functioning and goal achievement and minimize internal and interpersonal conflicts. The range of defense mechanisms is listed in Table 3.1.

Some of the defense mechanisms are similar to each other. *Displacement* and *sublimation* provide one example of this. In displacement, unacceptable feelings

TABLE 3.1   Common Defense Mechanisms

Denial	Negating an important aspect of reality that one may actually perceive (A woman with anorexia acknowledges her actual weight and dieting practices, but believes that she is maintaining good self-care by doing so.)
Displacement	Shifting negative feelings about one person or situation onto another (A student's anger at her professor, who is threatening as an authority figure, is transposed into anger at her boyfriend, a safer target.)
Intellectualization	Avoiding unacceptable emotions by thinking or talking about them rather than experiencing them directly (A person talks to her counselor about the fact that she is sad but shows no emotional evidence of sadness, which makes it harder for her to understand its effects on her life.)
Introjection	Taking characteristics of another person into the self in order to avoid direct conflict. The emotions originally felt about the other person are now felt toward the self. (An abused woman feels angry with herself rather than her abusing partner, because she has taken in his belief that she is an inadequate caregiver. Believing otherwise would make her more fearful that the desired relationship might end.)
Isolation of Affect	Consciously experiencing an emotion in a "safe" context rather than the threatening context in which it was first unconsciously experienced (A person does not experience sadness at the funeral of a family member, but the following week weeps uncontrollably at the death of a pet.)
Projection	Attributing unacceptable thoughts and feelings to others (A man does not want to be angry at his girlfriend, so when he is upset with her he avoids owning the emotion by assuming that she is instead angry with him.)
Rationalization	Using convincing reasons to justify ideas, feelings, or actions so as to avoid recognizing their true underlying motives (A student copes with the guilt normally associated with cheating on an exam by reasoning that he had been too ill the previous week to prepare for it.)
Reaction Formation	Replacing an unwanted unconscious impulse with its opposite in conscious behavior (A person cannot bear to be angry with his boss, so during a conflict he convinces himself that the boss is worthy of loyalty and goes out of his way to be kind.)

TABLE 3.1   Common Defense Mechanisms (Continued)

Regression	Resuming behaviors associated with an earlier developmental stage or level of functioning in order to avoid present anxiety. The behavior may help to resolve the anxiety (A young man throws a temper tantrum as a means of discharging his frustration when he cannot master a task on his computer. The startled computer technician, who had been reluctant to attend to the situation, now comes forth to provide assistance.)
Repression	Keeping unwanted thoughts and feelings entirely out of awareness (so that they are not expressed in any way.)
Somatization	Converting intolerable impulses into somatic symptoms (A person who is unable to express his negative emotions develops frequent stomachaches.)
Sublimation	Converting an impulse from a socially unacceptable aim to a socially acceptable one (An angry, aggressive young man becomes a star on his school's debate team.)
Undoing	Nullifying an undesired impulse with an act of reparation (A man who feels guilty about having lustful thoughts about a co-worker tries to make amends to his wife by purchasing a special gift for her.)

about one person or situation are consciously directed toward another person or situation. It is more "acceptable" to feel anger (for example) toward the *substitute* target than toward the *actual* one. A graduate student may take out her frustrations on a roommate rather than the professor with whom she is angry. Sublimation is similar to displacement but is considered more functional in that it enhances social functioning. It involves the channeling (displacement) of unacceptable impulses or feelings into socially acceptable outlets. One example is the aggressive adolescent who becomes a member of the school debate team.

A client's use of defenses can be evaluated in the following ways:

Flexibility versus rigidity—The behavior may or may not be appropriate to the social context. For example, at times anger should be suppressed (toward the boss during a staff meeting), and at other times it should be expressed (in a close personal relationship when feelings have been hurt). A rigidly defensive person will suppress—or express—angry feelings with insufficient regard for the context, and thus the behavior is more likely to create conflicts.

Future versus past orientation—Defenses should promote adaptive behavior in the present and future. When their use is based on past events that no longer affect the client, they may be maladaptive. For example, a young, married employee's rationalization of keeping a low-paying job for fear of not being able to find a better one may have been functional when he was just out of college and had little experience. Ongoing use of the defense may no longer serve the person once he has a master's degree and more marketable skills. The rationalization may be due to a fear of taking risks.

General reality adherence versus significant distortion—All defenses distort reality, but people can distort reality to such a degree that they lose basic awareness of their environment. A high school student, worried about an upcoming term paper, may use the defense of somatization, and ask the teacher for an extension due to illness. A more problematic use of the defense would be the student's becoming convinced that he has colon cancer and demanding hospital admission for emergency tests.

The Complexity of Defenses: Denial   Denial is defined in Table 3.1 as a person's negation (perhaps temporarily) of an important aspect of reality with which he or she is confronted. It is among the most common defenses. Whether denial is adaptive or maladaptive can be determined by several factors. First is the issue of its *timing*. When we are faced with traumatic news, it is quite common to deny it initially. This may be helpful, as it enables us to gradually come to terms with the seriousness of the issue, avoid becoming overwhelmed, and more carefully consider how to deal with it. If a man learns that he has potentially life-threatening liver damage due to years of substance abuse, he may deny the truth of the medical report for a period of time while he works through the implications of the news on his future. If he continues to deny the truth of the medical report for months, convinced of a misdiagnosis, he is using denial in a maladaptive way because he is avoiding treatment and putting his life in danger.

Second, denial may be a *positive* coping strategy when doing something about the event in question is not possible, but a *dysfunctional* strategy when rational action might be productive. If the man described above has a terminal liver disease that cannot be helped with treatment, his denial of its seriousness will not affect his mortality and may help him to live out the rest of his life with greater serenity. If the disease is treatable, his denial of its seriousness may unnecessarily lead to death.

Third, the adaptability of the defense depends on what aspect of an event is denied. Keeping with the above example, the man's ongoing denial of the *fact* of his illness is not adaptive, but his denial of its *implication* (probable death) might motivate him to seek out whatever treatments might prolong his life. It is not unusual to hear about medical patients who were initially told that they would probably die within several months, but who lived for years because of their determination to prove the doctors wrong.

THE NATURE OF PROBLEMS AND CHANGE

In ego psychology, problems or challenges may result from conflicts *within* the person or *between* the person and external world. That is, the stress a client experiences may result from excess environmental demands (an external focus), inadequate ego functioning (an internal focus), or reactions to normal life transitions (such as age and work transitions, parenthood, separation from significant others, and reactions to health problems). During ego-based intervention, the social worker helps the client either to build new ego strengths or use existing ego strengths more effectively. Change is manifested in the client's ability to utilize his or her ego functions to enhance self-understanding and achieve greater mastery of challenges, crises, or life transitions.

The goals of intervention are to enhance the client's inner capacities through ego development (which includes greater self-understanding, modify or change environmental conditions, or improve the fit between a person's ego capacities and environmental conditions by working on both areas. Clients are helped to acquire problem-solving and coping skills, and to achieve insight (self-understanding) through reflection about their strengths, limitations, and potential resources. Maladaptive defenses may be confronted and appropriate defenses strengthened. Clients are empowered with knowledge or movement toward more proactive stances with respect to their challenges. They should emerge from the intervention process with an improved capacity for self-direction.

ASSESSMENT AND INTERVENTION

Assessment

The social worker evaluates the strengths and limitations of *each* of the client's ego functions through a questioning of the client and perhaps his or her significant others, and a review of other available data sources. If possible, medical records or a medical evaluation should be sought to evaluate the possibility of physiological impairments that may affect certain ego functions, particularly the stimulus regulation and autonomous functions.

Assessment of a client's psychosocial development requires a review of significant past experiences. Ego psychology is a developmental theory; it assumes that all of us move through certain physical and emotional stages as we grow. Each new stage of personality development builds on previous stages. Any unsuccessful transitions can result in the onset of abnormal behavior as evidenced by problematic patterns of coping with new challenges. Such persons will experience difficulties mastering subsequent stages. In psychoanalytic theory, Freud wrote about psychosexual stages (oral, anal, phallic, latency, and genital stages), but ego psychology is more closely identified with stages that focus on environmental as well as internal processes. The best known of these is Erikson's (1968) psychosocial stages of development (see Table 3.2).

T A B L E 3.2   Erikson's Stages of Psychosocial Development

Life Stage	Psychosocial Challenge	Significant Others
Infancy	Trust vs. Mistrust	Maternal Person
Early Childhood	Autonomy vs. Shame and Doubt	Parental Persons
Play Age	Initiative vs. Guilt	Family
School Age	Industry vs. Inferiority	Neighborhood
Adolescence	Identity vs. Identity Diffusion	Peers
Young Adult	Intimacy vs. Isolation	Partners
Adulthood	Generativity vs. Self-Absorption	Household
Mature Age	Integrity vs. Disgust and Despair	Humanity

As an example of this theory, many older adolescents struggle with the two developmental stages of *identity versus identity diffusion* and *intimacy versus isolation*. Common challenges in the first of these stages include resolving issues of self-confidence (vs. apathy), positive role experimentation (vs. negative identity), and anticipation of achievement (vs. vocational paralysis). Challenges in the second phase include developing a capacity for intimacy as opposed to feeling socially empty or isolated within the family unit. The adolescent's successful transition into adult roles will depend on his or her successful passage through the preceding developmental phases.

Gathering information about relevant history can help the social worker determine whether the client may benefit from new skills associated with certain stages. Other examples of developmental stage theories include Levinson's (1978) stages of male development, Kohlberg's (1969) stages of moral development, and Gilligan's (1982) stages of moral development for women. Though all of these may be useful for understanding the person in context, there is an increasing appreciation in the social work profession for developmental differences among all people, especially members of different cultural, racial, and ethnic groups. Much remains to be learned about human development across populations, and social workers must be careful not to apply existing theories of development rigidly.

Intervention

The Social Worker/Client Relationship   The quality of the worker/client relationship is significant to clinical outcomes across theoretical perspectives (Horvath & Greenberg, 1994). The analytic theories are distinguished by the thoroughness of their attention to the nature of the worker/client relationship. In social work, Perlman (1979) has vividly articulated the ways in which unconscious processes can distort the social worker's understanding of a client's problems and their relationship, and vice-versa.

At a basic level, the working alliance should feature a positive emotional bond characterized by collaboration, agreement on goals, and some level of mutual comfort. For the social worker it requires skills of *empathy* (the ability to perceive accurately and sensitively the client's feelings, and to communicate that understanding to the client) and *authenticity* (relating in a natural and sincere manner). In ego psychology, relationship issues go beyond this, however, to include the social worker's ongoing management of the positive and negative aspects of the relationship. In fact, for some clients who seek help with relationship problems, examining the clinical relationship over time may serve as the primary intervention! Client factors that influence the nature of the clinical relationship may include voluntary status, level of motivation, ego stability, and cultural factors (Sexton & Whiston, 1994). The social worker may be challenged, particularly in longer-term interventions, to maintain a controlled level of emotional involvement with the client. The practitioner should also be alert to transference and countertransference issues, as described below.

Transference and Countertransference   The concepts of transference and countertransference emerged within psychodynamic theory during its beginning (Gabbard, 1995). They call attention to subtle effects of the worker/client relationship on all stages of the intervention. *Transference* was initially defined as a client's unconscious projection of feelings, thoughts, and wishes onto the practitioner, who comes to represent a person from the client's past such as a parent, sibling, other relative, or teacher (Jacobs, 1999). The practitioner does not actually possess those characteristics, but the client acts as if he or she does. The concept has gradually expanded to refer more broadly to *all* reactions that a client has to the clinical worker. These reactions may be based on patterns of interaction with similar types of people in the client's past or on the actual characteristics of the practitioner.

Countertransference was initially defined as a practitioner's unconscious reactions to the client's projections (Jacobs, 1999; Kocan, 1988). This concept has also broadened to refer to the effects of the practitioner's conscious *and* unconscious needs and wishes on his or her understanding of the client. It also refers to the conscious attitudes and tendencies that the worker has about *types* of clients (such as being drawn to working with children or having an aversion to older adults).

Transference and countertransference are not exotic ideas. They exist in *every* relationship. We do not experience others only in terms of an objective reality, but also in terms of how we wish them to be, or fear that they might be. These reactions may be taken into account in every clinical encounter with regard to how they influence the social worker's perception of the client (and vice versa). The social worker's awareness of his or her emotional reactions facilitates the intervention process, as it helps the practitioner better understand the rationales behind the clinical decisions he or she is making.

Some common countertransference reactions that social workers may experience include dreading *or* eagerly anticipating seeing a client, thinking excessively about a client during off hours, having trouble understanding a client's problems (they may be similar to the social worker's own), being either bored or unduly impressed with a client, feeling angry with a client for non-specific reasons, feeling hurt by a client's criticisms, doing things for the client that he or she is capable of, and feeling uncomfortable about discussing certain topics (Hepworth, Rooney, Rooney, Strom-Gottfried, & Larsen, 2005; Kocan, 1988; Schoenwolf, 1993). These reactions are only problematic when they cause the practitioner's decision making to be based on his or her feelings rather than the client's goals. Practitioners who work from the theoretical bases of ego psychology should monitor their own—and their clients'—transferences throughout the clinical intervention.

Specific Intervention Strategies   Ego psychology interventions are best understood as general strategies rather than concrete directives. This is sometimes frustrating to students and young practitioners who seek clearer guidance for intervention. Social workers need to tailor these general strategies to the specific needs of clients.

Ego psychology incorporates two basic types of intervention strategies (Woods & Hollis, 2000). The practitioner chooses *ego-sustaining* techniques after assessing the client's ego functions as relatively intact. These techniques help the client to understand his or her motivations and behaviors more clearly and then become mobilized to resolve present difficulties. They include *sustainment* (developing and maintaining a positive relationship), *exploration/description/ventilation* (encouraging the client's emotional expressions for stress relief and to gain objectivity about problems), and *person-situation reflection* (on solutions to present difficulties). The practitioner may also provide *education* to the client, often about environmental resources, and *direct influence*, particularly when the client is in crisis and temporarily unable to exercise good judgment about self-care.

The major *ego-modification technique*, which is used when clients experience maladaptive patterns of functioning that require an exploration of past experiences and unconscious processes, is *developmental reflection*. The social worker facilitates the client's self-understanding by exploring his or her patterns of behavior over time, providing new interpretations of relationship patterns, confronting maladaptive defenses, and guiding the client into corrective interpersonal experiences.

Each of these interventions is described in more detail below.

Exploration/Description/Ventilation   The social worker elicits the client's thoughts and feelings about an area of concern and helps the client to express and explore them. The practitioner keeps the client on the topic, but otherwise allows the client to drive the process. As a result, the client is helped to:

- Feel less alone and overwhelmed
- Gain control of incapacitating emotions
- See problems as more manageable
- Become motivated to take action
- Develop greater hope, confidence, motivation, and self-acceptance
- More clearly recognize and understand his or her emotional reactions
- Acquire greater insight
- Reduce his or her defensiveness
- Develop a positive transference to the social worker

For some clients with considerable ego strength who are anxious or in crisis, this intervention may be sufficient to resolve the problem.

Sustainment   This is a deceptively difficult intervention strategy that becomes more important over time in a clinical relationship. The social worker listens to the client actively and sympathetically, conveys a continuing attitude of good will (even when frustrated or angry), expresses confidence in the client, nonverbally communicates interest, and realistically reassures the client about his or her potential for goal achievement. This process can be challenging because the social worker must delicately balance supportive and demanding messages to the client. The purposes of the strategy are to:

- Promote a confiding relationship
- Instill a sense of the worker's caring

- Provide an antidote to alienation
- Enhance the client's morale and determination to persist
- Inspire and maintain the expectation of help
- Create a supportive atmosphere in which confrontation can be used constructively

Person-Situation Reflection   With this strategy the social worker first facilitates exploration/description/ventilation, and then guides the client into a focused, detailed review of thoughts and feelings related to the presenting issue. The social worker:

- Makes comments, asks questions, offers tentative explanations, and provides nonverbal communications that promote the client's reflective capacity
- Leads discussions of the pros and cons of the client's taking certain actions
- Assumes a moderately directive and structured stance, *perhaps* including confrontation
- Provides here-and-now interpretations of client behavior

Through this process the social worker promotes the client's abilities to evaluate feelings, self-concept, and attitudes; understand others or some external situation; develop insight into the nature of his or her behaviors and its effects on others; and use better judgment for considering a wider range of problem-solving options.

Advice and Guidance (Direct Influence)   No practice theory advocates that social workers routinely give advice to their clients. The values of the profession mandate that clients should be empowered to resolve their own problems. Still, social workers may occasionally need to give advice or make suggestions to a client about ways of thinking, reviewing feelings, or behaving. This is always done tentatively, and is reserved for situations in which the client is unable to exercise good judgment, such as periods of crisis, psychosis, or self-destructive ideation. It should always be done to meet the client's needs rather than the worker's needs (that is, desiring that the client behave in certain ways to comply with the worker's values).

The social worker's interventions may include stating an opinion, emphasizing a course of action the client is contemplating, or strongly cautioning the client. If a client requests advice, the social worker should explore the client's reasons for doing so. The social worker may choose to deny the request, and instead pursue a more reflective discussion. Even when provided, direct influence is given in a context of reflective discussion, if possible, and the social worker may guide the client to a decision rather than give direct advice. The social worker should avoid giving advice about major life decisions (whether to get married, drop out of school, accept or leave a particular job, etc.) and always review with the client the pros and cons of giving any advice.

Partializing (Structuring)   Many clients benefit from a social worker helping them break down presenting problems into discreet "units" that can be addressed sequentially. This is particularly helpful for clients who feel overwhelmed or have difficulty keeping focused on their concerns. The social worker's actions include focusing the client's attention, perhaps initiating time limits on their work, assigning tasks for completion outside the session, and outlining plans for using their time together. The social worker also engages the client in reflective discussion of the above strategies as a means of improving the client's orientation to problem solving. These interventions can benefit clients by relieving the sense of being overwhelmed, providing an action focus, and providing new opportunities for learning. Successes that result from partializing strategies enhance the client's sense of mastery and competence.

Education   Most theories acknowledge that the practitioner will act as a client educator for various purposes. In ego psychology the social worker may provide information to clients about environmental resources and issues related to the client's biological, psychological, or social functioning (such as diet, relaxation, the benefits of social interaction, or the actions of medications). The social worker may also educate clients about the effects of their behavior on others, and the needs and motivations of significant other people in their environments. These interventions help clients by increasing their options for change, their "fund of knowledge" for problem-solving activities, and their levels of insight. The manner in which education takes place in ego psychology is not fundamentally different from that of many other approaches, except that these practitioners may be more focused on reflective discussion of educational resources.

Developmental Reflection   This is the only strategy that is unique to the second level of ego psychology intervention, ego modification. The social worker engages the client in reflective discussions about his or her past life and relationships. The goal is for the client to develop greater insight into the ways in which his or her current sense of self and relationship patterns have their origins in past experiences and relationships. This is the only ego psychology strategy in which the social worker may intentionally arouse the client's anxiety. Doing so is sometimes necessary to help the client face and experience troubling emotions that may be suppressed and are associated with difficult interpersonal problems, so that he or she can stop being affected by them. In developmental reflection, the social worker:

- Explores connections between the client's present and past experiences with comments, questions, and tentative explanations
- Helps the client to better understand (interpret) past issues that may be influencing the present problem, and then find ways of dealing with these
- Confronts maladaptive ideas, feelings, and behaviors as appropriate
- Refers to the nature of the clinical relationship as an example of the nature of the client's other significant relationships

This strategy helps clients to identify long-standing patterns of functioning, including defenses and their effectiveness; develop new ways of thinking about the past and how it affects current behavior; develop insight into patterns of behavior that stem from irrational feelings or interpersonal conflict; and experiment with new ways of thinking and behaving.

Following a discussion of several more important issues in ego psychology, these intervention strategies will be applied to two case examples.

Endings in Ego Psychology   Given the abstract nature of ego psychology's assessment and intervention concepts, it should not be surprising that determining an appropriate end point with a client is not always easy. Several ending principles are offered here. First, in addition to evaluating the extent to which the presenting issue has been resolved, the social worker can review with the client the status of each ego function that has been a focus of intervention (Blanck & Blanck, 1979). It is important to communicate to the client that further strengthening of ego functions is possible after the relationship ends. Second, the social worker can help the client to devise strategies for continued self-reflection (Robb & Cameron, 1998).

The client should be helped to review his or her past, present, and future with regard to the presenting problem. The client's recent past can be addressed with a review of the intervention process. The present situation is reflected in the client's current status, focusing on the client's new knowledge and skills. Looking ahead to growth opportunities outside the clinical setting helps the client look constructively toward the future.

SPIRITUALITY AND THE PSYCHODYNAMIC THEORIES

Clients' spiritual or existential concerns can be addressed within the theories of ego psychology and object relations (discussed in the next chapter). Both of these psychodynamic theories assume the existence of drives, one of which is the drive to mastery and competence (Goldstein, 1995). It follows from the existence of this drive that people strive to make sense of the environment with the goal of finding satisfaction with, and seeking direction for, their lives. Spiritual issues are at the heart of this drive.

Logotherapy is a useful existential/spiritual perspective that derives from the psychodynamic theories (Frankl, 1988; Lantz & Walsh, 2007). In this clinical approach, the *will to meaning* is conceptualized as an aspect of the drive to mastery. It is a basic, enduring tendency to obtain what satisfies our nature. We all have this innate drive to create or discover meaning and purpose in life beyond our physical existence and survival. Many people do not often reflect on their spiritual selves, because recognizing purposes beyond the self also includes an awareness of vulnerability, responsibility, and the potential for loss. A person's experiences with suffering, guilt, and death, which are universal, can result in a suppression of this will.

Ego psychology and object relations theory assert that we utilize a variety of defense mechanisms to minimize the impact of anxiety on our lives. The drive toward mastery and competence is subject to the same defensive activities as other impulses. Likewise, the will to meaning may be relegated to the unconscious, with the result that we remain unaware of its influence while remaining consciously occupied with less threatening ideas. This is not a satisfactory resolution of the problem of anxiety, however, as we may then experience indirect symptoms of distress. For example, a client's depression may be related to the fact that he is avoiding making any personal commitments because of a fear of loss of those relationships. Perhaps that client has experienced a terrible loss and as a result has suppressed the will to meaning, or cut himself off from new relationship opportunities.

The social worker using an ego psychology or object relations approach may select from numerous strategies, including exploration and ventilation, education, direct advice, life structuring, and reflection to help clients address their spiritual concerns. The task of the practitioner should be to help the client become aware of spiritual impulses that are being unconsciously defended. Though growth-enhancing, this may unfold as a painful process for the client, because spiritual concerns can rarely be managed comfortably. Of course, it is always the client's decision whether such concerns are relevant to the clinical intervention process.

ATTENTION TO SOCIAL JUSTICE ISSUES

The National Association of Social Workers (NASW) Code of Ethics (1996) states that social workers should challenge social injustice. This can be done through social change activities, particularly with vulnerable and oppressed individuals and groups. Ego psychology can be provided to families and groups, but it is conceptually more focused on working with individuals. It attends to transactions between client systems and their environments, but its most highly developed concepts are based on the characteristics of individuals. This reflects its roots in psychoanalysis and appears to limit its facilitation of collective social change activities. There is nothing that prohibits a social worker who practices ego psychology from helping clients engage in larger system change activities, but nothing within the theory itself encourages these interventions.

Still, ego psychology can be empowering for clients. Enhanced self-understanding and greater awareness of one's strengths, limitations, and resources (enhanced mastery and competence) can be liberating for persons who have been oppressed and feel powerless. Further, the short-term strategies of ego psychology can be flexibly used to fit clients of varied backgrounds. Figure 3.2 summarizes the environmental issues to which the social worker must be attuned in attending to the special socio-cultural contexts of client's lives. Ego psychology, then, is not outstanding in its orientation to social justice activities, but it can be used to empower clients toward such ends.

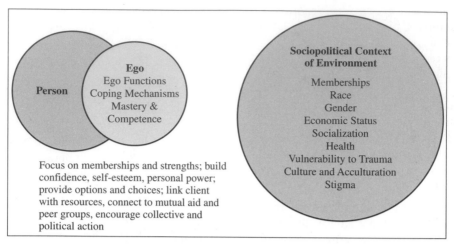

FIGURE 3.2 The Ego and the Environment: Diverse Populations

CASE ILLUSTRATIONS

The Angry Attorney

The following example describes Jacqui, a woman with a psychotic disorder. Ego psychology is not typically considered suitable for persons with such disorders, as these clients typically require concrete interventions such as medication, linkage, education, and social skills training. But ego psychology's emphasis on the importance of the client/worker relationship makes it useful for working with persons with thought disorders who characteristically have ambivalent attitudes about intervention. In this case it made the difference between successful engagement of the client and her refusal to participate in the process.

Jacqui had been released from a psychiatric hospital 45 days into her 90-day probation, and was legally required to comply with intervention at the mental health facility until her probation ended. She was a 40-year-old single Lebanese-American woman with a degree in law, and had a diagnosis of delusional disorder. This diagnosis is made when a person experiences non-bizarre delusions (false beliefs involving real-life situations) but no hallucinations, and functions well apart from events involving the delusions. Jacqui's probation was the result of her becoming paranoid and agitated, which severely disrupted her ability to work. She needed to be forcibly taken by her family to the hospital after a series of confrontations with neighbors and police officers.

Jacqui's impairments in ego functioning included poor reality testing and judgment (behaving in ways that jeopardized her career and reputation), maladaptive use of denial and projection (characteristic of paranoid persons), and problems with impulse control. Her strengths included a sense of mastery (several graduate degrees and a law practice focused on minority clients), good object relations (with a supportive family), and a coherent sense of identity. Jacqui, clearly a reluctant client, was outraged that her physicians expected her to take medications. She was convinced of the reality of her perceptions and felt that most other people were her intellectual inferiors, unwitting pawns in government conspiracies against her. She made it clear that she only came to the agency because of the legal mandate. Further, she warned agency staff to do nothing that might become the basis for a lawsuit.

Jacqui's perception of her situation was one of forced compliance with an unjust legal mandate. For that reason she felt she only needed to show up at her scheduled meetings and accept the injectable medication for the remaining 45 days. She expected the social worker to try to convince her of the need for treatment, as others at the hospital had done. Clearly, for her, the issue of unequal power was a major constraint to her potential to develop a cooperative relationship. It required that she subject herself to the will of the social worker and agency.

Nevertheless, within a month Jacqui and her social worker developed a solid working relationship. The social worker had relied on exploration/description/ventilation, person–situation reflection, and sustainment to engage the client. Understanding Jacqui's negative attitude about the agency, the worker encouraged her to ventilate her negative feelings about her incarceration and outpatient commitment. He asked nothing of her except regular meetings. They negotiated the details together, and agreed that they would meet biweekly, alternating between the agency and her home. The social worker was eager to allow Jacqui to remain on her "turf" so that she could relax and have more control of the situation. In this way he could also meet her father and sister, and assess their potential roles in Jacqui's treatment. For their first three visits the social worker did little more than ask Jacqui to share stories of her exciting life. She was happy to do this, feeling that she was being respected. The social worker behaved in as non-threatening a manner as possible. Jacqui soon calmed down, stopped the angry tirades, and began to value this new relationship, even as she continued to discount her need for services.

The social worker avoided participating in her medication appointments so as not to become involved in those power issues. He and the agency physician agreed for the client's benefit that the physician would assume the "bad guy" role by himself, to the extent that he expected Jacqui to take her medicines. With this strategy Jacqui could continue to see the social worker as supportive, and maintain her positive transference. In the long run Jacqui worked well with both staff members.

The social worker soon invited Jacqui to talk with him about some of her career frustrations and how she might try to work them out. The social worker listened attentively to her descriptions of persecution from others, neither agreeing nor disagreeing about their truth. He learned of her family relationships and how she planned to look for work after the probation. The social worker encouraged Jacqui to reflect on her current challenges in the context of her goals to return to work. Jacqui began to feel that the social worker sincerely wanted to understand her and had no intentions of using his power for coercive interventions such as referrals for vocational counseling, as others had done. He told her that when her probationary period ended he would report her compliance with the legal mandates to the appropriate authorities.

The social worker did not rush these interventions. He allowed this paranoid woman time to get to know him, and to test the validity of his interests in her. He continued encouraging ventilation and also person-situation reflection regarding her family and career. He asked her to think about what made others believe that she had a mental illness. The social worker became a trusted confidant, without being deceitful, and as a result Jacqui became willing to share more personal concerns with him.

As Jacqui became comfortable with the social worker he began offering other interventions, including education about job possibilities and partialization of her personal goals into more focused units. He provided some direct influence tentatively, offering opinions, for example, about how she might best prepare for job interviews. By the time her probationary period ended, Jacqui decided to stay involved with the mental health agency. She was still paranoid but less so (due in part to the medications), and became able to function well within a limited social and occupational range. She used the social worker as a sounding board for feedback when considering major life decisions (he gave no advice), and continued to take medications, which she perceived as useful for control of her anxiety as she dealt with new challenges. Jacqui had always been a churchgoer, but a new sense of spirituality emerged in her desire to become an advocate for other Lebanese-Americans. She decided to work toward initiating a monthly supportive discussion group for area Lebanese professionals. Jacqui eventually found part-time work as a college instructor and tax examiner. Her frequency of meetings with the social worker gradually diminished to monthly. He transferred her to another agency practitioner when he moved away several years later.

The Post-Traumatic Stress Survivor

Heidi was a 29-year-old married working mother (of a 12-year-old son) who came to the mental health center requesting help dealing with stresses associated with her job and marriage. Heidi, an assistant manager in charge of bookkeeping at a grocery store, wanted to function more effectively at work and qualify for a promotion. During his assessment the social worker took note of Heidi's history of sexual acting out prior to her marriage and her patterns of obsessive-compulsive behavior at work. He further noted Heidi's tendencies to intellectualize problems (a rigid defense). He was also impressed with her strengths of intelligence, motivation, and resilience.

In keeping with the client's stated goals, the social worker initiated a behavioral intervention strategy based on coping skill development. They agreed that Heidi would: (a) secure a comfortable, secluded space for reviewing her day's work once she returned home; (b) develop a daily pattern of communication with her husband (who was reluctant to come to the center) about their moods, mutual plans, and parenting responsibilities; and (c) learn a set of relaxation activities. The social worker set out to implement these strategies through education and structure. He also encouraged the client's reflections about her emotional life, because he did not want to support her tendencies to intellectualize.

The social worker also helped Heidi devise a regular exercise regimen (walking) to reduce her tension, and he encouraged her to contact several friends more regularly as a social outlet (Heidi was reluctant to reach out to others).

The social worker estimated that Heidi would achieve significant improvement in 6 to 10 sessions (the agency permitted a maximum of 16 sessions, unless special permission was granted), and they agreed to review their work after six weeks. Heidi made quick progress in her ability to manage her job responsibilities, as evidenced by her self-reports. The interactions with her husband were less successful, even though the social worker spent much time helping her rehearse strategies for better connecting with him. The worker noted that Heidi became more relaxed in their sessions over time and shared personal information more freely, which was evidence of their positive working alliance.

After their fourth session, however, Heidi's depression and anxiety increased. The worker observed that the more personal content she shared, the more negative feelings she experienced. Heidi eventually admitted that she was, in fact, a survivor of long-term sexual abuse by her father, beginning at the age of five and extending into her high school years. She added insightfully that she had learned as a young girl to suppress her emotions as a means of coping with that trauma. The present intervention had reawakened her range of emotions and she was losing the ability to control them (poor stimulus regulation). Heidi was experiencing insomnia, nightmares, and poor concentration. Most disturbingly, she began to experience additional memories of abuse. She became more aware of her father's actions and was overwhelmed with anger, despair, shame, guilt, and depression. She admitted to occasional suicidal wishes.

The social worker felt that their work was at a turning point. Heidi had sought help to deal with one set of problems, but another set of problems had emerged. Under this new stress her judgment was beginning to suffer and her sense of identity was becoming confused (feeling the strong influence of her father, though he was not physically present). The abuse memories made her less trusting of others, especially men, which negatively affected her everyday object relations. The social worker recognized that for Heidi to manage the effects of her abuse history she would need to explore her emotions rather than avoid them. In doing so she would likely become more distressed before developing new self-control. The social worker suggested, and Heidi agreed, that they expand their work together and use the ego psychology techniques of person-situation and developmental reflection in addition to the behavioral interventions, so that she could confront and manage the negative emotions stemming from her abuse. He also offered to refer Heidi at a later date to an abuse survivor's group led by a social worker at another agency.

The new, expanded set of goals included enhancing Heidi's external social supports (including communication with her husband), abuse history awareness, feelings of self-control, anger management skills, ability to manage negative emotions, and self-esteem. The social worker first helped Heidi solidify her friendships and positive family supports as resources to draw upon when she felt overwhelmed. He referred Heidi to the agency physician for a medication

evaluation when she requested medications, and an antidepressant was prescribed. The social worker also presented this case to the agency's peer review
team for extended care and was granted up to 16 additional sessions.

Together, Heidi and the social worker balanced her needs for nurturing and
support with her needs to face the facts of her abuse history and family trauma,
and learn to cope with them. From his ego psychology framework the social
worker encouraged a graduated process of reflection, providing Heidi with guidance and suggesting limits to the pacing of her self-exploration. He helped her to
give up some defenses and to strengthen others, build on her personal strengths,
and continue to develop stress-coping skills. Recognizing the agency's limits on
service delivery, they met three times monthly for six months. It was agreed that
Heidi could phone the social worker once weekly when in distress to ask what
she might do to calm herself.

The social worker needed to establish linkages with the agency psychiatrist,
staff at a local crisis facility (which Heidi attended three times), and staff at a psychiatric hospital, where she was admitted once for suicidal ideation. The social
worker monitored Heidi's progress by charting the frequency of her self-
reported anxiety attacks, feelings of self-harm, phone calls and visits with friends,
conversations with her spouse, and productive work days. The intervention contributed to Heidi's greater awareness of her needs, conflicts, and assets. It added
to her stress at times; Heidi's psychological growth was erratic but continuous.
She was able to make better decisions about her life goals and relationships
with family and friends.

The social worker integrated family and group work into the interventions.
He had observed that Heidi increasingly avoided sharing her feelings with her
husband. Also, she and her husband seemed to focus attention on their son rather
intrusively at times, largely to avoid a relationship with each other. Their son was
experiencing normal adolescent drives to separate from his parents, and he was
frustrated with their resistance to his changes. Three months into their clinical
relationship, Heidi agreed to the social worker's suggestion that her husband
come for several marital sessions. The social worker learned that she and her husband had developed avoidance patterns of dealing with intimacy. Heidi's relationship with her husband improved in that they could talk more openly in the
supportive atmosphere of the clinic about their needs and feelings. Heidi found
her husband to be more supportive than she had expected. Still, she made a decision near the end of her therapy to separate from him, allegedly as a means of
testing her ability to take care of herself, but also indicating that she was questioning her commitment to the marriage.

Near the end of Heidi's individual intervention she joined the group program
for survivors of sexual abuse, an open-ended group that met every two weeks. The
social worker leader organized the group as a mutual support rather than an insight-
development experience for the ten members. The social worker provided educational material for members about the prevalence of sexual abuse and the normalcy
of their reactions to the trauma. Heidi still struggled with her need to face the reality and consequences of her abuse history, but stated that the group helped her feel
much less alone. She developed additional supportive relationships there.

All of the interventions ended when Heidi made the decision to take a break from the intervention, after 24 total individual sessions. She had been confronting her abuse history for six months, and learned that she could integrate those facts into her sense of self without suppressing all of her emotions, losing herself in her work, or looking for others to rescue her. She was not completely at ease with herself and her past, but she had learned much and now wanted to focus her energies on other life pursuits, including her adjustment to living alone. The social worker agreed that her desire to end was indicative of Heidi's growth. She was ready to get on with her life without the support of a clinical practitioner. She had been following the leads of older men all her life, and now was ready to take control of herself.

EVIDENCE OF EFFECTIVENESS

The psychodynamic theories have a long tradition of the *case study* as a means of evaluating clinical process and outcomes (Lantz & Walsh, 2007). In case studies, practitioners discuss the characteristics of a client, family, or group, their own thoughts and actions, whether the client system improved, and whether the process was conducted appropriately. These studies are usually interesting, instructional, and rich in detail. They also tend to lack external sources of validation, except, at times, from the client. The literature includes hundreds of examples of ego psychology theorists and practitioners writing about single cases or summarizing a series of cases drawn from their own practices. The proponents of ego psychology are confident that this tradition provides a valid means of considering its effectiveness, and further maintain that many other theories overlook the complexity of the clinical process in their outcome studies. The validity of the theory is generally not questioned, although an author may conclude that certain approaches are not appropriate for a certain type of client.

It was noted in Chapter 2 that the case study method is unsatisfactory to some practitioners who feel that it is too subjective and not generalizable. Theories developed after the psychodynamic era have relied more on experimental, quasi-experimental, and structured single-subject methods. Another challenge to evaluating ego psychology is that its relatively non-specific intervention strategies make it difficult to determine whether a practitioner is, in fact, working strictly from the approach (although, as we shall see, this may be true of other theories as well). Practitioners do not see this as a problem as much as an acknowledgment that all clients are unique and deserve individualized interventions. It is interesting to note that the newest theory presented in this book, the narrative approach, also values the case study as a primary method of theory description and evaluation.

Listed here are examples of case study research in which ego psychology was found to be effective with various client populations. These include couples (Uhinki, 2001) and families (Nichols & Schwartz, 2007) in conflict, clients with schizophrenia (Leffel, 2000), children of alcoholic mothers (Dingledine, 2000), minority adolescents (Gibbs, 1998), adults experiencing grief reactions (Meuser,

1997), persons with substance abuse disorders (Murphy & Khantzian, 1996), persons with borderline personality disorder in groups (von Held, 1987), persons with mental illness in music therapy (Nolan, 1994), children with emotional and conduct disorders (Perris, 1992; Kernberg & Chazan, 1991; Ruttenberg, 1990), incest survivors (Kramer & Akhtar, 1991), people in crisis (Sands, 1984), and clients experiencing depression (Weiner, 1983).

Some efforts have been made to test the effectiveness of psychodynamic interventions using experimental designs. Falk Leichsenring and his associates have conducted several meta-analyses of randomized controlled (RCT) and quasi-experimental trials of psychodynamic therapy, of which ego psychology is a major derivative. In one study, Leichsenring (2005) reviewed the empirical evidence for the efficacy of psychodynamic therapy in specific psychiatric disorders. Studies of that therapy published between 1960 and 2004 revealed 22 randomized trials, and these provided evidence for the efficacy of psychodynamic therapy with depressive disorders (four trials), anxiety disorders (one trial), post-traumatic stress disorder (one trial), somatoform disorder (four trials), bulimia nervosa (three trials), anorexia nervosa (two trials), borderline personality disorder (one trial), Cluster C personality disorders (one trial), and substance-related disorders (four trials).

Leichsenring, Rabung, and Leibing (2004) tested the efficacy of short-term psychodynamic psychotherapy (STPP) in specific psychiatric disorders. They identified 17 studies of STPP published between 1970 and 2004 that used randomized controlled trials, treatment manuals (to insure the integrity and consistency of the interventions), experienced therapists, and reliable and valid diagnostic measures. STPP yielded significant effect sizes for clients' target problems, general psychiatric symptoms, and social functioning. Leichsenring and Leibing (2007) later reviewed the efficacy of STPP in depression, compared to cognitive-behavioral (CBT) or behavioral therapy (BT). Only studies in which at least 13 therapy sessions were performed were included. Six studies met the inclusion criteria, and in 58 of the 60 comparisons performed there were no significant differences between STPP and CBT/BT with regard to depressive symptoms, general psychiatric symptoms, and social functioning. Thus, STPP and CBT/BT seem to be equally effective methods in the treatment of depression.

While the above research is encouraging, ego psychology and other psychodynamic interventions continue to be criticized for a lack of sufficient evidence of effectiveness. Many professionals do not value the case study method of evaluation, and most practitioners would agree that more comparative research should be done on these interventions. Future process research should also address the complex interactions among interventions, clients' levels of functioning, and the nature of the helping alliance as well as concrete outcome measures.

CRITICISMS OF THE THEORY

Although it was once the social work profession's most widely used clinical theory, ego psychology (and all psychodynamic theories) has been increasingly criticized over the past 35 years (Rosen & Proctor, 2002; Goldfried & Wolfe, 1998; Conte, 1997; Myers & Thyer, 1997). Among the major criticisms are:

- The theory focuses on concepts that are rather vague (such as the ego, drives, and defense mechanisms).

- The intervention strategies are abstract and difficult to operationalize.

- Despite the drive to mastery and competence and its consideration of defense mechanisms as adaptive, the theory still appears to be deficits-oriented.

- The developmental theories that are commonly used in ego psychology (psychosexual, psychosocial, and moral, for example) do not adequately respect human diversity.

- Intervention strategies are open-ended and thus impractical in today's time-limited practice settings.

- Outcomes are difficult to evaluate without more concrete indicators. Practitioner reports of outcomes in case studies seem subjective. More controlled studies of the type described earlier are needed.

- Ego psychology may not adequately facilitate the pursuit of social change activities.

In response to some of these criticisms, proponents of ego psychology have made adjustments in recent years to address the changing face of clinical practice, primarily by devising focused, short-term approaches to intervention (Corwin, 2002).

SUMMARY

Ego psychology has been in existence longer than any other practice theory in this book. As a psychodynamic theory it appreciates the effects of unconscious mental processes on human behavior, and presents a comprehensive psychology of human development. Many of its intervention techniques are geared toward uncovering unconscious thought processes, but others maintain a concrete focus on the "here and now." Ego psychology is sensitive to the effect of the clinical relationship on the process of change, and emphasizes the importance of a client's reflecting on his or her thoughts and feelings as a means of developing mastery and competence with regard to presenting challenges. The theory has fallen out of favor somewhat in recent years because it has historically been an open-ended, abstract approach that does not easily lend itself to empirical examination. Still, many social workers use its concepts to guide their assessments, and many others find its intervention strategies useful to many types of clients.

TOPICS FOR DISCUSSION

1. Ego psychology considers that the quality of one's present functioning is in part the result of his or her mastery of prior developmental stages. Discuss from the perspective of Erikson's psychosocial theory how the manner in

which one has coped with a critical life stage in the past might affect present behavior without one being aware of that influence.

2. One major contribution of ego psychology to analytic thought is the concept of the drive to mastery and competence. Discuss what is implied by this drive, and whether you agree that it exists.

3. Consider each of the defense mechanisms (or a subset of them) and describe through examples how they can be utilized either as effective or ineffective coping strategies.

4. Briefly describe two types of clients: one for whom person-situation reflection might be a sufficient intervention, and another for whom developmental reflection might be needed in order to resolve the problem. What are the differences in these types of clients?

5. The intervention strategy of advice and guidance (direct influence) appears to run counter to ego psychology's emphasis on reflective techniques. Discuss examples of clinical situations in which this strategy might be appropriate.

IDEAS FOR CLASSROOM ACTIVITIES/ROLE PLAYS

1. Present a case scenario to the class, limiting the information to the nature of the presenting problem and type of agency. Divide the class into role-play groups of three students—a client, a social worker, and an observer. Assign to each group one, two, or three of the ego functions. Ask the student/social workers to assess the client *only* from the perspective of their assigned ego functions. Discuss afterward how the students sought information to accomplish this task. During the discussion ask if students from other groups have additional ideas for assessing the various ego functions.

2. List the ego psychology intervention strategies on the board. Ask students to consider the types of clients for whom each technique, either alone or in combination with one or more others, would be appropriate. Conversely, ask students to discuss types of clients for whom the strategies may not be suitable, either alone or in combination. What general themes seem to emerge in the students' perceptions of appropriateness?

3. Elicit from students a variety of presenting problem scenarios that might be suitable for ego psychology intervention. Select one scenario and write the client's relevant background information on the board. Ask students in small role-play groups (again with a client, one or more social workers, and one or more interviewers) to attempt an intervention that focuses on some combination of intervention strategies. Discuss the process afterward in the large group, including thoughts about what worked, what didn't work, and why. This activity can be repeated for various client types and combinations of intervention strategies.

APPENDIX: Ego Psychology Theory Outline

Focus	Ego: a mental structure that negotiates between a person's internal needs and the outside world
	Ego functions
	Unconscious thought
	Past and present person-environment transactions
Major Proponents	Hartmann, Erikson, Hollis, Goldstein
Origins and Social Context	Reaction to Freud's emphasis on instinct and his minimizing of ego and reality functions
	Efforts to extend psychoanalysis to build a psychology of normal development
	Development of the social and behavioral sciences
	Interest in adaptive capacities (strengths perspective)
	American culture (pragmatism)
	The rise of functional theory in the social work profession
Nature of the Individual	Ego contains all basic functions for adaptation: attention, concentration, learning, memory, perception
	Ego mediation of internal conflicts
	Drive to mastery and competence
	Stages of biopsychosocial (see p. 21) development
	Critical impact of life cycle events
Structural Concepts	Ego and its functions
	Reality testing
	Integration of internal and external stimuli
	Mastery and competence
	Direction of thought processes
	Drives (and their control)
	Defensive/coping functions
	Judgment
	Sense of the world and self
	Object (interpersonal) relations
	Superego: conscience
Developmental Concepts	Maturation of conflict-free, autonomous ego functioning
	Average expectable environment
	Psychosocial stages (Erikson)
	Object relations
	Processes of coping and adaptation
	Person-environment mutuality

APPENDIX: Ego Psychology Theory Outline (Continued)

Nature of Problems	Life events
	Heredity
	Health factors
	Ego deficits
	Maladaptive defenses
	Lack of fit between inner capacities and external conditions
	Maladaptive interpersonal patterns
Nature of Change	Ego mastery of developmental, crisis, transitional situations
	Learning new problem-solving, coping skills
	Emotionally corrective life experiences
	Better person-environment fit
	Conflict neutralization
	Reflection and insight
Goals of Intervention	Adjust defense mechanisms
	Increase adaptive capacities for ego functioning
	Modify maladaptive personality traits and patterns
	Improve fit between individual capabilities and environmental
	Conditions
Nature of the Worker/ Client Relationship	Genuineness, empathy, support
	Cultivation of positive transference
	Attention to countertransference
	Use of the relationship to address developmental needs
Intervention Principles and Techniques	Ego sustaining
	Exploration/description/ventilation
	Sustainment
	Person-situation reflection
	Structuring
	Education
	Direct influence
	Ego modification
	Developmental reflection (and some of the above)
	Focus first on conscious thoughts and feelings
	"Use of self" in providing feedback
	Use of the environment

APPENDIX: Ego Psychology Theory Outline (Continued)

Assessment Questions	What defenses is the client utilizing?
	How effective are the defenses?
	How is the client managing relationships?
	To what degree is the problem a matter of ego deficit versus conflict with other people or the environment?
	What circumstances are impeding the client's ability to manage the problem situation?
	To what extent is the client's stress a function of:
	– current life roles or developmental tasks
	– a traumatic event
	– a lack of environmental resources or supports?
	What inner capabilities and resources does the client have that can be mobilized to improve functioning?

4

Psychodynamic Theories II: Object Relations Theory

Each that we lose takes part of us;
A crescent still abides,
Which like the moon, some turbid night,
Is summoned by the tides*

As described in the previous chapter, clinical social workers have been using psychodynamic practice theories for almost a century. Those theories have experienced considerable evolution over the years in response to changing social values and ideas about the nature of human functioning. Psychoanalysis was followed by ego psychology, which in turn led to the development of object relations theory. In this chapter we will build upon the material presented on ego psychology and investigate object relations theory, a practice perspective that is distinguished by its attention to the role of relationships in people's lives.

Our first task is to clarify the meaning of the term *object relations*. It has almost a mechanical sound, but in fact "objects" refer to people, or portions of their personalities. The choice of that term is somewhat unfortunate for social work, which is more humanistic in its references to people. Beyond this issue, however, object relations has two meanings. Its general meaning is the quality of our interpersonal relationships. Ego psychology includes object relations as one of the ego functions, referring to our ability to maintain productive relationships with

* Reprinted by permission of the publishers and the Trustees of Amherst College from *The Poems of Emily Dickinson*, Thomas H. Johnson, ed., Cambridge, Mass.: The Belknap Press of Harvard University Press, Copyright © 1951, 1955, 1979, 1983 by the President and Fellows of Harvard College.

people in a variety of contexts. As a theory, however, object relations refers more specifically to our internalized attitudes toward others and the self, and how those attitudes determine our approach to new relationships. Object relations theory focuses on the internal world of our relationships and recognizes that these may be even more significant than relationships in the external world in shaping our thoughts, feelings, and behavior. One theorist refers to this as "the power of the situation in the person" (Goldstein, 2001, p. 131). The theory is concerned with how what is "outside" (relationships) gets "inside" (feelings about those relationships) and how our needs are met or not met in relationships. Object relations theory is also concerned with the effects of relationships on a person's ability to have a relationship with the self—that is, to perceive the self as continuous, feel good about the self, and feel comfortable when apart from others.

Object relations theory provides a bridge between the study of persons and family systems. It represents a shift in analytic thought from a focus on drives to a focus on relationships, and the relative weight given to each. Core issues in the theory include the nature of objects and how they become internalized (St. Clair, 1999). Like ego psychology, it is a developmental theory, and views stages in terms of unfolding object relations. The contributions of object relations theory to the science of human behavior include understanding attachments, how one's inner world becomes composed of representations of others, and the challenge of balancing being alone and being with others (Goldstein, 2001). Like the social work profession, it recognizes the influence of the environment on human development and social functioning, and values interpersonal connections over notions of independence.

ORIGINS AND SOCIAL CONTEXT

The emergence of object relations theory was in large part a natural evolution of psychoanalytic thought. No significant practice theory is static, of course. Theory evolution is a positive thing, indicating that many practitioners have adopted the theory and, through practice and research, discovered its areas of relative weakness as well as strength with regard to certain client populations and problems. As described in the previous chapter, psychoanalysis was initially focused on the drives and a rather pessimistic view of human nature featuring ongoing, inevitable conflict. Ego psychology represented an effort to build an analytic model of healthy human development. Object relations theorists, although varied in their particular contributions, attempted to correct the analytic focus on the individual and his or her drives, and bring the importance of relationships to the fore (Flanagan, 2007). There was such enthusiasm among practitioners for these developments that object relations became identified as a unique theory, rather than a development within psychoanalysis.

Other social influences on the development of object relations theory are described below.

The Effects of Early Nurturing

There is a large body of research devoted to studying the links between early life experiences and physical and mental health (Gerhardt, 2004; Gunnar, Broderson, Nachimas, Buss, & Rigatuso, 1996). This work demonstrates that negative infant experiences such as child abuse, family strife, poverty, and emotional neglect correlate with later health problems ranging from depression to drug abuse and heart disease. Relational elements of a person's early environments appear to alter the development of central nervous system structures that govern physiological and psychological responses to stress. These findings tend to support the lifelong significance of specific relationship interactions (Montgomery, 2002).

Animal models are common in this research, tracing the physiological aspects of rat and monkey stress all the way to the level of gene expression (Bredy, Weaver, Champagne, & Meaney, 2001; Lupien, King, Meaney, & McEwen, 2000). For example, it has been found that highly groomed young rats (pups) develop more receptors in their brains for the substances that inhibit the production of the corticotropin-releasing hormone (CRH), the master regulator of the stress response. As a result of tactile stimulation from their mothers, the pups' brains develop in a way that lowers their stress response throughout life. When the rats are switched at birth to different mothers, the pups' brain development matches the behavior of the mother who reared them, not their biological mothers. Further, high-licking and -grooming (nurturing) mother rats change their behavior significantly when given a substance that simulates the effects of chronic stress, raising their CRH and lowering oxytocin, a hormone related to the equanimity many human mothers feel after giving birth. Thus, under the influence of stress, the high-nurturing mothers behave like the low-nurturing mothers, and the pups in their care grow up the same way.

Many of you may be familiar with the tradition of research on the nurturing practices of rhesus monkeys, and research continues in this area (Suomi, 2005; Webb, Monk, & Nelson, 2001). In some of these experiments, monkeys are separated from their mothers at various intervals and raised in a group of other monkeys with a different mother. The infants who are separated later (three or six months) exhibit normal behavior in the new setting. Those separated earlier, however, show a variety of abnormalities. The monkeys separated at one month initially exhibit a profound depression and refusal to eat. Once they recover they show a deep need for attachments with other monkeys and great anxiety during social separation. The monkeys separated at one week showed no interest in social contact with other monkeys, and this did not change as they grew older. Autopsies of these monkeys show changes in brain development. The timing of separation from the primary caregiver seems to be significant to their later development.

This research has clear implications for human development in the concept of neural plasticity, or the capacity of the nervous system to be modified by experience (Knudson-Martin, 2004; Nelson, 2000). Humans may have a "window of opportunity," a critical period for altering neurological development, although this window varies for different areas of the nervous system. Even through the second decade of life, for example, external signals as well as internal biology influence neurological changes. Although stress can clearly affect brain development, any negative effects during the first three years of life are reversible (Nelson, 1999). A study of 2,600 undergraduate students found that, even in late adolescence and early adulthood, satisfying social relationships were associated with greater autonomic activity and restorative behaviors when confronting acute stress (Cacioppo, Bernston, Sheridan, & McClintock, 2000). Higher CRH levels characterized chronically lonely individuals. Secure emotional relationships with adults appear to be at least as critical as individual differences in temperament in determining stress reactivity and regulation.

In summary, secure attachments play a critical role in shaping the systems that underlie human reactivity to stressful situations. At the time infants begin to form specific attachments to adults, the presence of caregivers who are warm and responsive begins to buffer or prevent elevations in stress hormones, even in situations that elicit distress in the infant. In contrast, insecure relationships are associated with higher CRH levels in potentially threatening situations. Thus, one's object relations are critically important in one's development. Still, it must be emphasized that there is much to be learned in this area. Some people who have been subjected to serious early-life traumas become effective, highly functional adolescents and adults. Infants and children are resilient and have strengths that can help them overcome early-life stresses.

Attachment Theory

Attachment theory offers a beneficial foundation for understanding the connections between biology and social experience. It may be useful for us to consider one model of parent-child attachment here (Shorey & Snyder, 2006). All children seek close proximity to their parents, and they develop attachment styles suited to the types of parenting they encounter. Ainsworth and her colleagues (Ainsworth, Blehar, & Waters, 1978) identified three infant attachment styles—*secure, anxious-ambivalent*, and *avoidant* types. A fourth attachment style has been identified more recently—the *disorganized* type (Carlson, 1998; Main, 1996).

Parents of secure infants are sensitive and accepting. Securely attached infants act somewhat distressed when their mothers leave, but greet them eagerly and warmly upon return. Securely attached children are unconcerned about security needs, and are thus free to direct their energies toward non-attachment-related activities in the environment. Insecure infants, rather than engaging in exploratory behaviors, must direct their attention to maintaining their attachments to inconsistent, unavailable, or rejecting parents. Because these children are only able to maintain proximity to the parents by behaving as if the parents are not needed, the children may learn not to express needs for closeness or attention.

Anxious-ambivalently attached infants, in contrast, are distraught when their mothers leave. Upon their mothers' return, these infants continue to be distressed even as they want to be comforted and held. These children employ *hyperactivation* strategies. Their parents, while not overtly rejecting, are often unpredictable and inconsistent in their responses. Fearing potential caregiver abandonment, the children maximize their efforts to maintain close parental attachments and become hypervigilant for threat cues and any signs of rejection.

Avoidantly attached infants seem to be relatively undisturbed both when their mothers leave and when they return. These children want to maintain proximity to their mothers, but this attachment style enables the children to maintain a sense of proximity to parents who otherwise may reject them. Avoidant children thus suppress expressions of overt distress, and rather than risk further rejection in the face of attachment figure unavailability, may give up on their proximity-seeking efforts.

The disorganized attachment style is characterized by chaotic and conflicted behaviors. These children exhibit simultaneous approach and avoidance behaviors. Disorganized infants seem incapable of applying any consistent strategy to bond with their parents. Their conflicted and disorganized behaviors reflect their best attempts at gaining some sense of security from parents who are perceived as frightening. When afraid and needing reassurance, these children have no options but to seek support from a caregiver who also is frightening. The parents may be either hostile or fearful and unable to hide their apprehension from their children. In either case, the child's anxiety and distress are not lessened, and one source of stress is merely traded for another.

Although children with disorganized attachments typically do not attain the sense of being cared for, the avoidant and anxious-ambivalent children do experience some success in fulfilling their needs for care.

Contemporary Object Relations Theory

Recent developments in object relations theory include the emergence of relational-feminist and relational-cultural perspectives, which are not mutually exclusive. These will be discussed in greater detail in this chapter's section on major concepts.

Now we turn to the major concepts of object relations theory, all of which are considered in clinical assessment. These definitions are adapted from Flanagan (2007), Goldstein (2001), and St. Clair (1999).

MAJOR CONCEPTS

Many of the concepts associated with ego psychology are also used in object relations theory. In this section we will emphasize only concepts that are either unique to object relations theory or used in particular ways in the context of this theory.

The concept of *attachment*, described earlier, is central to object relations theory. It assumes that all people have an inherent biological need to form attachments with others in order to experience healthy development and to meet their emotional needs. Satisfactory human development is dependent on healthy early attachments. This is in contrast to earlier analytic theories, including ego psychology, that are more focused on drives than on relationships. As implied in the animal studies described earlier, there may be critical periods in which disruption of a key relationship can have long-term adverse consequences.

The process of *introjection* is the psychological "taking in" of the characteristics of other people. This is sometimes described as a defense mechanism in ego psychology, similar to internalization. For example, if a child is fearful of an aggressive parent, the child may take in (introject) characteristics of aggression so that he can better identify, and feel safe, with the parent. Introjection, more specifically, describes the process by which we become able to carry images of other people (our caregivers) within us when they are not physically present. We can maintain the sense of a parent's caring as we make our way through the limited environment of the household or neighborhood. Keep in mind that introjection refers to the process, not the content, of this activity.

A *representation* is the content, or result, of an introjection. It is a cognitive construction with deep emotional resonance; something like a "mental picture." It refers to the internal images of other people that we form and adhere to, perhaps consciously but often unconsciously. The quality of these images is crucial to our development of stable or unstable object relations. They are accompanied by affects, or strong feelings. An example is the individual who has a strong internal sense of a father figure, including the range of attitudes and behaviors (positive and negative) that such a person should display. The individual with that representation will experience strong emotions when encountering a (probably older) person with those qualities. People who develop frequent and significant interpersonal problems have a limited capacity to manage consistent and accurate representations of other people, and they tend to experience strong negative feelings when in conflict with them. The individual who is drawn to father figures, and who generally experiences strong positive emotions in their presence, may become extremely angry and rejecting when they feel disappointed by those people.

Object relations, described earlier, are the set of a person's internalized attitudes toward other people and toward the self. These develop through real interaction with significant other people in the context of facilitative or problematic environments. Our interactions with early caregivers are especially significant in determining later object relations with others.

The term *object* can be used to refer to an actual person in the physical world or one's mental representation of a person or a part of a person. An internal object is the same as a mental representation, but this is not true of an external object. I have an internal representation of my deceased father, and also of my living mother, but my living mother also exists as an external object. I have a real, ongoing relationship with her, even though we live far apart. The nature of an object and its emotional resonance is based in part on the actual characteristics of the external person and in part on our ideas and feelings about the individual. Its development depends on our internal temperament as well as the stability of the external environment in which we are located.

A *part object* refers to one or several characteristics that we have internalized about a person but not the "total" person. A client might maintain an internal representation of part of an individual that tends to be one-dimensional (good or bad) yet does not perceive the "total" person with both strengths and limitations. Early in the developmental process, a client may internalize his or her mother's caring qualities, or her hostile qualities, as part objects. *Splitting* others into part-objects can help the child avoid feelings of disappointment and rejection, perceiving the person as "bad." This is normal in children, but if it persists it can make the person fragile in relationships with others and even cause what they fear (rejection). A *whole object* is the internalization of all aspects of another person. In this instance the client is able to integrate experiences of gratification and frustration with the mother, father, or other primary caregiver. This ability to internalize a whole object represents a state of psychological maturity.

A *self-object* is an internal representation of one's own self. That is, we internalize aspects of ourselves (in whole or in part) as well as our experiences of others. We might internalize either a partial self-object or a whole self-object, with implications that we may feel positively, negatively, or both (at times) about ourselves. I may identify with my limitations (tending to be selfish at times, for example) and develop a negative self-object based on that characteristic, or I might have a more well-rounded self-representation. A *true self* is a self-image (or self-object representation) in which we recognize that we possess a variety of characteristics and needs, and we work to meet those needs. In contrast, a *false self* is a self-image in which one's personal needs are devalued and suppressed in deference to others. The person organizes his or her life around a desire to be compliant with, and pleasing to, other people. The true self is subjugated, with implications that the person never fulfils, or even consciously understands, his or her own needs.

Finally, *object constancy* is a mature psychological state in which we are able to maintain whole-object representations of significant people in our lives, even when separated from them. The person who experiences object constancy can maintain relationships even when separated from the other person for a long time. (Consider close friends who see each other only every few years.) With object constancy the person can balance being alone and being with others, and in either case maintain an awareness that there are available (or potential) people who care about them.

Additional Concepts from Contemporary
Object Relations Theory

Feminist Perspectives   Feminism does not refer to a single body of thought, but to a wide-ranging system of ideas about human experience developed from a woman-centered perspective (Lengermann & Niebrugge-Brantley, 2000). Among the psychological theories are psychoanalytic and gender feminism (Tong, 1998), both of which begin from the position that women and men approach relationships differently.

Psychoanalytic feminists assert that women's ways of acting are rooted in their unique ways of thinking. These differences may be biologically determined in part, but they are also influenced by cultural and social conditions. Feminine behavior, as Western culture understands it, features gentleness, humility, supportiveness, empathy, tenderness, nurturance, intuitiveness, and sensitivity. Masculine behavior in turn is characterized by strength of will, ambition, independence, assertiveness, rationality, and emotional control. Analytic feminists assert that these differences develop from early childhood relationships. Because women are the primary caregivers in our society, young girls tend to develop ongoing relationships with their mothers that promote their valuing of relatedness and the other feminine behaviors described above. For young boys the mother is eventually perceived as fundamentally different, particularly as they face social pressures to begin fulfilling male roles. This pressure to separate from the mother figure has long-range implications for boys, as they tend to lose what could otherwise become a learned capacity for intimacy and relatedness.

Gender feminists tend to be concerned with how values of separateness (for men) and connections (for women) lead to a different morality for women. Carol Gilligan (1982) elucidated a process by which women develop an ethic of care rather than an ethic of justice, based on their relational values. Gender feminists believe that these female ethics are equal to male ethics, although they have tended in patriarchal societies to be considered inferior.

In summary, psychological feminist theories promote the value of relationships and the importance of reciprocal interpersonal supports. Along with research on the importance of attachments, they have promoted ideas that are becoming central to object relations theory. In fact, many object relations theorists have appeared to value separation over relatedness in human relationships, and feminist thinkers are helping to counterbalance this notion.

Relational Perspectives

In recent years there has been an integration of the psychodynamic, object relations, and interpersonal theoretical perspectives, and this is broadly termed *relational theory* (Borden, 2009). The paradigm includes the relational-cultural and relational-feminist perspectives. In relational theory, the basic human tendency (or drive) is relationships with others, and our personalities are structured through ongoing interactions with others in the social environment. There is a strong value of recognizing and supporting diversity in human experience, avoiding the pathologizing of differences, and enlarging conceptions of gender and identity. It is assumed that all patterns of human behavior are learned in the give-and-take of relational life, and thus they are all adaptive, reasonable ways of our negotiating experience in the context of circumstances and the need to elicit care from others. Consistent with object relations concepts, serious problems in living are seen as self-perpetuating because we all have a tendency to preserve continuity, connections, and familiarity in our interpersonal worlds. Our problematic ways of being and relating are perpetuated because they preserve our ongoing experience of the self. What is new is threatening because it lays beyond the bounds of our experience in which we recognize ourselves as cohesive, continuous beings. That is, problematic interpersonal patterns are repeated because they preserve our connections to significant others in the past.

The relational perspective provides contexts of understanding for practitioners in their ongoing efforts to connect biological, psychological, and social domains of concern and to enlarge conceptions of persons in their environments. If this sounds to the reader like social work's longstanding focus on person-in-environment, it should! It seems, in this sense, that the psychodynamic thinkers have finally caught up to social work, although this connection is not often made in the literature. Still, relational theory differs from social work's overarching perspective in that it preserves analytic and object relations concepts while enlarging the scope of environmental concerns. Nonetheless, the similarity is striking, and relational practitioners encourage a variety of activities familiar to social workers, including brief intervention, case management, environmental development, and advocacy.

Regarding the therapeutic implications of the relational perspective, it is the client's subjective experience and sense of personal meaning that is always the focus of intervention. Both the client and practitioner participate actively in the helping process, and each influences the other in conscious and unconscious ways. Relational theorists encourage the social worker's natural, human, authentic manner of engagement with the client. Such practitioners engage in self-disclosure, and they encourage the client to regularly comment on the intervention process.

Contrary to traditional psychoanalytic notions, the relational social worker experiences and freely expresses a wide range of thoughts and feelings in the moment with a client, to facilitate a sense of mutual connection (Freedberg, 2007). Empathy is both a cognitive and emotional activity in which one person is able to experience the feelings and thoughts of another person as if they were one's own, while simultaneously being aware that his or her own feelings and thoughts are different from the other person's. This does not imply a neglect of appropriate boundaries, however. The mature practitioner will be capable of maintaining a relatively clear sense of self and flexible ego boundaries to allow for the high degree of emotional and cognitive integration necessary for empathy to be effective.

The relational-cultural approach enriches the concept of empathy by adding the notion of mutuality. The ability to participate in a mutual relationship through the use of empathic communication is seen as a goal for the client's growth and development, as well as a mechanism that allows for change in the worker/client relationship and beyond. Current social work literature reflects different views regarding the degree to which workers should remain emotionally detached with clients, but the general consensus calls for the worker to maintain a neutral, objective persona and a sense of separateness. In relational theory, the more the worker expends energy on keeping parts of herself or himself out of the process, the more rigid, and less spontaneous and genuine, he or she will be in relating to the client system. The worker/client relationship runs the risk of becoming organized into dominant and subordinate roles.

Relational theory incorporates an object relations perspective based on the inter-subjective aspects of self-development (Benjamin, 1990). This inter-subjectivity is a mutual recognition of the self and the other as people with unique subjective experiences and differences. The client gradually becomes able to recognize other people's subjectivity, developing the capacity for sensitivity and a tolerance of difference. Through relational intervention, the social worker is able to help the client to see others as distinct, rather than repetitions of others from the past, and thus the client is freed from the "pull" of past object relations.

The social worker continuously evaluates the relational context with regard to diversity issues such as age, race, culture, and gender, and their impact on the use of one's self in the empathic process. Comes-Diaz and Jacobsen (1991) have contributed greatly to social work's appreciation of these issues by analyzing the nature of ethno-cultural transference and countertransference in clinical practice (see Table 4.1) Building on relationship concepts discussed in the last chapter, these shared reactions of the social worker and client are related to perceived differences and similarities between the two parties. They are all assumptions, however, and only through open, empathic encounter can the parties become aware of the nature of their relationship and come to understand each other.

These are admittedly abstract, difficult concepts to understand. What follows are additional concepts from object relations theory that are specific to human development and that may help to clarify some of the above ideas.

DEVELOPMENTAL CONCEPTS

There are dozens of object relations theorists, and thus it is not easy to summarize what "the" theory says specifically about human development. In this section we will consider the ideas of two theorists who offer consistent but different accounts of the process: Donald Winnicott and Margaret Mahler.

TABLE 4.1   Issues in Ethnocultural Transference and Countertransference

Transference	
Inter-ethnic	**Intra-ethnic**
Over-compliance and friendliness	**Omniscient-omnipotent**
Denial of ethnicity and culture	**The traitor**
Mistrust, suspicion, hostility	**The auto-racist**
Ambivalence	**Ambivalence**
Countertransference	
Denial	**Over-identification**
Extreme curiosity	**Us vs. them**
Guilt	**Distancing**
Pity	**Cultural myopia**
Aggression	**Anger**
Ambivalence	**Survivor's guilt**

Donald Winnicott

Donald Winnicott was a British pediatrician who contributed much to the development of object relations theory. He was by all accounts a compassionate man, and his theoretical work features more of a strengths orientation than that of some of his contemporaries. His ideas are consistent with a social work perspective on the dynamics of infant development (in fact, his second wife was a social worker). His contributions include the following ideas (Winnicott, 1975):

A *facilitative environment* is one that flexibly adapts itself to the needs of the infant, rather than expecting the infant to adapt to it. This environment is comprised of people and resources that recognize the primacy of meeting the infant's needs so that he or she can develop in a healthy manner. This is an admittedly "fluid" concept that does not specify exactly what should be present in such an environment. This is open to the judgment of the practitioner.

Infant omnipotence refers to the infant's first perceptions, in which there is no perceived difference between the self and the world. This is a normal, functional stage in which the infant lives in a world of fantasy where, in a facilitative environment, his or her needs are met when they arise.

Good-enough mothering is another general term in which the mother is described as having a primary preoccupation with the child's welfare, or being focused on meeting the needs of the child above all else. This is a temporary situation in a facilitative environment, as the good mother will eventually resume attending to her other life demands and needs. Winnicott did not speak to the role of fathers, but we may suppose that the term "good-enough parenting" would be applicable in today's world of varied family constellations. Winnicott added that parental care should include the activities of holding the child (to give the child a sense of safety), handling the child (to develop his or her sense of uniqueness), and presenting other people and material objects to the child (to promote object relating). One of Winnicott's most famous contributions to object relations theory is the concept of the *holding environment*, a haven of security from which the child can begin to explore the world and take risks with a sense of confidence.

The *transitional object* is a physical object adopted by the child, representing an intermediate step between internal and external object relations. The object gives the child a sense of the parent being with him or her while being physically separate from that person. A commonly cited example is the blanket, although a variety of materials associated with the mother or father can serve such a function. Incidentally, transitional objects are not universal—they are specific to cultures that value independence (Goldstein, 2001).

Winnicott wrote that, in a facilitative environment, the child gradually moves from a position of dependence to one of independence. The stages in this process include *absolute dependence*, in which the child is completely passive in the relationship with the caregiver. The child moves into a state of *relative dependence* as he or she becomes—partly due to physical maturation and mobility—aware of his or her separateness. As the child develops social skills with family members and peers, he or she begins moving toward *independence*. The term *ego relatedness* refers to the child's increasing capacity to be alone.

Winnicott did not attach clear time lines to his developmental stages. As a contrast, the work of Margaret Mahler is described next.

Margaret Mahler

Margaret Mahler, born in Hungary, was trained as a pediatrician (like Winnicott), although she began practicing psychiatry soon after receiving her medical degree. She interacted with many of the original analysts in Europe prior to migrating to England and then to New York. Mahler's passion was working with children, and in her career she focused on the processes that lead to children's development of a "self." Her most famous work was *The Psychological Birth of the Human Infant* (Mahler, Pine, & Bergman 1975).

The twin concepts of *separation* and *individuation* describe the process by which an infant develops from a state of complete dependence on outside caregivers to one of object constancy, in approximately three years. The first two stages include *autism* (birth to three months), in which the infant senses no difference between the self and the external world; and *symbiosis* (one to five months), during which the infant senses a difference between the self and "other," but assumes that the other exists only to meet his or her needs. The third and final stage of separation and individuation occurs in the following four substages:

- *Differentiation* (5–8 months) represents the infant's awareness of his or her difference from the "other" and the capacity to function apart from that person.

- *Practicing* (8–16 months) is the period in which the infant applies his or her developing will to intentionally separate from the significant other for brief periods by, for example, crawling away.

- In *rapprochement* (16–24 months), the child learns that he or she can exist apart from the significant other, but that the other will be available to attend to the child's needs when the child returns or calls for help.

- *Object constancy* (24–36 months) is the mature stage of development in which the child has internalized the image of the significant other (object) and can spend longer periods of time alone without feeling abandoned.

Object relations theorists differ in their ideas about the specific stages involved in human development, but they tend to agree on the general process. It may be apparent to the reader that it would be impossible for a practitioner to assess the specific degree to which an adolescent or adult client's infant and early childhood environment was facilitative, or to what extent his or her development was healthy. This information would emerge from the family history and perhaps records from other providers, but it will always depend to some degree on the client's emotional memories. The client's needs will further be discovered through the nature of his or her relationship with the practitioner.

We have already noted the influence of relational theories on the idea that a person's capacity for relationships may be more important than his or her ability to separate or individuate. It is accepted among object relations theorists that a healthy person always seeks and maintains secure attachments, and that the process of becoming "independent" is not meant to suggest otherwise (Mitchell, 1988). In fact, as we have seen, the focus on the significance of relationships has become even more pronounced in contemporary object relations theory.

THE NATURE OF PROBLEMS

The development of healthy object relations is not an all-or-nothing process. When a person grows up with caregivers who are able to provide good-enough parenting, and in a facilitative environment, he or she will develop relatively intact and integrated object relations. The person will maintain the capacity throughout life to develop and sustain productive, satisfying relationships. The person may develop serious problems in living, and experience conflicted relationships, but will also have the capacity to manage interpersonal problems. Another person may grow up in an environment that is initially satisfactory, but becomes less so, due to abrupt changes in caregiving circumstances prior to the development of a stable internal environment. That individual will have "intermediate" success with object relations, developing problems managing some relationships, but probably not a major mental illness. A person who experiences early deprivation in both caregiving and the environment, however, will become unstable, anxious and fearful, and be at a greater risk of major mental illness and character disorders.

Persons with poor object relations tend to utilize the defense mechanism of splitting, which is a source of their chronic relationship conflicts. Splitting, described earlier, characterizes how a person sees others as "good" or "bad" prior to seeing them as "whole" (capable of having both types of elements) It is a universal defense (or coping) mechanism for young children. It is considered an "immature" defense because it is usually resolved by the parent figure demonstrating to the child that he or she can be loved without being gratified at all times. Splitting is used in adulthood when a person is incapable of tolerating ambivalent or mixed feelings about other people. The client perceives a "good" person as one who helps the client meet his immediate needs. The client cannot tolerate any negative feelings about a person who is perceived as being "good." Conversely, the client transforms any person who frustrates or angers him or her into a "bad" person. Thus, the client feels and believes that other people are either all good or all bad. He or she tends to alternate between idealizing and devaluing people. Once a person is devalued, it may be difficult for the client to feel positively about that person again.

Splitting always becomes an issue in clinical practice with persons who have poor object relations. A "good" person (a social worker, for example) who disappoints the client in some way (which is inevitable in anything other than a superficial relationship) becomes a "bad" person. The client completely and perhaps for a long time reverses his or her attitudes and actions toward that social worker. It is also common for the client to "split" the self into categories of good and bad, with an inability to integrate these perceptions of the self. As such the client may present to the social worker one day as attuned to the intervention process, and another day as detached or negative.

People with significantly impaired object relations, and who extensively utilize the defense mechanisms of denial, projection, splitting, and *projective identification* (discussed later), are frequently in conflict with their significant others. They cannot integrate the positive and negative aspects of those other people, and thus alternately love or hate them. In severe cases these clients may be diagnosed with personality disorders, enduring patterns of behavior with others that are pervasive and inflexible, leading to interpersonal distress and functional impairment (APA, 2000). The association of poor object relations with some personality disorders has been demonstrated in several studies (e.g. Fleischer, 1998). Practitioners will often move their focus from the specific presenting problem to the general personality disorder once it is diagnosed, and if they have the resources to address it.

THE NATURE OF CHANGE

For clients who experience problems stemming from fundamentally impaired object relations, change first requires that they develop insight into their repetitive negative interpersonal patterns. Second, they must modify their internal structures (objects) so that they can respond to others as unique human beings rather than as representations of past relationships (Masterson, 1972). This second task is addressed through initiating new relationships, or addressing existing relationships in new ways. The client must analyze and discuss his or her thoughts, feelings, and behaviors regarding these relationships with the social worker until new patterns become stable. For children and adolescents, insight is not a prerequisite for change. Young clients may be helped to change through environmental adjustments and practicing new behaviors.

ASSESSMENT AND INTERVENTION

The Social Worker/Client Relationship

The social worker's careful, consistent monitoring of the clinical relationship is critical in object relations theory (Goldstein, 1995). Remember that this is an interpersonal theory, with an assumption that a client's ongoing problems are related to a rigid replaying of old relationship dynamics with new people. The client will tend to act out his or her object relations patterns with the practitioner. For example, the angry man who is oppositional with authority figures will act the same way, sooner or later, toward the social worker. This is facilitative toward goal achievement because the practitioner can point out and discuss these dynamics with the client in a safe environment. It also ensures, however, that the social worker will experience a range of emotions in response to the client's behaviors that must be managed constructively. Thus there will be a strong focus on transference and countertransference issues in the clinical relationship (Hanna, 1993). This can be stressful for both parties, requiring clear structuring, limit setting, and occasional confrontation. The social worker will be challenged at times to provide an accepting, "holding" environment for the client.

An example of this challenge is seen in many clients' use of the coping/defense mechanism of projective identification (Ehrenberg, 1995). This mechanism also provides a good example of how people may interact unconsciously (on a level of affect) in addition to interacting on conscious levels. The client, when unconsciously experiencing an unacceptable emotion or impulse (such as despair or anger), will project that feeling onto the social worker, and behave in such a way that provokes the social worker to consciously experience that same emotion. The client then consciously (and verbally) identifies with the social worker's feeling, finally getting across his or her message. This can be thought of as a form of nonverbal communication.

A survivor of childhood sexual abuse, for example, may feel hopeless about her chances to ever feel stable and have relationships with men in which she will not be victimized. If the client is not verbally articulate, or is highly repressed, she may behave in ways that make the social worker feel helpless to assist her. She may speak with a quivering voice, express ambivalence, avoid eye contact, become tearful, ask to leave the session, and in other subtle ways exude a sense of despair. If the social worker acknowledges his or her own feeling of helplessness (and this really is how the social worker feels), the client may be able to admit that she feels the same way. The social worker needs to be alert to the possibility that his or her emotional status in the session reflects the client's emotional state, and be prepared to respond to this occurrence toward the goal of helping the client to become more self-aware and articulate. The social worker should also process these situations with the clinical supervisor to differentiate between his or her own emotional reactions and those that may be due to the client's projective identification.

Relationship management is central to intervention in object relations theory, but now we will consider a range of other assessment and intervention principles.

Assessment

The process of assessing clients from an object relations perspective is similar to that used in ego psychology, except for (as you might expect) a closer focus on the ego function of object relations. In order to maintain this focus, the social worker must provide "therapeutic space" to the client (not push the client too quickly to confide details of sensitive relationships). The practitioner then assesses the separation-individuation level of the client (as much as possible) from client reports and perhaps family reports or other available information. He or she also assesses the client's use of specific defense mechanisms that are common to persons with object relations problems. The social worker should also test the client's openness to interpretations, to find out whether he or she will be receptive to exploring the nature of significant relationships that carry a risk of high emotional reactivity.

The social worker should focus on the following types of questions in assessing a client's object relations:

- Does the client maintain positive relationships with some significant others (such as teachers, employers, and friends), or do most close relationships become conflicted?

- Regarding the client's interpersonal conflicts, are they rooted in present reality, or is an old relationship being repeated? Is the client tending to develop hostile interactions with significant others in the present as he or she did with a significant figure from early life?

- Do the client's behaviors seem to repeat early experiences with parents? For example, if the client felt neglected, is he establishing relationships today with people who are likely to be neglectful?

- Do the client's problem behaviors represent efforts to master old traumas by repeating them with other people? For example, if the client was abused by a primary caregiver, is she becoming involved with abusive others, and then trying unrealistically to demonstrate that she is worthy of affection?

- To what degree are the client's behaviors accurate renditions of what occurred in childhood? Does the client possess distorted memories of his or her past that need to be corrected?

- What cultural or environmental conditions are affecting the client's relationship-seeking behavior?

When relationship conflicts are assessed, they can be described in terms of three components: (a) the wishes, needs, or intentions expressed by the client, (b) the expected or actual responses from others, and (c) the client's own cognitive, emotional, or behavioral responses to the responses of others (Luborsky & Crits-Christoph, 1990).

Many instruments are available to aid in the assessment of clients' relationships. Several are mentioned here for descriptive purposes only, without data regarding their validity and reliability. The McGill Object Relations Scale measures relationships in the context of psychosocial development (Dymetryszyn, Bouchard, Bienvenu, de Carufel, & Gaston, 1997). The Krohn Object Representation Scale focuses on clients' adaptive and maladaptive mental representations (Levine & Tuber, 1993). The Blatt Object Relations Scale qualitatively measures a client's level of object representations (Daniels, 1994). Westen's Dimensions of Object Relations and Social Cognition Scale measures the content of a person's mental representations, affect tone, capacity for emotional investment, and sense of social causality (Schneider, 1990). The Self-Object Differentiation and Mutuality of Autonomy Scale measures the correspondence of children's and adolescents' levels of functioning with their developmental stage of object relations (Goldberg, 1989).

Intervention

The intervention strategies used in object relations theory are similar to those used in ego psychology, although there is a greater emphasis on sustainment and developmental reflection. These two strategies are especially important because, in object relations theory, there is a need to explore the client's interpersonal history and developmental milestones. This requires the social worker to be able to sustain a productive clinical relationship through periods of the client's anxiety, resistance, feeling confronted, mood changes, and testing of formal limits. If the practitioner is able to develop a "fund of empathy" with the client, the relationship will survive these likely ups and downs. Both of these strategies were introduced in the previous chapter and the reader is referred there to review them (pages 45 and 47).

Several object relations theorists have identified stages of intervention (Goldstein, 2001). In the early stage, the social worker provides a holding environment to reproduce positive early parenting experiences for the client. Whatever conflicts the client experiences in his or her life will be mirrored in the intervention. The social worker can then begin to model a different way of "being" with the client, which can help the client to develop a more consistent, integrated sense of self and sense of others.

The practitioner begins to interpret positive and negative patterns of interaction with people in various life contexts, suggesting their origins, intentions, and effects. The social worker interprets the clinical relationship in this way also, to demonstrate to the client that relationships can survive periods of conflict and negative interaction. In the middle stage, the social worker interprets the client's maladaptive defenses, such as splitting and projective identification, helping the client to look inward to understand what feelings and attitudes he or she is trying to disown and project. In the end phase, the client is helped to resolve major interpersonal conflicts and overcome developmental arrests. The client is guided into corrective experiences with people in his or her environment, using the success of the clinical relationship as a model for managing them.

As a part of these interventions, the clinical practitioner and client must agree on the limits of their relationship. They must negotiate how often they will meet, what the consequences are for any negative client behavior during or between sessions, the frequency of phone calls, and how crises will be managed. This must be done carefully because the social worker must enforce limits on the client's impulsive or demanding behaviors when they occur (which is likely). The practitioner should also intervene in the environment by helping the client bring structure to his or her daily life.

Ending Intervention

The process of ending intervention from the perspective of object relations theory may include one component not present in ego psychology. If the social worker has formed a constructive working relationship with a client who has had significant object relations deficits, the practitioner should openly explore with the client the *meaning* of the ending (Schermer & Klein, 1996). Reviewing the client's emotional reactions and stressing the positive gains that the client has made should make the transition out of the relationship less difficult for the client. The social worker should not assume that the ending will be difficult for the client, but raise the issue for discussion in order to minimize the possibility of difficulty.

ATTENTION TO SOCIAL JUSTICE ISSUES

Object relations theory is more facilitative of clients' pursuits of social justice-related goals than ego psychology because it is relational, rather than individually oriented. Within this theory the practitioner always attends to transactions between client systems and their environments, although the "environments" may at times be limited to the family and other close interpersonal systems. Object relations theorists in social work do not assume that clients who are vulnerable or oppressed in various ways, and who must deal with problems related to poverty, unemployment, and discrimination, experience those problems because of poor object relations. Still, like ego psychology, object relations is focused on small systems, and the social worker is not encouraged to look very far outward (except in the relational-cultural perspective) for types of influences on client functioning that tap into social justice issues. On the positive side, however, if clients who experience difficulties related to poor object relations receive help, they should develop an improved ability to manage important relationships in all facets of their lives, and be better able to address any challenges related to the environmental issues described above. One great challenge for object relations practitioners is to understand how interpersonal processes unfold for members of other cultures and ethnic backgrounds, so that those clients can be empowered by the resolution of their interpersonal problems.

CASE ILLUSTRATIONS

The Wild Child

Carolyn, a 15-year-old Caucasian adolescent, was "always in trouble," according to her mother. She had been referred to a social worker at the mental health center for an assessment after getting caught with several friends setting fire to dry brush along the side of a highway. No one had been hurt, but the blaze became large and took several hours for the fire department to extinguish. Carolyn faced legal charges for this incident, and was being considered for possible incarceration by the juvenile court. In the past, Carolyn had been in legal trouble for a series of petty theft incidents. Her mother had also become concerned that Carolyn was engaging in promiscuous sex, and possibly prostitution.

Carolyn was the third and youngest child (with two brothers) born to a middle-class couple from a large Midwestern city. Her parents complained that "she has no reason to behave as she does—she always had everything she needed." Still, Carolyn had frequently been in trouble with her parents, schoolteachers, and other authority figures since the first grade. She tended to be argumentative, moody, oppositional, and inconsistent in tending to her assigned responsibilities. Her father said, "she's an angry, unhappy, ungrateful kid." On the other hand, Carolyn was athletic, energetic, and had excellent social skills. She had many friends, although many of them shared her negative attitudes and were considered poor influences. Carolyn had average intelligence but did poorly in school, with no evident motivation to study. She had no sense that she should develop long-range goals.

The social worker's role was to make counseling recommendations to the court that would be taken into account regardless of her placement. She might have the opportunity to work with Carolyn over time, but this depended on the outcome of the court hearing. In conducting the assessment, the social worker learned that Carolyn's parents were about 50 years old and had been married for 30 years. Her father was an equipment technician at a local television station, and her mother worked part-time as a real estate agent. They reported that their marriage was stable, and that they had tried to raise Carolyn to be a responsible person. Her mother, in particular, felt that she had spent more time with Carolyn than her other two children, trying to help her develop appropriate values and interests. Carolyn was seven and nine years younger than her brothers. She had cordial relationships with them but, partly due to the age difference, they were not close. Carolyn saw her siblings only during holidays and family celebrations.

Carolyn expressed a different view of the relationship with her parents. She said her mother was overbearing and would never allow Carolyn out of her sight. Carolyn accused her mother of trying to keep her home as much as possible for as long as she could remember. She said that her father was "okay," but distant. In her words, he worked long hours and was not very involved in her life. Carolyn added that her father was not very involved in her mother's life, either. She complained that they stayed at home most of the time when not working, and that they didn't talk much.

The social worker learned that Carolyn's upbringing was affected by a critical event. Her mother, who had wanted a daughter very badly, had given birth to a stillborn girl three years before Carolyn was born. This was a traumatic event for the family. Her mother was depressed for a year after the event. When she became pregnant with Carolyn, she was thrilled but apprehensive. She and her husband learned of the baby's gender early during the pregnancy, and she became completely focused on having a safe pregnancy and delivery. She quit her job and stayed home. When Carolyn was born she was overjoyed, and then became a devoted but overprotective parent. Her husband admitted that his wife had been obsessed with Carolyn and wouldn't let her out of his sight. In fact, her husband was angry about his wife's attitude, and withdrew emotionally from her. This pattern of relationships seemed to characterize the family during Carolyn's life, up to this point. The social worker tentatively concluded that Carolyn was angry about the perceived overprotection. She had not developed a capacity to manage close relationships due to object relations deficits stemming from that experience.

The social worker had no way of objectively knowing the conditions of Carolyn's early upbringing. However, as she got to know the client over time, she saw a pattern emerge in which Carolyn was afraid of getting close to or trusting anyone for fear of being consumed by them—of losing her identity completely. At the same time, Carolyn felt empty and abandoned by caregivers and friends who would not provide her with the security she needed. Carolyn often described a "hole" in her abdomen that was painful to experience, and which she tried to fill with adventure, alcohol, and, more recently, sex. That is, though many of Carolyn's problem behaviors were related to present circumstances and the influence of her friends, they were also rooted in her inability to develop steady attachments, or stable object relations, with others. She tended to see people as "good" when she was friendly with but not close to them, and as "bad" when they became closer to her.

Interestingly, this pattern did not stem from a lack of parental attention—just the opposite! Carolyn did not have opportunities for age-appropriate movement toward independence because of her mother's well-meaning but intrusive presence. Carolyn's environment was positive in many ways but not facilitative of her needs for separation. Carolyn came to equate closeness with suffocation. Her defensiveness included a strong anger with which she acted out her fears with oppositional behavior.

Carolyn appeared to form a tentative attachment with her social worker, a young, single female. The social worker did not use the intervention technique of developmental reflection because the client was not reflective by nature. They instead focused on her current life concerns. The technique of sustainment was important, however, as Carolyn often became anxious, angry, and subversive of the intervention process as she became closer to the social worker and was challenged to disclose sensitive information about her life. The social worker accommodated the client's lability by being flexible with their schedule. She also allowed Carolyn to take the lead in formulating topics for their meetings, and she was confrontational only when it appeared that the client would not react negatively.

With person-situation reflection the social worker encouraged Carolyn to talk about the emotions she experienced in her current life activities, rather than project blame elsewhere. She helped Carolyn understand some of her relationship patterns, and helped her grasp the issue of her ambivalence in relationships. The social worker used their relationship to demonstrate how Carolyn tended to react to others when issues of intimacy emerged. The practitioner provided many structured interventions as well. Knowing that Carolyn had little self-confidence and was reluctant to take on any challenges, she encouraged the client to explore some of her talents and interests such as swimming and a school service club that included visiting nursing homes.

The social worker met with the client and her parents together only a few times. They were not requesting family intervention and Carolyn had asked for individual attention during this assessment for the courts. During their joint sessions the social worker was careful to maintain a positive atmosphere with the conflicted family. She pointed out the caring of the parents and educated them about the nature of Carolyn's interpersonal problems. The family was encouraged to talk more openly among themselves, and the parents were encouraged to support Carolyn's healthy activities. The social worker stated that she would like to provide regular family sessions if Carolyn remained at the agency.

The social worker formulated a set of recommendations for the professionals who would be working with the client if she was placed in a residential facility that reflected the spirit of object relations theory. The social worker emphasized Carolyn's problems in relationships but also her strengths, and noted that she would likely benefit from modeling by slightly older females, a combination of supportive and confrontational interactions, and peer counseling. In short, corrective relationships might help Carolyn break her "approach–threat–anger–acting out" cycle. In the end Carolyn was sentenced to time in a residential facility. The social worker was disappointed, but believed that with appropriate interactions Carolyn might become better able to understand that intimacy did not inevitably lead to a loss of identity. With this understanding her relationships might improve and her acting out behaviors might decrease.

The Group Therapy Intervention

Jordan was a 34-year-old single unemployed white male, living with his mother, sister, and brother-in-law in the latter couple's home. He complained of depression, poor self-esteem, and extreme discomfort around other people. Though he was intelligent, cared about others, and had a charming self-deprecating wit, Jordan had difficulty making and then sustaining relationships, and could not hold a job. During her assessment, the social worker learned that Jordan entered into relationships only if he felt he might receive unconditional positive regard. When he perceived that this was not forthcoming, he felt betrayed, became angry, and terminated the relationship. For these reasons he had no close friends and, when working, became so anxious with interpersonal pressures that he quit. Jordan visited prostitutes to satisfy his sex drive, and was particularly ashamed of this secretive practice. He was not comfortable with his living situation and sought counseling at a mental health center to see if he could become more independent.

The social worker diagnosed Jordan with dysthymic disorder and avoidant personality disorder. The client confided that his father had always been stern and critical, and though his mother was more outwardly caring, she was passive in the family unit. Jordan recounted many examples in his upbringing of his father forcing him to engage in tasks that might have been age-appropriate for some children but were beyond his developmental capability, such as giving a short presentation at a Boy Scout meeting. At these times the child cried with fear, but his mother stood by quietly. Jordan had felt insecure, inferior, and full of self-doubt his entire life. He always doubted the good will of others and, in keeping with his family pattern, assumed that other people looked down on him. From Jordan's perspective his older brother and younger sister seemed to be much better adjusted than he was.

For several months, the social worker intervened to help Jordan move toward his goal of self-sufficiency as he sought better social skills, employment, and junior college enrollment. She provided the interventions of sustainment, person-situation reflection, and, eventually, developmental reflection. She began challenging Jordan to face up to his anger and to recognize his maladaptive defenses (particularly splitting and projection). The social worker was careful not to be overly confrontational, however. She perceived that Jordan was always ready to reject others before he was rejected, and did not want the therapy to end for that reason.

Neither did she structure their time together or impose agendas on the client. She wanted Jordan to be in control of the process and to move at his own pace.

Jordan came to trust the social worker and became more comfortable in general. Over a period of several months he demonstrated progress by applying for jobs, attending interviews, and visiting a regional college campus to investigate part-time enrollment. Still, with each initiative he became incapacitated with anxiety and the fear of failure. The social worker referred him to an agency physician who prescribed a small dose of anti-depressant medication that helped Jordan sleep better at night, stabilized his mood, and reduced his anxiety. The social worker also referred Jordan to a therapy group that she co-led. The idea of talking in a group was traumatic for the client, and only after several months of considering the recommendation did he decide to participate.

It was in group therapy that Jordan made his greatest improvements. He attended an ongoing, relationship-oriented group that met weekly for 16 weeks. It included four women and two other men. All of the members faced different life challenges, but they shared difficulty with close relationships. The social worker and her co-leader were nondirective in their leadership, asking questions and making comments that promoted person-situation and developmental reflection. They helped the group develop an atmosphere of mutual sustainment, but in the spirit of developmental reflection also facilitated confrontations at times, generating anxiety in the members so that they faced up to their major defenses. Jordan was not initially pushed to participate with the others, but soon after beginning the group he decided that his interpersonal skills and comfort level were greater than he had assumed.

The group followed Goldstein's (2001) three-stage model. In the early stage, the social workers provided a holding environment to reproduce positive early parenting experiences for the members. The co-leaders interpreted positive and negative patterns of interaction among the members, suggesting their origins, intentions, and effects. The social workers tried to model for the clients through their own behavior that relationships can survive conflict. In the middle stage of the process the practitioners interpreted the members' maladaptive defenses (splitting and projection), helping them to understand the feelings they were trying to disown. In the end stages the social workers emphasized that each member's relationships with the others represented corrective experiences to their earlier patterns. The leaders also began to generalize the members' intra-group experiences to their other life conflicts.

During the course of attending the group, Jordan developed positive feelings about most of the members and even became a friend of one other male member. At the time the group ended, he was taking classes at the community college in preparation for a career as an electrician. Interestingly, he experienced a relapse when the group ended. The end coincided with one leader unexpectedly leaving the agency to take another job. Jordan became upset and accused the co-leader of not caring about the members after all this time together. It was an awkward final session for Jordan, but the social worker felt confident that the relapse would be short-term and that the client would be able, with the support of others, to resolve his anger and turn his attention to his remaining vocational work.

EVIDENCE OF EFFECTIVENESS

Some research efforts to test the effectiveness of psychodynamic theory, of which object relations is a major type, were summarized in the last chapter. Here we will review evidence of effectiveness of object relations theory more specifically. Despite its limitations with regard to large-scale research validation, object relations theory has been successfully used with clients who face a variety of problems and challenges in meeting their goals. The literature demonstrates that its interventions have been effective with adult daughters of alcoholic mothers (Dingledine, 2000), persons in methadone treatment programs (Wood, 2000), persons struggling with chronic loneliness (Coe, 1999; Feldman, 1998), children in foster care (Metzger, 1997), sexually abused inner-city children (Josephson, 1997), survivors of child abuse (Ornduff, 1997), young girls with depression (Goldberg, 1989), persons recovering from the trauma of heart disease (Hartstein, 1990), persons with psychotic disorders in group settings (Takahashi, Lipson, & Chazdon, 1999), juvenile delinquents (Loftis, 1997), young inpatients with serious emotional disorders (Blatt, Ford, Berman, Cook, Cramer, et al., 1994), women in groups who have been sexually abused (Burns, 1997), and persons with borderline personality disorder (Levine, 2002). Interventions based on object relations theory have also been effectively used in a multicultural context, with clients from Puerto Rico (Rosario, 1998).

Although a majority of reports about the effectiveness of object relations interventions are based on client outcomes in case studies, some are based on research designs that include larger numbers of clients. In a pre-test/post-test study of 23 clients with borderline personality disorder receiving transference-focused psychotherapy for 12 months, client measures of suicidality, self-injury, and medical and psychiatric service utilization dropped significantly (Clarkin, Foelsch, Levy, Hull, Delaney, et al., 2001). Another pre-experimental study followed 20 clients receiving brief therapy to investigate whether their *quality of object relations* (QOR) would increase during clinical intervention (Schneider, 1990). Measures were taken at intake, termination, and six months later of the clients' complexity of representations and capacity for emotional investment. The finding of a significant correlation between improved QOR and positive therapy outcome supported the hypothesis at all data collection points. Another study investigated the relationship between the mastery of maladaptive interpersonal patterns and the outcome of intervention (Grenyer & Laborsky, 1996). Transcripts from the psychodynamic psychotherapy of 41 clients were scored using a content analysis mastery scale. Changes in mastery of interpersonal conflicts over the course of therapy were significantly related to changes in observer, practitioner, and clients' reports of problem resolution. These results are consistent with the object relations proposition that symptoms abate with the mastery of core interpersonal conflicts.

Another study followed clients at six- and twelve-month intervals to investigate the efficacy of both interpretive and supportive forms of short-term therapy, and the interaction of each type of therapy with the client's QOR (Piper, McCallum, Joyce, Azim, & Ogrodniczuk, 1999). Clients receiving both forms of therapy maintained intervention gains across both time intervals, although there was a direct relationship only between QOR measures and favorable outcome in the interpretive therapy that focused on patterns of the clients' relationships. The authors concluded that QOR was an important predictor of outcome for persons receiving that intervention.

Several studies have focused on children and adolescents. Tuber (1992) reviewed the literature on the association between assessment of children's object representations and intervention outcomes. He concluded that accurate assessment in this regard did tend to increase the likelihood of positive outcomes for children. A study of 100 inner-city females between 8 and 16 years old concluded that girls reporting more depression had significantly earlier developmental levels of object relations than did girls reporting less depression, regardless of their chronological ages (Goldberg, 1989). In a quasi-experimental study of six families (three of which served as controls), the potential for an object relations family intervention including components of cognitive therapy to increase anger control in aggressive male adolescents was investigated (Kipps-Vaughan, 2000). Program effectiveness measures were collected over a five-month period from teachers, parents, and the adolescents. Comparative measures indicated that the intervention had a positive effect on the adolescents' anger control, family relationships, problem-solving skills, quality of communication, and school grades, and that clients experienced a decrease in school suspensions. Changes in QOR were also studied among 90 adolescents in a long-term, psychodynamic inpatient program (Blatt & Ford, 1999). Clients were divided into two diagnostic categories based on their pathology: disorders related to interpersonal relationships and disorders related to the sense of self. Based on responses to projective tests, the researchers concluded that the adolescents' improvements were characterized by a decrease in inaccurately perceived relationships with others.

Finally, in an unusual study conducted at a religiously oriented inpatient facility, an object relations intervention was evaluated with 99 primarily depressed clients (Tisdale, Key, Edwards, & Brokaw, 1997). Effectiveness was measured by changes in the personal adjustment and positive "God image," with measures taken at admission, discharge, and six and twelve months after discharge. The researchers concluded that the hospital program had a significant positive impact on both variables and that there was a positive correlation between object relations and the clients' God image.

CRITICISMS OF THE THEORY

Object relations theory has been subjected to many of the same criticisms as has ego psychology. Johnson (1991) summarizes several of these. First, the theory features concepts that many social workers believe are vague (such as objects, object relations, object constancy, and projective identification). Further, its intervention strategies appear to some practitioners to be difficult to operationalize and systematically evaluate. Other social work authors have expressed additional concerns. Object relations theory may promote client assessment from the perspective of developmental theories that do not reflect cultural diversity (Applegate, 1990). Practitioners working from this perspective may tend to see problems only within people and their intimate relationships rather than in the context of a larger environment. The theory focuses attention on processes of early development that are often difficult to validate due to possible biases in client or family reporting (Payne, 2005). As a depth approach to intervention it may not be useful in many traditional social work settings (Cooper & Lesser, 2002). Finally, because the first wave of object relations theorists wrote in the 1950s and 1960s, when the nuclear family was more prominent and gender roles were rigid, it is seen as a mother-blaming approach to problems in living (Coleman, Avis, & Turin, 1990). More recently, practitioners and theorists have attempted to apply object relations interventions to members of diverse client populations. They have also attended to issues of time limits in clinical practice (Goldstein & Noonan, 1999).

SUMMARY

This concludes our review of two psychodynamic theories, ego psychology and object relations, each of which emphasizes the importance of the practitioner attending (when possible) to clients' unconscious mental processes as a means of helping them resolve challenges and experience psychological growth. Few theories in this book deny the possible existence of an unconscious (except behaviorism), but in these theories it is given greater relevance as a determinant of social functioning. For practitioners who value empirically based practice, these two theories are problematic because they include concepts that are difficult to operationalize. Still, the ego psychology and object relations theories continue to be used as the primary perspectives of many clinical social work practitioners, who find that they provide a basis for flexible interventions with a range of clients.

TOPICS FOR DISCUSSION

1. It is not unusual for some people to have difficulty developing satisfactory relationships with certain types of others, such as authority figures, members of the opposite sex, or work peers. Yet these people may not have pervasive relationship problems. Do these recurrent but specific problems represent object relations deficiencies, or something less fundamental? If these specific problems are different, what might be their sources?
2. Discuss what you perceive to be the characteristics of people who maintain appropriate balances between "independent" and "relational" life. How do different perspectives on this point reflect personal values or cultural differences?

3. Discuss what is meant by the following abstract terms, and provide examples of how they might "appear" in one's life: *introjection, representation, object, part object, whole object,* and *self-object.*

4. What do you perceive to be the characteristics of a facilitative environment for an infant or young child? How might cultural differences lead to different ideas about such an environment?

5. Consider the concept of projective identification. Try to recall if you have been the recipient of this phenomenon at any time in your life, with clients or otherwise. Describe the process and the feelings you experienced.

IDEAS FOR CLASSROOM ACTIVITIES/ROLE-PLAYS

Each role-play activity can be done with one set of students (and perhaps the instructor) in front of the class, or in small groups. The roles of social worker, client, and observer should all be represented, and each role may include more than one person.

1. Present a real (from a student) or hypothetical situation in which a client with object relations deficits experiences conflict with the social worker. Play out the session for some period of time (15 minutes should be sufficient). Afterward, ask the observer in each group to describe any evidence of the social worker's frustrations with the interaction. Ask the social workers how they tried to sustain the client, even when confrontation was necessary. Finally, ask the clients how they experienced the behavior of the social worker.

2. Present a situation featuring a client who has fundamental object relations deficits, and whose presenting problem is being fired from a series of jobs due to interpersonal conflicts. Present as much information to the class as is available (using students' own cases is always preferable). Ask the students to devise a guiding intervention strategy, and then act out a role-play in which that strategy is implemented. Discuss afterward what worked well and what didn't work so well in each group.

3. Present a situation in which the identified client is a child or adolescent who displays aggressive acting-out behaviors with other children at school. Ask the students to identify possible sources of information to determine whether the client has significant object relations deficits, including specific questions the social worker could ask the family, other primary caregivers, or school personnel.

4. Consider Comes-Diaz's list of possible ethnocultural transferences and countertransferences in the client/worker relationship. Identify issues from the list that you have experienced with clients or other acquaintances. Try to identify the sources of your (or the other person's) feelings, and what you did, or might have done, to process them with the other person. (This item could be used as a written course assignment.)

APPENDIX: Object Relations Theory Outline

Focus	Interpersonal relationship patterns
	Internalized perceptions of the self and others
	Re-enactments of early relationships
Major Proponents	Jacobson, Klein, Fairbairn, Mahler, Kernberg, Winnicott, Bowlby, Ainsworth, Goldstein, Benjamin, Mitchell
Origins and Social Context	Studies of early childhood deprivation and its effects
	Interest in the role of early relationships (attachment theory)
	Studies of infant–mother interactions (1940s, 1950s)
	Feminism
Nature of the Individual	Healthy development requires a nurturing early environment
	People are relationship-seeking from birth
	People internalize their early relationship patterns
Structural Concepts	Same as ego psychology (id, ego, superego, ego functions)
	Attachment
	Introjection
	Object relations (whole, part, and self-objects)
	Object constancy
Developmental Concepts	Facilitative environment
	"Good-enough" parenting
	Holding environment (for safety and security)
	Transitional objects
	Stages of object relations development
	Winnicott
	Absolute dependence
	Relative dependence
	Toward independence
	Mahler
	Autism
	Symbiosis
	Separation/individuation (differentiation practicing, rapprochement, object constancy)
	From feminism
	Relationship differentiation (vs. separation/individuation)
Nature of Problems	Internalization of "bad" self and object (other people) perceptions
	Extensive use of splitting and projection in relationships
	Repetitive self-defeating behavior

APPENDIX: Object Relations Theory Outline (Continued)

Nature of Change	Insight
	Modification of faulty "internalizations"
	Development of positive internalized self and object perceptions
	Adjustment of defense mechanisms
Goals of Intervention	Modification of internalized relationship patterns
	Modification of defenses
	Growth in areas of ego deficit
	Acceptance of new experiences as new, rather than as repetitions of older ones
Nature of Social Worker/Client Relationship	Emphasis on transference, countertransference
	Emphasis on the present relationship and how it is affected by the client's interpersonal patterns
	Provision of a holding environment
	Inter-subjectivity
Intervention Principles and Techniques	"Here-and-now" reality testing
	Set limits on impulsive and demanding behavior
	Bring structure to the client's life
	Developmental reflection
	Interpret the nature of relationships in new ways
	Interpret transference
	Confront primitive defenses
	Provide a corrective relationship
	Guide into corrective experiences
Assessment Questions	Does the client maintain positive relationships with some significant others, or are most close relationships conflicted?
	What old relationship is being repeated?
	Do behaviors repeat early experiences with parents?
	Do problem behaviors represent efforts to master old traumas by repeating them with others?
	To what degree are the client's behaviors accurate renditions of what occurred in childhood?
	What cultural conditions are affecting the client's relationship-seeking behavior?
	What environmental conditions are affecting the client's relationship-seeking behavior?

5

Family Emotional Systems Theory

Alone, I cannot be –
For Hosts – do visit me –
Recordless Company
Who baffle Key –
Their Coming may be known
By couriers within –
Their going – is not –
For they're never gone★

S ince its introduction in the 1960s, *family systems theory* has thrived as an influential and widely used theory of family assessment and intervention. The
theory provides a comprehensive conceptual framework for understanding how
emotional ties within families of origin (including extended family members) influence the lives of individuals in ways they often fail to appreciate and may tend
to minimize. The theory is sometimes called *family emotional systems* theory to
underscore this point, and to distinguish it from the generic "family systems"
term. This theory is unique in its attention to multigenerational family processes
and also in its prescriptions for working with individual clients in a family context (Bowen, 1978; Kerr & Bowen, 1988). It is placed directly after the psychodynamic theories in this book because its creator, Murray Bowen, was trained as
an analyst and, in my view, the theory can be understood as an extension of

some analytic ideas (such as unconscious mental processes) to the study of family systems.

Bowen asserted that the nature of healthy human functioning includes one's acquisition of a balance between emotional and rational life. The concept of differentiation characterizes one's ability to achieve this balance. The concept also describes one's ability to function effectively both apart from and within the family of origin. Differentiation is made possible by a facilitative family environment in which the person can establish an identity related to, but also separate from, the identity of the nuclear family. Within most cultures of American society, people typically accelerate the processes of physical and emotional separation from their families of origin during late adolescence. This is a major life transition for those who leave and those who stay behind. People who have achieved a high level of differentiation will be successful in this transition, and those who have not will experience difficulty establishing a stable sense of identity outside the family. Each person's capacity to develop positive relationships in adulthood is driven by his or her learned patterns of managing family of origin relationships. That is, the influence of that family is pervasive throughout life.

The concepts from family systems theory may be useful to social work practice, with all types of presenting problems, as a means of assessing the nature of family interactions. Understanding the subtle aspects of family relationships may be significant in treatment planning, regardless of the family's specific needs. The intervention strategies, however, are not appropriate for all problem situations. Family systems interventions are generally appropriate when the focus will be on the quality of nuclear or extended family interpersonal processes, and the desire for one or more family members to become more differentiated. These families often appear to the outside observer to be functioning well. It is their interpersonal lives that are the sources of their difficulties. Some structural stability in the family is necessary for the social worker to help members explore any patterns of behavior that may be contributing to problem situations.

Titelman (1998) edited a book that includes examples of a range of problems for which family systems interventions may be appropriate. These include family problems related to marital fusion, emotional dysfunction in children, a child with a medical problem, college students with adjustment problems, concerns about elderly members, depression, phobias and obsessive compulsive disorder, alcoholism, incest, divorce, and remarriage. More recently the theory and its interventions have been found useful for issues encountered in adolescent substance abuse and other risky behaviors (Knauth, Skowron, & Escobar, 2006), child abuse (Skowron, 2005), homelessness (Hertlein & Killmer, 2004), and couples violence (Walker, 2007; Stith, McCollum, Rosen, & Locke, 2003).

ORIGINS AND SOCIAL CONTEXT

Murray Bowen was a member of the first generation of family theorists who emerged in the United States during the 1940s (Guerin & Guerin, 2002). He was trained in psychodynamic theory, but he shared a concern with his peers (including Nathan Ackerman, John Bell, Don Jackson, and Carl Whittaker) that existing clinical practices were not adequate to treat certain disorders such as schizophrenia. Also, like his peers, Bowen was influenced by general systems theory (see below).

Analytic Theory

The field of psychoanalysis was slow to recognize the importance of family dynamics on individual functioning (Mullahy, 1970). Freud had never involved families in treatment, but Alfred Adler stressed the importance of family constellations (including birth order and sibling rivalry) on personality formation. Harry Stack Sullivan, a mentor of Bowen, argued that people were the products of their relatively enduring patterns of interpersonal interaction. He believed that the role of the family during one's transition to adolescence was especially significant, and his interpersonal theory of schizophrenia (1962) was based on the nature of those interactions.

Systems Theory

Bowen's other influence was *general systems theory*. This way of thinking, so central to the social work profession today, challenged prevailing attitudes in science at the time that complex phenomena could be broken down into series of simpler cause-and-effect relations. Systems theory argued instead for a circular causality, in which all elements of a system simultaneously are influenced by, and influence, each other. During the 1940s, general systems theory was adapted to phenomena at all levels—plant, animal, human life, and even inanimate phenomena such as galaxies (Von Bertalanffy, 1968).

Systems theory had existed since at least the late 1800s, when economist Herbert Spencer formulated his evolutionary perspectives on society (Buckley, 1967; Klein & White, 1996). Its concepts found practical applications in the new science of information technology in the early twentieth century, spurred by observations of the workings of the telegraph, telephone, and other inventions. This new technology gave rise to such concepts as inputs, outputs, and feedback loops. An even greater impetus for systems theory was the growth of information technology during World War II and the need for widely dispersed weapons systems that could be coordinated. The new field of *cybernetics* focused on the analysis of the flow of information in electronic, mechanical, and biological systems (Wiener, 1948). The first family theorists were influenced by the communications aspects of systems theory and the sociologist Parsons's concept of functionalism, which postulated that every social structure now or at one time performed a necessary function for system maintenance (Ritzer, 2000).

The basic principles of systems theory now seem rather simple, but they were once quite innovative in the fields of clinical practice. One of these is connectedness, the principle that all parts of a system are interconnected, and changes in one part will influence the functioning of all other parts. A second principle is wholeness, the idea that any phenomenon can be understood only by viewing the entire system. Finally, the *feedback principle* states that a system's behavior affects its external environment, and that environment affects the system. These ideas are still evident in the social work profession's person-in-environment, psychosocial, and generalist practice concepts. Through the work of Bowen and his contemporaries they also became the basis for family systems theories.

Bowen's Career

Bowen began his family research in 1948 at the Menninger Clinic in Kansas. He observed the interactions of mothers and their children with schizophrenia, hoping to gain a better understanding of their *symbiosis*. This systems term from biology describes a state of co-existence between two organisms in which each is dependent on the other for a continuation of its existence. In psychology, the term refers to a relationship in which the attachment is so intense that physical or emotional separation compromises each party's abilities to function.

Bowen's schizophrenia research in the late 1950s at the National Institute of Mental Health focused on families that he studied for lengthy periods of six months to three years (Bowen, 1959; Dysinger & Bowen, 1959; Howells & Guirguis, 1985). Bowen concluded that the type of family anxiety that results in one member's developing schizophrenia required three generations to unfold. In his sample, the first generation's parents were relatively mature, but the child acquired their combined immaturity, manifested as anxiety and fusion (similar to symbiosis). The same process, repeated in the next generation, produced sufficient emotional fusion for schizophrenia to develop. These observations were the source of his recommended three-generation assessment of families.

Bowen is criticized for being one of a group of influential family theorists who blamed the development of schizophrenia on parents' behavior. It is now known that schizophrenia is largely biological in origin. Still, Bowen's work was helpful to family theorists in understanding the manner in which anxiety can be passed down through generations. Eventually, Bowen went to Georgetown University, where he continued his work until his death in 1990.

It is ironic that family systems theory provides such a rich understanding of the emotional lives of people within their families, because it emphasizes the importance of rationality in the formulation of "health." This is consistent with the psychodynamic theory in which Bowen was trained. It is the function of the ego to channel the drives into healthy outlets. Bowen felt that it was important for one's reasoning ability to develop, so that it could keep emotional experience from becoming the only basis on which decisions are made.

The influence of systems thinking on Bowen's theory will become more evident as we consider its major concepts.

MAJOR CONCEPTS

What follows are the major concepts of family systems theory that are central to the process of assessment. These are drawn primarily from Bowen (1978) and others, as noted.

The Multigenerational Perspective

One of Bowen's greatest contributions to the field of family theory was his principle that individual personalities and patterns of interaction among family members have their origins in previous generations. Additionally, he demonstrated that extended family relationships might be as important to personal development as nuclear family relationships. In these ways Bowen foreshadowed recent developments in the field of family therapy, of moving beyond the nuclear family unit into a consideration of other influences on family life. His broad definition of "family" also accommodates diverse family forms.

Bowen recommended a three-generation assessment of families, partly because of realistic limits on the availability of information, and also because of his early career work with families who included a member with schizophrenia (Bowen, 1959; Dysinger & Bowen, 1959; Howells & Guirguis, 1985). Bowen's work of that time was helpful to family therapists in understanding the manner in which anxiety can be passed down through generations. For example, McKnight (2003) found in a study of 60 mothers that a cutoff of parents from the previous generation has an impact on their parental functioning and the well-being of their adolescent children. The more cut off a mother is from her own mother, the less well she functions, and cutoff between a mother and father is likely to result in a child who is cut off from his or her own father.

The social worker does not need information about three generations to effectively provide family interventions. Family structures are more diverse and fragmented today than they have ever been in American life. Social workers experience reconstituted families, dissolving families, single-parent families, and gay and lesbian families. Geographic mobility is such that many people have limited awareness of their blood or territorial origins. It is always important to acquire as much information as possible about nuclear, extended, and cross-generation family relationships, but the practitioner can proceed with whatever data are available. In fact, the trend in family systems theory in the past 20 years has been to develop strategies to work with families with a focus on only one or two generations (Titelman, 1998).

Differentiation of Self

Healthy or adaptive individual functioning is characterized by *differentiation of self*. This is a key concept in family systems theory that has two meanings. First, it represents a person's capacity to distinguish between and balance his or her thinking and feeling selves. Both aspects of experience are important. The thinking process represents one's ability to detach from, or look objectively at, personal reactions or biases. Emotional processes provide important information about the significance of the situation. The "total" human experience involves both emotion and reason. While Bowen advocated for a balance of reason and emotion, he thought this was really not an attainable condition because emotional feeling, unlike intellect, was a pervasive life force. For that reason it must also be emphasized that differentiation is an ideal that can never be fully attained.

The term *differentiation* also refers to the ability of an individual to physically differentiate from his or her family of origin in a manner that preserves aspects of those emotional ties while not being constrained by them. Differentiation is thus a characteristic not of a person, but of a relationship. The person develops the capacity to maintain a balance in being able to separate self and maintaining old and new emotional ties. It will be shown later that this idea has been amended by some feminist thinkers who perceive the self as being more connected than separate in nature (e.g., Knudson-Martin, 2002).

In one major review of the literature, Bowen's concept of differentiation was supported, as a consistent relationship was found between differentiation and chronic anxiety, marital satisfaction, and psychological distress (Miller, Anderson, & Keala, 2004). Further, more differentiated persons experience more intimate relationships with their parents. In a study of 23 men and women over the age of 30, the more differentiated group's greater intimacy resulted in a deeper sense of loss during the initial grief response to a parent's death, but also a corresponding absence of regret and guilt in the months that followed (Edmonson, 2002). Higher levels of differentiation even have an effect on one's response to physical illness, as the severity of the symptoms of fibromyalgia have been correlated with lower levels of differentiation and perceived stress (Murray, Daniels, & Murray, 2006).

Highly charged emotional interactions can cloud a person's ability to appropriately separate his or her feelings from those of others and to have an independent existence. Bowen felt that it was important for one's reasoning ability to develop, so that it could keep emotional experience from becoming the only basis on which decisions are made.

Triangles

In family systems theory, the interpersonal triangle is the primary unit of analysis. All intimate relationships are inherently unstable; they require the availability of a third party to maintain their stability. On first glance this might seem to be a paradoxical notion, but it makes common sense. The price of intimacy in any relationship is the experience of occasional conflict. People cannot exist in harmony all the time. When in conflict, people usually rely on a third person (or different third persons, depending on the circumstances) for mediation, ventilation, or problem-solving assistance. (One author has written about the "pet-focused" family, in which the pet can become a part of the triangle in these same ways [Entin, 2001].) This is a natural, healthy process. Serious problems related to one's differentiation may develop, however, when he or she is drawn into certain types of triangles within the family. When a "weaker" (undifferentiated) person is drawn into a triangle in a way that does not facilitate the original two people's resolution of their conflict, the person may be deprived of the opportunity to become a unique individual. He or she may assume the ongoing role of helping the other two people avoid their problems with each other. For example, in one study of 150 families in Japan and the United States, it was found that triangulated daughters in both cultures had lower scores on a measure of ego development (Bell, Bell, & Nakata, 2001). Problematic triangulation in families occurs when conflicted adults draw in weaker family members, often the children, to maintain the stability of their relationship.

Anxiety and the Nuclear Family Emotional System

Anxiety is an unpleasant but normal and functional affect that provides people with warning signs for perceived threats (Marks, 1987). Its symptoms include tension and nervous system hyperactivity. An anxiety-producing situation may be perceived as an opportunity for growth or as a threat to well-being. Anxiety becomes problematic when it interferes with one's capacity for problem solving. The concept of anxiety is central to psychodynamic theory, and Bowen adapted it to family systems theory. Family systems possess levels of anxiety, just as individuals do.

The nuclear family emotional system includes four relationship patterns that may foster problem development (Georgetown Family Center, 2008). With marital conflict, each spouse projects his or her anxiety onto the other and attempts to control the other person. With the problematic emotional functioning of one spouse, the other spouse makes accommodations to preserve relationship harmony, but may develop heightened anxiety as a result. If one or more children exhibit a physical or emotional functional impairment, the parents will focus their anxieties on that child, who in turn may become emotionally reactive to them. With emotional fusion, family members distance themselves from one another to reduce the intensity of their relationships, and they may become isolated in the process.

A family system that is characterized by psychological tension for any of the above reasons may produce an atmosphere of anxiety that is shared by all members. As described earlier, this system anxiety can be passed on and increased through generations. An individual who is not differentiated experiences relatively high levels of tension in family relationships and will tend to be drawn to friends, spouses, and partners with similar levels of anxiety. In fact, one recent study concluded that anxiety is the best predictor of differentiation of self, emotional reactivity, and emotional fusion (Cocoli, 2006).

Parental Projection

As described in Chapter 3, psychological defenses are processes by which people protect themselves from intolerable anxiety by keeping unacceptable impulses out of their awareness (Goldstein, 1995). Defenses are positive coping mechanisms when they help the person function effectively and do not significantly distort reality. Projection is a common defense mechanism in which one person attributes to someone else his or her unacceptable thoughts and feelings. The projector is not aware of having the feelings or thoughts, but believes instead that the person on whom they are projected is experiencing them. For example, a wife may feel anger toward her husband for spending too little time in the household. If she is threatened by the idea of being angry with her spouse, she may project that feeling onto a child. She may decide that the child is angry with the father and report that "fact" to her husband.

Projection may involve significant distortions of others' feelings, attitudes, and behaviors. Parents often use the projection defense with their children as "targets," because children are vulnerable family members. Children tend to accept and internalize the pronouncements, insights, and beliefs of their parents. Within family systems, children may suffer if the parents project negative feelings and ideas onto them. They may believe that they possess the negative thoughts and feelings attributed to them, and behave as such. In family systems theory, parental projection is a major source of transmitted family anxiety.

Fusion and Emotional Cutoff

Emotional cutoff is an instinctual process between generations. It deals with the ways people separate themselves from the past in order to start their lives in the present generation (Illick, Hilbert-McAllister, Jefferies, & White, 2003). Cutoff may be manifested in physical distance, internal distance, or a combination of both (Friesen, 2003). While emotional cutoffs may be natural and healthy, emotional fusion is the opposite of differentiation. It is a shared state involving two or more people, the result of a triangulation in which one member sacrifices his or her striving toward differentiation in the service of balancing the relationship of two other people. When one person is emotionally fused with another, his or her emotional reactivity to the other person becomes strong. The person does not "think," but "feels," and does so in response to the emotional state of the other person. The feelings of the mother, for example, become those of the son. When she is happy, he is happy, and when she is sad, he is sad. The son does not have an emotional life apart from that of his mother. Neither person is consciously aware of this state because they lack the capacity to reason about or reflect on the situation. This happens because, for a significant length of time during childhood and adolescence, prior to having an opportunity to differentiate, the fused person began to serve an ongoing function within a triangle that served the needs of two other family members.

People tend not to have insight into the fact that they are fused, but they experience high levels of emotional reactivity to the other person and may attempt to extricate themselves from the relationship. A common strategy is the emotional cutoff, a person's attempts to emotionally distance him- or herself from certain members of the family or from the entire family. Emotional cutoff is the result of a person's inability to directly resolve issues of fusion, which in turn prevents him or her from forming a unique identity or satisfying relationships with others.

In situations where the family is living together, emotional cutoff may be characterized by physical avoidance of another person or, more commonly, not discussing emotionally charged topics. For example, a son in conflict with his mother may be pleased to talk about what happened at school, but they may avoid discussing how they feel about each other or the family. This pattern can continue after the family member leaves home. The son and mother may enjoy each other's company to an extent, but have superficial interactions. The son may look for substitute families at work, at college, or at church.

Emotional cutoff is often seen in physical distance. Adolescents may be eager to leave home as a solution to their family problems. Again, this may represent a normal family transition. However, when distance alone is seen as a solution to ongoing family tensions, the person may be disappointed. A first-year college student may feel that he can at last become his own person, when in fact his fusion with another family member prevents him from fully experiencing other people. An important aspect of emotional cutoff is that the person experiencing it is usually not aware of the strength of the pull of the primary relationship. The process is denied or minimized.

Other Concepts

Bowen believed that sibling position within a nuclear family is a partial predictor of a child's personality development. For example, oldest children tend to be more responsible and conservative, whereas younger children are more sociable and rebellious. These differences are due in part to the constellations of triangles that exist in families of different sizes. Research during the past 15 years, however, has tended to dispel the notion that personality types can be validly predicted on the basis of family position alone (Steelman, Powell, Werum, & Carter, 2002). There are many other variables to be considered, including gender, number of years between siblings, innate temperaments, and the nature of external environments. Still, being alert to the different triangulation possibilities for each sibling is useful in assessing family systems.

Societal emotional processes are the manner in which social systems can be conceptualized as analogous to those of the family with regard to the rules that govern interpersonal behavior within and among them. Family systems concepts may be helpful for understanding these other systems. For example, the social service delivery system itself has been described as one-third of a triangle, along with participating individual members and the family, with implications for the differentiation and fusion of participants (Moore, 1990). The church congregation has also been conceptualized as a family (Howe, 1998). Each member's relationship patterns acquired in the family of origin may be replicated with the congregation, and it is this body from which the individual must strive for appropriate differentiation. Although interesting, the concept of societal emotional processes is not yet as well-developed as those concepts that are specific to the family unit.

THE NATURE OF PROBLEMS AND CHANGE

The nature of problems was discussed in the section above. The nature of change involves an opening up of the family system (Kerr & Bowen, 1988). Presenting problems may be quite varied but represent difficulties related to triangles, fusion, and emotional cutoff. These emotional processes may be manifested either by too much or too little investment in family activities among some or all members. Change requires detriangulation and new alliance building among members of the nuclear and extended family. The social worker attends to the following goals:

- Lowering the anxiety present in the family system
- Increasing the reflective capacity (insight) of all members
- Promoting differentiation of self by emotionally realigning the family system, which includes identifying and adjusting symptomatic triangles and opening up cut off relationships
- Instilling member sensitivity to the influences of multigenerational family patterns on their present interactions
- Improving the family's ability to share their systemic concerns with each other
- Redressing inequalities within the family by inhibiting members who are behaving in inappropriately dominant ways

ASSESSMENT AND INTERVENTION

Family systems therapists do not work with a set of explicit, concrete intervention techniques. Like ego psychology, the theory offers broad intervention strategies with which the social worker can design techniques in accordance with a family's particular concerns (Bowen, 1978; Kerr & Bowen, 1988). These strategies are summarized below.

The Social Worker/Client Relationship

As a prerequisite to change, family members must experience the clinical setting as safe, comfortable, and relatively free of the anxiety that tends to characterize their natural environment. The practitioner acts as a coach. He or she remains on the sidelines of family interaction, asking questions and making suggestions that the family members discuss and enact with each other. The practitioner strives to be the focus of the family's attention and to set the tone of their exchanges. He or she must be calm, promote an unheated atmosphere, and maintain professional detachment. The purposes of this posture are to avoid emotional reactivity and negative triangulation with family members. The practitioner also serves as a model for rational interaction.

In the early stages of intervention, the social worker may ask family members to talk directly to him or her about sensitive issues, rather than to one another, to minimize interpersonal tensions. If tensions are so high that productive interactions cannot proceed, the practitioner can use displacement stories as a means of taking the family's focus off itself and giving it some distance from its own concerns. This is a technique in which the practitioner provides an example of a hypothetical family with processes and problems similar to those of the actual family. The social worker asks the actual family to share observations and suggest interventions.

The Genogram

A major tool for both assessment and intervention is the multigenerational *genogram* (see Figures 5.1 and 5.2). This is a visual representation on one sheet of paper of a family's composition, structure, member characteristics, and relationships (Kerr & Bowen, 1988; McGoldrick, Gerson, & Petry, 2008). It typically covers a span of three generations. Information provided on a genogram includes basic facts about family members (such as dates of birth and death, marriages, moves, and illnesses), the primary characteristics and levels of functioning of each member (education, occupation, health status, talents, successes, and failures), and relationship patterns among members (closeness, conflicts, and cutoffs). Overall family characteristics that may be assessed include structure (roles, rules, and boundaries) and the impact of life events, life transitions, and relationship patterns across generations. The advantage of the genogram as an assessment tool is its presentation of complex family data on one page. It is also an excellent means of eliciting family medical information (Sawin & Harrigan, 1995).

By participating in the construction of the genogram, family members gain insight into their family processes. They learn about interpersonal patterns and how triangles operate within the family. With these insights, family members learn to recognize that their behavior is related to larger system processes, and the ways in which those processes support or inhibit member functioning. This normalizes some family problems, particularly those related to transitions. With the information provided, family members may be able to offer their own ideas for enhancing family functioning. The genogram often stimulates a process of life

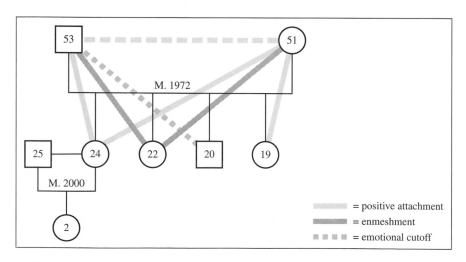

FIGURE 5.1 The Reeves Family

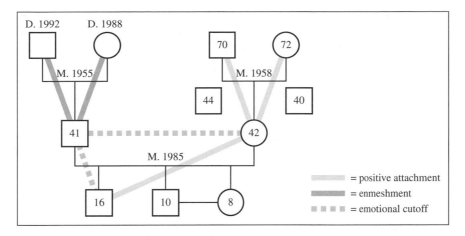

FIGURE 5.2 The Charles Family

review among older adults. Another way in which the genogram serves as an effective early intervention is that, during its construction, each member is physically observing a diagram, rather than each other. This brings a shared focus to the discussion and displaces any negative feelings onto an object rather than onto another person.

Some social workers may be reluctant to construct genograms at the level of detail suggested by family systems theory because it is time-consuming and may be annoying to clients who are eager to move into problem resolution activities (McGoldrick, 1996). Despite these concerns, it is important to understand that, in the first session, genogram construction engages all family members in the discussion, and usually offers a new way for them to think about their family system.

Detriangulation

This represents any strategy by which the practitioner disrupts one triangle and opens up the family members to new, more functional alliances or triangles. There are many ways in which the social worker can detriangulate the family (Guerin, Fogarty, Fay, & Kautto, 1996). He or she can shift alliances with tasks to be performed within the session or when members are at home. Within the session, the social worker might encourage role reversals, or situations in which members interact with each other in different ways. A child who is accustomed to complaining to his mother about the annoying behavior of a sibling might be asked to confront the sibling. When a couple triangles with a child as a means of avoiding issues in their relationship, they might be instructed to spend a certain amount of time together talking about whatever is on their minds that day. If they need the assistance of a third party to bring an issue to resolution, they might be encouraged to talk with a different adult family member. In these ways members are guided into new functional attachments with nuclear or extended family members. Any strategy that contributes to members' opening up the family to new attachments can be pursued. The practitioner should always encourage the development of new attachments that have the possibility of promoting a member's differentiation.

Increasing Insight

Family systems theory holds that understanding can lead to change. The social worker facilitates reflective discussions that promote insight about the effects of relationships on one's personality and behavior. Children and adolescents may appear to have less capacity for reflection, but insight can be defined for them simply as understanding that one person's behavior always affects another person's feelings and behavior. Two techniques that promote insight are *person-situation reflection*, focused on the present, and *developmental reflection*, focused on the history of the family and its patterns (Woods & Hollis, 2000). These techniques were discussed in Chapters 3 and 4 but will be summarized here with regard to their family applications. With the first technique, the social worker makes comments, asks questions, and offers tentative explanations that promote the family members' reflective capacity. For example, two family members in conflict may be helped to carry on a calm discussion of their differences and mutually decide how to resolve them. The social worker assumes a moderately directive stance and provides here-and-now interpretations of behavior. The technique improves the family members' capacity to evaluate feelings and attitudes, understand each other and the nature of their behaviors, and consider a range of problem-solving options. With developmental reflection, the social worker uses comments, questions, and tentative explanations to explore connections between the family's present and past patterns of behavior. If an adolescent is displaying oppositional behavior within the family, the social worker may lead a discussion of how this represents a pattern with all the children over time, and the circumstances that perpetuate the pattern. The practitioner may intentionally arouse anxiety to help the family face and confront their ingrained maladaptive behaviors. The family may develop insight into patterns of behavior that stem from irrational feelings and be able to consider new ways of thinking in the present.

Two related techniques that the social worker might use are externalizing the thinking (helping each member put into words what is generally kept inside) and encouraging the "I" position. In the latter practice the social worker asks each person to speak about his or her own feelings and label them as such, rather than reacting to negative feelings with critical comments toward others. For example, a father who generally accuses his son of being grossly insensitive might be helped to say, "Dan, I feel angry when you walk away when I'm trying to talk to you. I feel like you're mocking me." This works against the tendencies of many family members to blame others for what they feel, and helps the recipient of the comment be less defensive.

Education

Families often benefit from understanding that their patterns of interaction have sources in the family's history, and that improving family life may involve "going backwards" to revisit relationships with various extended family members. This helps family members feel less confused and guilty about their behaviors. In teaching families about family system processes, the social worker helps each member to observe the self within triangles and to examine behavior in terms of family themes. This also serves as a normalizing strategy for families who worry that they are uniquely dysfunctional or beyond help. The social worker must decide when to integrate teaching moments with other interventions. The practitioner should always provide this information in terms that the family can understand.

Working with Individuals

One of the strengths of family systems theory is its utility for working with any subset of a family or even with individual clients (McGoldrick & Carter, 2001). Family systems intervention requires an awareness, but not necessarily the presence, of all family members. In individual therapy, the social worker can construct a genogram with the client and examine the client's behavior in terms of emerging family themes. The practitioner helps the client observe the self in triangles and then detriangulate by developing new or different relationships with family members who are available. The social worker can also help the client develop insight and use this knowledge of the effects of family relationships to disrupt the repetitions of unsatisfactory relationship patterns with others.

Endings in Family Emotional Systems Theory

The major family emotional systems theorists do not clearly address issues related to ending intervention. A review of the major concepts, however, suggests some methods for determining an appropriate ending point (Walsh & Harrigan, 2003). Several family assessment instruments are suitable as measures of change. The genogram can be redrawn with the family at intervals to see if desired changes are occurring, or the family can be asked at intake to draw two genograms: one as they see themselves, and the other as they wish themselves to be. The products can be reviewed at times to track progress. The Family Adaptability and Cohesion Scale includes one subscale (of two) that provides a measure of family cohesion (Walsh, 2003). A social worker might ask families to complete the cohesion scale from this instrument at intervals to help members see how they are progressing toward emotional cohesion.

Lower observed system anxiety levels can serve as an indicator of positive change. The social worker can informally monitor the family's ability to communicate without tension, interruptions, and defensiveness. He or she can also monitor changes in anxiety outside the session by soliciting reports of the tone and content of family interactions. Levels of emotional cutoff can be monitored as members' extent of interaction, the content of their interactions, and their ability to be physically together without reported anxiety or conflict. Finally, because insight is important for lasting change, a family's ability to accurately articulate its relationship patterns, potential problem areas, and options for creating change is significant. If a family develops and sustains a constructive, shared understanding of its system dynamics, the social worker and family may decide to initiate the ending process.

SPIRITUALITY AND FAMILY EMOTIONAL SYSTEMS THEORY

Children usually develop their early values and spiritual beliefs in the context of family life. In fact, Lantz and Walsh (2007) write that the family is the major source of meaning development for all people. Shared spirituality in family life might be seen in religious activities, community service activities, and how the members perceive appropriate ways to support each other's personal and social development. For these reasons, family systems interventions can (and should) incorporate topics about spirituality, understood as the shared meanings members develop about the purposes of their lives, both apart and together. These issues have great emotional resonance with all people.

Bowen did not write extensively about spirituality, but emotional connections among family members are often tied to issues of meaning and purpose. During intervention, the social worker should encourage family members to discuss such topics when they arise. As family members strive toward differentiation they may develop different spiritual perspectives from their significant others, and when these concerns are not addressed the possibility of fusion or emotional cutoff may increase. Sharing spiritual concerns may also present a fragmenting family with opportunities to find common ground. About ten years ago I conducted a small study on this topic and found that families in conflict related to the mental illness of one member were sometimes able to preserve a sense of cohesion through attention to spiritual topics (Walsh, 1995). The second case illustration in this chapter also shows how a family used its religious affiliation as a means of resolving some conflicts.

ATTENTION TO SOCIAL JUSTICE ISSUES

We have noted that effective intervention with family emotional systems theory requires at least moderate structural stability within a family. Thus the theory's interventions may not be suitable with families who are experiencing problems directly related to such issues as poverty, unemployment, discrimination, and inequality of opportunity. Still, as a systems perspective, it encourages the social worker to consider external events that might be affecting family cohesion. Ego psychology focused on individuals, object relations focused on relationships, and family systems theory considers the entire multigenerational family and also its social context. The social worker's professional detachment will prevent him or her from being an advocate, but the possibility of family social action exists through the social worker's coaching of discussions of related topics, when appropriate.

On one other point related to social justice, family emotional systems theory has been criticized for not being sensitive enough to cultural and ethnic family diversity (McGoldrick, 1998). This reasonable criticism is leveled against most theories that profess uniform principles of development across populations. In fairness, the theory's current proponents have worked to expand its applicability to diverse family forms.

CASE ILLUSTRATIONS

Two examples of family systems intervention are described below. The first involves a family with marital conflict and substance abuse, and represents a two-generation intervention. The second, three-generation, example involves emotional fusion, the functional impairment of an adolescent member, and issues related to the adult children of elderly family members.

The Reeves Family

Though every family system is unique, some dynamics are common in families characterized by the alcohol abuse of an adult member. There is often an enmeshment, or co-dependency, of the adults. This pattern has its origins in the adults' families of origin (Bowen, 1991a; Prest, Benson, & Protinsky, 1998). Spousal interactions tend to be characterized by fusion, control and defiance patterns, inadequate conflict resolution habits, and tendencies for the negative triangulation of others (Scaturo, Hayes, Sagula, & Walter, 2000). The non-alcoholic spouse may be over-responsible. This refers to a form of pursuit that diverts the person away from his or her own self by focusing instead on the behavior of another person. It features boundary crossing and an avoidance of issues central to the relationship. The alcoholism may keep the couple's focus away from core relationship issues.

There are common patterns of triangulation in alcoholic families. One child becomes a hero. Typically the oldest child, the hero stabilizes the family, as his or her responsible behavior ensures that no additional problems occur in the system. The hero becomes the pride of each parent and a refuge from their conflicts. Such a child may be detached from his or her feelings, however. The scapegoat is the child whose negative behaviors divert others in the family from the problem of alcoholism. This person acts out and is often in trouble. Substance abuse may be among this child's problems. The parents are often upset with the scapegoat, but they need the negative behaviors to maintain their own façade of cohesion. The lost child copes with family anxiety by separating him- or herself from the family, emotionally and perhaps physically. Whereas this may seem to be a healthy strategy, the lost child is undifferentiated, and lacks a stable sense of self on which to build an independent life. Finally, the mascot also diverts the couple's attention from each other, but is more of an entertainer or clown. This person is well-liked in the family, but is superficial and seems immature. The parents resist the mascot's efforts to grow up.

Marcia was the identified client of the Reeves family. She was 22, living at home, working part-time, and attending community college. She was referred for individual therapy following a short-term hospitalization for depression. Marcia had been anxious, crying frequently, and failing her courses. She admitted to feelings of dread about finishing school, but added that it wasn't "right" to feel that way. Her stated goals were to finish school and then get her own apartment and full-time job in the business field. Marcia was likable and had a good sense of humor. She said her family had always been supportive of her. She got along particularly well with her father, the only child to do so.

The social worker, whose agency encouraged work with individuals, did not meet with the family for several months, but he eventually came to know them all (see Figure 5.1). Mr. Reeves, 53, owned Reeves Roofing Services, a successful local business. The family was financially well-off. He was an alcohol abuser with daily heavy drinking and generally kept to himself. He verbally berated his wife of 31 years when angry, often within earshot of the children. Mr. Reeves was a domineering man who intimidated his family. Mrs. Reeves, 51, was attractive and sociable, but passive and prone to anxiety. She voiced no complaints about the family. She was nurturing of the children and bought them gifts frequently. She talked with them about anything but their emotional lives.

There were three other children. Carolyn, 24, was married and had a two-year-old daughter. She was in contact with the family mostly on formal occasions such as holidays, but also during family crises. She saw her role in the family as that of a peacemaker. She became frustrated with her siblings and parents whenever conflicts developed. Patrick, 20, worked for his father as a manager and lived with friends. He had been the "problem child" in the past, engaging in substance abuse and oppositional behavior. Dad had bailed him out of trouble many times. Patrick was loyal to the family, but not close to any of them. He and his father were often in conflict, but since he moved out of the house they experienced less friction. Kathleen, 19, lived with a cousin and attended modeling school. She was attractive and socially sophisticated. She had been away from home for most of the past three years, attending boarding schools. She was a favorite of her mother, who was impressed with her career direction and personal style. Kathleen tended to be parental with her sister Marcia.

The social worker's assessment of Marcia included an exploration of her coping style, dependency issues, and the circumstances of her depression. He suggested that Marcia keep a diary of her emotional experiences to help her become aware of any patterns to her stresses and mood cycles. He helped Marcia, through graduated tasks, to resume her previous level of part-time school, part-time work, and social interaction with friends and family. A psychiatrist prescribed anti-depressant medications for Marcia, but supported counseling as the primary intervention. The social worker quickly developed a close relationship with Marcia. Therapy intensified, focusing on developing Marcia's insight about her fears, lack of confidence, interpersonal patterns, and self-image.

When Marcia came to feel safe with the practitioner, she admitted that her "goals" of self-sufficiency were false, and that she wanted to maintain dependence on her parents. She was strongly enmeshed. Marcia viewed her college graduation as the end of an adolescence, beyond which she could not function. She was reluctant to share these fears with anyone because, she said, she did not want to be "found out." The pull of the family system was enormous. Late adolescent and early adult depression is frequently related to a lack of differentiation and "sacrificial roles" fulfilled in triangulation with parents (Lastoria, 1990). The social worker realized that he needed to slow down the pace of his interventions and initiate a family focus.

Marcia's parents and siblings reluctantly agreed to participate in family therapy. Her father was particularly ambivalent, and seemed to attend primarily to make sure that nothing negative was said about him. For these reasons, only six family meetings were held, and at two of them one or the other parent was not present. The family's conversations during the genogram process and other interventions tended to be superficial and non-critical. Still, the social worker came to understand that, because the other children had left home, Marcia's parents were dependent on her presence to keep themselves in balance with each other. They sabotaged her initiatives toward independence with critical comments. Marcia had previously revealed to the practitioner that they were privately critical of his own interventions.

Despite this relatively short-term family intervention, the social worker had an impact on the system. He educated the family about systems influences by discussing in a positive way their mutual roles in helping each other function. He did not directly confront Mr. and Mrs. Reeves about their triangulation of the children, as this would have been destructive to the intervention. He framed family conflicts in terms of stage-of-life issues (empty nesting, children leaving home) to which the parents could relate and that also kept the focus off Marcia. He encouraged new functional alliances and triangles by enforcing the value of sibling relationships. He encouraged Mrs. Reeves to spend time together with Marcia and her oldest daughter. This might weaken the triangle of Marcia and her parents and also allow Mrs. Reeves to have time away from her husband. No members of the extended family lived in the area, so Marcia was encouraged to join social groups as a structured means of developing extra-family relationships. One of these was an Al-Anon group (Marcia had privately admitted to the practitioner her concern about her dad's drinking).

None of these task activities included Mr. Reeves, but the social worker was careful to engage him in discussions, recognize his contributions to the family's financial stability, and suggest new ways for him to interact with his children outside the home (to de-emphasize his dominance). The practitioner was not sure whether Mr. Reeves did these things, as he continued to seem withdrawn. Neither did the practitioner assume that he had any influence over Mr. Reeves's drinking. Some of the practitioner's questions in family sessions gave opportunities for the issue of Mr. Reeves's drinking to be raised by the others, but it never was.

The social worker continued to see Marcia individually, and she made progress. She slowly adjusted her role within the family in response to the practitioner's interventions: She pursued her education, made small changes in her family interactions, and developed relationships outside the family. The social worker needed patience to give Marcia the time she needed to work toward differentiation. Marcia never graduated from college, but she did move into an apartment with a friend from work and thereafter spent less time in the company of her parents.

The Charles Family

Normal life transitions can create problems in functioning for individuals and families. Among family systems theorists, Carter and McGoldrick (1989) have identified six general stages of a family's lifespan, including young adulthood (between families), the young couple, families with young children, families with adolescents, families at midlife (including launching children), and families in later life. As families enter each new stage, they may experience difficulty coping with the challenges inherent in that stage. The following case provides an example of a bi-racial family's stresses related to two lifespan stages—adolescence and the declining health of older members. Concepts from family systems theory are useful for understanding the heightened anxiety and emotional tumult that creep into a family with aging or dying members (Bowen, 1991b; Margles, 1995). The illustration includes excerpts from the social worker's dialogues with the family (indicators of many of the intervention strategies are included in parentheses).

Dan Charles was a 16-year-old high school sophomore referred to the mental health center because of poor grades, negative attitudes about school and his peers, and reports by his parents of suicidal thinking. The Charles family (Figure 5.2) had moved from Ohio to Virginia six months earlier when Dan's father, Jeff (age 41), accepted new employment. The Charles family was bi-racial, as Jeff was a Caucasian-American and his wife Jinhee was Japanese-American. This was not mentioned as an issue with regard to the presenting problem, however. According to Dan and his parents, Dan was unhappy about living in Virginia. He was irritable, argumentative, and in persistent power struggles with them. Dan usually stayed in the house when he was not in school and had made no friends. He complained about life in Virginia and said he wanted to move back home. Dan complained about his classmates and refused to participate in school activities. Dan's two younger siblings (Adam, 10, and Kim, 8) resented Dan's anger and how he took it out on them. They enjoyed living in Virginia and had made new friends.

During the practitioner's assessment, however, other family issues emerged as significant to the present situation. She learned that Jin (age 42), Dan's mother, was concerned about the health of her aging parents back in Ohio. Jin's mother was in the middle stages of Alzheimer's disease, and her father was physically limited by congestive heart failure. For that reason, Jin felt guilty about moving away from Ohio.

Jeff was a Caucasian, middle-class native of Ohio, who grew up in a rural community where he learned skills primarily related to hunting, farming, and construction. His interests and values reflected his "outdoorsy" upbringing, and his parents had not emphasized higher education. Jeff was an only child born to parents who were highly nurturing but "doting," investing most of their energies into Jeff's happiness. Jeff was a popular child and adolescent, but he had never excelled at school. He stayed close to home and became a successful unskilled laborer who worked a series of factory jobs.

Jin was the middle child and only daughter of a Japanese-American couple from California. Her parents were first-generation Japanese natives who had moved to the West Coast from Japan in the 1930s. Sadly, they had been interned as children with their own families in a camp for Japanese persons during World War II, and spent two years in confinement. When they were released at the end of the war, their families continued to live in the Oakland area. The couple met in high school and married several years later. Jin's father was an auto mechanic and eventually found work at a truck production plant in Ohio, where Jin and her brothers grew up. Jin met Jeff in high school and they married after Jeff finished his technical school training. He had been a devoted husband, and while Jin was embraced by the Charles extended family, her own parents had trouble accepting Jeff as a suitable husband to their daughter. He was not Japanese and was not, in their minds, sufficiently "upwardly mobile."

Additional relevant family cultural dynamics will be described in the context of the intervention.

The practitioner met with the family ten times over a period of four months, focusing on systems issues rather than the presenting problem of one member's maladjustment. She framed the family's functioning in a context of everyone's need to better adjust to the move, and the family was agreeable to working on this.

SOCIAL WORKER (REFRAMING): "Obviously, things have been tense in the home for all of you. But consider that you've had to move several times in the last few years, and there have been real worries about money and health. Considering all that, you've done well in some ways. I can see that you all care about each other, and that you'd all like the atmosphere at home to improve."

JEFF: "That's not quite true, though. We're not all trying [he looks at Dan]."

SOCIAL WORKER: "But you said he's been a good kid in the past. I wonder if you're all clear about what this experience has meant to him. Dan?"

DAN: "My folks should know."

SOCIAL WORKER: "Maybe they do, and maybe they don't. Perhaps you'll become able to tell them more about that."

One motivator for the family was that, because they were now rooted in a new location, they had few choices but to support one another. The practitioner introduced the theme of life-cycle stresses and complimented all of them on the good decisions they had made in their transition. Dan was pleased to have the focus taken off him.

SOCIAL WORKER   "All families go through transition periods. When there is a
(EDUCATION):   new child born, when a parent dies, when a child goes to
school or moves away. Those things all have a big effect on
everyone, even though you may not be aware of it at first. I
think that, among other things, your family is in a transition
period. Family members have to take some responsibility for
themselves, of course, but I think you are all affected by these
changes. Some of what you're concerned about is related to
that. I hope you all recognize that and can maybe make some
decisions about how to make this transition easier."

As they reviewed the genogram, the practitioner suggested that they could
help each other with their adjustment by dealing more directly with their feelings and interacting with each other in new ways. She included attention to the
grandparents in this process. Recognizing the entire family's concern for the aging couple, she integrated strategies to see that all of their needs were addressed.

SOCIAL WORKER   "It's clear to me that you share a sense of family, especially since
(EDUCATION,   you're all concerned about Jin's parents. It has to be hard to be
LOWERING   this far away from them. Again, I'm not sure if you are all aware
SYSTEM   of what each other are experiencing, not only with this move,
ANXIETY):   but with other challenges over the past few years, like the family
finances. With people close to us, if we don't regularly 'check
in,' we may begin to make assumptions that aren't true. Or we
may decide that not talking is the easiest way to avoid stress."

The social worker then asked the family if she could share some of her observations about the genogram. She did so as a means of encouraging the family
members to consider the entire system, but she also wanted to raise the issue of
their bi-racial family, to see if this might reveal any underlying dynamics significant to the presenting problem. The process was successful on both counts, and
the following story emerged.

The couple's racial difference had several significant effects on their relationship (Romanucci-Ross, De Vos, & Tsuda, 2006). In Japanese spousal relationships the wife takes on the mothering role toward the husband, and Jeff admitted
to having been attracted by this quality in Jin, given how his own parents doted
on him. And while father-and-child relationships in Japan are traditionally characterized as distant, parents in later life often rejoin their children's families to be
cared for. This extended Jin's caregiving role beyond that of her current family,
and created some adjustment challenges for all three generations. This was complicated by the fact that Jin and her brothers had agreed that their parents were
too ill to move, even though Jin had acted as the primary caregiver.

Japanese family values are characterized by a focus on connection and a desire
to be part of the broad racial group. American family values, in contrast, focus on
the immediate family, a single generation, individual achievement, and autonomy.
This values conflict created some strain in the Charles family. Jeff, in fact, viewed

his parents-in-law's desire to be near Jin as related to their desire to interfere with them. Further, in Japanese culture communication patterns are such that women are hesitant to discuss their emotions and are careful not to be offensive to others. Jin did possess these characteristics, and thus had trouble expressing any frustrations she was feeling to Jeff and the children. Jeff was outspoken in his negative reactions to what was happening in the family, but Jin was not as expressive.

Further discussion revealed that Jin's parents' confinement in an internment camp may have set up belief systems and patterns of interaction that affected Jin negatively. During World War II 120,000 Japanese persons were interned in these camps, 60% of whom were United States citizens (Nagata, 1991). They were abruptly removed from their homes and had to give up whatever business and careers they had established. The emotional effects of such traumatic experiences shaped the lives of their children. Common outcomes were inhibited family communication, self-esteem problems, a lack of assertiveness, an emphasis on the importance collective identity, and the belief that children (especially sons) should "vindicate" the family's honor thought external achievement. Parents who had been interred usually maintained silence about their experiences in the camps, inhibiting cross-generational communication and creating a sense of secrecy. The messages children tended to receive from their parents were that the children must finish the unfulfilled dreams of the parents, to heal the pain of past loss. A strong sense of living within Japanese culture was emphasized, which caused those who married outside the race to feel guilty. Jin discussed these issues with great difficulty, and Jeff appeared anxious as she spoke.

SOCIAL WORKER (USE OF THE GENOGRAM): "As we have just seen, genograms sometimes lay out family relationships in a way that is more clear than just talking about them. For example, Jin, it looks like your brothers have put you in charge of your parents, even though they live closer. Is that accurate?"

JIN: "Men aren't as thoughtful that way. It's my job to make sure my folks get what they need and don't become isolated. You know what it's like for older folks—if they get lonely, they give up and die. My brothers need to be concerned about their own careers. They want to do the family proud."

JEFF: "Men aren't thoughtful? You think I'm like your brothers?"

JIN: "Well, look [pointing at the genogram]. It was just you and your parents. They took care of you. They died before you were able to repay that."

SOCIAL WORKER: "Since we're all looking at the genogram, do any of you see anything interesting?"

JIN: "Yes. I take care of my folks, and Jeff is used to being taken care of. So now he expects me to take care of him. I want to take care of him, but I can't do everything. I have our own children, too."

JEFF (DEFENSIVELY): "Jin goes overboard worrying about her parents. She gives them more attention than she gives the rest of us. Shouldn't we be number one now?"

SOCIAL WORKER (REDIRECTING THE INTERACTION): "I suggest that all of you direct your comments to each other rather than to me. You're really speaking to each other. Don't worry about me, I'll follow along and participate."

Jeff and Jin argued about this issue often. Jeff was the only child in his family of origin. He was born when his parents, now deceased, were in their forties. They had been quite doting, and Jeff was accustomed to being taken care of. Jeff seemed to want Jin to attend to him in the ways she did for her parents. Jin, being a natural peacemaker, tried to see Jeff's side of the issue. Still, she resented his insensitivity to her experiencing this midlife role reversal with her parents.

JIN: "He just doesn't know what it's like for me."

SOCIAL WORKER (USE OF "I" STATEMENTS): "I don't know if he does or not. It's important for you to make it clear to Jeff how you feel, Jin. In fact, all of you should try to make clear how the behavior of you parents and brothers and sister makes you feel, both good and bad. You can best get your feelings across by using what are called 'I' statements. That is, always say, 'I feel this way' or 'I feel that way' when something happens."

ADAM: "I don't get it."

SOCIAL WORKER: "For example, if your sister makes a lot of noise and keeps you from getting your homework done, you might say, 'I get mad when you make such a racket because I can't study,' instead of only saying something like, 'Stop making such a racket!'"

The practitioner suspected that Dan tended to be caught in a triangle with his parents as a diversion from their conflicts. When they were angry with each other they found fault with Dan and vented their feelings at him.

JIN: "He used to be a good kid. But, now look. The rest of us are trying our hardest to make all these adjustments, and he goes off and sulks, not helping at all."

SOCIAL WORKER (USE OF 'I' STATEMENTS): "Make sure you talk to Dan instead of to me. And tell him how his behavior makes you feel."

JIN: "Okay. Dan, I feel frustrated when you go off by yourself when I'm trying to talk to you. I feel like you're mocking me. [To the social worker] Is that okay?"

The practitioner wondered if Dan willingly took on the role of trouble-maker when his parents were in conflict. It was true that the recent move was hard on Dan, more so than the other children, due to his stage of life. But the combined family stress may have resulted in Dan's increased efforts to divert his parents' attention from each other, his mother from her guilt about not fulfilling her role in her nuclear family, and his father's anger toward his in-laws and about his unmet needs to be cared for.

SOCIAL WORKER (DETRIANGULATION DISCUSSION): "It's normal that there would be a lot of tension in a household after a major move. Dan, I know your parents are concerned about your welfare. I'm wondering, though, how you see them reacting to, for example, a failing grade at school or your staying in your room all day."

DAN: "Well, they yell. They yell at me. It can go on for days."

SOCIAL WORKER: "Are things pretty calm between them otherwise?"

KIM: "Oh no."

SOCIAL WORKER: "What's that, Kim?"

KIM: "They yell at each other a lot."

SOCIAL WORKER: "You think so? Adam, what do you observe?"

ADAM: "Yeah. That's just the way it is. But it's okay, it doesn't bother me much."

SOCIAL WORKER: "So things can get tense in the house. That's not necessarily a problem unless you lose sight of what you are really upset about."

JEFF: "I don't follow you."

SOCIAL WORKER: "Sometimes people use each other as outlets when they're upset but maybe not sure what, exactly, they're upset about. With all that's happened, is it possible that you take out some feelings on each other that might be related to your mixed feelings about moving?"

[AND LATER] SOCIAL WORKER (DISPLACEMENT): "Sometimes kids might become concerned about their parents arguing and actually do things to take the parents' attention away from each other, or give them something to agree on."

While the younger children did not seem to be as obviously affected by the family anxiety, the practitioner was concerned that their "staying out" of the situation put them at risk for emotional cutoff.

KIM: "I'm doing fine. Nobody seems mad at me, except Dan sometimes. I can get away from it. It doesn't bother me, really. I can go to my room."

SOCIAL WORKER: "That helps, sure. And it's okay to have your private space. But I wonder if you are able to feel comfortable being around your parents and brothers. I hope you do, most of the time."

The practitioner eventually helped the family develop plans for groups of them to travel to Ohio every three weeks to look after Jin's parents. These represented detriangulation exercises and an effort to open up the nuclear family to the extended family system. This might also help Jeff's relationship with his parents-in-law, as it seemed their lack of full acceptance of him into their family had produced an underlying resentment in him.

SOCIAL WORKER: "Jin, you like to visit your parents. Have you considered taking other family members along?"

JIN: "Not much. They're all trying to get adjusted here, and it's my problem, really."

SOCIAL WORKER: "But they might be interested in going along. Have you asked them?"

JIN: "No. I've been preoccupied and ... [hesitating] I thought Jeff might get annoyed and think I was trying to keep the kids from getting settled here."

JEFF: "Oh, come on, I'd never say that!"

JIN: "You might think I was planning to get us all back home."

SOCIAL WORKER (OPENING UP THE SYSTEM TO EXTENDED FAMILY MEMBERS): "Jeff and Jin, if you agree that you're going to live here, as you said before, and make the best of it, perhaps you don't have to have such doubts. These short trips can be a good way for you to connect with each other and stay connected to the grandparents."

The family decided that Jin and two of the children might make one trip, enabling them to spend two full days together. Jeff and two of the children might travel to Ohio on another weekend. Jeff and Jin could not take long trips together without the entire family, so the practitioner encouraged them to spend time together close to home but away from the children. Their lives had centered on the children for years. The couple reluctantly decided to meet once a week for lunch.

JEFF: "I'm not sure that lunch together can help. It seems kind of trite. We have most suppers together as it is."

SOCIAL WORKER: "With the kids, though."

JIN: "Jeff, there's less of a chance we'll get upset if the kids aren't around, sulking."

Jin felt good about this plan, and it lowered her anxiety. The practitioner helped the family appreciate Jin's need to provide support to members of two generations. In the spirit of developing new family tasks, Jeff and the children decided that they could undertake minor home renovation projects during the absences of the other members.

SOCIAL WORKER (COACHING): "Jeff, you've mentioned that you and Dan don't spend time together anymore. What did you used to do?"

JEFF: "We camped, played sports. I don't know, he's getting older, he doesn't do as much of that stuff anymore."

DAN: "There's the carpentry stuff, too."

JEFF: "Yeah, we used to work on the house some. Sanding the floors, building cabinets."

SOCIAL WORKER: "Might you enjoy sanding floors together again?"

JEFF: "Actually, there's a lot to do in the new place. But he won't help."

DAN: "I might."

The practitioner hoped that this would both enhance their sense of mastery and positively change the nature of their relationships. In all of these strategies the practitioner was helping the family to form new alliances and to differentiate. The children, with the encouragement of the social worker, spent some of their time in Ohio talking with their grandparents about their mother's and father's lives when they were younger. This strengthened their relationships with their grandparents. The grandparents had been rather silent about certain traumatic aspects of their history, but, with Jin's encouragement, became able to share more of those stories. All three children were fascinated, and came to know their grandparents in a very different light.

Another effective intervention strategy was the practitioner's support of the family's following through with a vague desire to join a church in Virginia. The family had not been active in their church in Ohio but was more interested in doing so now, partly because of their relative social isolation. Jin had become more conscious of her religious roots since her parents had become ill and were facing existential concerns more directly. Interestingly, she had become more interested in Christianity over the years, another issue which had disappointed her parents. She decided to embrace her religion more openly, with her parents being farther away.

SOCIAL WORKER: "I'm getting the feeling that there's a lot of … intensity to what happens in the house. Is there anything that you all do that involves other people? I know you don't have family in the area."

JIN: "We go to church. Sometimes. We haven't spent much time there, really."

SOCIAL WORKER: "Did you ever? I mean, before you moved here?"

JEFF: "Sure. I volunteered on Sundays, too, to clean up after services."

SOCIAL WORKER: "Churches have family activities, too. Is there anything fun the kids might do there?"

The practitioner supported the idea, as it might provide the family with a bonding experience. This activity could also help them consider family functioning within a spiritual context. The family did participate in several church activity groups that helped them to initiate social ties. In the past, their church affiliations had not provided them with a basis for family-focused activity, but it became more a part of their lives now.

When therapy ended, the family had made a better adjustment to life in Virginia. Relationships improved among the members, and Dan was feeling better about his parents, his siblings, and his school. Jeff had helped Jin confront her brothers about their need to be more attentive to her parents, and Jeff and Dan continued to spend recreational time together. The family had talked about possibly moving Jin's parents to Virginia if their health continued to deteriorate. They continued to make monthly trips to Ohio.

EVIDENCE OF EFFECTIVENESS

Evaluating the effectiveness of family theories is generally difficult, and family systems theory is among the most difficult to operationalize. Bowen did not believe that empirical study was an appropriate way to determine the usefulness of his theory. He believed that such methods overlooked its richness in focusing on limited variables. He believed that what people say they do is not always the same as what they do, so he did not put great faith in standardized clinical self-report measures (Georgetown Family Center, 2008).

Family systems theorists emphasize research on process rather than outcome, and on single cases or small samples. Such studies have been conducted at the Georgetown Family Center (2008) and include the topics of family violence, families and cancer, families with substance-abusing adolescents, family processes in immigrant families, relationships and physiology, relationship processes and reproductive functioning, the process of differentiation, and the workplace as an emotional system. Previous Center studies have focused on AIDs and the family (Maloney-Schara, 1990), aging and the family (Kerr, 1984), family violence, and managing diabetes. The theory is also used as a model for adolescent group work to promote member growth through differentiation (Nims, 1998).

The literature includes examples of tests of the utility of the theory's concepts, and several are presented here. Roberts (2003) tested 125 college undergraduates to examine whether level of differentiation (defined as moderate levels of autonomy and intimacy with the family of origin) was associated with life stressors and social resources. She found that higher levels of differentiation correlated with lower levels of perceived life stress and more social resources; further, lower social class status was significantly associated with more life stressors, but not fewer social resources. The author concluded that social class influences the number of one's stressors but not one's social resources. Kim-Appel (2003) examined the relationship between differentiation and psychological symptom status (somatization, interpersonal problems, depression, anxiety, hostility, and a global symptom measure) in persons aged 62 and older. Her hypotheses were confirmed, as measures of differentiation correlated negatively with emotional reactivity and emotional cutoff, and correlated positively with "I" position statements. She concluded that differentiation is significant to social functioning across the life span, and that intervention with older adults can productively utilize family systems concepts.

Other studies have supported the validity of this theory's concepts. Correlations have been found between level of differentiation and risks for substance abuse and other risk behavior. Adult chemically dependent persons have lower differentiation than the control population. People who begin using substances at age 13 or younger have significantly higher levels of emotional reactivity than persons who start using at age 14 or older (Pham, 2006). Among individuals in substance abuse treatment, those who report lower levels of differentiation of self are more likely to report violence in their intimate relationships, while those who report more emotional reactivity (overwhelmed by emotions of the moment) and greater emotional cutoff (threatened by intimacy) are more likely to report one instance of violence in intimate relationships during the past year (Walker, 2007). Higher levels of differentiation related to lower levels of chronic anxiety and higher levels of social problem solving. Higher chronic anxiety was related to lower problem solving, indicating that differentiation influences social problem solving through chronic anxiety. Higher levels of social problem solving were related to less drug use, less high-risk sexual behavior, and an increase in academic engagement (Knauth, Skowron, & Escobar, 2006).

Several studies have focused on family-of-origin influences on career decision making. Keller (2007) studied college students and found that differentiation (and the ability to take an I-position) was positively predictive of a student's proactive career exploration. Dodge (2001) investigated the effects of differentiation (and, from another theory, the concept of personal authority) on career development outcomes for 243 college students. Each concept was positively associated with a sense of vocational identity and self-efficacy in career decision making. Further, family of origin conflict was inversely associated with low self-efficacy in career decision making, low individuation, and dysfunctional career thoughts. The author concluded that addressing family conflict in therapy could have a positive impact on career development in young adults. In another study of this type, 1,006 college students were surveyed using measures of fusion, triangulation, intimidation, anxiety, and career decision making (Larson & Wilson, 1998). Results indicated that anxiety (from fusion) inhibits career development, but triangulation is not related to career decision problems.

A number of studies have considered the effects of family systems on a person's later degree of satisfaction with intimate relationships. In a study of 60 married couples it was found that higher-differentiated couples described higher levels of marital satisfaction than lower-differentiated couples (Racite, 2001). Couples who demonstrated different levels of differentiation reported more marital problems than couples who were similar in differentiation. In one research project, men's and women's emotional cutoff scores were predictive of the nature and quality of their relationships and related depressive episodes over time (Glade, 2005). Larson, Benson, Wilson, & Medora (1998) studied the effects of the intergenerational transmission of anxiety on 977 late adolescents' attitudes about marriage. The participants' experiences of fusion and triangulation were found to be related to negative opinions about marriage. Timmer & Veroff (2000) studied the relationship of family of origin ties to marital happiness after four years of marriage for 199 black and 173 white couples. One predictor of marital happiness for wives, particularly those from disrupted families, was closeness to the husbands' families of origin. When husbands' or wives' parents were divorced or separated, closeness to the husband's family reduced the risk of divorce. Avnir and Shor

(1998) operationalized the concept of differentiation with a set of indicators, so that the concept may be qualitatively assessed during family intervention. Regarding parenting potential, Skowron (2005) found that greater differentiation of self (lower reactivity, emotional cutoff, or fusion, and better ability to take an I-position) predicted lower child abuse potential.

The clinical practitioner can evaluate his or her own effectiveness with family systems theory through the application of single systems (comparing baseline and treatment measures) or pre-experimental (comparing pretreatment with posttreatment measures) measures. All that is required is a background in basic research methods. The practitioner can translate a family's goals into observable indicators that can be monitored. Coco and Courtney (1998) provide one example. They initiated and evaluated a family systems intervention for preventing adolescent runaway behavior using pre- and postintervention measures of family satisfaction and cohesion.

CRITICISMS OF THE THEORY

Family systems theory has been criticized for two related reasons (Bartle-Haring, 1997; Knudson-Martin, 1994; Levant & Silverstein, 2001). First, it has not adequately attended to variations in how men and women experience differentiation and fusion. The theory has incorporated a male bias in its valuing of reason over emotion and prioritization of separation over connection. Beginning with Gilligan (1982), developmental theories about women have considered their relational and communication styles to be different from those of men. Women are typically brought up to empower others in the family—to respond to the thoughts and feelings of others and foster their growth and well-being. Men are programmed to seek extra-familial success, while women are programmed to nurture and support them, often at the expense of their own development. While these are culturally supported roles, they may create a tendency to see women as enmeshed. A gender-neutral family theory would place greater emphasis on helping men increase their capacity for intimacy and balance their achievement and relationship needs.

Second, even with its attention to societal emotional processes, the theory has not been sufficiently contextual in its identification of males as the dominant cultural group and their uses of power in family systems (Nichols, 2009). Although these criticisms are valid, they began to be addressed by theorists in the 1990s. Family issues of gender difference and power can be productively addressed in therapy (McGoldrick, 1996).

SUMMARY

Family systems theory is unique in its attention to the subtle emotional family processes that develop over several generations. It is an appropriate guide to assessment and interventions that focus on the quality of nuclear and extended family relationships and the desire for members to become differentiated. The theory provides a useful means of working on issues related to boundaries, enmeshment, and emotional distance. It is versatile in its applicability to individuals and subsets of families. Its potential for use across cultures has been articulated, although not yet extensively (Skowron, 2004).

Family systems theory interventions require that the client, whether an individual or a family, have the capacity to interact in an atmosphere of relative calm, and be able to reflect on relationships. There must be a stable-enough family structure that the majority of members are not in crisis. For these reasons the theory might not be appropriate for families whose primary concerns involve meeting basic material and support needs. The urgency of such needs suggests interventions that do not require sustained reflection. Likewise, families characterized by chaos from structural instability would require a higher level of worker activity than is consistent with the family systems perspective.

Family systems theory might be appropriate for intervention with the above types of families after their initial problems are resolved. After a family acquires access to basic needs, its members may struggle with issues related to enmeshments or cutoff. A structural breakdown may be related to a triangulation in which an adolescent accedes to an inappropriate position of power. The social worker's ability to assess those dynamics may be helpful in determining how to help the family organize problem-solving activities, strengthen certain subsystems, or plan for growth after the primary intervention ends.

TOPICS FOR DISCUSSION

1. Think about your own family of origin, and try to identify one or two examples of "relationship patterns" that characterized that system. How did these develop, and when? It might be interesting to talk with some other family members about these patterns.

2. What are the characteristics of a person who is differentiated? As you consider this question, think about any value biases that might be reflected in your response.

3. The ideal position of the social worker in family emotional systems work achieves both engagement and therapeutic distance. Think about clinical situations that might test your ability to assume or retain this ideal position. How can you manage these challenges?

4. Describe a point of fusion you have observed in your work with an individual, family, or family subsystem. Describe how you might (or did) proceed to modify that relationship.

5. Think of some ways that you could use displacement stories or activities as part of an intervention. Try to be creative in how you select and implement these.

IDEAS FOR ROLE-PLAYS

(The instructor or students should fill in the details of these vignettes however they deem appropriate.)

1. A single mother, divorced two years ago, has ongoing conflicts with her ex-spouse, and is also having trouble "letting go" of a supportive 19-year-old daughter who is moving toward independence in a normal way. There are two other children, aged 14 and 10, in the household (all the children live with their mother). Focus the intervention on helping the mother to appropriately "let go."

2. An individual adult client is troubled by his inability to risk intimacy (however you define it) in relationships with significant others. The assessment indicates that this person was the hero child in a family in which the father was an alcohol abuser.

3. In a family that includes a father, mother, and two children, the mother is dying of ovarian cancer. The father has withdrawn emotionally from her because he does not perceive himself as having adequate caregiving capabilities. He feels guilty about this withdrawal. The adult son and daughter (living independently in the same city) have good relationships with both parents and want to help reverse their father's withdrawal.

APPENDIX: Family Emotional Systems Theory Outline

Focus	The lifelong influence of nuclear family relationships ("You can run, but you can't hide")
	The "hearts and minds" of family members
Major Proponents	Bowen, McGoldrick, Carter, Kerr, Guerin, Titelman
Origins and Social Context	Schizophrenia research (family dynamics)
	Cybernetics
	Natural systems theory
	Psychodynamic theory
Nature of the Individual	A striving to balance intellectual and emotional experience
	Nuclear family processes influence functioning throughout life
Major Concepts	Multigenerational perspective (three generations)
	Nuclear family emotional system
	The triangle
	Differentiation of self (in emotional and cognitive functioning)
	Fusion (of emotions and intellect)

APPENDIX: Family Emotional Systems Theory Outline (Continued)

	Emotional cutoff
	Parental projection
	Sibling position
	Anxiety
Family Development Stages	Young adults leaving home
	Couples
	Families with children
	Families with adolescents
	Older members with young adults leaving home
Nature of Problems	Triangulation (adults in conflict draw in "weaker" family members to maintain stability, and thus elicit symptoms in them)
	Emotional fusion (anxious attachment)
	Emotional reactivity
	Too much or too little investment in family relationships
Nature of Change	"Opening up" the family system
	Detriangulation
	Changing the relationship of primary couples
	Going backwards through the extended family to find solutions
	Less family anxiety
Goals of Intervention	Lower family system anxiety
	Identify and adjust the central symptomatic triangle(s)
	Put problems in the context of the multigenerational family system
	Promote an awareness of the relevance of all family members
	Redress inequalities within the family
	Emotionally realign the family system (includes opening any "closed" relationships)
	Promote differentiation (requires each member to have relationships with all other family members)
	Enhance habits of problem sharing
	Increase the reflective capacity of all members
Nature of Worker/ Client Relationship	Worker as "coach"
	Professional detachment (to avoid reactivity, triangulation)
	Worker provides a calm atmosphere
Intervention Strategies	Review of the multigenerational genogram (education)
	Discuss behavior in terms of family themes

APPENDIX: Family Emotional Systems Theory Outline (Continued)

	Externalize the thinking (increase quality of communication)
	Lead detriangulation conversations
	Shift alliances within triangles with tasks
	The displacement story
	Guide members into functional attachments with nuclear and extended family members
	Increase insight (help each member observe the self within triangles)
	Person-situation reflection
	Developmental reflection
Assessment Questions	What are the current stresses? How are they expressed?
	How has the family handled stresses historically?
	What physical and emotional symptoms are evident in the family?
	How do the symptoms affect family relationships?
	How does the nuclear family interact with the extended family?
	How well does the family manage anxiety?
	How well-differentiated are the family members?
	What triangles exist? Which are primary?
	Are any emotional cutoffs operating?

6

Behavior Theory

I gained it so –
By Climbing slow –
By Catching at the Twigs that grow
Between the Bliss – and me*

In this chapter we will review a practice theory that is very unlike the reflective theories described in the previous three chapters. *Behavior theory* consists of ideas about how human actions and emotions develop, are sustained, and are extinguished through principles of learning. Behavioral practitioners are distinguished by their relative lack of concern with a client's internal mental processes and their focus on physical, observable, "objective" behavior. Behavioral practice is also distinguished by a commitment to the principles of the traditional "scientific method" for helping clients to eliminate unwanted behaviors or acquire desired behaviors. Some behaviorists actually reject its status as a "theory" because of their distrust of any concepts (abstractions) as explanations for thoughts, feelings, or behavior. Behavioral practitioners have always been concerned with the empirical evidence for the effectiveness of their interventions, and thus third-party payers value these approaches. Because implementing behavioral strategies does not require that the client be able to think abstractly, it is a popular practice approach with children and persons with cognitive and developmental disabilities. But it can be used with *all* client populations.

Three major approaches to behavior therapy include *applied behavior analysis* (focused on the consequences of behavior), the *stimulus-response* model (focused

---

*Reprinted by permission of the publishers and the Trustees of Amherst College from The Poems of Emily Dickinson, Thomas H. Johnson, ed., Cambridge, Mass.: The Belknap Press of Harvard University Press, Copyright © 1951, 1955, 1979, 1983 by the President and Fellows of Harvard College.

on environmental factors that elicit and maintain a behavior), and *social learning theory*, which adds a concern with *cognitive mediational* processes (Wilson, 2000). This chapter will concentrate primarily on the first two approaches, as the third is more closely related to *cognitive theory* (the subject of Chapter 7). Additionally, the intervention model of *dialectical behavior therapy* will be discussed in the next chapter, as it includes some cognitive techniques.

ORIGINS AND SOCIAL CONTEXT

Behaviorism has been prominent in the social sciences since the first half of the twentieth century, and it became a popular theory among clinical practitioners by the 1960s. Its rise was closely linked with the advancement of logical empiricism, first in the field of philosophy and later in the sciences (Thyer & Wodarski, 1998). Beginning with the French philosopher Descartes in the seventeenth century, empiricism has referred to knowledge that is based on observation or sensory experience. In the late 1800s its definitions (there are several) were refined to incorporate the process of basing knowledge on evidence that is rooted in "objective" reality (it is now disputed that any such thing exists) and gathered systematically by observation, experience, or experiment (Spiegler, 1993). A major principle of behaviorism is that all claims to knowledge should withstand testing and verification.

The first major innovator of behaviorism in psychology was Wilhelm Wundt in Germany, the late-nineteenth-century "father of experimental psychology" (Taylor, 1972). He believed that "laws" of cognitive and emotional experience could be derived with the same research methods that were being used to study human physiology. His thinking was influenced by developments in the physical sciences that emphasized exact measurement of phenomena as well as the importance of inter-subjective verification. Wundt set up the first psychology laboratory for experiments with animals. In Russia, Ivan Pavlov's (1927) discovery of the laws of classical conditioning represented a major step forward for this new science. American educational psychologist Edward Thorndike (1911) was another major contributor, inventing the "puzzle box" for experiments with rats and developing the first principles of operant conditioning.

Contemporary discussion of behaviorism begins with the work of American John Watson (1924). He coined the term "behaviorism," conducted experiments on humans, and brought the approach into mainstream psychology. Watson set out to establish psychology as a science. Protesting against what he viewed as the subjectivism of introspective psychology, he urged his discipline to give up its concern with understanding consciousness and to focus instead on observable facts. He believed that psychology as scientific enterprise should seek to be able to predict and control events, and that only "objective" methods, enabling two or more scientists to observe the same objects and events, would further the achievement of those goals. He reasoned that because states of consciousness are private, observation of behavior alone was able to provide the clear data needed for scientific activity. Watson felt that human behavior should be reducible to the laws of physics, and that eventually psychologists would be able to explain behavior at the molecular level.

B. F. Skinner (1953) disagreed with Watson about the ultimate aim of behaviorism, arguing that the behaviorist should focus at the level of the person. Skinner's work advanced the field tremendously. He refined the principles of operant conditioning, and his many publications, some of which were geared toward general audiences, brought behaviorism into the public consciousness. The *radical* behaviorists, including both Watson and Skinner, acknowledged the existence of mental processes but were not concerned with them. *Moderate* behaviorists such as Edward Tolman (1948) and Clark Hull (1943) were interested in mental processes as intervening variables between a stimulus and response. Albert Bandura's (1977) social learning theory brought mental processes further into the realm of behaviorism. A major learning principle that Bandura presented was that of *modeling*: people learn not only by direct reinforcement, but also by seeing how the behavior of others is reinforced.

Research on conditioning and learning principles became a dominant part of experimental psychology in the United States following World War II, but this research was largely confined to animal laboratories. Several studies of humans, however, bolstered the belief that behaviorism could be an effective therapy for humans. South African Joseph Wolpe (1958) was among the first to conduct research that applied learning principles to the eradication of adult neurotic disorders. In so doing he developed the intervention method of systematic desensitization. In London, Hans Eysenck also popularized behavior therapy as a means of treating behavioral and emotional disorders (Eysenck & Rachman, 1965). In 1963, he founded the first journal devoted to behaviorism, *Behavior Research and Therapy*, which remains a respected publication today.

Behavior theory and its related interventions are prominent in the social work profession. The first social worker to extensively advocate for the behavioral perspective in direct practice was Edwin Thomas (1974, 1968), who conducted research on intervention with substance abusers and couples, among other client populations. Bruce Thyer has advocated the philosophy of logical positivism and its adoption by social work practitioners for more than three decades (Thyer & Wodarski, 2007). While some social workers believe that a focus on observable behavior runs contrary to the profession's increasingly holistic perspective, Thyer has eloquently demonstrated its utility for promoting positive outcomes with a variety of client populations. He also argues that the application of behavioral intervention is critical in the development of evidence-based practice standards for social workers. Mark Mattaini (1997) has developed an *ecobehavioral* model of practice that he argues is fully consistent with social work professional values. While his model is firmly rooted in empirical practice, it encourages social workers to assess human behavior in a broader context than some behaviorists would consider, including all relevant social systems with which clients interact. The goal of the model is to expose clients to new *cultures*, defined as family members, friends, organizations, and communities, that can provide ongoing support for the acquisition of new behaviors. We will review this model in more detail later in the chapter.

MAJOR CONCEPTS

The basic principles and assumptions of behavior theory are as follows (Gambrill, 1994; Wilson, 2000; Wodarski & Bagarozzi, 1979):

- Behavior is what a person does, thinks, or feels that can be observed. Inferences about a person's mental activity should be minimized because it cannot be directly observed. Clinical assessment should focus on observable events with a minimum of interpretation.

- People are motivated by nature to seek pleasure and avoid pain. They are likely to behave in ways that produce encouraging responses, or positive reinforcement. (It must be emphasized, however, that it is not always easy to determine what constitutes pleasure and pain for a specific client.)

- People behave based on their learning, by direct environmental feedback, and also by watching others behave and interact.

- Behavior is amenable to change. A prerequisite for clinical change is that the behavior of concern must be defined in terms of measurable indicators.

- Intervention should focus on influencing reinforcements or punishments for client behaviors. Consistent and immediate reinforcement produces change most rapidly.

- Thoughts and feelings are behaviors subject to reinforcement principles.

- The simplest explanations for behavior are preferred. Practitioners should avoid reification (giving "life" to esoteric concepts such as the "ego" and searching for "ultimate" causes of behavior).

Behaviorists do not offer a theory of human development. They do acknowledge, however, that genetic and biological factors are relevant to a person's sensitivity to stimuli and attraction to certain reinforcers. Knowledge of the person, however, is only relevant to intervention insofar as it helps to specify environmental circumstances that serve as significant reinforcers.

THE NATURE OF PROBLEMS AND CHANGE

All behavior is influenced by the same principles of learning, which include *classical conditioning, operant conditioning*, and *modeling*. These are described below. No behavior is considered inherently healthy or unhealthy, or normal or abnormal. It is all developed and maintained because of a person's unique reinforcement schedules. *Reinforcement* can be understood as any environmental feedback that encourages the continuation of a behavior. An aggressive adolescent's fighting behaviors may be reinforced by his enhanced status within a peer group. *Punishment* is feedback that discourages the continuation of a behavior. That same adolescent's aggression may be discouraged by a loss of driving privileges. Put simply, a person's behaviors change when the reinforcements in his or her environment change and are consistently applied. Clinical intervention always involves the rearrangement of a client's reinforcements so that more desirable or functional behaviors will result.

Classical Conditioning

Conditioning is a process of developing patterns of behavior through responses to environmental stimuli or specific behavioral consequences (Kazdin, 2000). The earliest behavioral research involved classical conditioning, in which an initially neutral stimulus comes to produce a certain response after being paired repeatedly with a certain stimulus. In Pavlov's famous research with dogs, the sight of food (the conditioned stimulus) naturally produced salivation (an involuntary response). A bell (the unconditioned stimulus) initially failed to evoke salivation. However, after the bell was paired with the food, over time the dogs salivated when presented with the bell alone. The bell at this point attained the status of a conditioned stimulus because it was capable of producing a response by itself.

Classical conditioning plays a role in understanding many problems that clients experience. For example, previously neutral cues, such as certain places (restaurants or bars), people, or feeling states (e.g. boredom) may become associated with problem behaviors. A person who is accustomed to abuse alcohol when in the company of friends at a particular location will be inclined to drink when at that location, whether or not other incentives are present. Many anxiety-related disorders are classically conditioned. For instance, a bite by a dog might generalize to a fear of all dogs. A series of stressful classroom presentations in grade school might generalize to a person's long-standing fear of public speaking or social interaction.

During clinical intervention, the principles of classical conditioning are reversed. For example, a client struggling with a drug problem may experience urges to use when experiencing a particular emotion, such as boredom. The conditional pairing between boredom and drug use may eventually lose its association if the person abstains from using drugs to counteract boredom over a period of time, and learns instead to manage boredom in a new way (for example, with exercise, reading, or listening to music). For anxiety, fear-laden situations such as those involving public speaking are often rank-ordered by the client and practitioner according to the level of fear they invoke. Clients learn to face each event or item on the list, starting with the least anxiety-provoking, by learning to pair relaxation exercises rather than anxiety with the event. Relaxation processes might include deep breathing, deep muscle relaxation, and visualization. In this process of *systematic desensitization*, a form of *exposure*, a conditioned stimulus that usually produces a negative response (anxiety) becomes paired with a new, incompatible response (relaxation). Clients work their way through the rank ordering of fears until they are no longer plagued by the most disabling anxiety.

An essential issue with any kind of conditioning, and one that presents a major challenge to behavioral practitioners, is that all significant other persons in the client's life must consistently support new reinforcement contingencies over a period of time in order to sustain a long-term effect. If the client's behavior changes are reinforced by some persons (family, teachers) but not others (peers, co-workers), those new behaviors may fade.

Operant Conditioning

The main premise of operant conditioning is that future behavior is determined by the consequences of present behavior (Gambrill, 1994). The practitioner also pays attention to the *antecedent*, or prior, conditions that may trigger the behavior. Two types of reinforcement are postulated in this model: *positive* and *negative*. Both positive and negative reinforcement encourage the continuation of a behavior. Positive reinforcement encourages the continuation of a behavior preceding it. For instance, alcohol use is positively reinforced by the resultant feelings of well-being and pleasant social interaction with others. *Negative* reinforcement is the process by which an aversive event is terminated by the individual's behavior and, therefore, the behavior is reinforced. Alcohol use, for example, is negatively reinforcing if it leads to escape from feelings of boredom or sadness. Compulsive behaviors, such as overeating or substance abuse, are reinforced positively by the feelings of well-being that are created and the social interaction with others involving the food or substance. (Similarly, positive and negative punishment is distinguished by either *adding* a negative consequence that eliminates a behavior, or *eliminating* a reinforcer that then eliminates the behavior.) In practice, clients are helped to seek out behaviors that can offer alternative reinforcements, that is, other activities such as relationships, work, or hobbies, so they will not be as prone to indulge in the problem behavior.

Operant conditioning principles can also be enacted when people assume environmental control over the behavior of others. *Parenting skills development* offers one example of operant behaviorism for parents of children with behavior problems. Parents are taught to reinforce their children's pro-social behaviors and extinguish negative behaviors through either ignoring them or using punishments (providing adverse consequences for the target negative behavior). An extended example of parenting skills development is provided later in this chapter.

Modeling

People also learn behaviors by *modeling*, or watching others engage in behaviors and be reinforced or punished for them (Bandura, 1977). Modeling is a pervasive means of learning for all people, but especially children and adolescents. For instance, children may learn to act appropriately in school by seeing classmates praised for listening to the teacher and criticized for talking while the teacher is lecturing. Adolescents may begin using alcohol or acting aggressively because they have seen their parents and other relatives act this way and be positively reinforced for doing so. Along with didactic instruction and discussion, modeling is a chief method of behavior change. In modeling, the practitioner shows the client how to enact a new behavior. The client then practices the new behavior (called *behavioral rehearsal*), receiving supportive feedback and suggestions for its refinement.

Covert modeling can also be used for intervention purposes. In covert rehearsal, the social worker guides the client through a process of *imagining* the completion of steps toward a successful outcome (Beck, 1995). For example, an anxious client who must give a formal presentation may imagine herself approaching the public speaking situation with ease, and with the expectation that she will do well. She visualizes and feels herself speaking in a confident and calm manner, and receiving a warm reception from the audience. The practitioner "walks" the client through this process, and then the client rehearses it herself prior to and during the actual event. Though artificial, this helps the client anticipate and manage the anxiety that he or she will experience during each step.

Practitioners tend to prefer *coping* (satisfactory progress) rather than *mastery* (perfection) approaches to behavior change through modeling and rehearsal. Coping more openly manifests the struggles a person might expect when performing the new behavior, including the free expression of anxiety, hesitation, and making errors. Clients identify more easily with a coping model (Hepworth, Rooney, Rooney, Strom-Gottfried, & Larsen, 2005). The social worker's rehearsal of new skills with clients is important because confidence to carry out tasks is enhanced by practice.

To summarize, all situations in which people find themselves (except for truly novel ones), "cue" or prompt behaviors based on principles of classical conditioning (paired associations with certain aspects of the setting), operant conditioning (prior experiences in similar situations), or modeling (watching others behave and receive feedback). During the first day of a new academic year at a new school, for example, a student may be inclined to socialize with classmates based in part on conditioned positive associations of the classroom setting with other peer situations. She may respond eagerly to the instructor's questions due to her anticipation of positive reinforcement for doing so. Finally, she will watch how students behave in this new school to learn what other classroom behaviors are reinforced by other students and the instructor.

The goal of behavioral intervention can be stated rather simply: to change behavior. This is accomplished through the use of reinforcers and punishments. The social worker helps the client achieve new, desirable behaviors by manipulating the environment to alter reinforcement patterns or by providing new opportunities for positive modeling. For example, returning to the above scenario, if a child behaves in school in ways that are disruptive to the classroom process, the practitioner can devise a plan in which those negative behaviors are extinguished (punished) and new, more acceptable classroom behaviors are reinforced. One of the challenges in behavior therapy is to identify the specific antecedent conditions and responses that are reinforcing to the client from among the numerous influences on the client's behavior. A teacher's displeasure with acting out behaviors might serve as punishment to some students, but as reinforcement to others.

ASSESSMENT AND INTERVENTION

Assessment

The Social Worker/Client Relationship   Although behavioral therapy is highly structured, the importance of a positive social worker/client relationship should not be underestimated. The social worker needs to be perceived as competent, caring, and trustworthy, because he or she will be encouraging the client to engage in some behaviors that will feel uncomfortable or threatening. Further, the behavior of both parties in the clinical relationship is subject to the same conditioning principles described above (Wodarski & Bagarozzi, 1979). The client will be initially attracted to the social worker if their interactions result in less anxiety and the practitioner is perceived as having the ability to secure rewards for the client. The practitioner's empathic understanding will facilitate these conditions. The social worker must be careful not to use *punishing* behaviors with the client, at least initially, as these tend to be alienating and result in a loss of perceived reinforcing potential. The social worker must be collaborative with the client as they devise intervention strategies because the client needs to have a strong investment in change strategies. Over time, the client will evaluate the relationship on the basis of its rewards and costs relative to alternative behaviors (such as different intervention approaches, a different social worker, or no intervention at all), and the perceived likelihood of future rewards and costs. Regular discussions about how the client is reacting to the intervention help to sustain his or her sense of reward for participation.

After orienting the client to the principles of behavioral intervention, the practitioner can perform a comprehensive assessment through *functional behavior analysis*. First, the client's problem behavior is specified as clearly and concretely as possible. Next, the environmental conditions (cues) that enhance or maintain the behavior are identified. Finally, the consequences of the behavior are considered. The practitioner asks questions of the client about cues that may occur in each of five life domains that may be related to the problem situation, including the environmental, social, physical, cognitive, and emotional domains (Carroll, 1995).

Listed below are examples of the types of questions the social worker asks during assessment (Bertolino & O'Hanlon, 2002):

When do you experience the behavior?

Where do you experience the behavior?

Who are you with when the behavior occurs?

How long does the behavior typically last?

What happens immediately after the behavior occurs? That is, what do you do, or what does someone else do to or with you?

What bodily reactions do you experience with the behavior?

How long do these reactions last?

How often does the behavior typically happen (hourly, d.

What is the typical *timing* (of the day, the week, the mon
the behavior?

What do the people around you usually do when the behavior i.

Table 6.1 includes a more detailed list of cues, behaviors, and cc   ᴐ to investigate in each of the five domains.

The *ecobehavioral assessment* (Mattaini, 1997) is similar to the functional behavior analysis in that it considers the client's behavior in a broad context. It is different, however, in that it uses an eco-map to illustrate the particular domains with which a client interacts and focuses more on systems that are external to the client. Figure 6.1 provides a simple eco-map of a young woman who is having problems adjusting to living away from home at college for the first

TABLE 6.1   Five Domains of Behavior Analysis

Domain	Antecedents (Triggers, Cues)	Consequences (Reinforcers)
Environmental	What people, places, and things act as cues for the problem?	What people, places, and things have been affected by the problem?
	What is the level of the client's day-to-day exposure to these cues?	Has the client's environment changed as a result of the problem?
	Can some of these cues be easily avoided?	
Social	With whom does the client spend most of his time?	Has the client's social network changed since the problem began or escalated?
	Does he have relationships with people who do not have the problem?	How have his relationships been affected?
	Does he live with someone who is involved in the problem?	
Physical	What uncomfortable physical states precede the problem occurrence?	How does the client feel physically afterward?
		How is her physical health as a result?
Emotional	What feeling states precede the occurrence of the problem?	How does the client feel afterward?
		How does she feel about herself?
Cognitive	What thoughts run through the client's mind, or what beliefs does he have about the problem?	What is he thinking afterward?
		What does he say to himself?

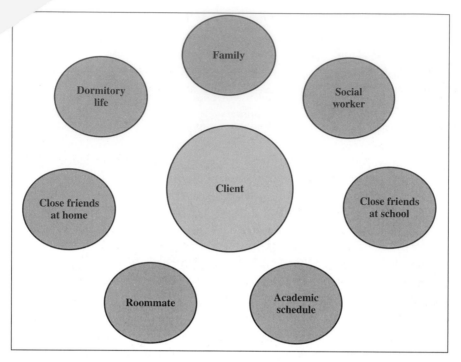

FIGURE 6.1 Eco-Map for an Ecobehavioral Assessment

time. The circles represent her particular environmental contexts, and the lines indicate whether she is having positive or negative exchanges within those domains.

From these behavior assessments the practitioner determines the reinforcers and triggers that are maintaining the problem behavior. This assessment leads to the *planning* step, in which the practitioner and client construct concrete target behaviors (goals) that include attention to the antecedent conditions and contingencies required to bring about desired new behaviors. The success of the process mandates that the client (and perhaps other relevant persons, such as a spouse, friend, or teacher) agree to task assignments in which these new conditions are applied.

Intervention

The process of intervention in behavior theory is systematic, and includes the following steps:

- The client's problems are stated in behavioral terms.
- Measurable outcomes related to problem reduction are developed.
- The practitioner and client gather baseline data (its current occurrence) on the problem behavior.

- The steps required to reach problem resolution are specified.

- The client's personal and environmental resources for making changes are specified. Any other people who will participate in the intervention are identified and sought out for consultation (often to act as reinforcers).

- Possible obstacles to goal achievement are identified in advance, and plans are made to minimize them.

- An appropriate intervention strategy is chosen with the participation of the client and with an emphasis on positive consequences for new behaviors. As a rule, behavioral practice focuses on rewarding positive behavior rather than punishing negative behavior whenever possible (Gambrill, 1994).

- The practitioner, client, or other persons collect data about the client's activities. The client's behavior changes are documented regularly.

- The client and practitioner evaluate the intervention process regularly, comparing baseline conditions to current "counts" of desired behavior.

- The intervention ends after the client achieves his or her goals and demonstrates the likelihood of goal maintenance.

Ending intervention in behavior theory is a process of *fading*. That is, after an intervention has been under way for some length of time and the client has acquired the desired new behaviors, any artificial supports (including meetings with the practitioner and the reinforcement schedule) are gradually eliminated.

SPIRITUALITY AND BEHAVIOR THEORY

Because behaviorism is focused on concrete observable events, it gives no particular attention to ideas related to spirituality or purpose in life. These topics are often abstract and refer to a person's internal belief systems, which are out of the realm of the practitioner's concern. Remember that the behavioral practitioner is not concerned with *any* aspects of mental life except as they are represented in external behavior. Behavioral social workers would not deny the significance of spirituality in clients' lives, but spiritual matters are only relevant to the extent that they may serve as antecedent conditions and reinforcers in the context of a presenting problem. A social worker might operationalize aspects of a client's spirituality (such as the number of church services attended or the amount of time spent on goal activities that are intended to enhance personal fulfillment) if the client articulates goals related to it. But the social worker would not otherwise explore these concerns with a client.

ATTENTION TO SOCIAL JUSTICE ISSUES

Behavior theorists argue that their methodology can be effectively used to promote a range of social justice issues. Wodarski and Bagarozzi (1979) write that the behavioral practitioner can determine "what reinforcers social workers and their clients possess that can be utilized to manipulate other individuals who distribute such reinforcers as housing, medical care, and other social services" (p. 264). The authors note that social workers themselves possess important *collective reinforcers*, such as knowledge and money. If politicians, for example, do not agree to secure more adequate social conditions for certain disadvantaged groups in return for political support (positive reinforcement), an intervention strategy might include punishment contingencies, such as demonstrations and negative advertising. Wodarski and Bagarozzi describe a number of behavioral interventions with individuals and small groups that have targeted social justice issues, including efficient household energy consumption, trash control, and comfort with racial integration. More recently, Thyer and Wodarski (2007, 1998) describe behavioral interventions for a variety of social problems, such as child maltreatment, children with educational disadvantages, school violence, adolescent sexuality, HIV disease, substance abuse, crime, unemployment, marital conflict and domestic violence, race, older adult issues, chronic medical problems, and hospice care.

Whereas the term "manipulation," as used in behavioral therapy, has a negative connotation for many social workers (compared with "collaboration"), Gambrill (1994) argues that many practitioners misunderstand the philosophical basis of behaviorism. She writes that "behavioral methods, if effective, increase clients' skills in influencing their environment (a large part of which may be provided by other people), but they do not teach them to manipulate this environment in an insidious or unfair way" (p. 56). She provides examples of intervention that focus on empowering clients, including enhancing advocacy skills, and notes that social skills training helps clients acquire interpersonal skills that can enhance their advocacy potential.

Behaviorism requires that social workers become familiar with the life experiences of oppressed and culturally diverse groups because they need to understand each person's unique set of reinforcers. Behavioral practitioners also routinely use outside resources, such as information about resources and opportunities for new activities, to help clients learn and to change their behavior. Thus it can be argued that behaviorism can be used in service to the values of the social work profession (Thyer & Wodarski, 2007).

CASE ILLUSTRATIONS

There are many behavioral interventions that the practitioner might select depending on the client's presenting problem, the client's preferences, and the time and resources available. Described below are two examples of behavioral interventions, each of which incorporates several target strategies.

Mama's Boy

In the *coercive cycle* of aggressive children, children and adults get caught up in a pattern that tends to increase undesired behavior. The adult makes a request, the child reacts with hostility, the adult in turn acts with hostility and withdraws, and the child averts the request. Parent training, or parenting skills development, is a model of operant behavioral intervention that teaches parents to apply the principles of reinforcement to change their children's behavior and break these frustrating patterns. Parents learn to reinforce desirable behaviors in their children and ignore or punish negative behavior. The interventions can be provided in individual, family, or group formats. Successful parenting skills development involves the following steps:

- Parents select a priority goal related to the child's behavior.
- Goals are broken down into smaller, observable components, called *tasks*.
- Tasks are specified to encourage the presence of positive behavior, rather than the absence of negative behaviors.
- A baseline measure of the desired behavior is determined (in numbers).
- A target goal is established.

Ms. Rosman was participating in a parenting skills development program because her 10-year-old son Andy would not do his homework, and he also engaged in disruptive behaviors at bedtime. In order to determine a reasonable target for the desired behaviors, *the baseline*, or current occurrence of the behaviors, must be determined. Its occurrence can be measured in different ways: through its frequency (Ms. Rosman said that Andy never did his homework, so his baseline would be zero) or duration (Ms. Rosman observed his behavior for a week and said that Andy showed "appropriate homework behaviors" for only two minutes at a time).

The behavioral term *shaping* refers to reinforcing successive approximations of a desired behavior to eventually meet a goal that is initially out of reach for a client. In parenting skills development the practitioner may provide parents with a handout on command giving, which includes the following points (Webster-Stratton, 2001):

- Only use commands that are necessary; giving too many different commands may confuse, agitate, or alienate the child.
- Issue only one command at a time.
- Issue clear and specific commands ("Look both ways before you cross the street") rather than vague warnings ("Be careful" or "Watch out").
- Issue statements ("Please clean up your toys and put them in the box") rather than questions ("Why don't you pick up your toys?") or "Let's" commands ("Let's clean up the toys"), unless the parent plans on being a permanent part of the effort.
- Phrase commands as to what the child should do ("Please play in the kitchen rather than in the living room") rather than on what the child should not do ("Don't play in the living room").
- Keep commands brief (do not lecture).
- Praise compliance with a command.

Preferred reinforcement systems include the use of high-probability behaviors, social reinforcement, and token economies. *High-probability behaviors* are those in which children frequently engage, such as playing outside, talking on the phone, using the Internet, playing video games, and watching television. *Social reinforcements* include interpersonal rewards such as praise, hugs, pats on the shoulder, a smile, a wink, or a thumbs-up sign.

With Ms. Rosman, the practitioner provided education on the benefits of praising her child. They went down a list of "things to do" and "things not to do" (Webster-Stratton, 2001) that demonstrated how Ms. Rosman could enact the principles of praise with Andy. The list of "things to do" included the following:

- Describe specifically what he does to deserve praise
- Pair verbal praise with eye contact, a smile, or physical affection
- Praise effort and progress rather than total achievement
- Praise his positive behavior immediately after it is performed

The list of "things not to do" included:

- Use unlabeled praise (global statements about Andy, such as "What a good boy!")
- Couple praise and criticism ("You did a good job washing the dishes, but why can't you dry them right?")
- Wait too long after the behavior to praise him
- Take his feelings of awkwardness as a sign to stop praising

Another type of reinforcement system to use with children involves *token economies*, in which points or tokens are given for desirable behaviors and are then traded in for an agreed-upon reward (Barkley, 2000). A token economy involves the use of tangible reinforcers, such as chips, coins, tickets, stars, points, stickers, or check marks, for desirable behaviors that are earned, compiled, and then traded for an agreed-upon reward.

Punishment involves the presentation of negative events (e.g., physical discipline, harsh words, criticism) or the removal of positive events (e.g., privileges) that decrease the occurrence of a response (Kazdin, 2000). These can be effective, although parenting skills development experts recommend that positive reinforcements be provided at three times the ratio of punishments (Barkley, 2000). The definition of *extinction* involves no longer reinforcing a behavior, resulting in a decrease or eradication of the behavior. Kazdin (2000) states that before undertaking extinction, it is important to understand the reinforcer that is maintaining the behavior with some certainty, and whether it can be controlled. When applying extinction to a particular behavior, one must first examine its function. In Ms. Rosman's situation, Andy engaged in disruptive behavior at bedtime to prolong his time awake and to get special attention from his mother. Ms. Rosman was told about the importance of being consistent, and to ignore Andy's behaviors every time they occurred. She was also asked to practice in the session, after watching the practitioner model them, appropriate behaviors during a child's tantrum, such as looking away, maintaining a neutral facial expression, and avoiding any verbal or physical contact.

Time-out, or *isolation*, is a form of punishment that involves physically removing a child from the source of reinforcement for a brief period (Hodges, 1994). The time-out should be structured around a certain amount of time, observing the general guideline of one minute per year of the child's age. Its purposes are to extinguish the negative behavior through punishment, help the child calm down, and help the child understand why the behavior is unacceptable. It is important to follow a time-out with a *time-in* activity; either a supportive conversation with the parent or re-engagement in a previous activity that the child enjoys.

The location for a time-out should be free from reinforcement; there should be no activities available, and the child is to do nothing. Ms. Rosman said she could move a stool for Andy to the front hallway of their home for a time-out, although he could see other family members in the living room from there and might call out to them. The practitioner reminded Mrs. Rosman that Andy's attempts to engage family members in annoying behaviors should be ignored. If Andy's disruptive behaviors escalated there, the time out period should only resume after he got his behavior under control. The time-out should end with the child's being reminded why he was punished, and with a resumption of normal activities so that the child has an opportunity to feel good again and perhaps show that he can behave appropriately.

Parents must be warned that they will likely experience an initial increase in the undesirable behavior when they first begin employing extinction techniques. Ms. Rosman was told to take the inevitable "extinction burst" as a sign that the technique was working. She was assured that Andy's behavior would improve and that gains would last if Ms. Rosman consistently ignored any recurrence of the undesirable behaviors. She was reminded to pair her extinction behaviors with positive reinforcement for appropriate behaviors. Ms. Rosman worried that ignoring "bad" behavior seemed to implicitly encourage it. The practitioner emphasized that refusing to give in to the behaviors would help Andy learn over time that they had no effect. If reinforcement of desirable behaviors and ignoring undesirable behaviors didn't stamp out the problems, then they would consider using punishments.

The technique of *distraction* paired with ignoring negative behavior can be effective with young children (Webster-Stratton, 2001). For instance, if a young child cries because he wants to play with the television remote control, rather than shouting at him, the parent could take the remote control away and divert his attention to a brightly colored ball: "Here's something else you can play with. See if you can catch it!" Distraction helps to avoid arguments about a parental command.

The example of parenting skills development incorporates a number of operant behavior intervention principles, as well as modeling. Ms. Rosman was able to help her son make some improvements in his homework behavior as a result of their ongoing application, with occasional directives from the social worker.

Another common behavioral intervention with children and adolescents is *social skills development*. It was not used in the illustration above, but is worth summarizing here. Social skills development is simply a process of teaching clients how to engage in socially appropriate behaviors. An assumption of the technique is that the client is capable of improved social behavior, but, due to a lack of learning or a reinforcement of antisocial behaviors, does not currently practice it. It is associated with social learning theory, briefly mentioned earlier, because of its use of modeling. Social skills development involves a series of steps, each of which must be thoroughly addressed before moving to the next one:

- Through assessment, determine what skill the client wants or needs.
- Describe the skill and its utility to the client.
- Outline all parts of the skill separately (there may be more parts than you first think).
- Model the skill for the client.
- Role-play each part of the skill with the client.
- Evaluate the role-plays.
- Combine the parts of the role-plays into a full rehearsal.
- Encourage the client to apply the skill in real-life formats.
- Evaluate and refine the skill.

The following example of intervention with an older adult includes strategies related to classical conditioning.

The Smart Shopper

Systematic desensitization was described earlier as a process by which a client gradually overcomes his or her anxieties by confronting them in a series of steps, from less to more incapacitating. It is a type of *exposure therapy* (another type is *flooding*, in which the client is overwhelmed with a feared object or situation in order to learn that he or she can tolerate it). This behavioral intervention technique was helpful to Mr. Tucker, an older adult who had developed panic disorder with agoraphobia. Mr. Tucker was a 72-year-old widower, living alone in a small house he had shared with his wife for more than 40 years prior to her death three years previously. His son, living in a nearby city, had become concerned about Mr. Tucker's well-being, noticing that he was isolating himself at home and not tending to his physical health. The previously robust man appeared to be malnourished and physically weak, and his diabetes was going unattended. His son initially thought that Mr. Tucker's condition was related to grieving the death of his wife, but his father had by now achieved a stable mood, even as his avoidance behaviors were increasing.

A social worker who agreed to make home visits assessed Mr. Tucker as having an anxiety disorder, concluding that, through a process of classical conditioning, he had become fearful of being outside the house. Mr. Tucker had been a healthy working man most of his adult life, keeping long hours at a printing company, and leaving most domestic responsibilities to his wife. Mrs. Tucker developed breast cancer in her mid-60s and experienced a slow decline until her death four years later. Mr. Tucker dutifully cared for his wife during the illness, assuming such responsibilities as grocery shopping and escorting his wife to her doctor's appointments.

As his wife's condition worsened, Mr. Tucker understandably became more upset. He came to associate his relatively new activities of going to the doctor's office and shopping with feelings of fear. After his wife's death, as he adjusted to living alone, Mr. Tucker continued to associate common activities of daily living outside the home with his anxiety states. Mr. Tucker gradually stopped going outside, except for rare instances when he felt it absolutely necessary to purchase household supplies. He welcomed friends and family into his home, and was clear-headed and personable there. But, because he was an aging man who would not attend to his physical needs, his health was suffering greatly.

The social worker's functional behavior analysis of Mr. Tucker's anxiety revealed that his avoidant behaviors were primarily related to environmental cues, and his responses featured physical symptoms such as nausea, dizziness, and mild hand tremor. Following the practitioner's education of Mr. Tucker about the rationale underlying systematic desensitization, the client agreed to work toward overcoming his panic disorder. It should be emphasized that Mr. Tucker's isolative lifestyle was also being reinforced through operant conditioning, as his family and friends indulged his requests to visit him at his home rather than expect him to venture outdoors. Still, the social worker identified the desensitization strategy, to work against his classically conditioned panic reactions, as having a strong potential for success.

The practitioner invited Mr. Tucker to select specific activities as a focus of their intervention. He chose grocery shopping and going to the doctor's office for check-ups, with the former activity as a starting point, thinking he would have a better chance of success. Mr. Tucker articulated a goal of being able to independently go shopping for all of his groceries once per week. He and the practitioner constructed a list of ten tasks associated with grocery shopping. They included making a shopping list, searching the day's newspaper for coupons, getting into the car and driving onto the road, driving to the outskirts of the neighborhood, driving past the grocery store, driving into the lot and parking, walking from the car to the store, selecting a pushcart and walking through the store, selecting items for purchase, and paying at the cash register. Mr. Tucker opted to address the tasks in sequence, beginning with the first task. The social worker suggested that Mr. Tucker select a time of day when he felt most able to tolerate these tasks. The client chose early morning when there would be fewer people on the road and in the store. The practitioner also suggested that Mr. Tucker consider asking his son to go to the store with him during his first attempts. The client agreed that this would be helpful.

Before Mr. Tucker addressed the first task on the list, the practitioner taught him a *relaxation* technique and rehearsed it with him at some length. A client needs to feel calm when approaching a stressful activity, and must be able to relax *during* the activity if anxiety escalates (Meichenbaum & Deffenbacher, 1988).

If this process is successful, the client will begin to dissociate the task from the anxiety and fear once paired with it. Relaxation techniques are often used by themselves to help clients manage certain types of anxiety, such as that which contributes to insomnia. The practitioner helped Mr. Tucker master a basic natural breathing technique that includes the following steps (Davis, Eshelman, & McKay, 2000):

- Sit comfortably and close one's eyes.

- Breathe through the nose.

- At a pace that is slow but comfortable, gradually inhale, concentrating internally on how the lower third, middle third, and upper third of the lungs are filling with air.

- When inhalation is complete, hold the breath for a few seconds.

- Exhale slowly, pulling in the abdomen as the air leaves the lungs.

- Relax the abdomen and chest.

- Repeat the technique up to five times.

It is crucial that the client have mastery of the relaxation technique and be able to use it in "abbreviated" form in public situations prior to confronting anxiety-provoking situations. In the final step in preparation, the practitioner reminds the client not to expect complete success on the first attempts at task completion (Thyer & Bursinger, 1994), as confronting one's fears is never easy. This helps prevent the client from becoming demoralized if he experiences difficulty. The practitioner assures the client that he can terminate an activity at any time if it seems overwhelming. If the client is unable to successfully complete a task, the practitioner takes responsibility for the failure (due to initiating a step prematurely or to inadequate preparation) and then moves to an easier task for the client. Finally, the client is helped to identify rewards for successful task completion. This builds operant reinforcement into the process. Mr. Tucker, an avid music listener, decided to treat himself to a compact disk from his mail-order record club following his successful completion of two "repetitions" of a task.

Systematic desensitization interventions often work relatively quickly (Thyer & Bursinger, 1994). Positive results often occur by the third or fourth session (although each session may be several hours long, depending on particular circumstances). The social worker is intensively involved during the early stages, in person or perhaps by phone, to "coach" the client and revise steps as necessary. Mr. Tucker was able to achieve his goal of weekly shopping trips within three weeks. He had the most trouble with the step of walking into the store and selecting a pushcart. His son accompanied him to the grocery store three times before Mr. Tucker was able to follow through with that step. The practitioner reviewed the client's physiological reactions that accompanied those failures and helped Mr. Tucker practice the relaxation technique until he felt relief from those reactions. Mr. Tucker's son was also present for the client's first two successful shopping trips before absenting himself from the process.

Mr. Tucker accomplished his second goal of keeping doctor's appointments more quickly, his confidence bolstered by the earlier success. The social worker then "faded" from Mr. Tucker's life, gradually reducing the frequency of his visits, and finally keeping contact with occasional phone calls until the client was able to maintain his behaviors independently. The practitioner felt that Mr. Tucker's achievements would generalize to other areas of his life outside the house, and that he no longer experienced symptoms of an anxiety disorder.

EVIDENCE OF EFFECTIVENESS

Behavioral interventions maintain popularity among practitioners, administrators, and third-party payers because their effectiveness is often supported by quantitative research methodologies. We must recognize, however, that some other theoretical perspectives do not lend themselves as easily to experimental, quasi-experimental, and single-subject research designs. Psychodynamic practitioners, for example, place a higher value on case studies and qualitative studies of outcome. Thus, though behavior theory cannot necessarily claim superiority on this basis (although its proponents might do so), its effectiveness in many instances can be concretely demonstrated. In this section we will review the findings of experimental and quasi-experimental research studies.

In Chapter 1, we reviewed the American Psychological Association's criteria for *well-established* and *probably efficacious* clinical interventions. Chambless and Ollendick (2001) have compiled a list of empirically validated behavioral treatments using those criteria. *Well-established* interventions have been documented for persons with agoraphobia, panic disorder, generalized anxiety disorder, posttraumatic stress disorder, social anxiety, geriatric depression, major depression, anorexia, sexual dysfunction related to anxiety, behavioral problems related to dementia, behavioral problems related to schizophrenia, family stress when one member has schizophrenia, attention-deficit hyperactivity disorder, encopresis, and enuresis. *Probably efficacious* behavioral interventions are documented for persons with blood injury phobia, specific phobia, alcohol abuse and dependence, cocaine abuse, opioid dependence, chronic pain, headache, smoking cessation concerns, avoidant personality disorder, anger control problems, obesity, and other phobias.

Other literature reviews add more detail to the above findings. Two research meta-analyses concluded that the most comprehensive treatment for ADHD in children is medication in combination with behavioral interventions (specifically including negative reinforcers) to improve the appropriateness of social behaviors (Hinshaw, Klein, & Abikoff, 2002; Turchiano, 2000). A meta-analysis of interventions for obsessive compulsive disorder found that behavioral methods were as effective as drugs (Kobak, Griest, Jefferson, Katzelnick, & Henk, 1998). As one example, a seven-week group intervention for persons with the disorder, which focused on exposure and relaxation for improved self-control, significantly improved participant ratings of obsession, compulsions, and depression (Himle, Rassi, Haghighatgou, Krone, Nesse, et al., 2001). A review of 24 studies of intervention for social phobia concluded that exposure in combination with cognitive restructuring (described in the next chapter) produced the best outcomes compared to waiting list, placebo, and cognitive restructuring alone (Taylor, 1996). For childhood anxiety disorders in general, medication with behavior therapy provided higher effectiveness rates (65.3%) than drugs alone (42.8%) or drugs with supportive counseling (27.7%). A meta-analysis of treatment for sleep problems concluded that behavior therapy produces greater sleep quality over time than drug therapy (Smith, Perlis, Park, Smith, Pennington, et al., 2002). Similar results have been found with regard to insomnia in older adults (Pallesen, Nordhux, & Kvale, 1999) and bedtime refusal and night waking in young children (using extinction and prevention strategies) (Mindell, 1999).

Behavioral interventions are often used with children who demonstrate problem behaviors. These interventions have been found to be effective in reducing selective mutism (Pionek-Stone, Kratochwill, Sladezcek, & Serlin, 2002) and managing constipation and fecal incontinence (McGrath, Mellon, & Murphy, 2000). A review of 26 parenting skills development programs indicates that these programs have short-term positive effects on antisocial behavior in children, although long-term effects are not as clear (Serkeitch & Dumas, 1996). A meta-analysis of 32 treatment programs in Europe found that behavioral and cognitive behavioral programs reduced the recidivism of juvenile and adult offenders by 12% (Redondo, Sanchez-Meca, & Garrido, 1999).

To provide more details about what interventions may be used effectively in behavior theory, we will look at four recent meta-analyses. In one such review of 51 studies of the treatment of insomnia, effective behavioral interventions included relaxation strategies, improved sleep hygiene (implementing conducive lifestyle habits), and sleep scheduling activities (learning to associate the bedroom with sleep, and restricting the amount of daytime sleep) (Irwin, Cole, & Nicassio, 2006). A review of 30 studies of behavioral marital therapy found that relationship improvements were associated with the development of communication, problem solving, and emotional expressiveness skills, desensitization to negative emotional reactions, and contingency contracting (each member agreeing to perform certain desired activities for the other) (Shadish & Baldwin, 2005). A review of 30 studies of the use of vouchers or money-based incentives for substance abusers, contingent on their satisfying predetermined therapeutic goals (generally abstinence, staying in treatment, medication compliance, and workplace productivity), found that incentives of between $5–$17 dollars per day, given immediately after completion of the desired behavior, were effective (Lussier, Heil, Mongeon, Badger, & Higgins, 2006). Finally, a review of 194 studies about the effectiveness of HIV-prevention interventions (appropriate use of condoms) found that active (behavioral) interventions were far more effective than passive (informational) ones (Albarracín, Gillette, Earl, Glasman, Durantini, et al., 2006). The most effective behavioral interventions included role-plays, learning to apply condoms, regularly taking HIV tests, and sexual self-management strategies.

CRITICISMS OF THE THEORY

Behavior therapy has been described as empowering because it educates clients about processes of change that can be generalized (Cooper & Lesser, 2002), but it has also been criticized for not adequately attending to the broad biopsychosocial-spiritual perspective on human behavior (Nichols, 2009). It is sometimes seen as dehumanizing, overlooking aspects of life that may be important to the client. A second criticism of behaviorism is that its interventions rely on a "controlled environment" in which a client's reinforcements (or punishments) must be consistently applied to create and sustain new behaviors (Allen-Meares, 1995). It is often difficult for social workers to plan for and monitor such consistency of reinforcement when a client interacts with many people in many life domains. A child who demonstrates aggressive behavior may be reinforced for alternative behaviors at home or at school, but with his friends the aggression may still be reinforced. Behavioral practitioners work hard to establish effective reinforcement schedules but are rarely able to engage all relevant persons in the process. Finally, it is difficult to isolate the significant antecedents and reinforcers that surround many problem behaviors (Walters, 2000). Is a man's reluctance to get out of bed in the morning a consequence of his wife's verbal comments the day before, his anticipation of his boss's comments at work that day, or something else? We are commonly unaware of the range of stimuli and reinforcers that govern our behaviors. At times these are discoverable, but they can also remain unclear. For these reasons, behaviorism has fallen short of its original goal to become a generalizable science of human behavior.

SUMMARY

Behavior theory offers an approach to clinical practice that focuses on observable concrete client behaviors and outcomes, rather than internal mental processes. It provides a potentially effective basis for social work practice, particularly among children and other client populations with a limited potential for abstract thought. Some social workers do not consider behaviorism a practice "theory" because it is purely focused on stimulus-response issues (Thyer & Wodarski, 2007). Though it certainly has a "Spartan" conceptual basis, behaviorism does incorporate ideas about the nature of problems and change. Behaviorism is pre-eminent among practice theories in its attention to empirical research on its effectiveness. Though often criticized by social workers for being overly reductionistic, its emphasis on monitoring human action has been adapted within other theoretical perspectives. When practiced by social workers, behavior theory is often combined with cognitive theory, which is the focus of the next chapter.

TOPICS FOR DISCUSSION

1. Some behavioral practitioners argue that a major strength of their approach is its not being a theory at all. That is, by limiting their focus to questions of

stimulus and response they avoid abstractions inherent in other practice approaches that lack validity. Review the definition of practice theory given in Chapter 1 and decide whether, in your view, behaviorism qualifies as a theory. As you discuss this topic, consider whether any conceptual processes are required of a practitioner when identifying certain phenomena in clients' lives as "stimuli" and "responses."

2. Do you think that behavioral approaches are reductionistic—that they fail to elicit aspects of social functioning that may be important to clients? Can a behavioral practitioner organize his or her work to show an appreciation for the "whole" person?

3. Behaviorists assert that interventions should focus, when possible, on reinforcing rather than punishing behaviors. Why is this? Think about client populations such as substance abusers or aggressive children. How can social workers develop interventions that reinforce certain client behaviors while extinguishing others?

4. Recall any clients you have worked with or observed in the past in the context of the five domains of behavior analysis in Table 6.1. How would your client's responses to the various questions have helped you to devise a focused behavioral intervention?

5. What values, if any, are inherent in behaviorism? Do you think that it can be used in the service of social justice? Discuss some clients you have worked with who faced oppressive circumstances, and whether behaviorism could have offered (or did offer) them the capacity to better confront those problems.

IDEAS FOR ROLE-PLAYS

(The instructor and students should fill in the details of these vignettes however they deem appropriate.)

1. Role-play an intervention with a grade school or middle school student who is frequently in trouble for aggressive behavior with peers and teachers in the schoolyard before school, at recess, and after school. The student does not behave aggressively in the classroom. Be specific in the assessment about determining target behaviors and goals.

2. Select a type of client with one or more behavior problems that all students can use for small group (or one large group) role-plays. As usual, include the social worker, client, and observer roles in each group. Perform an assessment that is based on the five domains of behavioral assessment. After the role-plays compare how the social workers were able to get the information needed from the client or perhaps the client's significant others.

3. Select one or more examples from students' field placements of clients whose presenting problems are described as more "emotional" than behavioral

(such as depression, anger, guilt, or a desire for greater closenesswith a spouse or partner). Role-play the first session to see how a behavioral practitioner would attempt to orient the client(s) to the behavioral approach, and develop appropriate goals and objectives for intervention.

APPENDIX: Behavior Theory Outline

Focus	Observable behavior
	Reinforcements
	Punishments
	Principles of conditioning (modeling, classical, operant)
Major Proponents	Pavlov, Watson, Skinner, Thomas, Thyer, Wodarski, Mattaini
Origins and Social Context	Experimental psychology
	Interventions with children and other non-cognitively oriented populations
	Empiricism (emphasis on observable evidence)
	Parsimony (simple vs. complex explanations)
	Avoidance of "reification" (giving substance to abstract ideas)
	Distrust of "inferences" about mental activity
Nature of the Individual	Genetic and biological factors are relevant
	Trait theory
	Human nature is to seek pleasure and avoid pain
	All behavior is accounted for by contingencies of:
	Survival
	Reinforcement
	Social evaluation
	Thoughts and feelings are behaviors in need of explanation
	No behavior is pathological by nature; it is all influenced by the same principles
Structural Concepts	None (unobservable events are disregarded)
Developmental Concepts	None
Nature of Problems	Reinforcement of negative behavior
Nature of Change	Changing or adjusting reinforcers (reconditioning)
	Concrete measurement of behavioral responses
Goals of Intervention	Develop new, desirable behaviors via new reinforcement patterns
Social Worker/ Client Relationship	Worker must be trustworthy, demonstrate positive regard, be collaborative

APPENDIX: Behavior Theory Outline (Continued)

Intervention Principles and Techniques	State problems in behavioral terms
	Establish clear, measurable objectives
	Gather baseline data
	Specify steps toward problem resolution
	Specify personal and environmental resources
	Identify relevant significant others for participation
	Identify possible obstacles in advance
	Interventions (emphasize positive consequences)
	Modeling
	Behavioral rehearsal (includes role-playing)
	Reinforcement control (positive and negative)
	Stimulus control (rearranging antecedents)
	Systematic desensitization
	Shaping
	Overcorrection
	Relaxation training
	Collect data
	Document changes over time
Assessment Questions	Is the client's problem stated specifically?
	Can the problem be translated into concrete behaviors?
	Is the client motivated to work actively on the problem?
	What reinforcers tend to be most influential in the client's life?
	What persons are available to assist the client in problem resolution?
	What resources can the client mobilize to resolve the problem?
	How can the client's behaviors be measured over time?

7

Cognitive Theory

A Deed knocks first at Thought
And then — it knocks at Will
That is the manufacturing spot*

Many behaviorists eventually turned their attention to clients' *internal inter-pretations* of events as they respond to stimuli and reinforcers. *Social learning theory* (Bandura, 1977) was instrumental in developing the concept of *cognitive mediation*, defined as the influence of one's thinking between the occurrence of a stimulus and response. Learned patterns of evaluating environmental stimuli help to explain why each of us adopts unique behaviors in response to similar stimuli. This and other developments in the cognitive sciences (described below) accounted for the development of cognitive theory in clinical social work practice. This approach is consistent with behaviorism in many ways and, as we shall see, the two theories can be used together.

Cognitive theory for clinical practice emerged in the 1960s and continues to be a popular and effective basis for intervention by social workers. It is quite different from the ego psychology and object relations theories in its assertion that *conscious thinking* is the basis for most human behavior and emotional experience. It is different from behavioral theory in its focus on internal mental processes. Whereas some of these processes might be categorized as unconscious (or *preconscious*), they are presumed to maintain a minor influence on behavior and can readily be brought to the surface with reflection or the social worker's probing (Lantz, 1996).

For example: You are driving down the interstate, ten miles over the speed limit. Suddenly you see flashing lights and hear the siren of a police car behind

---

*Reprinted by permission of the publishers and the Trustees of Amherst College from The Poems of Emily Dickinson, Thomas H. Johnson, ed., Cambridge, Mass.: The Belknap Press of Harvard University Press, Copyright © 1951, 1955, 1979, 1983 by the President and Fellows of Harvard College.

you. How do you feel? Scared! You pull over. The police car proceeds to follow the car that was in front of you. Now you feel relieved, even happy. What changed? The police car was always following the car in front of you. What changed was the nature of your thoughts about what you had observed.

Cognitions include our beliefs, assumptions, expectations, and ideas about the causes of events, attitudes, and perceptions in our lives. Cognitive theory postulates that we develop habits of thinking that form the basis for our screening and coding of environmental input, categorizing and evaluating that experience, and making judgments about how to behave. *Emotions* are defined within this theory as physiological responses that follow our cognitive evaluation of input (Lazarus & Lazarus, 1994). Thus, thoughts occur prior to most emotions, and, in fact, produce them.

The relationship between thoughts, feelings, and behaviors can be illustrated as follows (Beck, 1995):

An activating **event**—produces a **belief or thought**—that produces an **emotion or action**.

Cognitive interventions are focused on enhancing the rationality of a client's thinking patterns, the degree to which conclusions about the self and the world are based on external evidence, and the linear connections among a person's thoughts, feelings, and behaviors.

ORIGINS AND SOCIAL CONTEXT

Cognitive theory is consistent with trends in American thought that have existed since the late 1800s. It did not work its way into clinical practice, however, until the 1950s. Its influences included developments in American philosophy, information processing theory in the computer sciences, and social learning theory in psychology.

Pragmatism and Logical Positivism

American philosophers have always tended to evaluate ideas pragmatically, with reference to practical applications, compared to their European cohorts (Kurtz, 1972). One example is John Dewey (1938), the most influential American *pragmatist* of the early twentieth century. He wrote that when a person's experiences present challenges to understanding, the natural response is to initiate a process of problem solving, or "inquiry." Dewey maintained that ideas are arrived at through plans of action that are evaluated for "truth" by their expected consequences. His work influenced the systematic procedures seen in the problem-solving model, described later in this chapter. *Logical positivism* was another major philosophical movement that became prominent in the United States in the 1930s (Popper, 1968). Focused on language, the positivists perceived the task of philosophy to be analysis and clarification of meaning, and they looked to logic and the sciences as their models for constructing formally perfect languages. The positivists' *verifiability principle* maintained that a statement was meaningful only if it was empirically verifiable. They were critical of ideas that could not be tested, and these ideas influenced theorists from other fields who became concerned with verifiability.

Information Processing Theory

The advance of computer and information technology was particularly influential on the development of a "science of cognition" in the social sciences (Bara, 1995). Human service practitioners became interested in how people processed information and in correcting cognitive "errors." In retrospect, these ideas may seem rather simplistic accounts of how the mind works, but they emerged at a time when little was understood about the functioning of the nervous system.

Information processing theory maintains that there is a clear distinction between the thinker and the external environment (Ingram, 1986). People receive stimulation from the outside, and code this with sensory receptors in the nervous system. The information is then integrated and stored for purposes of present and future adaptation to the environment. We develop increasingly sophisticated problem-solving processes through the evolution of cognitive patterns that enable us to attend to particular inputs as significant. Information processing is a *sensory* theory in that information from the external world flows passively inward through the senses to the mind. The mind is viewed as having distinct parts, including a sensory register, short-term memory, and long-term memory, which make unique contributions to our thinking in a specific sequence.

Information processing theory eventually gave way to *motor theories*, in which the mind is thought to play an active role in processing input; not merely recording, but also constructing its nature. This was replaced, in turn, by models of the mind as engaging in *parallel* processes, organizing multiple activities in perception, learning, and memory while it receives external information. That is, the mind is interactive with its environment.

Personal Construct Theory

The American psychologist George Kelly introduced a theory of personality in 1955 in which a person's core tendency is to attempt to predict and control the events of experience (Maddi, 1996). He described the essence of human nature as the scientific pursuit of truth—an engagement in empirical procedures of formulating hypotheses and testing them in the tangible world. This "truth" is not absolute, but represents a state in which perceptions are consistent with our internal construct system. *Constructs* are interpretations of events arrived at through natural processes of reasoning. The only important difference between laypersons and professional scientists is that the latter are more self-conscious and precise about their procedures.

Kelly's model of the "person as empirical scientist" influenced the ideas of cognitive theorists who followed him. These included Leon Festinger and *cognitive dissonance* theory, Seymour Epstein's *hierarchical organizations of personal constructs*, and David McClellan's explorations of *motives, traits*, and *schemas*. All of these theorists, in turn, had direct influence on the psychotherapies of Albert Ellis and Aaron Beck.

Albert Ellis and Aaron Beck

Albert Ellis was the first cognitive therapist, publishing *Reason and Emotion in Psychotherapy* in 1962. He believed that people can consciously adopt principles of reasoning, and he viewed the client's underlying assumptions about him- or herself and the world as targets of intervention. The major theme of Ellis's work is that our understandings of how we need to conduct ourselves to maintain security are often narrow and irrational. Behind most distressing emotions one can find irrational beliefs about how things *should* or *must* be. Ellis's therapy involved helping people become more "reasonable" about how they approached their problems. He was known to be a confrontational practitioner, actively persuading clients that some of the principles they lived by were unrealistic.

Cognitive therapy became a more prominent practice theory with the publication of Aaron Beck's *Cognitive Therapy and the Emotional Disorders* in 1976. Beck had been trained as a psychoanalyst and was interested in the problem of depression. He initially attempted to validate Freud's theory of depression as "anger turned toward the self." Instead, his observations led him to conclude that depressed people maintain a negative bias in their cognitive processing. He conceptualized this negativism in terms of cognitive *schemas*—memory structures made up of three basic themes of personal ineffectiveness, personal degradation, and the world as an essentially unpleasant place. Beck was less confrontational than Ellis, seeing clients as "colleagues" with whom he researched the nature of "verifiable" reality.

In the past 40 years, many cognitive practitioners have integrated techniques from cognitive theory with strategies from other approaches. As one prominent example, Donald Meichenbaum's work (1977) combined cognitive modification and skills training in a therapy model that is useful in treating anxiety, anger, and stress.

Cognitive Theory in Social Work

Social workers have been using cognitive theory extensively for thirty years. Reid and Epstein's (1977) *Task-centered Practice*, while not strictly cognitive in theoretical orientation, incorporated many elements of the structured, rational, behavioral-outcome-focused intervention that characterize the approach. The following year, Lantz (1978) published a comprehensive summary of cognitive theory and its related interventions in *Social Work*. Several years later, Sharon Berlin (1982) began her work integrating the theory with the unique perspective of the social work profession, which culminated in her book *Cognitive Theory: An Integrative Approach* in 2002. Berlin's work addresses a gap in the literature on cognitive therapy that stems from its almost exclusive focus on personal meanings and lack of attention to the ways people acquire information from their social environments. That is, cognitive therapy approaches in social work must incorporate clients' life conditions and interpersonal events, particularly those who experience severe deprivation, threats, and vulnerability. More recently, Corcoran (2005), in *Building Strengths and Skills: A Collaborative Approach to Working with Clients*, constructed an eclectic practice approach for social workers that interweaves both strength-based and skills-based practice approaches through a creative integration of motivational interviewing, solution-focused therapy, and cognitive-behavioral therapy.

MAJOR CONCEPTS

Within cognitive theory there are no assumed innate drives or motivations that propel people to act in particular ways. We all develop patterns of thinking and behavior through habit, but these patterns can be adjusted as we acquire new information. A central concept in cognitive theory is that of the *schema*, defined as our internalized representation of the world, or patterns of thought, action, and problem solving (Granvold, 1994). Schemas include the ways we organize thought processes, store information, and process new information, and also the products of those operations (knowledge). Schemas are the necessary biases with which we view the world, based on our early learning. They develop through direct learning (our own experiences) or social learning (watching and absorbing the experiences of others). When we encounter a new situation we either *assimilate* it to "fit" our existing schema, or *accommodate* it, changing the schema if, for some reason, we can't incorporate the experience into our belief patterns. A flexible schema is desirable, but all schemas tend to be somewhat rigid by nature.

Piaget's (1977) theory of cognitive development is the most influential in social work and psychology. It describes the first schema that an infant possesses as a body schema, because a small child is unable to differentiate between the self and the external world. Cognitive development involves a gradual diminishing of this egocentricity. In Piaget's system, the capacity for reasoning develops in stages, from infancy through adolescence and early adulthood. These stages are sequential, evolving from *activity without thought* to *thought with less emphasis on activity*. We evolve from being toddlers who scream out when hungry, to adults who patiently prepare our own meals. That is, cognitive behavior evolves from *doing* to *doing knowingly*, and finally to *conceptualization*. Normal maturation in one's physical and neurological development is necessary for full cognitive development.

Figure 7.1 illustrates how our core beliefs (schemas) influence the manner in which we perceive particular situations throughout life. Our internal perspectives about the world, based on unique life experiences, lead to assumptions and related coping strategies. These core beliefs have a direct influence on how we perceive and react to specific life situations. Our assumptions and related strategies are not "correct" or "incorrect" as much as they are "functional" or

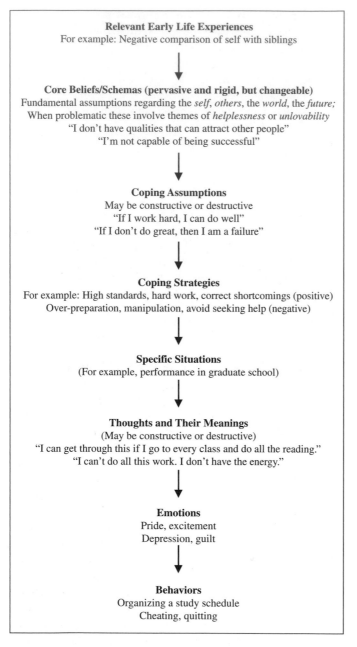

Relevant Early Life Experiences
For example: Negative comparison of self with siblings

Core Beliefs/Schemas (pervasive and rigid, but changeable)
Fundamental assumptions regarding the *self*, *others*, the *world*, the *future*;
When problematic these involve themes of *helplessness* or *unlovability*
"I don't have qualities that can attract other people"
"I'm not capable of being successful"

Coping Assumptions
May be constructive or destructive
"If I work hard, I can do well"
"If I don't do great, then I am a failure"

Coping Strategies
For example: High standards, hard work, correct shortcomings (positive)
Over-preparation, manipulation, avoid seeking help (negative)

Specific Situations
(For example, performance in graduate school)

Thoughts and Their Meanings
(May be constructive or destructive)
"I can get through this if I go to every class and do all the reading."
"I can't do all this work. I don't have the energy."

Emotions
Pride, excitement
Depression, guilt

Behaviors
Organizing a study schedule
Cheating, quitting

FIGURE 7.1 The Influence of Core Beliefs

"non-functional" for our ability to achieve our goals. Schemas can change, but not always easily.

It was mentioned earlier that cognitive theory is a *motor* theory, asserting that we do not merely receive and process external stimuli, but are active in constructing the reality we seek to apprehend. There is no singular way to perceive reality; still, rational thinking can be understood as thinking that (Ellis & McLaren, 1998):

- Is based on external evidence
- Is life-preserving
- Keeps one directed toward personal goals
- Decreases internal conflicts

A person's thoughts can accurately reflect what is happening in the external world, or be *distorted* to some degree. These distortions, called *cognitive errors*, will be described below.

Cognitive interventions are applicable to clients over the age of approximately 12 years because the person must be able to engage in abstract thought. Of course, some adults with cognitive limitations, such as mental retardation, dementia, and some psychotic disorders, may not be responsive to the approach. To benefit from these interventions, clients must also be able to follow through with directions, not require an intensely emotional encounter with the social worker, demonstrate stability in some life activities, and not be in an active crisis (Lantz, 1996).

Other concepts that are central to cognitive theory will be introduced in the section below.

THE NATURE OF PROBLEMS AND CHANGE

Many problems in living result from misconceptions—conclusions that are based more on habits of thought rather than external evidence—that people have about themselves, other people, and their life situations. These misconceptions may develop for any of three reasons. The first is the simplest: The person has not acquired the information necessary to manage a new situation. This is often evident in the lives of children and adolescents. They face many situations at school, at play, and with their families that they have not experienced before, and they are not sure how to respond. This lack of information is known as a cognitive *deficit*, and can be remedied with education. A child who has trouble getting along with other children may not have learned social skills, and teaching that child about social expectations may help to resolve the problem.

The other two sources of misperception are rooted in schemas that have become too rigid to manage new situations. That is, the schema cannot accommodate the situation. An adolescent who can manage conflicts with his friends suddenly realizes that he cannot use those same strategies to manage conflict with his new girlfriend.

As a part of one's schema, *causal attributions* refer to three kinds of assumptions that people hold about themselves in relation to the environment. First, a person might function from a premise that life situations are *more* or *less* changeable. (I'm unhappy with my job, and there is nothing I can do about it.) Second, a person may believe that, if change is possible, the source of power to make changes exists either *within* or *outside* the self. (Only my supervisor can do anything to make my job better.) Finally, a person might assume that the implications of his or her experiences are limited to the *specific situation*, or that they are *global*. (My supervisor didn't like how I managed that client with a substance abuse problem. He doesn't think I can be a good social worker.)

The final sources of misperceptions are specific *cognitive distortions* of reality. Because of our tendency to develop thinking habits, we often interpret new situations in biased ways. These patterns are generally functional because many situations we face in life are similar to previous ones, and can be managed with patterned responses. These habits become a source of difficulty, however, when they are too rigid to accommodate our considering new information. For example, a low-income community resident may believe that he lacks the ability to advocate for certain medication benefits and, as a result, continues to live without them. This belief may be rooted in a distorted sense that other people will never respect him. The client may have had real difficulties over the years with failure and discrimination, but the belief that this will happen in all circumstances in the future may be arbitrary. Table 7.1 lists some widely held cognitive distortions, also known as "irrational beliefs" (Beck, 1967), with examples.

T A B L E 7.1   Common Cognitive Distortions

Irrational Beliefs	Examples
Arbitrary inference: Drawing a conclusion about an event with no evidence, little evidence, or even contradictory evidence	"I'm not going to do well in this course. I have a bad feeling about it." "The staff at this agency seem to have a different practice approach than mine. They aren't going to respect my work."
Selective abstraction: Judging a situation on the basis of one or a few details taken out of a broader context	"Did you see how our supervisor yawned when I was describing my assessment of the client? He must think my work is superficial."
Magnification or *minimization:* Concluding that an event is either far more significant, or far less significant, than the evidence seems to indicate	"I got a B on the first assignment. There is a good chance I will fail this course." "I don't really need to get to work on time every day. My clients don't seem to mind waiting, and the administrative meeting isn't relevant to my work."
Overgeneralization: Concluding that all instances of a certain kind of situation or event will turn out a particular way because one or two such situations did	"My supervisor thinks that my depressed client client dropped out because I was too confrontational. I don't have enough empathy to be a decent social worker."
Personalization: Attributing the cause, or accepting responsibility for, an external event without evidence of a connection	"The instructor didn't say this, but our group presentation got a mediocre evaluation because of my poor delivery."
Dichotomous thinking: Categorizing experiences as one of two extremes: complete success or utter failure (usually the latter)	"I didn't get an A on my final exam. I blew it! I'm not competent to move on to the next course." "I got an A on the mid-term. I can coast the rest of the way through this course."

Interventions within cognitive theory can help clients change in three ways. Clients can change their personal goals to become more consistent with their capabilities, adjust their cognitive assumptions (beliefs and expectations), or change their habits of thinking (which includes giving up cognitive distortions). Even when some of a person's beliefs are distorted, the potential to correct them in light of contradictory evidence is great. In clinical assessment, the social worker observes the client's schema, identifies thinking patterns with respect to the presenting situation, and considers the evidence supporting the client's conclusions about the situation. When those conclusions seem valid, the social worker helps the client develop better problem-solving or coping skills. When the conclusions are distorted, the social worker uses techniques to help the client adjust his or her cognitive processes in ways that will facilitate goal attainment.

ASSESSMENT AND INTERVENTION

The Social Worker/Client Relationship

Cognitive intervention is always an *active* process. Intervention often resembles a conversation between the social worker and the client. (I often tell students that if they like to talk, this is a good theoretical perspective to adopt.) The social worker serves as an *educator* in situations where clients experience cognitive deficits, and as an "objective" voice of reason (to the extent that this is possible) when the client experiences cognitive distortions.

The practitioner is a collaborator—goals, objectives, and interventions are developed with the client's ongoing input. The client's desired outcomes are often written down so that they may be followed consistently over time or revised. Beyond this, the social worker may serve as a *model* of rational thinking and problem solving for the client, or as a *coach*, leading the client thorough a process of guided reasoning. The social worker needs to demonstrate empathy with the client's problem situation, in part because confrontation is frequently a part of the interventions. Confrontation involves the social worker pointing out discrepancies between a client's statements and actions (Hepworth, Rooney, Rooney, Strom-Gottfried, & Larsen, 2005), which can sometimes be difficult for a client to tolerate. The social worker's perceived positive regard will help the client understand that these confrontations are being presented constructively.

Cognitive interventions are highly structured, and it is the responsibility of the social worker to establish and maintain that structure (Beck, 1995). The structure of the first session includes the social worker's setting an agenda, doing a mood check, reviewing and specifying the presenting problem, setting goals, educating the client about the cognitive model, eliciting the client's expectations for the intervention, educating the client about the nature of his or her problem, setting up homework assignments, providing a session summary, and eliciting the client's feedback about the session. Subsequent sessions include brief updates and checks on the client's mood, the social worker's linking issues between the previous and current session, setting the agenda, reviewing homework, discussing issues on the agenda, setting up new homework tasks, providing a final session summary, and eliciting the client's feedback about the session.

The social worker must always be aware that his or her clinical assessments are also subject to cognitive biases. To minimize the possibility of his or her own distortions when working with a client, the social worker should:

- Consistently examine his or her own beliefs and attitudes about the client through supervision
- Generate and evaluate a *variety* of hypotheses about a client's problem situation
- Consider and "rank" the evidence for and against the "working hypotheses" about a client
- Use clear evaluation measures of client change (standardized or personalized)
- Use various sources of feedback, including peers and supervisors

Assessment

The practitioner initially educates the client in the logic of cognitive theory and then assesses the client's cognitive assumptions, identifying any distortions that may contribute to problem persistence. The rationality of a client's thinking is assessed through a process known as *Socratic questioning* (Granvold, 1994). This term derives from the work of the philosopher, whose teaching technique involved asking questions of his students until they came upon the answers by themselves. The social worker assesses the validity of a client's assumptions associated with a problem issue through detailed, focused questioning. After the client describes the presenting problem and some of the relevant history surrounding it, the following types of questions guide the social worker's assessment:

- First, tease out the client's core beliefs relative to the presenting problem ("What were you thinking when…?" "How did you conclude that…?" "What did it mean to you when…?")
- What is the *logic* behind the client's beliefs regarding the significance of the problem situation?
- What is the *evidence* to support the client's views?
- What *other explanations* for the client's perceptions are possible?
- How do particular *beliefs* influence the client's attachment of significance to specific events? Emotions? Behaviors?

To maximize the reliability of the client's self-reports during assessment and intervention, the social worker should (Berlin, 2002):

- Inquire about a client's cognitive events of concern as soon as possible after the event

- Analyze the internal consistency of a client's statements
- Minimize the kind of probing that may influence a client's ability to reflect "objectively" on his or her thoughts and feelings
- Help the client acquire cognitive retrieval skills (through imagery and relaxation)

At the end of the assessment the social worker helps the client to arrive at a tentative conclusion about the rationality of his or her thought patterns, and, if any distortions are apparent, examines the client's willingness to consider alternative perspectives.

Intervention

When a client's perceptions and beliefs seem valid, the practitioner intervenes by providing education about the presenting issue and implementing problem-solving or coping exercises. When the client exhibits significant cognitive distortions, the practitioner and client must identify the situations that trigger the misconceptions, determine how they can be most efficiently adjusted or replaced with new thinking patterns, and then implement corrective tasks. Various specific intervention strategies are presented below. Not *all* possible interventions are described in this chapter (there are many), but what follows is representative of the theory.

Cognitive Restructuring   Strategies for cognitive intervention fit into three general categories. The first of these is *cognitive restructuring*. This technique is used when the client's thinking patterns are distorted and contribute to problem development and persistence (Emery, 1985). Through a series of discussions and exercises, the social worker helps the client experiment with alternative ways of approaching challenges that will promote goal attainment.

The ABC model (presented earlier in this chapter on page 148) is the basis of the cognitive restructuring approach. "A" represents an activating event; "B" is the client's belief about, or interpretation of, the event; and "C" is the emotional and behavioral consequence of A and B. For example, if A is an event (a rainy day) and C, the consequence, is the person's feeling of depression, then the B (belief) might be: "Everything looks so gray and ugly, and I wanted to go out. Nothing can go well for me on a day like this." If the same activating event (rain) occurs, but the resulting emotion (consequence, or C) is contentment, the client's belief might be: "How peaceful. Today I can stay home and read. It'll be really cozy." The ABC process occurs so quickly that clients often make the assumption that A directly causes C, but except in certain reflexive actions (such as placing a finger on a hot stove and then abruptly pulling it back) there is always a cognitive event, B, that intervenes between them.

In order to change a client's belief systems, three steps are necessary. The first is to help the person identify the thoughts preceding and accompanying the distressing emotions and non-productive action ("What was going through your mind...?"). It is important to put the client into a frame of mind in which he or she can reflect on thoughts and feelings *as if the event is occurring at the present moment*. Some clients may require assistance in grasping their thinking patterns. The practitioner might engage the client in *imagery* ("Close your eyes, take a deep breath, and see yourself in that situation. What are you doing? ...What are you feeling? ...What are you thinking?"). The social worker may invite other clients to participate in role-plays toward the same end ("Let's pretend that we are at work, and I am your boss..."). By re-enacting the problem situation, clients can more accurately retrieve the thought patterns that are maintaining the problem.

The second step is to assess the client's willingness to consider alternative thoughts in response to the problem situation. One means of addressing this is the point/counterpoint or cost/benefit analysis, in which the social worker asks the client to consider the costs and benefits of maintaining his or her current beliefs pertaining to the problem (Leahy, 1996). This can be accomplished through simple conversation, but is often more effective with pen and paper. Writing down the pros and cons of an argument can help the client visualize whether his or her goals are being well-served by the current perspectives. It must be emphasized that the mere number of pros and cons will not influence the client's thinking in one direction or the other, as some will carry more "weight" than others.

The third step is to challenge the client's irrational beliefs by designing natural experiments, or tasks, that he or she can carry out in daily life to test their validity. For instance, if a college student believes that if she speaks out in class everyone will laugh at her, she might be asked to volunteer one answer in class to see the reactions of others. By changing clients' actions, their cognitions and emotions may be indirectly modified. The actions may provide new data to refute clients' illogical beliefs about themselves and the world.

The ABC Review   This cognitive intervention technique requires a client to fill out a form over a specified period of time (Beck, 1976). Its purpose is to help the client become more aware of his or her automatic thoughts and subsequently work toward modifying them so that emotions and behaviors can become more productive. Following an assessment of the client's cognitive patterns, the social worker prepares a sheet of paper with four columns (see Figure 7.2). The first column is headed "situations that produce stress" (the A component of the ABC process). The client is instructed to write down during the course of a day the situations that produce the negative emotions or behaviors for which he or she is seeking help. The next column is headed "automatic thoughts" (the B component), and here the client records the thoughts that accompany the situation. This step is difficult and takes practice for many clients. Some tend to overlook their interpretations that intervene between situations and emotional and behavioral responses. Others tend to record emotions rather than thoughts. During the intervention the social worker can help the client learn to distinguish between thoughts and feelings. Next, the client is asked to think about and record in the third column the assumptions that seem to underlie the automatic thought. For example, a client who is rejected for a job (the situation) may think

Situation that produces stress	Automatic thought	Assumption behind automatic thought	Feeling/Behavior

Situation that produces stress	Automatic thought	Assumption behind automatic thought	Feeling/ Behavior	Alternative thought	Feeling/Behavior

F I G U R E 7.2   The ABC Work Sheets

that he "will never get a good job" (automatic thought) because "I am worthless" (the underlying assumption). Finally, the client is asked to record the emotional response to the automatic thought, such as depression or panic (the C component).

The social worker asks the client to fill out the form with some mutually agreed-on frequency, depending on the nature of the problem and the ability of the client to maintain a structured task focus. Often, the social worker will ask the client to fill out the form every day between their appointments, when they can review it together. Over time, the social worker helps the client clarify his or her automatic thoughts and understand which of them are arbitrary. The social worker then asks the client, with an expanded form, to experiment with alternative rational thoughts about his or her problem situation that might be more constructive (see Figure 7.2 again). These alternative thoughts, and the feelings that follow them, can be written in fourth and fifth columns on the page. The client and social worker can then monitor how the client's feelings and behaviors change.

Cognitive Coping   A second category of interventions is *cognitive coping*. The practitioner helps the client learn and practice new or more effective ways of dealing with stress and negative moods. All of these involve step-by-step procedures for the client to master new skills. (Here we begin to see the convergence of the cognitive and behavior theories: combining new thinking patterns with new situations that may provide reinforcement of new behaviors.) Cognitive coping involves education and skills development that targets both covert and overt cognitive operations, with the goal of helping clients become more effective at managing their challenges. Clients can modify their cognitive distortions when they experience positive results from practicing new coping skills. That is, if clients develop good coping skills, they may elicit positive reinforcement from the environment. Several interventions are presented here in detail.

Self-Instruction Skills Development   This is a means of giving clients an internal cognitive framework for instructing themselves in how to cope more effectively with problem situations (Meichenbaum, 1999). It is based in part on the premise that many people, as a matter of course, engage in internal speech, giving themselves "pep talks" to prepare for certain challenges. For example, one good friend of mine, a respected social worker, stands in front of the mirror every morning and lectures herself about what she needs to do to manage the most difficult parts of her work day. She feels energized by this practice.

Often, when people find themselves in difficult situations that evoke tension or other negative emotions, their thinking may become confused, and their ability to cope diminishes. Some people have a lack of positive cues in their self-dialogue. Having a prepared internal (or written) script for problem situations can help a client recall and implement a coping strategy. Self-instruction training has mainly been studied in relation to children and school task completion, but it can also be used with adults.

When using this technique, the social worker assesses the client's behavior and its relationship to deficits in sub-vocal dialogue. The client and social worker develop a step-by-step self-instruction script, including overt self-directed speech, following their plan for confronting a problem. Such a script may be written down or memorized by the client. The social worker and client visualize and walk through the problem situation together so the client can rehearse its implementation. During rehearsal, the client gradually moves from *overt* self-dialogue to *covert* self-talk. The client then uses the script in the natural environment, either before or during a challenging situation.

As an example, Beth (who will be introduced later in more detail) felt guilty about dropping her young son off at the day care center every morning on her way to classes, feeling that she was a poor mother for indulging herself at the expense of time with her son. This negative feeling stayed with her much of the day. She developed a self-instruction script with the social worker that included the following statements: "My son will be well cared for. Many good parents take their children to day care when they go to work every day. I spend every evening and every weekend with my son. When I get my degree I will be a better provider for my son and myself. It is good for my son to learn to interact with people other than myself. He has a chance to play with other children while there. I will be a better parent if I take care of myself as well as him." Beth initially wrote down these statements, but quickly memorized them. She recited them to herself internally every morning and anytime during the day that she began to feel guilty about her son.

Communication Skills Development   The teaching and rehearsal of these skills cover a wide spectrum of interventions that includes attention to clients' social, assertiveness, and negotiation skills. Positive communication builds relationships and closeness with others, which in turn helps improve mood and feelings about oneself (Hargie, 1997). Social support is a source of positive reinforcement and buffers individuals from stressful life events. In addition, when a person can articulate his or her concerns, other people may constructively suggest how that person might adjust his or her attitudes and behaviors.

The components of communication skills training include using "I" messages, reflective and empathic listening, and making clear behavior change requests. (These were discussed in Chapter 5, as an intervention with family emotional systems theory.) "I" messages are those in which a person talks about his or her own position and feelings in a situation, rather than making accusatory comments about another person. The basic format for giving "I" messages is: "I feel (the reaction) about what happened (a specific activating event)." For example: "I feel angry when you break curfew on Saturday night. I also worry about you." These statements help the speaker to maintain clarity about his or her own thoughts and feelings. This is a clearer communication than saying, "How dare you stay out so late!" which generally makes the other person feel defensive.

Listening skills include both reflective listening and validation of the other person's intent. The purpose of reflective listening is to ensure that one understands the speaker's perspective. It decreases the tendency of people to draw premature conclusions about the intentions and meaning of another's statement (Brownell, 1986). Reflective listening involves paraphrasing back the feelings and content of the speaker's message with the format: "What I hear you saying is…" or "You seem to feel [*feeling word*] when I…" Beyond reflection, validation involves conveying a message that, given the other person's perspectives and assumptions, his or her experiences are legitimate and understandable ("I can see that if you were thinking I had done that, you would feel that way.").

A third component of communication skill development involves teaching people to make clear behavior requests of others. Such requests should always be *specific* ("pick up your toys") rather than global ("clean up this room"), *measurable* ("I would like you to call me once per week"), and *stated in terms of positive behavior* rather than the absence of negative behavior ("Give me a chance to look at the mail when I come home" rather than "Stop bothering me with your questions").

Problem-Solving Skills Development   The third category of intervention is *problem solving*. This is a structured, five-step method for helping clients who do not experience distortions but nevertheless struggle with the problems that they clearly perceive. Clients learn how to produce a variety of potentially effective responses to their problems (McClam & Woodside, 1994). The first step is *defining the problem* that the client wishes to overcome. As the poet Emerson (1958) wrote, "a problem well defined is a problem half solved." Solutions are easier to formulate when problems are clearly delineated. Only one problem should be targeted at a time (Wheeler, Christensen, & Jacobson, 2001).

The next step in problem-solving training involves the client and social worker's *brainstorming* to generate as many possible solutions for a presenting problem as they can imagine. At this point, evaluative comments are not allowed, so that spontaneity and creativity are encouraged. All possibilities are written down, even those that seem impossible or silly. Some supposedly ridiculous ideas may contain useful elements on closer examination. It is important in this step for the social worker to encourage additional responses after clients decide they are finished. Clients often stop participating when a list contains as few as five alternatives, but when pressed they can usually suggest more.

The third stage of the problem-solving process involves *evaluating the alternatives*. Any patently irrelevant or impossible items are crossed out. Each viable alternative is then discussed as to its advantages and disadvantages. More information about the situation may need to be gathered as a result of the work in this stage. For instance, information might be gathered about other agencies and resources (including other people in the client's life) that can assist in making some of the choices more viable.

Choosing and implementing an alternative involves selecting a strategy for problem resolution that appears to maximize benefits over costs. Although the outcome of any alternative is always uncertain, the client is praised for exercising good judgment in the process thus far, and is reminded that making any effort to address the problem is the most significant aspect of this step. The social worker should remind the client that there is no guarantee that the alternative will succeed, and that other alternatives are available if needed.

During the following session, the social worker helps the client to *evaluate the implemented option*. If successful, the process is complete except for the important discussion about how to generalize problem solving to other situations in the client's life. "Failures" must be examined closely for elements that went well in addition to those still needing work. If a strategy has not been successful, it can be attempted again with adjustments or the social worker and client can go back to the fourth step and select another option.

Role-playing is an effective teaching strategy that can be used with all of the above interventions (Hepworth Rooney, Rooney, Strom-Gottfried, & Larsen, 2005). This involves the social worker first modeling a skill, then the worker and client rehearsing it together. Role-playing offers a number of advantages for intervention. First, the social worker demonstrates new skills for the client, which usually is a more powerful way of conveying information than verbal instruction. Second, by portraying the client in a role-play, the social worker gains a fuller appreciation of the challenges faced by the client. At the same time, the client's taking on the perspective of another significant person in his or her life (family member, boss, or friend) allows the client to better understand the other person's position. Assuming the roles of others also introduces a note of playfulness to situations that may have been previously viewed with grim seriousness.

SPIRITUALITY AND COGNITIVE THEORY

Unlike behavior theory, the concepts of cognitive theory can facilitate an understanding of clients' spirituality and promote their reflections on the topic. Remember that spirituality refers here to a client's search for, and adherence to, meanings that extend beyond the self. Cognitive theory emphasizes each person's natural inclination to make sense of reality, and the idea that values can change through reflection and action. The theory further asserts that we are active participants in constructing our realities. Thinking represents our organized efforts to create meaning from personal experience.

In the context of cognitive theory, then, spirituality can be understood as the core beliefs (including values) that provide us with meaning and motivate our actions. Effective social functioning depends on our developing patterns of *shared meaning* with others, and thus we tend to seek out others who share our deepest concerns. Cognitive deficits or distortions may contribute to a person's disillusionment in striving for spiritual goal attainment. Interventions relevant to spirituality include Socratic questioning, which helps clients reflect on long-term goals and the significance of problem situations in that context. *Any* cognitive interventions that encourage a client's reconsideration of ways of understanding and acting on challenges may be relevant to his or her spirituality.

An example may help to clarify these points. Terri was a grade school teacher with a clear commitment to helping children develop positive social and academic skills. Her strong values about children were related in part to a personal background in which she had felt unfairly demeaned. Along with this core value was a core belief that she was socially incompetent, less intelligent, and less worthy of affection than other people. This core belief led to serious cognitive distortions in which Terri believed herself to be untalented and inept professionally. Acting on these distortions, Terri received unsatisfactory evaluations from the school principal and was at risk of losing her job. While the social worker helped Terri to address her distortions with cognitive intervention strategies, he also helped her to maintain a focus on her ultimate value so that she would persist toward her goal of success in the classroom.

ATTENTION TO SOCIAL JUSTICE ISSUES

Cognitive theory includes many features that may facilitate the social worker's promotion of social justice activities with clients. The theory incorporates an empowerment approach, with its premise that people are competent problem solvers, and can be taught to generalize problem-solving strategies to other life challenges. In examining core beliefs the social worker will likely encourage the client's examination of personal and social values. The concept of "social construction of reality" underscores the social worker's obligation to be sensitive to issues of cultural and ethnic diversity. The theory is applicable to many client populations—actually, to all people who have the capacity for cognition and reflection. The theory may have particular appeal to members of diverse populations who seek concrete, practical approaches to problem solving, such as persons in lower socioeconomic groups, Latino clients, and African-American clients (Fong & Furuto, 2001).

On the other hand, cognitive theory focuses on individuals and tends to limit its attention to the *immediate* rather than the *macro* environment. It does not encourage the social worker to look outside the client, except to consider environmental evidence for his or her beliefs about the world. In considering the "rationality" of a client's thinking, practitioners may be as likely to support the acceptance of social conventions as to encourage social change activities when working with vulnerable or oppressed client groups (Payne, 2005). Second, though the theory encourages sensitivity to diversity, the social worker must always make difficult judgments about the "rationality" of a client's thinking. The less the social worker understands the client's world, the more difficult will be the task of assessing the client's rationality.

CASE ILLUSTRATIONS

Problem Solving and the Adolescent Girls Group

Ridgedale High School was located in a lower-class section of a large city and served neighborhoods that experienced much criminal activity. Drug dealing, prostitution, grand and petty theft, and burglaries occurred frequently. As one preventive measure, the school offered a number of coping groups for students who were considered at risk for developing delinquent behaviors. One such group was offered to female adolescents who demonstrated chronic school truancy. This eight-week time-limited group, like others at the school, was led by a social worker. This "academic and personal success" group used the problem-solving model as a basis for intervention.

The social worker devoted the first meeting to the girls' getting acquainted with each other and generating topics for discussion. Subsequent meetings included structured discussions among the girls about ways to problem solve with regard to the topic for that day. During one group session, the issue of safe sex was selected as a topic for discussion. The girls agreed that they did not want to become pregnant and some were opposed to the idea of having sex, but all of them had faced difficulty with boys who were sexually aggressive.

The social worker's responsibilities each week included teaching and implementing the problem-solving process to address a variety of problems in living. She emphasized that engaging in this practice was often more effective when done in the group setting, with the benefit of immediate input from others. In the first part of this meeting the girls were asked to specify a problem related to the general topic of safe sex. They quickly agreed that they wanted to learn how to reject the advances of boys who tried to talk them into sex. The social worker asked the girls to role-play several scenarios during the meeting to get a clearer idea of the situations they had in mind. This was helpful and also provided the girls with some amusement as they acted out the parts.

The girls next brainstormed possible solutions to the challenge. Because all ideas are welcomed and none are censored, this task was fun for the girls. They could laugh and be outrageous with each other while also sharing suggestions about physically protecting themselves, making specific and assertive verbal responses to boys, limiting their dates to certain kinds of settings, avoiding certain topics of conversation, addressing their preferences before a date began, and dealing with other situations.

In the group setting, it is not necessary for all members to choose the same solution to implement. Each girl can select her own solution, and it is supported as long as she can articulate reasons for the choice that represent a logical cost/benefit thought process. The social worker, whose goal was to teach generalizable problem-solving skills, asked the girls to make a commitment to implement their solutions, if and when the problem situation arose. In this instance, the girls agreed that greater assertiveness would help them maintain control of the situation when alone with a boyfriend. The girls could not all implement their strategy in the context of a date situation during the next week, but they could practice assertiveness skills in other contexts with boys.

The following week the girls shared their experiences in exercising assertive behavior with boys at school and over the weekend, and stated whether they considered these episodes successes or failures. Several of the girls had, in fact, been on dates. One had specifically experienced the problem of aggressive behavior with a boy and described how she had responded. The girls helped each other evaluate their task implementation, and again were constructive in their comments. As a final stage in this process they helped each other refine their approaches to assertiveness and consider new strategies for the coming week.

Cognitive Restructuring and the Single Parent

Beth was a 26-year-old single parent who was raising a four-year-old son while attending college to get a business degree. She maintained an apartment with money acquired from a computer programming job she kept during school breaks. Her parents, both of whom lived in town and were divorced, helped Beth with occasional money and babysitting assistance. Her son attended a day care center while Beth went to school. She had many friends, most of whom did not have children. Beth sought counseling because she was overwhelmed with stress related to managing her responsibilities. She had little time to relax, lived on a tight budget, had an unsatisfying social life, and felt that she was a bad parent because she was preoccupied with school and often lost her temper with her son. She could not sleep well, was often irritable, and had trouble concentrating on her schoolwork. Despite her goal of being a businesswoman, Beth wondered if the material and emotional costs were worthwhile. The social worker acknowledged that this was a difficult time in Beth's life, but also pointed out her personal strengths of persistence, resilience, and love for her child. The social worker educated Beth about several community agencies that might provide material assistance to her household.

Beth was a suitable candidate for coping skills training, which will be discussed later in this chapter. Still, much of her difficulty was rooted in her *causal attributions* and *cognitive distortions*. The social worker concluded after the assessment that Beth had a basic sense of powerlessness to change any aspect of her life situation. Further, Beth had a tendency to engage in *overgeneralization*, believing that any failures implied complete incompetence on her part. She also *personalized* negative events in her life, believing that anything negative that happened was due to her own inadequacies, and ignoring the parts that other people or circumstances played in those situations.

The social worker organized a cognitive restructuring intervention with Beth. He initially educated Beth in the ABC sequence of cognitive operations. This helped her see that her appraisal of life situations, based on core beliefs that were not always consistent with external evidence related to the event of concern, had a role in producing her emotional experiences. Like many clients, Beth was able to grasp this point after some discussion and reflection. She could see, for example, that her father's high expectations of her as a child and adolescent resulted in her belief that she should be competent to manage every aspect of her life.

It was more difficult for Beth to see that she might have the power to change some of her problem situations. She had to cope with multiple stresses, but the social worker eventually helped Beth see that there were some areas of life in which she could proactively make adjustments. As one example, Beth had become reluctant to ask her grandparents to babysit her son on weekends, thinking that they resented the intrusion on their time. Beth had reported, however, both that the grandparents loved her son, and that they seemed to feel lonely as they got older. The social worker explored these contradictory statements with Beth and helped her work out a flexible "schedule" of family babysitting requests so that she would call on her mother, father, and grandparents every few weeks in rotation for that purpose. This worked out well, providing Beth with more predictable time for study and even a few hours for working. The process also taught Beth that she could have an effect on her environment.

In the process of *Socratic questioning*, the social worker and client reviewed specific situations in Beth's life that made her feel sad or upset and looked at alternative interpretations of those situations. It is important to understand in cognitive intervention that some negative emotional responses to situations reflect a client's accurate appraisals. For example, Beth discussed with the social worker her frustrations with several professors which appeared to accurately reflect their insensitivity to her learning style. On the other hand, Beth's anger at her friends for their alleged unwillingness to understand her limited availability for social outings seemed (to the social worker) to indicate an oversensitivity to rejection. Beth believed that her friends did not want to spend time with her anymore, and thus she tended not to seek them out. Through questioning the social worker helped Beth see that there was limited external evidence for Beth's assumption. The practitioner suggested that, possibly, Beth's friends were well aware of her busy schedule, and called less often so as not to intrude.

Beth agreed to engage in the pen-and-paper ABC review for several weeks. The social worker asked her to record for one week every situation in which she felt rejected by her friends and to record her accompanying thoughts and feelings. In a relatively short time Beth was able to see that she quickly jumped to self-denigrating conclusions whenever a friend was not available to spend time with her (which, to Beth's surprise, did not happen as often as she had supposed). The social worker noted that many times people learn that they have made erroneous estimates of the frequency of their problem situations when they record them. Beth changed her thinking about her friends' behaviors and resumed more comfortable relationships with several of them.

Managing Family Friction with Communication
Skills Development

Nigel and Nita Bourne sought family counseling because of conflicts that had become more prominent since Nigel, a recovering alcoholic, had stopped drinking six months previously. Nigel, age 50, was a successful small businessman in his community and had been married to Nita, 47, for 24 years. Three children lived in the household: Diane, 22, Peter, 20, and Christina, 19. Whereas all members of the family were pleased with Nigel's decision to stop drinking, he had become more tense and moody, and their longstanding but "subtle" communication problems had become prominent. Nigel tended to be authoritarian with his family, and Nita tried to "make up" for his brusque manner by being overly agreeable with the children, rarely disagreeing with or confronting them. The siblings tended to be argumentative with each other. Nigel was receiving alcoholism treatment in addition to seeking family counseling. Their goal was to become able to air their feelings and process their disagreements without falling into arguments. They agreed that a calmer atmosphere would also help their father to maintain his sobriety.

Following his assessment, the social worker agreed that communication skills training would be an important intervention. He explained his rationale for this strategy, and the family agreed to participate. The social worker took control of a chaotic situation and modeled the skills he was trying to teach. He assured all family members that they would have the opportunity each week to make their thoughts and feelings known to each other. He set a "ground rule" that no one could be interrupted when expressing a thought or feeling. The social worker did, however, reserve the right to intervene if he perceived that communication was breaking down. This directive made a significant difference in reducing escalating tensions during the family's interactions.

The social worker next taught listening skills by asking each person to repeat back what someone had said to him or her each time, making sure the listener had received the message accurately. The family members felt awkward following this directive, but they were amazed to learn how often they misunderstood each other. The practitioner pointed out that this represented a learned family pattern. The receiver of a message began to defensively formulate a response for the sender before the sender had completed the message.

When the family had made some progress in these ways the social worker taught the use of "I" messages. For example, Nigel, instead of angrily saying to his son, "You need to get a job and get out of the house!" was asked to formulate the message as "I feel angry when you are not working because a young man of your age should take on more responsibility." His son was instructed to say, even though Nigel would not agree, "Sometimes I feel uncomfortable living here when I am not working, but I also think parents should always support their kids." These messages resulted in a clearer articulation of each member's assumptions about family life. The members had great difficulty learning to communicate in these ways, and the practitioner gave them homework assignments for practice using "I" messages.

As a final component of this four-session intervention the family members were asked to role-play a variety of conflicted interactions that occurred in the household. Members usually portrayed themselves in these role-plays, and other members were asked to comment afterward on the quality of the communication and problem solving demonstrated and to make suggestions for more effective ways to interact. During the role-plays members were helped to make clearer and more specific requests of each other. For example, Diane tended to be negative in her interactions with her younger sister, saying, "You are so controlling all of the time. You're never considerate of Peter or myself." She was encouraged to give the same message in a more constructive way, saying, "It feels to me like you are ignoring my ideas when you make decisions for all three of us. Peter and I would like to be considered more often. You know, we might still agree with you."

The social worker had moderate success with this family. The level of tension in the household did diminish, and each member seemed to acquire improved communications skills. Nita became able to confront her husband about his authoritarian manner, which was one of her goals. Interestingly, this assertive behavior ran counter to her family's cultural value of women as passive, and it seemed that she would only be likely to "speak out" occasionally. The family members remained mutually supportive, although Nigel was having difficulty containing his temper. He planned to get help for this problem from his substance abuse counselor.

COMBINING COGNITIVE AND BEHAVIORAL
INTERVENTION

Many social workers *combine* intervention approaches from cognitive theory and behavior theory when working with clients. The two theories are often compatible because cognitive interventions help clients develop alternative ways of thinking, and behavioral approaches help reinforce clients' new thought patterns with effective new behaviors.

Consider Makita, a new university student commuting from a small town, who felt depressed because she did not "fit in" to the large campus environment. Through *arbitrary inference*, she concluded that the other university students were not friendly because none of them ever approached her in the crowded student commons. She also concluded that she would continue to be lonely and sad because she was a dull person. To help adjust her thoughts, a social worker helped Makita learn to evaluate her external environment differently. She was helped to change some of her beliefs and expectations about how to make friends in an environment more impersonal than the one she came from. Makita's thinking was adjusted through the techniques of education (about the typical behaviors of college students on a large campus) and an ABC review of her thoughts and feelings. She concluded that the commons was not an appropriate place to meet people because it is crowded and students tend to hurry through lunch and off to classes. There might be more appropriate settings for Makita to meet people. She also learned that she would benefit from assertiveness in her desire to make friends.

In addition to assessing and adjusting Makita's thought patterns, behavioral strategies such as *desensitization* and *behavioral rehearsal* helped to adjust her present reinforcers. Makita and her social worker designed and practiced a series of steps whereby she approached a small group of students at a lunch table and asked to join them. Positive reinforcers included the other students obliging her and later asking Makita to join them in other activities. Combining these interventions allowed the social worker to help Makita cognitively (to assess and adjust her assumptions about the behavior of college students) and behaviorally (to spend increasingly long time periods in the crowded commons, and saying "hello" to a certain number of students in her classes).

Makita's story features several aspects of a cognitive-behavioral approach known as *social skills training*. This was described in the previous chapter, but its cognitive aspects are presented here. The full range of its components is listed below (Richey, 1994).

Improving Cognitive Capacity

- Providing knowledge about relationships (what they are, why they are important, how they develop, social norms)
- Enhancing perceptual skills (how to more accurately interpret the social world)
- Improving decision-making skills (when it is appropriate to approach others)
- Improving assessment skills (how to consider a variety of explanations for the observed behavior of others)

Improving Behavioral Skills

- Self-presentation (to enhance likelihood of positive responses)
- Social initiatives (includes how to start conversations)
- Conversation (talking, listening, turn-taking)
- Maintenance (of relationships over time)
- Conflict resolution (handling disagreements, disappointments)

Although cognitive interventions often include task assignments, *true* behavioral interventions require the social worker to take a highly systematic approach to organizing environmental activities and measure progress carefully. In a pure sense, cognitive-behavioral interventions are generally more cognitive than behavioral.

Another example of combining cognitive and behavioral intervention is seen in *dialectical behavior therapy* (DBT). This intervention approach, often associated with the treatment of borderline personality disorder but also used with substance abusers and other client populations, assumes that the core difficulty of clients is *affective instability* (Robins, 2002). DBT is based on cognitive, behavioral, and learning theories, and is (in its "pure" form) an intensive, one-year intervention that combines weekly individual sessions with weekly skills-training groups. The purposes of the groups are to teach adaptive coping skills in the areas of emotional regulation, distress tolerance, interpersonal effectiveness, and identity confusion, and to correct maladaptive cognitions. The individual sessions, conducted by the same practitioner, address maladaptive behaviors while strengthening and generalizing the client's coping skills. Some client-practitioner phone contact is permitted between sessions for support and crisis intervention. An important component in DBT is the consultation team that can help the practitioner maintain objectivity during the often intensive intervention process.

Dialectical behavior therapy can be considered a *well-established* intervention for clients with borderline personality disorder, as evidenced by seven randomized clinical trials across four different research teams (Lynch, Chapman, Rosenthal, Kuo, & Linehan, 2006). Another summary of studies that compared DBT to other treatments indicated that DBT is more effective than less structured interventions in reducing client suicidality, although overall differences are modest (Binks, Fenton, McCarthy, Lee, Adams, et al., 2006).

EVIDENCE OF EFFECTIVENESS

A strength of cognitive theory is that its interventions lend themselves to empirical research methods. A number of meta-analyses of the professional literature, produced during the past ten years, and based on critical reviews of dozens of studies, provide evidence of the effectiveness of cognitive-behavioral interventions for a variety of psychological problems. These analyses support the effectiveness of cognitive or cognitive-behavioral interventions for HIV-infected persons' mental health and immune system functioning (Crepaz, Passin, & Herbst, 2008), obsessive-compulsive disorder (Prazeres, de Souza, & Fontenelle, 2007), generalized anxiety disorder and panic disorder (Siev & Chambless, 2007; Mitte, 2005), unipolar depression (Vittengl, Clark, & Dunn, 2007), breast cancer pain control (Tatrow & Montgomery, 2006), depression (Haby, Donnelly, & Corry, 2006; Gregory, Canning, & Lee, 2004), behavior disorders in children and adolescents (Gresham, 2005; Gonzalez, Nelson, & Gutkin, 2004), major depression in children and adolescents (Haby, Tonge, Littlefield, Carter, & Vos, 2004), and task performance for persons with schizophrenia (Krabbendam & Aleman, 2003).

Another literature review by Butler and Beck (2001) provides a good summary of the research on cognitive interventions up to that time. They reviewed 14 meta-analyses that covered 9,138 subjects in 325 studies. The researchers found that cognitive therapy was substantially superior to no treatment, waiting list, and placebo controls for adult and adolescent depression, generalized anxiety disorder, panic disorder (with or without agoraphobia), social phobia, and childhood depressive and anxiety disorders. Cognitive interventions were moderately superior in the treatment of marital distress, anger, childhood somatic disorders, and chronic pain.

Cognitive therapies were mildly superior to anti-depressant medication in treating adult depression. A year after treatment discontinuation, depressed clients treated with cognitive therapy had half the relapse rate of depressed persons who had been treated with anti-depressants. Cognitive therapy was equally effective as behavior interventions in the treatment of adult depression and obsessive-compulsive disorder. In the small number of direct comparisons with supportive and nondirective therapy (two for adolescent depression and two for generalized anxiety disorder), cognitive therapies were superior. They were mildly superior to miscellaneous psychosocial treatments for sexual offending.

Chambless and Ollendick (2001) compiled a list of validated cognitive interventions using the American Psychological Association's criteria for *well-established* or *probably efficacious* interventions. These criteria are described in detail in Chapter 1 (and the reader is reminded that the validity of these studies is often limited by their failure to discuss the circumstances of client dropouts). The authors note *well-established* cognitive interventions for geriatric depression, major depression, anorexia, bulimia, and conduct disorder, and *well-established* cognitive-behavioral interventions for agoraphobia, panic disorder, generalized anxiety disorder, post-traumatic stress disorder, social anxiety, chemical abuse and dependence, binge-eating disorder, smoking cessation, avoidant personality disorder, schizophrenia, conduct disorder, ADHD, and childhood anxiety.

Probably efficacious cognitive interventions are described for obsessive compulsive disorder, and *probably efficacious* cognitive-behavioral interventions are included for opiate dependence, irritable bowel syndrome, sickle-cell disease pain, marital discord, geriatric caregiver distress, sleep disorders, and disorders of childhood and adolescence (depression and recurrent abdominal pain).

CRITICISMS OF THE THEORY

Five criticisms have been made about cognitive theory, as discussed below.

Thought is prior to most emotional experience All practitioners agree that both cognition and emotion are essential to human functioning, but some give greater importance to emotional life. Magai (1996), for example, asserts that emotional traits form the core of human personality. She states that people possess five primary human emotions that originate in their neurophysiology: happiness, sadness, fear, anger, and excitement. These emotions are instinctual and the sources of one's motivations. They activate cognition and behavior in ways that are adaptive for survival. To illustrate, a person's propensity toward sadness may be elicited by the experience of a personal loss. This leads to a temporary physical slowing down, a decrease in general effort, and withdrawal in situations where efforts to cope with the loss would be ineffective. The sadness allows the person time to process his or her needs and regain energy for more focused application to achievable goals. It also provides a signal to others in their social networks to offer support. This idea that emotions influence cognition is antithetical to the principle stressed in cognitive theory.

The emphasis is on conscious rather than unconscious thought The content of conscious thought is certainly more readily accessible to people than their more subtle ideas and emotions, but this does not imply that they are more relevant to social functioning. Psychodynamic practitioners attribute great influence to unconscious thought processes, and even some social theorists state that significant mental activity may occur "beneath the surface" of conscious thought (Ritzer, 2000). Cognitive theorists do attempt to locate a "core belief" in a client, but spend relatively little time on the client's past to do so. By ignoring what is less concrete and accessible, social workers may never fully understand the basis of a person's thoughts and emotions.

Cognitive theory has an "individual" rather than a relational focus Cognitive theory maintains an emphasis on the individual rather than on interpersonal processes located within the family, group, or community. Object relations, systems theorists, and feminist thinkers, on the other hand, place greater value on the interpersonal aspects of human experience (families, groups, and communities), and assert that the essence of human life is most evident in relationship capacity (DeYoung, 2003). In fairness, it must be acknowledged that some prominent cognitive theorists have developed strategies for marital intervention (e.g. Baucom, Epstein, Rankin, & Burnett, 1996; Beck, 1988).

Cognitive theory overemphasizes objectivity and rationality Cognitive practitioners apply a kind of "scientific method" to their direct practice. The philosophy of this positivist method (ideas about external reality, what can be "known," and the "politics of knowledge") has come under fire since the 1980s. Post-positivist thinkers do not trust the value-free nature of this approach, and claim that all types of "rational" knowledge, in fact, incorporate the perspectives of those in positions of social power (Foucault, 1966).

Cognitive theory employs overly structured approaches Many cognitive interventions include systematic procedures, and researchers sometimes require the use of formal "manuals" for the appropriate provision of an intervention. Some argue that standardized protocols represent a strength of cognitive theory, as they bring great clarity to clinical practice. An alternative view, however, is that highly systematized approaches dehumanize intervention and create a rigidity that prohibits the social worker from attending to clients as unique people (Payne, 2005).

SUMMARY

Cognitive theory focuses on conscious thought as the primary determinant of most human emotions and behaviors. It has had great appeal to social work practitioners because of its utility for working with many types of people and problem situations. For social workers who may have appreciated the systematic nature of behavioral practice but were uncomfortable with its narrow focus, cognitive theory initially offered a related but more humanistic alternative. Cognitive interventions tend to be more systematic than those from ego psychology and object relations theory in helping a client explore his or her basic assumptions, ideas, and values as they relate to a problem. The basic assumptions of cognitive theory can be readily grasped by most clients, which facilitates a practitioner's desire for collaborative intervention. Cognitive theory has maintained relevance over the past 50 years by evolving from a position of seeking "objectivity" in thought to incorporating ideas from social constructivism. Its techniques also lend themselves to empirical validation, which makes the theory attractive to third-party payers.

TOPICS FOR DISCUSSION

1. Describe two examples of (different) cognitive distortions you have observed in your clients. Discuss plausible intervention strategies for changing them.

2. Depression is an unpleasant mood for anyone to experience, but we all know people who seem to be depressed much of the time without evident external stressors. Describe how a person might develop a cognitive pattern that produces depressed moods.

3. Consider a client who, for you, would represent a special population (based on age, race, gender, sexual orientation, disability, or socioeconomic status). Note one cognitive pattern of the client that might be different from yours but would not represent a distortion. How can a social worker guard against mistakenly assessing such a pattern as a distortion?

4. Share examples of how a social worker's own cognitive biases might become problematic in working with clients. How might the social worker guard against this?

5. How can cognitive/behavior theory guide a social worker's intervention with an otherwise well-adjusted client who spends three days in a hospital recovering from a heart attack?

IDEAS FOR CLASSROOM ACTIVITIES/ROLE-PLAYS

1. Organize role-plays featuring any type of client who has a presenting problem that might be suitable for cognitive intervention. The social worker should assess the client's cognitive patterns with the ultimate goal of uncovering one or several core beliefs. Discuss afterward the kinds of questions that seemed to facilitate this goal.

2. Organize a role-play featuring any kind of client (the same client may be used from the previous exercise). Begin from the point of having identified a cognitive distortion. The social worker should introduce and use the

pen-and-paper ABC intervention to help the client examine his or her cognitive patterns and perhaps consider alternative interpretations of a significant event. Students can share the challenges they faced in conducting this intervention, which may (in the role-play) span several sessions.

3.   Many agencies provide education and support groups for the families of clients who have certain long-term disorders, such as schizophrenia, bipolar disorder, and ADHD. Assign students to develop a brief psychoeducational program for families of a client who experiences one such problem, based on the principles of cognitive theory. Students must decide what material to include that might correct cognitive deficits, help to confront cognitive distortions, and assist in family problem-solving activities.

APPENDIX: Cognitive Theory Outline

Focus	Cognition, including:
	Structure (how thought processes are organized)
	Propositions ("stored" information)
	Operations (patterns of information processing)
	Products (beliefs, attitudes, values)
Major Proponents	Beck, Ellis, Lantz, Lazarus, Meichenbaum, Berlin, Corcoran
Origins and Social Context	Development of the cognitive sciences
	Pragmatism/Logical positivism
	Cognitive mediation in behaviorism
	De-emphasis of the unconscious
	Social learning theory
	Emphasis on concrete goals and objectives in human services
Nature of the Individual	Thought is the origin of most emotions and behaviors
	Emotions result from cognitive evaluations
	Human nature is neutral (neither good nor evil)
	"Reality" as a human construction
Structural Concepts	Schemas (via direct and social learning)
Developmental Concepts	Biological maturation of cognitive capacities
	Core beliefs
	Capacity for symbolization
	Development of the self through self-talk

APPENDIX: Cognitive Theory Outline (Continued)

	Conditioning
	Cognitive pattern (schema) development
Nature of Problems	Patterns of causal attribution
	Life situations are more or less changeable
	Internal versus external locus of control
	Specific versus global implications of perceptions
	Cognitive distortions (faulty information processing)
	Arbitrary inference
	Overgeneralization
	Magnification
	Minimization
	Selective abstraction
	Personalization
	Dichotomous thinking
Nature of Change	Changing personal goals
	Adjusting cognitive assumptions
	Beliefs
	Expectations
	Meanings attached to events
	Adjusting cognitive processes
	Selection of input
	Memory retrieval
	Thought patterns
Goals of Intervention	Promote the adjustments noted above
	Increase self-regard
	Enhance the sense of internal control
Nature of Social Worker/	Positive regard
Client Relationship	Social worker provides and enforces structure Worker is:
	A model
	A coach (through guided reasoning)
	A collaborator
	Objective
	Active

APPENDIX: Cognitive Theory Outline (Continued)

Intervention Principles	General:
	Socratic questioning
	Reframing
	More specific categories of intervention:
	Cognitive restructuring
	Self-instruction training
	Triple column technique
	Point/counterpoint (cost/benefit analysis)
	Education (particularly for children and adolescents)
	Cognitive coping
	Problem solving
	Communications skills development
	Social skills development
	Stress management skills development
Assessment Questions	What is the logic behind the client's beliefs?
	What is the evidence to support the client's views?
	What other explanations for the client's perceptions are possible?
	How do particular beliefs influence the client's attachment of significance to specific events? To emotions? To behaviors?
	How strongly does the client believe that approval from others is necessary to feel good about himself or herself?

8

Interpersonal Therapy

An Hour is a Sea
Between a few, and me –
With them would Harbor be –*

*I*nterpersonal psychotherapy (IPT) is a short-term, manual-based intervention modality that exclusively addresses the nature of a client's interpersonal problems in the treatment of depression and other emotional disorders (Weissman, 2006). IPT is *not* theoretically unique. It is distinctive in its clinical applications, but consists of elements of *psychodynamic theory* (emphasizing a broad exploration of the client's emotional and interpersonal life) and *cognitive and behavior theories* (using behavior change techniques and a review of the rationality of the client's perceptions). IPT focuses on three issues: the client's use of defenses, the underlying thought patterns that influence one's evaluation of the self and others, and the client/practitioner relationship as a model for other relationships. The goals of the therapy are to enhance clients' mastery of current social roles and adaptation to interpersonal situations. IPT is usually provided in 12 to 16 one-hour weekly sessions. It is almost always provided to individual clients but has been occasionally used in group formats (e.g., Tasca, Balfour, Ritchie, & Bissada, 2007; Wilfley, MacKenzie, Welch, Ayres, & Weissman, 2000).

Interpersonal therapy is included in this book for several reasons. First, it represents a link between the analytic and cognitive/behavioral intervention approaches described earlier. Second, it is consistent with the social work value perspective in its emphasis on the relationship "environment." Third, it has been empirically tested for effectiveness more extensively than many other

---

*Reprinted by permission of the publishers and the Trustees of Amherst College from *The Poems of Emily Dickinson*, Thomas H. Johnson, ed., Cambridge, Mass.: The Belknap Press of Harvard University Press, Copyright © 1951, 1955, 1979, 1983 by the President and Fellows of Harvard College.

interventions. IPT has been used to treat depression among a variety of client populations, including new mothers, adolescents, persons with HIV, persons with medical problems, couples experiencing marital disputes, older adults, and persons with early-stage Alzheimer's disease (Weissman, Markowitz, & Klerman, 2000). The therapy has been used more recently with persons experiencing anorexia, bulimia, substance abuse problems, and bipolar disorder.

Formal training programs for IPT are available at several universities, including Cornell University, the University of Pittsburgh, the University of Iowa, and the Clarke Institute in Toronto. To complete the training process, a practitioner must read the appropriate instructional manual (Frank, 2005; Mufson, Dorta, Moreau, & Weissman, 2004; Markowitz, 2001), attend a day-long training seminar, and receive supervision in the modality for a period of time. Because training program availability is limited, however, practitioners have been known to simply read the manuals and implement the approach along with clinical peers as an informal mutual training group.

ORIGINS AND SOCIAL CONTEXT

The interpersonal perspective on treating depression and other emotional disorders originated in the Washington-Baltimore area during the first half of the twentieth century (Klerman, Weissman, Rounsaville, & Chevron, 1984). At that time, and especially after the onset of the Great Depression, the nation's capital was a center of new ideas about the effects of the environment on the social functioning of individuals. The proponents of interpersonal therapy cite its beginnings in the work of Adolph Meyer, the most influential psychiatrist in the United States from the late 1800s until the Depression years. Working in Baltimore, Meyer coined the term "psychobiology" to describe his approach to treating mental illness, which included a focus on the person's adaptation to the social environment. Although Meyer never clearly operationalized his term, he participated in many Progressive-Era social reform movements and influenced all of the mental health professions to look away from the person toward the social environment for both causal and curative factors for a client's emotional problems. Harry Stack Sullivan, the well-known psychiatrist who also practiced in the Washington, D.C. area, more clearly articulated an interpersonal paradigm for mental health intervention. Beginning in the 1930s he actually defined psychiatry as a field of interpersonal relations. He and his associates developed a comprehensive theory of the connections between psychiatric disorders and interpersonal relations for the developing child (in the family) and for the adult (in major life transactions). Sullivan's perspective paved the way for the family studies of the 1950s and 1960s related to mental illnesses such as schizophrenia, bipolar disorder, and severe depression.

During the early 1900s there was also an emerging emphasis on interpersonal relations in the field of sociology, especially at the University of Chicago (Abbott, 1999). These sociologists (including George Herbert Mead and Robert Park) were concerned about the effects of urbanization on social life, and argued that the "self" was a changeable consciousness that arises out of interaction with significant others. The child was initially most influenced by the family, while the adult self was sustained by ongoing interactions with "significant others." *Role theory* was another important contribution from sociology to the study of people in the context of their social and life stage activities. Interpersonal theorists in psychiatry utilized these ideas to explore relationships between social roles (family member, student, employee, spouse, friend, etc.) and psychopathology. Disturbances in role functioning could serve as antecedents to pathology and, conversely, emotional problems could produce impairments in one's ability to perform certain social roles.

In the 1960s the work of John Bowlby (1979) on attachment theory furthered the development of interpersonal therapy. He wrote that people are innately inclined to form attachments, and that these are necessary for the survival of the species. For humans, intense emotions are associated with the formation, maintenance, disruption, and renewal of attachment bonds. The family determines the way emotional bonds are made during childhood, and many mental disorders result from one's inability to make and keep those bonds. For most people in Western society, strong attachments are maintained with relatively few people such as partners, children, close relatives, and friends. A task of psychotherapy became helping the client examine current interpersonal relationships and understanding how they developed from prior experiences with key attachment figures.

Myrna Weissman and Gerald Klerman developed the specific modality of interpersonal therapy for treating people with depression in the early 1970s (Weissman, 2006). The basic assumption was that there is a relationship between the onset and recurrence of a depressive episode and the client's social and interpersonal relationships. In their model, which was developed to treat depression, the unit of intervention is the primary social group, or the face-to-face involvement of the individual with one or more significant others. In IPT, clients learn to understand the relationship between their symptoms and what is currently going on in their lives, especially their current interpersonal problems. Weissman and Klerman wrote a manual for the use of IPT and tested its effectiveness with a series of studies on depression conducted primarily through the New Haven–Boston Collaborative Depression Research Project. Their desire was to develop a specific therapeutic method with demonstrable effectiveness. As it evolved, IPT lacked a unique theoretical basis, but adapted concepts from psychodynamic and cognitive theories. As such, it is a good example of theory integration. Since the 1980s, IPT has been modified for a variety of problems, including bulimia, substance abuse, somatization, and depression (Klerman & Weissman, 1993). Studies of its use with anorexia, bipolar disorder, post–traumatic stress disorder (PTSD), and some anxiety disorders are underway. In each adaptation the fundamentals of the treatment manual are adhered to, but different components are emphasized.

Interpersonal therapy assumes that depression is a *medical illness* (Klerman, Weissman, Rounsaville, & Chevron, 1984). It also assumes, somewhat paradoxically, that life events affect one's mood, and that improving one's life situation promotes a greater sense of control and satisfaction. IPT does not presume that psychopathology arises exclusively from problems within the interpersonal realm.

It does emphasize, however, that these problems occur within an interpersonal context that is intertwined with the illness process. A client receiving the therapy may be referred for a medication evaluation for his or her depression, but this does not affect the clinical practitioner's use of the IPT model. Depression is conceptualized as being manifested in a client's *symptoms*, quality of *social functioning*, and *personality style*. IPT aims to intervene specifically in the area of social functioning, with subsequent benefits to the client in reduced symptoms. Personality is *not* a focus in IPT, given the brevity of the intervention.

The profession of social work has not yet produced any major proponents of IPT, although the social work literature does include examples of its applications (e.g., Coleman, 2006; Levinsky, 2002).

In summary, IPT can be described as *time-limited*, *focused* on specific problem areas, focused on *current* (rather than past) interpersonal relationships, and *interpersonal*, rather than purely intrapsychic or cognitive/behavioral. A client's social functioning problems are conceptualized as originating in one or more of the following four areas:

- Interpersonal disputes
- Role transitions
- Grief processes
- Interpersonal deficits

MAJOR CONCEPTS

Interpersonal practitioners do not postulate any unique concepts about internal mental processes, and we have seen that the intervention is based on concepts from psychodynamic and cognitive-behavioral theory (Stuart & Robertson, 2002). Described below are examples of how the model is related to the two theories.

Elements of Psychodynamic Theory

Interpersonal therapy tries to change way a client thinks, feels, and acts in problematic interpersonal relationships. The practitioner focuses on issues such as non-assertiveness, guilt, poor social skills, and an overemphasis on unpleasant events. Negative emotions, and the way these feelings affect relationships, may become the clinical focus. IPT recognizes the significance of the client's personality, although this is not a primary clinical focus. Instead, the practitioner relies on strategies such as reassurance, clarification of feelings, communication training, and testing perceptions and performance through interpersonal contacts.

Like the psychodynamic theories, IPT emphasizes the significance of the worker/client relationship to the client's growth process (Weissman, 2006). Unlike psychodynamic theory, IPT assumes that unconscious processes can be brought into a client's awareness relatively quickly. Practitioners also assume, of course, that the quality of interpersonal life is key to human functioning. People are conceptualized as social beings more than as individuals. In this way, the therapy is consistent with object relations and feminist theories, though with a short-term focus. The types of interpersonal relationships that are of major interest to IPT practitioners occur within the nuclear family, extended family, friendship group, work group, and community. The importance of *emotional expression* in IPT with depressed persons was examined as part of the NIMH Treatment of Depression Collaboration Research Project (Coombs, Coleman, & Jones, 2003). Transcripts from 128 IPT and CBT sessions were studied, and three relevant factors in emotionality were found. First, collaborative emotional expression was significantly related to positive outcome. Second, the practitioner's educative-directive factor was unrelated to outcome. Third, clients with higher levels of painful emotional expression tended to have poorer outcomes, which supports the modality's focus on *controlled* emotional expression.

Interestingly, the researchers found that while emotional arousal tended to be higher at the beginning and end of each cognitive-behavioral session, it is higher in the middle portion of the IPT sessions. These findings support the greater emphasis on emotional expression in IPT. In another comparative study of 27 clients, IPT practitioners made more interpersonal linkages during clients' reflections, and there was a positive correlation between these linkages and client improvement in the areas of self-esteem and social adaptation (Kerr, Goldfried, Hayes, Castonguay & Goldsamt, 1992).

To summarize, one literature review reported on seven IPT interventions that resemble psychodynamic therapies (Blagys & Hilsenroth, 2000). They include:

- A focus on affect and the expression of emotions
- An exploration of clients' attempts to avoid topics or engage in activities that hinder the intervention process
- The identification of patterns in clients' actions, thoughts, feelings, experiences, and relationships
- A focus on interpersonal experiences
- An emphasis on the therapeutic relationship
- An exploration of the client's wishes and dreams

Elements of Cognitive/Behavior Theory

Interpersonal therapy has much in common with cognitive/behavioral therapy (CBT) in its concern with a client's distorted thinking about the self and others and his or her options for managing those concerns. Unlike CBT, however, IPT makes no attempt to systematically uncover distorted thoughts or develop alternative thought patterns. The practitioner calls attention to distorted thinking only as it pertains to relationships with significant others.

Interpersonal therapy has often been compared to cognitive/behavioral intervention in research studies, and some differences have been noted. In a study of 548 taped sessions involving 72 clients, persons receiving IPT contributed significantly more extensive narratives to the sessions, while in the CBT sessions a higher number of practitioner words per narrative were noted (Crits-Christoph, Connolly, Shappell, Elkin, Krupnick, et al., 1999). This suggests that IPT clients are encouraged to be more verbally involved in the process with fewer directives. Another group of researchers reviewed videotapes of 18 sessions of IPT and CBT that the practitioners identified as productive (Mackay, Barkham, Stiles, & Goldfried, 2002). As expected, they found that client emotions expressed during the IPT sessions were less pleasant on average than client emotions in CBT sessions.

Two studies attempted to clarify types of clients who might be better suited for either IPT or CBT based on their personality styles. Using the data set from the NIMH Project, it was found that IPT is particularly effective for persons with avoidant personality styles, while CBT is more effective for persons with obsessive personality styles (Barber & Muenz, 1996). Interestingly, the researchers also found that married clients did better with CBT, and single and non-cohabiting clients responded better to IPT. Two other researchers reviewed a clinical data set and concluded that depressed clients with higher social functioning skills responded more positively to IPT, while clients with higher cognitive functioning did so with CBT interventions (Blatt & Felsen, 1993). This finding supports the general notion that therapy models may be more or less suited to personality types, and that IPT is suited to clients with a general tendency to avoid addressing their relationships in depth.

THE NATURE OF PROBLEMS AND CHANGE

Interpersonal therapy conceptualizes four types of problems on which to focus all change efforts, as described below (Blanco, Clougherty, Lipsits, Mufson, & Weissman, 2006; Markowitz, 2001).

Interpersonal disputes are significant conflicts that arise when the client and some other person(s) have different expectations of a situation that involves them both. They tend to occur in marital, partner, family, social, work, and school settings. One example is a marital dispute in which a wife's attempt to take initiative in decision making leads to conflict with her spouse. In this circumstance the practitioner would attempt to determine the seriousness of the dispute and identify sources of the misunderstanding in faulty communication and invalid or unreasonable expectations. The focus of change might include clarifying the nature of the dispute, making choices about a plan of action, modifying communication patterns, or reassessing expectations for conflict resolution.

Role transitions are situations in which the client must adapt to normal, expectable changes in life circumstances. They may include developmental crises (for example, moving from adolescence to adulthood), changes in one's work or social setting, problems adapting to major life events, or the end of a relationship. In people who develop depression, these transitions are experienced as losses that may contribute to serious problems in social functioning. Change involves the client's reappraising the old and new roles, identifying sources of difficulty in the new role, finding solutions for those difficulties, and developing new attachments as sources of support.

Grief is defined in IPT as "loss through death," and the term is reserved for interpersonal bereavement. When grief is an issue of clinical relevance, the practitioner assesses how the client's relationship capacity has been affected by minimizing or feeling overwhelmed by the loss. The client may change by reconstructing his or her relationship with the deceased person, experiencing feelings more directly, clarifying cognitions to facilitate the mourning process, and establishing new relationships that can substitute (in part) for what was lost.

Interpersonal deficits are diagnosed when a client reports impoverished relationships in terms of their number or quality. This type of problem is common in the chronic affective disorders such as dysthymic disorder, in which significant social withdrawal occurs either before or after their onset. In many cases change requires the client and practitioner to focus both on external relationships and the clinical relationship. The client's relationship patterns and goals are identified, and the practitioner helps the client to modify any problematic patterns, such as excess dependency or hostility. The therapeutic relationship often serves as a template for further relationships that the practitioner will help the client to initiate.

ASSESSMENT AND INTERVENTION

The social worker/client relationship. The "working alliance" between the social worker and client is key to the effectiveness of interpersonal therapy. In one study, for example, it was determined that the alliance was more significant to clinical outcomes than the relationship in solution-focused therapy (Wettersten, Lichtenberg, & Mallinckrodt, 2005). The social worker provides a warm and collaborative presentation to the client while adhering to the prescribed therapeutic structure. He or she maintains a relaxed, conversational tone throughout the process, validating the client's perspective on issues of concern. Clearly, clinical skill is required to balance attention to the client's immediate concerns with the need to keep the short-term process moving forward. The practitioner maintains a focus on termination criteria from the outset. Discussions that are past-focused and non-specific are avoided as much as possible. Although transference and countertransference are not interpreted, they are assessed and used as a tool for identifying the client's interpersonal patterns.

Assessment

The social worker begins the assessment by gathering information about the client's presenting problem and symptoms. This serves the purposes of establishing a diagnosis, reassuring the client that his or her problems fit into a recognizable syndrome for which help is available, and placing the problem into an interpersonal context. Following the diagnosis the practitioner emphasizes (if clinically appropriate) that the client's problem represents a mental disorder. This helps the client distance him or herself somewhat from the problem, and helps to mobilize energy for addressing it.

Next, the social worker conducts, over several sessions, an *interpersonal inventory*, the standard protocol for assessment in the IPT approach (Markowitz, 1997). The client is asked to list all significant current and past relationships, especially those from the family of origin, family of choice, workplace, school, intimate relationships, other friendships, and community activities. The following information is gathered about each person:

- The nature of the interactions (frequency of contact and activities shared)
- The perceived expectations of each person in the relationship, and whether these are or were being fulfilled
- The satisfactory and unsatisfactory aspects of the relationship, with specific examples
- How the client would like to change the relationship, either by changing his or her own behavior, or by bringing about changes in the other person

During this inventory, the social worker is alert to the thoughts and emotions that the client demonstrates about the significant other persons. The practitioner looks for and documents patterns of interaction with specific types of people (such as authority figures) and patterns of behavior related to dominance and submission, dependency and autonomy, intimacy and trust, demonstrations of affection, divisions of labor (within families and at the workplace), religious, recreational, and community activities, and responses to separation and loss. Following this assessment, the client and social worker agree on a primary problem area for intervention. They set only two or three goals so that the intervention can maintain a focus.

Intervention

There is some debate about how actively practitioners should conduct sessions, other than to keep the focus on interpersonal issues. There are no distinct guidelines in this regard, although a goal of IPT (like cognitive therapy) is to facilitate the process of clients generating their own interventions, and thus phasing the practitioner out of the process.

Intervention Outline

In interpersonal therapy, a client is helped over a period of 12 to 16 weekly sessions to see connections between his or her disorder and life events, and then choose among available options to improve the situation. Change occurs in three phases. In the first phase, the client's presenting problem is diagnosed within a medical model. In phase two (the intermediate phase), the client and practitioner work on the major interpersonal problem areas. In the termination stage, the client's progress is reviewed and the remaining work to be done after the intervention is outlined. Progress is monitored regularly (every 2 to 4 sessions) with the use of a formal instrument. What follows is a summary outline of the assessment and intervention process (the numbers of sessions devoted to each stage are approximations) (Weissman, Markowitz, & Klerman, 2000).

The Initial Sessions (Sessions 1 through 3 or 4)   The social worker reviews the client's symptoms, diagnoses the problem, explains the nature of the intervention, allows the client to assume the sick role (to reduce feelings of shame or guilt), and considers whether a referral for medication is indicated. Further, the social worker relates the client's problem to an interpersonal context through the interpersonal inventory, identifies the major problem areas and sets goals (focusing on relationships that are significant to the problem), and collaborates with the client on an intervention contract.

The Intermediate Sessions—The Problem Area (Sessions 4 or 5 through 8)   *For interpersonal disputes*. The goal is to modify expectations or communication practices to bring about a satisfactory dispute resolution. Strategies include relating symptom onset to overt or covert disputes with the significant other, determining the stage of the dispute, understanding how non-reciprocal role expectations may contribute to the dispute, looking for parallel patterns in other relationships (including the clinical relationship), determining how the dispute is perpetuated, and then problem solving.

For role transitions. Goals are to help the client mourn and accept the loss of the old role, regard a new role more positively, and restore self-esteem with mastery of new demands. Strategies included relating symptoms to difficulties in coping with a recent life change, reviewing positive and negative aspects of old and new roles, exploring feelings about what is lost and opportunities in the new role, evaluating what is lost, encouraging the release of feelings, and developing social support systems and skills needed in the new role.

For grief. Goals are to facilitate the mourning process and help the client re-establish interests in new or other relationships to substitute for what has been lost. Strategies include relating symptom onset to the death of the significant other, reconstructing the client's relationship to the deceased, describing sequences and consequences of interpersonal events prior to, during, and after the death, exploring the client's associated feelings, and considering new ways for the client to become involved with others.

For interpersonal deficits. Goals are to reduce the client's social isolation and encourage the formation of new relationships. Strategies include relating the client's symptoms to social isolation and a lack of fulfillment, reviewing the positive and negative aspects of past relationships, discussing feelings about the practitioner, and seeking parallels in other relationships.

Termination (Sessions 9 through 12)   The social worker explicitly discusses the ending of intervention, acknowledges termination as a time of grieving, and moves the client toward recognition of competence. The practitioner calls attention to the client's successes—to the range of available supports (such as friends, family, and the church) and the ways in which the client has shown the ability to handle his or her own difficulties. The practitioner bolsters the client's sense of being able to handle future problems through discussions of how various situations could be handled. Early warning signs of stress should be identified along with ways of coping.

With this overview of the intervention process, we will now consider the specific change strategies that the social worker can use, adapted from ego psychology and cognitive/behavioral theory.

Specific Intervention Techniques

Non-directive exploration—This unstructured strategy is used during parts of each session. The social worker encourages the client to take initiative in presenting issues of concern, identifying problem areas, reviewing emotions, and searching for solutions. The practitioner provides directives for the client's exploration when his or her focus appears to wander. This strategy includes supportive listening to affirm the client's sense of worth, normalize the experience of problems, and develop trust.

Encouragement of affect—The social worker allows, and sometimes encourages, the client to experience unpleasant emotions that may have previously resulted in the use of problematic defense mechanisms. This allows the client, especially one who is more "cognitive" in orientation, to acknowledge the emotional aspects of an interpersonal encounter.

Clarification of beliefs and perceptions—In order to minimize the client's biases in describing interpersonal concerns, and to promote logical thinking, the social worker asks the client to rephrase comments (to seek confirmation) and calls attention to both the logical extensions and contradictions of the client's statements. The practitioner hopes to bring consistency to the client's cognitive and emotional experiences and to reduce cognitive distortions.

Communication analysis—This is a means of assessing the nature of a client's interpersonal conflicts and suggesting more effective communication strategies. The social worker challenges the client's ambiguous and indirect communications, faulty assumptions about what has been communicated or understood, indirect verbal communications, and tendencies to close down communications with silence. The practitioner helps the client to consider and try out new communication practices.

Use of the therapeutic relationship—This is a strategy to make the client's feelings about the practitioner or the intervention process a focus of discussion. These thoughts and feelings are examined because they represent a model of the client's typical ways of thinking and feeling in other relationships. This is similar to the psychodynamic practitioner's use of transference, except that discussions do not probe beneath the surface (for their origins) and do not become the entire focus of the intervention.

Behavior change strategies—These include all concrete strategies to help the client work on interpersonal changes outside the clinical setting. They include the social worker's advice and suggestions, behavioral limit setting (for impulsive clients), education, and modeling. Decision analysis (problem solving) is a means by which the practitioner helps the client consider a range of alternative behaviors in certain situations. Role-playing is often used to assess the nature of the client's interpersonal processes and to practice new social skills.

It should be evident that, although IPT is a structured intervention model, the practitioner has discretion in deciding how much time to spend in its various stages. Each client's intervention will be unique, although when sufficiently focused it will never exceed the 16-session limit.

ATTENTION TO SOCIAL JUSTICE ISSUES

Interpersonal therapy focuses on individuals (or small groups) and problems that can be resolved through changing interpersonal behaviors. Despite its strengths, the modality is not inherently well-suited to clients' focus on larger systems issues that might promote their social justice interests. Its conceptualization of the environment is limited to interpersonal relationships, primarily those involving family, friend, work, and social contacts, with the immediate community as the "outer" limit. There is no prohibition against addressing relationships with people who may be oppressors (for example, abusive spouses or people who engage in discriminatory practices against the client), but organizations and communities—targets that represent groups of people—would not likely become intervention targets. The developers of the model were clearly interested in the individual client's struggles. The social worker could combine IPT with other interventions, of course, in the promotion of social justice ends, when desired. Most practically, the ways in which cognitive theory can be used to promote social justice issues would be applicable because of the overlap of the two approaches.

Because of its similarities to cognitive theory, the reader is referred to Chapter 7 for a consideration of ways in which spirituality can be addressed within IPT.

CASE ILLUSTRATION

Following is an example of how interpersonal therapy can be used with a client who is experiencing depression. Notice that, though the practitioner follows the guidelines of the model, he is flexible in addressing the client's particular presentation.

The Rose from Spanish Harlem

Connie was a self-referred 21-year-old single psychology major in her final year of college who also worked 30 hours per week as a retail makeup artist. She lived in a southeastern city with her mother. Both of her parents were born in Puerto Rico, and Connie was born and raised in Spanish Harlem, New York City.

The Initial Sessions (3 Visits) The social worker used the strategies of *exploration*, *encouragement of affect*, and *clarification* to understand the client's problems and help her focus on specific goals. Connie shared her concerns about having a "pessimistic outlook," a lack of trust in other people, and general feelings of negativity. She said that these feelings were intensified by a romantic relationship that was "going bad." Connie described herself as generally unhappy, and said that she "worried too much about a lot of things." She admitted to jealousy and chronic fears about unfaithfulness in all of her relationships, and to angry outbursts when feeling insecure. The client often resorted to sarcastic comments toward people close to her, and admitted this had driven away many of her friends. Connie also reported excessive worrying about tuition debt and school performance, but these were not primary concerns (she was passing all of her courses).

The client explained that her unhappiness became worse after seeing her boyfriend casually talking with another woman at a party. She and her boyfriend (also of Puerto Rican heritage) had been seeing each other exclusively for four months, and she described the relationship in mostly positive terms. She was unsure whether there was a factual basis for her jealousy. Connie felt that this episode represented a recurring pattern in her life that needed to be addressed in counseling.

During the next two sessions the social worker encouraged Connie to share details of her personal history and complete an interpersonal inventory (she had already begun the process in describing her presenting problems). Connie was an only child. Her parents were married for 14 years before divorcing when Connie was eight years old. Her mother moved to their current city of residence at that time. Connie, however, remained in the custody of her father, now 48, who worked as a computer programmer in New York City.

Although Connie lived with her father until finishing high school, she described their relationship as "not good." She said that he was not affectionate toward her and was still bitter about the divorce. She said, "He sees me as an obligation," "He has no feelings of love toward me," and that he had not offered any financial support for her schooling. She described him as having a problem with alcohol, and added that several members of her extended family had substance abuse problems. Connie's mother, 46, with whom she got along well, worked full-time as an aide for a city councilman. She had not remarried. Connie's grandparents were deceased, but she had an extensive network of aunts, uncles, and cousins in New York City with whom she remained in regular contact.

School and her job occupied most of Connie's time (she was on schedule to graduate in three months), but she maintained an active social life. She reported knowing "a lot of people," but had only two close friends, one male and one female, besides her boyfriend. These relationships were not as intense as the one with her boyfriend, but Connie admitted to insecurity about their feelings toward her. Socially, Connie liked to shop, dance, work, go to movies, and visit parks. Her strengths included a strong work ethic, great talent in cosmetic work, intelligence, and social skills.

Connie had no health or medical problems and did not take any medications. She added that she would not consider using medications to deal with her problems. She felt strongly that people should learn to overcome their problems without using drugs of any type.

The social worker diagnosed Connie on Axis I with dysthymic disorder, early onset, and a partner relational problem. She had felt depressed for most days since mid-adolescence. Her symptoms included low self-esteem (feeling inferior to and detached from her friends and peers), difficulty in making decisions to a degree that she regularly felt overwhelmed, overeating, and feelings of hopelessness with occasional ruminations about self-harm. The relationship between her and her boyfriend was characterized by many arguments. On Axis IV the social worker noted problems with the primary support group (her father and boyfriend).

Near the end of the third session the social worker explained his diagnosis to the client, and supported her decision not to use medications. He related Connie's depression to her relationships, including concerns she had about her father, boyfriend, former boyfriends, and close friends. He asked Connie to review the positive and negative aspects of those relationships as well as her expectations about them. She was able to do so and thus demonstrate good insight. She hoped that her father might change his attitude toward her, but otherwise stated that she wanted to change her own attitudes and expectations about the people close to her.

Connie initially articulated three goals for her counseling: to improve her ability to cope with negative feelings about herself, to develop a more positive outlook on her life, and to manage her relationships more satisfactorily. The social worker helped her to articulate and expand these in a manner that would more clearly suggest outcome indicators, as follows:

1. I will resolve the status of my current romantic relationship, as evidenced by my self-report of satisfaction with how my boyfriend and I are relating to one another (this includes the possibility of our relationship ending).

2. I will develop a positive sense of self-worth, as evidenced by making positive statements to my social worker about my actions when reviewing interpersonal events of significance.

3. I will develop improved relationship patterns, as evidenced by (a) spending more time with people other than my boyfriend and two close friends and (b) arguing less with all of my friends.

4. I will clarify the nature of my relationship with my father, as evidenced by (a) sharing my feelings about our relationship with him and (b) attempting to reach a mutual agreement about how we will organize our relationship.

The client accepted the social worker's suggestion that they monitor her mood every two sessions with the Beck Depression Inventory (BDI) (Beck, Steer, Bell, & Ramieri, 1996). Connie had already completed the measure during her first session.

The social worker had previously described the procedures involved in IPT, but did so at this time in more detail. He explained that he had assessed her depression as being rooted in *interpersonal disputes*, and this would be the focus of their work in the coming weeks. The social worker and client would meet once per week for one hour of individual counseling. The social worker shared his concern with Connie that she was so obsessively self-analytical that exclusively reflective interventions might be detrimental to her. He would concentrate instead on *clarification, communication analysis, behavior change*, and *use of their own relationship*.

Members of ethnic groups often have unique perspectives on the world and the nature of clinical intervention. Prior to the second session, the social worker, a Caucasian male from a small Midwestern city, consulted one book for information about persons from Puerto Rico so that he could be more sensitive to Connie's personal inclinations (Fong & Furuto, 2001). He learned that Puerto Rican culture emphasizes spirituality, the importance of extended family, and the values of community, children, respect, and cooperation. Latino people tend to have a heightened sensitivity to the nonverbal behaviors of others and value informality and warmth in relationships, rather than observing formal roles.

The Intermediate Sessions (5 Visits)   The social worker's strategies during these sessions were to help Connie clarify beliefs about herself and others (primarily her father and boyfriend), modify expectations about herself and others, and improve her communication practices. Regarding the last goal, Connie was highly verbal but often unclear about the feelings behind her comments. Due to Connie's ability to maintain a focus on goals with moderate prompting, the social worker did not need to enforce high levels of structure during their sessions. He observed that it was most productive to follow her lead as she addressed the first three of her four goals each week. They discussed and clarified Connie's negative cognitive patterns, and the social worker affirmed her capacity to re-evaluate the external evidence for her beliefs about the motives of others. The social worker's clarification questions helped Connie identify and curtail her tendency to mistakenly "read" the thoughts of others. To further affirm the client's changes, the social worker (during this and every subsequent meeting) asked Connie to summarize her movement toward each goal (as well as complete the BDI).

The social worker regularly used their relationship to illustrate how Connie's habits of seeing herself through the eyes of others were skewed negatively. This was practical because Connie often played out her relationship problems with the social worker, wondering openly if he cared about her, was bored with her, thought she was stupid, or thought she was "whiny." The social worker challenged Connie's basis for making these statements. He also showed Connie how her expectations of complete attention, loyalty, and availability from others was not realistic. Their discussions next focused on Connie's fears of losing friends by driving them away with her demands and complaints. The social worker suggested a behavioral strategy in which Connie would limit the amount of time she talked about her worries with those close to her. She agreed and decided herself that she would carry a watch and limit herself to five minutes per interaction.

Over the weeks Connie continued to demonstrate progress. She developed insight into her unrealistic suspiciousness and jealousy. The social worker praised Connie's accomplishments. Despite this, she continued to perceive rejection frequently. In fact, she admitted a continuing mistrust of the social worker's interest in her. He had noted in the beginning of their work that she was sensitive to nonverbal cues and he had been vigilant in this regard. Still, he was tired one particular morning, and the client interpreted his affect as boredom. The social worker was careful to reassure the client by listening actively, conveying an attitude of goodwill, and expressing confidence in her.

The client canceled her next session because of a work conflict. One week later she returned and announced that she had broken up with her boyfriend. She had decided that she did not want to be in an intense relationship at this time of her life. Still, she was having difficulty maintaining boundaries with her boyfriend. Connie had been calling him five or more times per day to check on his whereabouts and mood. The social worker processed this behavior with Connie and suggested she set limits on her extent of phone and in-person contact for at least two weeks as she made the transition out of the relationship. She was agreeable to limiting her calls to no more than two per day. They role-played phone conversations in which Connie tried to minimize her tendency to be controlling.

By their eighth session, the client showed more confidence than the social worker had yet seen. For the first time, Connie appeared calm. She reported that the relationship with her boyfriend was indeed over and they were having no further contact. Connie felt good about her decision and was regaining a sense of independence. The social worker guided her through a discussion about what she had learned from the boyfriend experience and from therapy thus far. Connie expressed her awareness that she could not control the behavior of others and that she needed to accept herself without so much external reassurance. It appeared that she had met her most immediate goals, but Connie wanted to spend more time discussing the relationship with her father and also to see if her changing attitudes would persist. They agreed to meet for another 3 to 5 weeks.

One week later, Connie was continuing to function well. She described several recent stressful scenarios involving family and friends and described them to the social worker for his input about the "reality basis" of her thoughts, feelings, and behaviors. Connie spoke at length for the first time about her parents, particularly her father. She hoped that she could share her concerns about their relationship more openly with him now that her self-confidence was higher. The social worker knew that Connie would be having contact with her father during the coming week and engaged her in several role-plays so that she could practice her communications and test how she might react to his behavior.

Termination (2 Visits)   The next week Connie announced that she felt ready to end her therapy. Though this occurred earlier than the practitioner expected, the decision seemed appropriate. She had confronted her father on the telephone about her perceptions of his minimal interest in her life, and he had responded constructively. They would be meeting to talk more at Connie's graduation in three weeks. The social worker wondered if Connie should stop her therapy at this early stage of reconciliation with her dad. Connie responded that she wanted to focus her energies on the upcoming graduation, including arranging for several extended family members to join her at school.

The social worker and client used part of this session to review her progress over the past nine weeks. He used the techniques of *clarification* and *exploration* in these two sessions. He sketched a graph of Connie's BDI scores to emphasize her steady positive movement. He asked Connie to review her progress with regard to each of her four goals and explain how she had specifically addressed each of them. They agreed that she had satisfactorily resolved her presenting problems and that her gains had persisted. She no longer met the DSM-IV criteria for dysthymic disorder, but the social worker recommended to Connie that she self-monitor her mood on a weekly basis for several months, using the same scale, as a precaution against backsliding. He asked questions to explore her feelings about ending the treatment relationship but, as he expected, Connie was not experiencing it as a loss. She had maintained a perspective on that relationship as short-term, and focused more intently on relationships outside the office.

During the final session Connie and the social worker reviewed her activities during the past week and her plans for the near future. He described a number of possible scenarios regarding her father and friends that might threaten Connie's progress, and then helped her formulate adaptive responses for those scenarios. He also reviewed their own relationship (*the therapeutic relationship*), reminding Connie how he had witnessed some of her problematic interpersonal patterns playing out between them, especially her suspiciousness and tendency to make negative assumptions about others' motives. He reviewed the *behavior change* strategies they had rehearsed of checking the validity of her assumptions with the other people.

Since dysthymia tends to be a chronic, relapsing disorder and life stress events can bring about major depressive disorder (Moerk & Klein, 2000), continuation with treatment or maintenance of treatment gains is critically important (Oxman, Barrett, Sengupta, Katon, Williams, et al., 2001). As they ended, the social worker invited Connie to return if she so desired (she would retain service eligibility for two months after graduation), but he did not hear from her again.

EVIDENCE OF EFFECTIVENESS

A task force of the American Psychological Association found interpersonal therapy to meet its highest standard for empirical effectiveness (two rigorous, randomized, controlled trials showing superiority to placebo or another intervention) in the treatment of major depression and bulimia, and its second-highest standard for effectiveness (at least one randomized trial showing superiority to a control or comparison intervention) in the treatment of geriatric depression and binge-eating disorder (Chambless & Ollendick, 2001). A variety of other literature reviews and single studies have further demonstrated the effectiveness of the modality with these and other disorders, and these are summarized below.

Studies of Depression

In a systematic review of research findings on the efficacy of interpersonal therapy for depressive disorders, IPT was found to be superior to placebo, similar to medication, and more effective than cognitive-behavioral therapy (de Mello, de Jesus Mari, Bacaltchuk, Verdeli, & Neugebauer, 2005). Several large-scale randomized control group trials support interpersonal therapy's efficacy in treating depression. The New Haven–Boston Collaborative study in 1973 found that IPT was comparably effective to the anti-depressant amitriptyline in treating major depression (Weissman, Prusoff, & DiMascio, 1979). Using both strategies in combination had an additive effect. A larger National Institute of Mental Health (NIMH) project several years later studied 250 outpatients with depression who were randomized to receive cognitive-behavioral therapy (CBT), IPT, the anti-depressant medication imipramine, or supportive clinical management (Elkin, Shea, Watkins, Imber, Sotsky, et al., 1989). It was found that CBT, IPT, and medication were equal in efficacy after 12 weeks. Clients rated as severely depressed responded as well to IPT as to imipramine, while clients receiving CBT for severe depression did not respond as well. A University of Pittsburgh Group led by Kupfer, Frank, and Perel (1992) later studied the maintenance treatments of depression and found that both "low-dose IPT" (provided monthly) and high-dose imipramine seemed to be effective in preventing relapse compared with placebo. As a result of these and some other supportive findings (e.g., Stuart, 1999), the Australian and New Zealand Clinical Practice Guidelines for the Treatment of Depression cite IPT and CBT as equal to medication for treating clients with some depressions (Ellis, Hickie, & Smith, 2003).

IPT has been effective for women experiencing postpartum depression. A literature review of nine randomized trials concluded that both psychosocial (peer support) and psychological interventions (cognitive-behavioral and interpersonal therapy) were effective in reducing their major symptoms (Dennis & Hodnett, 2007). In a four-session preventive program including 35 pregnant women receiving public assistance, 17 persons receiving IPT were compared with 18 controls (receiving unspecified treatment as usual) on measures of depression before and after delivery (Zlotnick, Johnson, Miller, Pearlstein, & Howard, 2001). Six of the controls developed depression three months after childbirth; none of the women receiving IPT did so.

IPT has been evaluated with older adult clients (Scocco & Frank, 2002). One literature review of studies conducted during the past 20 years concluded that IPT and CBT, combined with anti-depressant medication, have the largest base of evidence for treating late-life depression (Arean & Cook, 2002). A pilot study that incorporated IPT in the treatment of early-stage Alzheimer's disease noted that outcomes were more positive than with approaches not featuring IPT (Brierley, Guthrie, Busby, Marino-Francis, Byrne, et al., 2003). Components of the intervention include the client and family's increased ability to pick up on interpersonal cues, staying with feelings, and developing a shared interpersonal understanding of here-and-now challenges.

Several studies have focused on intervention with adolescents (Mufson, Weissman, Moreau, & Garfinkel, 1999). In a study of 25 adolescents with moderate to severe depression, 12 sessions of supervised IPT by novice practitioners resulted in a substantial improvement for more than half of the clients as indicated by pre- and posttreatment scores on a variety of established instruments (Santor & Kusumakar, 2001). A major implication of the study is that relatively inexperienced practitioners, with supervision, can effectively deliver IPT. In another study with inexperienced trainees, 54 clients were randomly assigned to 12 weeks of IPT or to a wait-list condition (these people would eventually receive IPT) (Shaw, Margison, Guthrie, & Tomenson, 2001). Thirty-three clients completed the intervention, and the experimental group demonstrated significant positive changes compared with the controls. The second group also experienced benefits once they received the intervention. It was noted that clients with a history of childhood abuse were difficult for the trainees to engage in treatment. A recently published IPT treatment manual focuses specifically on intervention with adolescents (Mufson, Dorta, Moreau, & Weissman, 2004).

There is some evidence that the progress made by depressed persons who receive IPT persists over time (Blanco, Lipsitz, & Caligor, 2001; Frank, Kupfer, & Perel, 1990). The retention of gains was examined for 104 clients with depression who had received either IPT or CBT (Shapiro, Rees, Barkham, & Hardy, 1995). After one year all clients had generally sustained their gains, although 79% of clients continued to have some symptoms of depression. Only 11% of clients who had been asymptomatic at the end of their interventions, however, experienced a recurrence of depression. The authors conclude that their findings support the importance of postintervention follow-up for clients with depression.

In one study, IPT was provided to 23 depressed adults who were HIV-positive (Markowitz, Klerman, & Perry, 1993). Twenty of those clients were symptom-free after an average of 16 sessions. Aspects of the intervention that were considered useful for this population included psychoeducation about ways of managing the sick role.

Clients presenting to an emergency services facility in New Zealand who were deliberately self-poisoning were randomly assigned to two treatment groups, one of which featured IPT (Guthrie, Kapur, Mackway-Jones, Chew-Graham, Moorey, et al., 2003). Four sessions of IPT were effective in reducing suicidal ideation for persons with moderate depression, no prior history of self-harm, and who had not consumed alcohol with the overdose. Another study of 91 clients with depression discovered a relationship between pre-treatment normalcy of sleep EEG scores and response to IPT (Thase, Buysse, Frank, & Cherry, 1997). It was hypothesized that the abnormal EEG profiles were related to more severe depression. Clients with abnormal EEG sleep profiles had poorer outcomes than clients with normal profiles. Those clients who were later given medication tended to experience remission, however.

Other Applications

Interpersonal therapy has been used to treat clients with bulimia in both individual and group settings (Levinsky, 2002; Wilfley, Agras, Telch, Rossiter, Schneider, et al., 1993). It is hypothesized that the intervention may be especially effective for persons whose bulimic symptoms are associated with problematic relationships and who can benefit from structure and clear behavioral directives (Apple, 1999). One study examined the relationship between changes in attachment insecurity and target symptom outcomes in women with depression and binge-eating disorder (Tasca, Balfour, Ritchie, & Bissada, 2007). Women treated with IPT and cognitive-behavioral therapy all showed improvement in levels attachment security, but for women treated with IPT, greater changes in mood levels were also noted. Researchers in England found IPT and CBT to be equal in efficacy, with IPT continuing to show benefits after the end of therapy (Fairburn, Jones, Peveler, Hope, & O'Connor, 1993). The researchers noted that IPT helped to improve clients' dysfunctional cognitions in terms of weight and body image, even though these were not openly addressed during the intervention. In another study, IPT was provided to clients with bulimia who had not benefited from 12 weeks of a CBT group (Agras, Telch, Arnow, & Eldridge, 1995). There was no further improvement noted for those clients.

Some applications of IPT are relatively new and less well tested. For example, the modality is hypothesized as having utility in the treatment of some personality disorders because of its focus on interpersonal behavior patterns (Safran & McMain, 1992). A more recent study showed that while both IPT and cognitive therapy were, along with medication, effective with clients who have borderline personality disorder, IPT was more effective in improving client satisfaction with social functioning and reducing their controlling behaviors (Bellino, Zizza, Rinaldi, & Bogetto, 2007). Combining IPT with social rhythm therapy, an intervention that concentrates on a client's time organization, appears to promote mood stability in clients with bipolar disorder (Frank, 2005).

Finally, interpersonal therapy may be cost-effective compared with some other clinical approaches. In one study of 110 clients classified as "high users" of psychiatric services in England, the introduction of IPT resulted in a significant improvement in psychological status and a reduction in overall health care utilization and costs up to six months following the intervention (Guthrie, Moorey, Margison, Barker, Palmer, et al., 1999).

CRITICISMS OF THE THERAPY

Several important criticisms have been directed at interpersonal therapy. One is that it subscribes to a medical model of diagnosis and problem conceptualization. Its assumption of this model to remove the sense of stigma from clients seeking help may be functional, but it also works against social work's biopsychosocial perspective. Use of the model, in fact, represents an inconsistency in IPT, because it clearly promotes a psychosocial perspective on intervention. Another criticism pointed out early in this chapter is IPT's historical focus on clients with depression. Its applications have been expanded, but less research is available to evaluate the modality with other disorders. On a positive note, IPT practitioners can rightly claim that, inherent in their modality, unlike some others, is a focus on systematic evaluation.

One limitation of interpersonal therapy is the need for clinical practitioners to be formally trained in the modality. Training seminars are not accessible to all potentially interested practitioners, and thus IPT is probably not used as pervasively as it might be. It is estimated that fewer than 10% of clinical psychology internship programs provide supervision or instruction in IPT (Weissman, 2001). Some practitioners, of course, have begun using the therapy without such training, relying on published works and peer supervision.

Another limitation of IPT applies to all manualized approaches to clinical intervention. Some argue that standardized protocols represent a strength of the modality, as they bring clarity to clinical applications. On the other hand, manualized approaches often do not unfold as efficiently in "natural" clinical settings as they do in controlled trials in which clients are carefully selected and supervision is extensive. Further, manualized clinical approaches are said to de-emphasize the "human" element in intervention, creating a rigidity that prohibits the social worker from attending to clients as unique people (Payne, 2005).

SUMMARY

Interpersonal therapy provides a good example of a theoretically integrated, manual-based, relatively short-term intervention that has been empirically tested for more than three decades for its utility in helping clients who experience depression and some other disorders. It combines psychodynamic and cognitive/behavioral ideas into a unique model of intervention. In IPT, a client's social functioning problems are conceptualized as stemming from interpersonal disputes, role transitions, grief processes, and interpersonal deficits. With IPT, the practitioner helps the client change the way he or she thinks, feels, and acts in problematic interpersonal relationships. As the social work profession moves toward empirically based practice, IPT is likely to become more widely used in the field. The intervention is limited in its range of applicability, but its tradition of evaluation continues as it is applied to disorders other than depression.

TOPICS FOR DISCUSSION

1. Does IPT's simultaneous emphasis on the medical model for diagnosis and relationships as the focus for intervention represent an inconsistency in the model? Can a social worker reconcile these two apparently conflicting ideas?

2. Consider the types of problems for which IPT has been used. Given its focus on relationships, for what other types of client diagnoses might it be suitable?

3. List the types of presenting problems social workers face that are significantly related to interpersonal disputes, role transitions, grief processes, and interpersonal deficits, but do not seem to fit a medical model. Can IPT, or perhaps an attenuated form of the model, be useful?

4. IPT is the only "manualized" intervention featured in this book, although the practitioner does retain leeway in how the intervention is provided. What would be the benefits and limitations of manualized interventions at your agency?

5. Consider a couple of any type who was seeking help with a problem that appeared to be primarily relationship-based. Could IPT be adapted for use with them if they have different expectations of the relationship?

IDEAS FOR CLASSROOM ACTIVITIES/ROLE-PLAYS

1. Have students pair off and practice conducting an interpersonal inventory. The student who plays the client can use his or her own life situation or those of clients for this material. Discuss afterward the ease or difficulty of gathering the information.

2. Have one or more students present to the class the cases of former clients whose presenting problems featured depression. Discuss how the client might have been assessed, and what interventions might have been provided, if the practitioner had been working from the IPT model. Discuss similarities to and differences from what was actually provided.

3. Using the IPT model as a basis, have the class devise a structured group program for a population of high school students who are experiencing relationship problems due to either interpersonal deficits or disputes.

APPENDIX: Interpersonal Therapy Outline

Focus	The here-and-now nature of interpersonal relationships that contributes to problems and their resolution
	The disease model of mental, emotional, and behavioral disorders
Major Proponents	Sullivan, Meyer, Bowlby, Klerman, Weissman
Origins and Social Context	Urban sociology and social psychology
	Progressivism (in psychiatry)
	Systems theory
	Attachment theory
	Psychoanalysis and cognitive theory
Nature of the Individual	Not specified, although the relevance of genetic, biochemical, developmental, and personality factors in social functioning is acknowledged
Structural Concepts	Defenses
	Cognitive structures
	Transference
Developmental Concepts	None
Nature of Problems	Interpersonal disputes
	Role transitions
	Grief
	Interpersonal deficits

APPENDIX: Interpersonal Therapy Outline (Continued)

Nature of Change	Developing alternative behaviors in interpersonal relationships
Goals of Intervention	To improve the client's quality of perceived interpersonal functioning relative to the presenting problem
Nature of Social Worker/ Client Relationship	Relaxed, conversational
	Collaborative
	Practitioner provides the focus of the intervention
Intervention Principles	The interpersonal inventory
	Exploration and clarification of beliefs and perceptions
	Supportive listening
	Communication analysis
	Encouragement of affect
	Use of the clinical relationship (to examine relationship patterns)
	Behavioral change techniques
	Directives (suggestions, limit setting, education, modeling)
	Decision analysis (problem solving)
	Role-playing
Assessment Questions	What has contributed to the client's problem right now?
	What are the client's current interpersonal stresses?
	Who are the key persons involved in the client's life?
	What are the current disputes and disappointments?
	Is the client learning to cope with the problem?
	What are the client's relationship assets?
	Is the client able to ventilate painful emotions, and talk about situations that evoke guilt, shame, and resentment?
	Is the client functioning with significant misinformation about his or her current relationships?

9

Structural Family Theory

To mend each tattered Faith
There is a needle fair
Though no appearance indicate –
'Tis threaded in the Air –
And though it do not wear
As if it never Tore
'Tis very comfortable indeed
And spacious as before –*

*S*tructural family theory* is a popular and useful perspective for organizing clinical interventions with families. It offers an alternative and complementary perspective to family emotional systems theory (discussed in Chapter 5). Structural family practice is not quite as rich theoretically, but it includes more concrete intervention techniques. Whereas interventions from family emotional systems theory tend to be *reflective* in nature, those from structural theory demand *action* from both the family and the social worker. In fact, this approach to intervention has much in common with the cognitive and behavioral theories.

Structural family theory was developed by Salvador Minuchin in the 1960s, and has continued to evolve through his ongoing work and that of others (Minuchin, 1974; Minuchin, Lee, & Simon, 1996; Minuchin, Nichols, & Lee, 2007). The focus of the theory is family *structure*, a concept that refers to *the invisible and often unspoken rules* that organize how family members interact. During assessment, the social worker evaluates these patterns of interaction for their system utility. Structural family theory does not focus on the emotional lives of family members as much as on the external "architecture" of the family. Structural practitioners assert that when a family establishes appropriate authority, rules, subsystems, and boundaries, the emotional lives and behaviors of its members will develop in ways that are mutually satisfactory.

Minuchin's work was influenced by social worker Virginia Satir (1964), whose own family intervention methods were evolving during the 1960s. Satir's family intervention is most often called *experiential*, and goes beyond a focus on family structure. Still, her interventions required a high level of practitioner activity, and she was particularly influential in her development of family communication interventions and sculpting techniques, which will be described later.

Structural theory developed in response to a perceived need among practitioners for intervention methods that could be used with families experiencing multiple problems, including non-traditional inner-city families dealing with poverty and other issues contributing to family disruption. This flexible theory can be used with any type of family, but its interventions seem particularly suitable for families plagued by physical or mental illness, acting-out members, drug addiction, crime, single parenthood, and violence.

ORIGINS AND SOCIAL CONTEXT

We saw in Chapter 5 how family systems theories became popular among human service professionals in the years after World War II. Structural family theory emerged several years after that first wave, in the mid-1960s. Its perspective is derived from the influences of its founder's background, social developments in American society, and the status of structural theory in the field of sociology.

Salvador Minuchin maintained an interest in social action throughout his life (Aponte & DiCesare, 2002; Nichols, 2009). He was born in Argentina in the 1920s and became a pediatric physician. Always interested in travel and public service, Minuchin served as a physician in the Israeli army in the late 1940s. He later came to the United States and studied child psychiatry with the noted family theorist Nathan Ackerman. In 1954 he underwent training for psychoanalytic practice, and was particularly influenced by Sullivan's interpersonal theories.

In the major turning point of his professional life, Minuchin accepted a job in the late 1950s as a psychiatrist at the Wiltwyck School for Boys in New York State. At Wiltwyck, where he stayed for eight years, Minuchin worked with a challenging population of institutionalized delinquent boys, many of whom were African-American and Puerto Rican. He decided that family intervention was the most useful way to help these adolescents, and thus became the first of the major family theorists to work with multi-problem families. Throughout these years he maintained contact with other notable family theorists of the time. Minuchin left Wiltwyck in 1965 to become the director of the Philadelphia Child Guidance Center for ten years. His national reputation was established with the publication of *Families of the Slums* (Minuchin, Montalvo, Guerney, Rosman, & Schumer, 1967), which outlined his theory of structural family intervention in detail. He continued to practice and write until his retirement in 1996.

Minuchin's interest in working with children and multi-problem families from poor urban areas was timely, given changing social conditions in the United States during the 1960s. Those were years in which poverty, unemployment, delinquency, out-of-wedlock births, and discrimination in the cities emerged as major public policy concerns (Reisch, 2000). The Kennedy and Johnson administrations attempted to address these social issues through such initiatives as the War on Poverty and the Great Society (Day, 2000). Related programs included the Economic Opportunity Act, Job Corps, VISTA, Upward Bound, Neighborhood Youth Corps, and Head Start. The spirit of the times supported the efforts of human service practitioners to reach out to persons who experienced problems related to oppressive urban conditions. Minuchin's theory was well-suited to this challenge. He was the only major family theorist of the time who had extensive experience with these client populations, and there were underserved populations in the cities that might benefit from his models of family intervention.

A third influence on Minuchin's theory was the systems perspective in the field of sociology known as *structural functionalism* (Parsons, 1977). Developed by Talcott Parsons, this theory was dominant in American sociology from the 1940s through the 1960s. It conceptualized societies as social systems featuring *structures* (repetitive patterns of behavior) that should be evaluated in terms of their contribution to the maintenance of the system. Structural functionalism emphasized the importance of shared norms and values among actors in a system. The foundations of any system were said to be motivated actors whose behaviors are held in check by role expectations, the power of sanctions, and their shared desire to uphold institutional values.

In structural functionalism a *social institution* (such as the family) is defined as an established order comprising rule-bound behavioral patterns of people guided by shared values. Institutions are necessary in all societies for members to meet their social needs and maintain social order. They tend toward self-maintenance with boundaries, rules about relationships, and control of internal tendencies to change. The purposes of the family institution are to regulate reproduction, socialize and educate children, provide economic and psychological support to members, transmit values, and care for sick and elderly persons. Minuchin was aware of Parsons, and even called his own therapy *structural* (Kassop, 1987). His outlook was compatible with many principles of structural functionalism. The family is conceptualized as a social unit situated in a hierarchy composed of individuals and established social structures.

Family structural interventions have been prominently featured in the social work literature through the work of Harry Aponte, who has developed a model of multi-systemic therapy that combines structural and larger systems interventions (Aponte, Zarski, Bixenstine, & Cibik, 1991). This will be described in a later section of the chapter.

With this brief introduction to the theory's development, the logic behind its major concepts that inform family assessment can be better understood.

MAJOR CONCEPTS

The family structure concept was described earlier. The other major concepts, all of which make up that structure, are described below.

Subsystems

In any family that is composed of more than two people, some members develop patterns of interaction in certain contexts that exclude other members. Examples of these *subsystems* include parents, adult members, nuclear- versus extended-family members, siblings, older and younger siblings, and some adult/child alliances. Subsystems are normal and usually functional. For example, adult members need to act as a subsystem in establishing behavioral standards for children, and siblings learn social skills and ways of negotiating conflict through their interactions. Subsystems may be problematic, however, when serious conflicts develop between them (parents versus children, for example) or if they inappropriately exclude certain other members. A problematic parent/child subsystem may develop as a strategy by one parent to avoid interacting with, or dilute the influence of, the other parent.

Executive Authority

Effective family structure requires that some person or persons assume a position of primary decision-making power. This *executive authority* characterizes the persons in that role. Structural theory asserts that in every family consisting of more than one generation, adult members should exercise primary authority. As an example of the appropriateness of such authority, a study of European-American adolescents found a positive link between the nature of the parent-adolescent hierarchy and the capacity of both boys and girls to experience intimacy with their best friends (Updegraff, Madden-Derdich, Estrada, Sales, & Leonard, 2002). Other family members may share authority in some circumstances, such as in deciding how to spend a weekend or what kind of restaurant to visit.

During assessment, the social worker should determine who has power, whether power shifts depending on circumstances, and how decisions are made. Regarding decision making, the social worker should assess the extent to which the opinions and needs of all members are taken into account, the ability of the family to problem solve as a unit, and the family's flexibility in adjusting decisions when appropriate.

Boundaries

Families are systems, but they must preserve some physical and emotional separateness for each member in order to ensure their effective functioning. These *boundaries* are both internal and external. *Internal* boundaries are the barriers that regulate the amounts of contact that members or subsystems are expected to have with each other. In some families, for example, each member is entitled to the privacy of his or her own room, while in others it is desired that the members share rooms. Likewise, some families engage in many social activities together; in others, the members interact infrequently. Boundaries may be rigid (members being physically or emotionally isolated) or fluid (members being too close to each other, and therefore denied privacy or separateness). A study of adolescents from diverse ethnic backgrounds revealed that appropriate parent/child boundaries promoted the young adolescents' maturity, ability to form coalitions, and communicating well with peers (Madden-Derdich, Estrada, Updegraff, & Leonard, 2002). *External* boundaries refer to the separation of the family unit from outside systems such as community groups. Most families believe that much of their internal business (finances, conflicts, illnesses, religious practices, child-rearing practices) should be kept private from persons (and agencies) outside the family.

Rules

Rules are the behaviors and responsibilities to which each family member is expected to adhere. They are different for each member depending on life stage and family position (parent, child, extended-family member, etc.) and are usually established with reference to age-appropriate social norms. The executive authority has primary responsibility for rule development, but all members may participate in the process. A parent may decide rules about driving practices among adolescent members, but the adolescent may be permitted to set rules about his or her study and work routines. Rules may pertain to such issues as curfew, household upkeep, academic standards, who is expected to work, how money will be spent, and with which other people family members may interact. Some rules are openly articulated while others may be acquired through habit. For effective family functioning, rules should be clearly understood by all members.

Roles

A family member's *roles* refer to his or her functions within the system. Each family member must manage several roles. These may be *assigned* by the executive or some external source (usually reflecting social norms) or be *assumed* by members because of particular family circumstances. Examples of typical roles include the breadwinner, money manager, caregiver, housekeeper, and "social director." Other roles may include the family "hero" (who presents a positive image of the family to the outside world) or "scapegoat" (the source of all family problems). Roles change over time and in different contexts. The social worker needs to assess how a family's roles are defined, whether they seem appropriate, how satisfied members are with their roles, and whether any members experience stress due to "role overload" or being responsible for a number of possibly conflicting roles.

Alliances

Alliances are conditions in which two family members or subsystems interact cooperatively. These are positive when they contribute to the overall well-being of the persons involved and to the family unit. In families that include two spouses, their alliance around child-rearing practices is positive if those practices contribute to the health of the children. Alliances are negative when they are rigid, exclusionary, or otherwise contribute to family problems. Two siblings can form an alliance against a third sibling or against a parent, with the purpose of enhancing their power and the result being cruel or unfair treatment of the third person. Two terms that reflect family problems in this regard are *enmeshment* (two or more members behaving in collusion with one another to the extent that they cannot function with autonomy) and *disengagement* (two members being isolated from one another). You may recall that these terms are also used in family emotional systems theory.

Triangles

Triangles were described in Chapter 5 and represent a type of alliance in which two family members turn their attention to a third member for relief or support when in conflict with each other. As examples, two adults in conflict may choose to blame a child member for creating their problem (that is, scapegoating) or an adult and a child member may join forces to block the power of another adult member. Negative triangles often develop outside of the parties' awareness. Family emotional systems theory focuses on the emotional outcomes for the most vulnerable member of a triangle, whereas structural theory focuses on triangles' long-term threats to family organization. Triangles are often a natural process of seeking relief from tension, but they may cause structural problems if they become disruptive to other members in a family system.

Flexibility

For effective functioning, all families frequently need to adjust their structures to accommodate the predictable and unpredictable changes in the lives of their members and in the environment. Predictable changes may include the movement of members into new life stages (childhood to adolescence, adulthood to older adulthood) or the addition and loss of members through birth, death, coming home, and moving away. Unpredictable changes may include a member's abrupt job loss, physical injury, illness, incarceration, pregnancy, or changed relationship with significant others in the external environment. *Flexibility* refers to the ability of the family system to make adjustments that preserve its positive functions. Flexibility is not in opposition to structure. The opposite of structure is chaos, which represents a family's structural breakdown in the face of system challenges.

Communication

The ability of people in relationships to engage in clear and direct *communication*, the practice of conveying messages, is important in every practice theory. It receives extensive attention in structural family theory, however, because the practitioner is interested in the *structure* of communication. Functional family communications are characterized by verbal and nonverbal congruence and consistently observed rules. The structural practitioner will assess and may help the family to become aware of its "rules"; for example, *who* is permitted to talk to *whom* about *what issues* at *what times* and in *what tones of voice*. Many family problems are caused or sustained by unclear or unbalanced communication, or by its absence. If communication skills are enhanced, other restructuring activities are facilitated.

Other Concepts

Other factors not specific to structural theory must also be taken into account during structural family assessment. These include:

Cultural Considerations   Diverse family cultures may feature differences in structure regarding communication style, family hierarchy and power structure, how much authority the family wishes to grant the practitioner, member preferences for formal or informal interaction (with each other and the practitioner), and the issue of dual identity (the family's relationship to the dominant external culture) (Fong & Furuto, 2001). Social work practitioners need to be aware of cultural norms when a family's background is different from their own, so that the assessment will not be biased. Structural family interventions have recently been found to be effective with such populations as Hispanic and African-American youth (Santisteban, Coatsworth, Perez-Vidal, Mitrani, Jean-Gilles, et al., 1997), gay men (Long, 2004), and Asian–Americans (Kim, 2003), among others.

   As an example of how structural family theory can and should take into account the family's cultural context, a review of the process with LGBT families is presented here. Note that concepts from family emotional systems theory (discussed in Chapter 5) are also included in this example.

   Lesbian, gay, bisexual, and transgendered (LGBT) individuals are present in many families as partners, parents, or children. The term "LGBT families" describes families in which one or two of the adult heads of the family identify as lesbian, gay, bisexual, or transgender. In many aspects, LGBT families, and the challenges that bring them to counseling, are similar to most other families. LGBT families may seek counseling for assistance with communication issues, parenting issues, infidelity issues, sexual issues, and substance abuse (Connolly, 2004). Although these general themes are common in practice with many families, the specifics of how they are manifest in LGBT families are important to recognize. Additionally, LGBT families may seek intervention to deal with specific LGBT issues, such as coming out or disclosure issues; problems relating to families of origin and their reactions to the LGBT family; dealing with cultural oppressions, including homophobia, transphobia, or heterosexism; and internalized homophobia or transphobia. LGBT families of color or interracial families often face additional issues that may bring them to family intervention, including dealing with the intersecting oppressions of racism, homophobia, or transphobia, and, in the case of interracial families, dealing with issues arising from family members having differing cultural identities and expectations surrounding family life (Green & Boyd-Franklin, 1996).

Family intervention for LGBT families is a relatively new focus in the family practice literature. Prior to the 1980s, much of the literature regarding LGBT individuals in families focused on the alleged treatment of homosexuality, attempting to shift individuals' same-sex desires and behaviors to heterosexual desires and behaviors (Spitalnick & McNair, 2005). Since then, more literature around the treatment of LGBT families is focusing on positive and affirmative practices that address the specific needs of the population. A number of family theory concepts from structural family and Bowenian theory can be used when these issues may present themselves in LGBT families. These include family and gender roles, boundaries, and differentiation of self.

Traditionally, roles within a family are strongly influenced by members' cultural backgrounds and personal family histories. For LGBT families, the creation of roles and division of tasks is not necessarily based on gendered divisions. Being composed of two men or two women, a same-sex couple cannot rely on traditional male-female role divisions to structure their interactional patterns (Green & Mitchell, 2002). Instead, same-sex couples must work to negotiate and develop family and relationship roles that account for the individual desires, strengths, and preferences of all involved. It is important to note that, despite the stereotype, only a small minority of LGBT couples divides relationship roles in a manner in which one member plays the role of the "wife/mother" and the other plays the role of the "husband/father." Structural family practitioners working with LGBT families need to be aware of issues surrounding family roles, as they are often working to create family roles without the aid of models (Coates & Sullivan, 2006). In-session enactments (described later) are a powerful tool in aiding LGBT families in both recognizing the roles they currently hold in the family, as well as identifying potential alternative family structures (Greenan & Tunnell, 2003).

Creating or maintaining healthy family boundaries is a significant issue in LGBT families for a variety of reasons. Families of origin and society at large may devalue the commitment that same-sex partners have made to one another, and their shared roles as parents or stepparents to children. This can cause split loyalties in which each partner remains loyal and connected to her or his family of origin to the exclusion of the partner, thus destabilizing the relationship and its boundaries (Greenan & Tunnell, 2003). LGBT parents may also adopt alternative parenting roles, such as having their children call them by their first names, in an attempt to create a post-heterosexist family (Coates & Sullivan, 2006). Although well-intentioned, this parenting style can potentially lead to disengagement, as it does not provide for well-defined boundaries between family members. Conversely, in LGBT families, as with other minorities who perceive their families to be operating in an ambivalent or hostile social environment, a greater risk of enmeshment exists. Social workers practicing with LGBT families need to be aware of patterns of enmeshment or disengagement so that they can intervene to assist families in developing appropriate boundaries among family members and between the family and outside systems.

The Bowen family systems concepts of differentiation of self and fusion are often discussed in family practice with LGBT families, particularly with lesbian couples. Beginning in the 1980s, family theorists looking at lesbian couples asserted that these dyads had high levels of fusion, leading to relationship and sexual problems, to the extent that issues stemming from fusion were attributed as the primary cause of the termination of these relationships (Laird, 1993). More recently, scholars such as Spaulding (1999) and Basham (1999) have asserted that the typification of lesbian relationships as pathologically fused stems from sexist biases regarding appropriate levels of connection between partners. In contrast, gay male couples are often perceived as more emotionally distant from their partners. Within gay male couples, open or non-monogamous relationships are not uncommon, which has led some individuals to make the assumption that gay couples are therefore less committed and caring than other couples. In gay male couples with negotiated open relationships, the meaning of sex with others is viewed differently, as simply a pleasurable act rather than a betrayal of commitment (Green & Mitchell, 2002). In working with LGBT families and couples, social workers need to be conscious of potential fusion, but at the same time recognize that heterosexist views about family relations may influence their assessment of the family's level of differentiation. The use of genograms with LGBT families has been noted as an important tool that opens up space for dialogue about issues such as the impact of homophobia and heterosexism on the family (Swainson & Tasker, 2006).

Providing culturally competent social work practice is critical to working with all minority or oppressed populations, including LGBT individuals and families. Wetchler (2004) suggests that all practitioners, regardless of sexual orientation and gender identity, are raised and live in a heterosexist society, which may shape their values and attitudes towards LGBT couples. At times, a social worker's personal values may differ from those of LGBT clients they are working with. A family practitioner may have strong values regarding the importance of fidelity and monogamy in relationships, and thus be challenged in working with an LGBT family whose values regarding monogamy are different. Green (2007) states that the most important prerequisite for helping same-sex couples is the practitioner's personal comfort with love and sexuality between two women or two men. Additionally, practitioners working with LGBT families need to be aware of their personal beliefs regarding LGBT people as parents, and its potential effects on family intervention.

Particularly relevant to cross-cultural awareness with LGBT families is an awareness of the many forms families may take within the LGBT community. This includes an understanding of the concepts of family of origin, or the family in which LGBT individuals were raised, and family of choice, which can encompass non-biological relations including partners, children, friends, and chosen biological family members (Green, 2007). In a sense, LGBT people are bicultural.

The majority of LGBT people were raised in the dominant, heterosexual culture, but as part of the LGBT community they may have beliefs, values, and behaviors that may differ from those of the dominant culture (Johnson & Keren, 1998). Social workers need to have knowledge regarding the LGBT community, and use practice techniques that demonstrate understanding and respect. Cross-cultural skills can run the range from following clients' leads with regard to how they identify themselves and their relationships, to openly and honestly discussing with clients how larger social oppression, such as homophobia, may be affecting their relationship (Green, 2007).

Family Goals   Families do not always openly articulate a set of goals, but members nevertheless tend to develop a sense of purpose regarding their place in the family and how they can be mutually supportive of those goals (Hepworth, Rooney, Rooney, Strom-Gottfried, & Larsen, 2005). Family goals may include raising responsible children, developing loving bonds, developing a shared sense of spirituality, or amassing material resources. The social worker should assess the family's awareness of and level of consensus about goals, and their functionality.

Family Life Cycle Stage   The nature and quality of a family's functioning varies depending partly on its composition, which may include unattached adults, new partners, young children, adolescents, adult children, or persons in later life. It would be expected, for example, that a family with adolescents features more ongoing tension than one composed only of new partners. Social work has been significant in demonstrating the utility of the life model perspective through the work of Germain and Gitterman (1996), whose ecological perspective focuses on the complex relationship between people and their environmental systems during predictable and unpredictable life transitions

Family Myths   This refers to shared family beliefs that evolve in a family's effort to define itself, set boundaries with the outside community, and perhaps protect members from both internal and external conflict (Hepworth, Rooney, Rooney, Strom-Gottfried, & Larsen, 2005). They are called myths because they are not "true" in an objective sense, but reflect traditions and possibly cultural factors. Examples of family myths are: "outsiders are not to be trusted"; "people should always stay close to home"; "children should take care of their parents"; "Dad's violent behaviors are not to be questioned"; and "Mom doesn't really abuse drugs." Myths tend to be problematic for outsiders (including social workers) when they serve a defensive function.

External Systems Influences   It has been noted that the family is a primary social institution, but there are others with which families routinely interact, including religious, educational, economic, and political institutions. Further, families exist in the midst of other identifiable systems, such as the neighborhood and the larger community. All of these entities contribute to conditions that influence a family's structure and the quality of life of its members. Recall that structural family theory developed in a context of serving the needs of families that were socially disadvantaged by external systems. The social worker must always assess the effects of a family's interactions with these other systems, and possibly direct some of his or her interventions toward creating a more mutually facilitative environment. The social worker's extra-family activities may include linkage, referral, mediation, and advocacy activities. Social worker Carol Meyer (1970) brought attention to these processes in her development of the eco-map, a graphic representation in which the family is placed within the context of the larger social system.

THE NATURE OF PROBLEMS AND CHANGE

The above concepts direct the manner in which structural practitioners define the problems experienced by their clients. Many problem situations are on a "continuum of functionality." It is not easy to conclude without a careful assessment whether, for example, a boundary is rigid or fluid.

Power imbalances describe situations in which the "wrong" (less mature or responsible) members have the most power in a family system. Perhaps young members of the family can get adult members to acquiesce by throwing temper tantrums or making threats. Young members may also assume power when the adult members choose not to exercise it. Further, adult members in a family may be inconsistent in their expectations of members or disagree about major decisions and behavior limits. When the "wrong" family members have the most power, the system often moves toward chaos (a lack of structure), because it lacks an executive authority with reasonably mature judgment about family functioning.

Subsystem boundaries that are too rigid or too diffuse produce situations in which some members are either emotionally or physically isolated from each other or too involved in each other's lives. Examples of problems related to diffuse boundaries include the sexual abuse of a child by an adult and parental over-involvement that prevents adolescent members from developing age-appropriate independent living skills. Adult and child subsystems may intrude into each other's personal affairs to the extent that none are assured of privacy, and as a result they act out their frustrations with negative behaviors. Problems related to rigid boundaries include adult members being unavailable to their children and lack of communication and interaction among members of subsystems (adults, children, extended family, etc). When boundaries are rigid, members may experience high levels of tension due to an inability to find support to manage their everyday challenges at school, with peers, or at work. Members of subsystems also fail to benefit from the learning that might otherwise come from their interaction.

The following two sources of family problems are related to the boundary issues described above, but refer to the behaviors of individuals rather than of subsystems. *Disengaged (isolated) members* do not interact with other members or with the family system in general. When one spouse is disengaged from the other, each person may feel lonely or depressed. Another example is commonly seen in an adolescent member "shutting out" the rest of the family and organizing her or his life around peer activities. This diminishment of the family's influence prevents it from providing appropriate guidance and limits to the disengaged member. Of course, the person may feel angry with or "pushed away" by the family. On the other hand, *enmeshed members* rely too much on one other for support and assistance, instead of developing their own life skills. They may be at risk for failure to progress through expected stages of social development and become unable to assume socially appropriate roles.

When members of a family lack good communication skills, they may develop a family atmosphere of *pervasive conflict or tension* related to the *avoidance* of processing conflict. It was noted earlier that good communication practices are an essential component of successful family systems. Communication is the "currency" of family interaction. Because conflict is also a natural part of interpersonal life, an inability to process it sustains even small problems. For example, if a parent cannot resolve anger with a child related to poor grades in school, the resulting tension may persist and spiral into resentments that "blow up" at times into harsh physical punishments.

Family problems may derive from a *failure of the system to realign* (or resume productive and cooperative individual and family roles) after a stressful event such as the birth, death, injury, illness, or separation of a member. Although making adjustments to change can be challenging for any family, rigid families have particular trouble, essentially holding onto roles and rules that are no longer functional. With the death of one parent, for example, the other parent may be unable to make changes in his or her roles and routines to devote more time to nurturing the children. The children may not be inclined to increase their support of the remaining parent by taking over some household responsibilities. This failure to adjust may result in a variety of presenting problems, such as increased tension, other emotional distress among members, substance abuse as a coping strategy, and behavioral acting out.

Member resistance to normal family change processes is related to the issue above but indicates a lack of flexibility in the family system to accommodate *any* changes. This issue presents a challenge for many families: being able to recognize when one member is moving into appropriate new roles and a changed relationship with the family, and making adjustments in the rest of the family to accommodate that change. Parents typically struggle with these change issues when considering when to allow younger members to work, drive, stay out later, and spend more time away from home. Siblings struggle to adjust to one member's moving away, and to the changing expectations for those remaining in the household.

The goals of intervention in structural family theory are to change the existing family structure so that it becomes more functional. Change may also involve increasing the available supports for members outside the family system. A basic principle of structural family intervention is that *action precedes understanding*. One or more family members must take action, with the guidance of the social worker, to change the nature of family interactions, rather than simply *talk* about taking action. Through restructuring processes that include practicing new ways of interacting and communicating, family members may experience permanent relief from the presenting problem. Insight about the problem situation may occur after the fact, but is not considered a necessary aspect of change. This perspective is consistent with (but not identical to) those of the cognitive and behavior theories.

ASSESSMENT AND INTERVENTION

The Social Worker/Client Relationship

In structural family intervention, the social worker is highly directive. From the first meeting, he or she must "take charge" and lead the family's process of problem resolution. In contrast to some other theories we have reviewed, the social worker's relationship with the family is not always collaborative. Minuchin felt that the practitioner was the "expert" in that he or she, as a trained observer, was in the best position to understand a family's structure. At the same time, the social worker must make efforts to connect with each family member, be perceived as credible and empathetic, and promote an atmosphere of family competence. A recent study of videotaped structural family sessions revealed that not only was practitioner empathy evident, it was an essential ingredient in facilitating within session change (Nichols, 2009).

Assessment

Prior to problem exploration, it is often useful for the social worker to conduct a structured warm-up exercise to promote the family's comfort. Such exercises may include traditional "ice breakers," such as having members introduce each other, talk about their favorite hobbies, describe the figures from popular culture they most admire, and so on (see Barlow, Blythe, & Edmonds, 1999).

Structural family theory does not rely on a lengthy process of formal information gathering in the form of specific questions. The social worker does ask all members of the family to describe the issue that brought them all to the agency and give some details about its background, but always in a conversational tone. The social worker then attempts to get information about the following issues, not by asking the questions specifically, but by observation and a non-threatening interchange:

- What are this family's patterns of interacting? Who spends time with whom, what do they do together, and what do they talk about?

- How does the family present itself structurally? What roles do the members seem to occupy? How do these roles play out in the session?

- Where does power lie in this family? Who makes decisions and who enforces them? Is authority or decision making shared in any ways?

- What subsystems appear to be prominent? Which members appear to be bonded, and for what reasons? Are alliances rigid or fluid?

- Does the presenting problem appear to serve a function for the family? Does one member's, or several members', behaviors absorb the family's attention?

- What are this family's typical patterns of managing stress? How do they respond as a unit to everyday stress, as well as to crises and members' normal life transitions?

- How sensitive are family members to each other's feelings and needs? Do they listen to each other and take each other seriously? Are certain members ignored?

- What do members seem to expect from each other? What is their sense of shared responsibility for any family functions?

- Do members accommodate each other's needs? Are they capable of flexibility in their responses to each other?

- Is the family involved with external systems? With what formal and informal institutions do they interact, like churches, civic associations, recreational centers, or perhaps legal and welfare agencies? Are they welcoming or suspicious of outsiders?

The social worker begins rather quickly to assess the family structure and presenting issue by encouraging members to *enact* rather than merely *describe* their significant interactions. This is facilitated through role-plays. During these enactments the social worker focuses on the nature of member interactions with respect to the questions listed above.

During enactments, the social worker begins to identify both positive and negative patterns of interaction within the family. The practitioner alerts family members to any observed problematic communication patterns and asks if they wish to change them. The practitioner also identifies and articulates any structural characteristics of concern such as weak bonds between spouses or others, conflicts between subsystems, alienation or enmeshment of any members, and alliances outside the family that contribute to internal problems. What follows next are the strategies that help to promote the change effort.

Intervention

It must be emphasized here that, when implementing all of the interventions described below, *repetition* is often necessary for structural changes to become internalized in a family system.

Supporting system strengths refers to the social worker providing compliments about aspects of family functioning that are going well. This includes affirming the dignity of the family with empathetic responses and nonjudgmental comments about its behaviors.

Relabeling, or normalizing, a problem helps family members develop a new perspective about themselves that is more constructive. Behaviors that are currently problematic may have initially represented members' caring for each other. For example, a parent's harsh verbal treatment of a child may now be a problem, but it may also indicate that the parent cares about the child. When relabeling, the social worker does not excuse behavior, but places it into a context that reduces defensiveness and the stigmatization of any member as "the problem."

Problem tracking encourages the family to track its target behaviors between sessions so that members can more clearly identify their structural patterns and get accustomed to working actively on problem resolution. A part of each family meeting will include a review of these observations as well as reports of new activities undertaken between sessions. At the same time, members are asked to give up an exclusive focus on past events that have been problematic and look toward their future family life.

Teaching stress management skills can enhance the self-control of members prior to initiating any anxiety-provoking interactions. The most basic means of supporting stress management is to find out what healthful means of relaxation members already have and prescribe more of those activities. Other practices, such as deep breathing and progressive relaxation, can help members manage tensions that may emerge during family intervention. Several of these techniques are described in the chapters on cognitive theory and behavior theory.

Helping the family modify its rules is achieved through *discussion and mutual decision-making*. The potential for a family to resolve its presenting problems is usually high, particularly in the relatively formal environment of the social worker's office, where interactions may be less emotionally charged. As a part of this process, the social worker should help to correct any cognitive distortions or myths regarding what family life should or should not provide for the members (see Chapter 7).

Manipulating space, or assigning family members to stand or sit in certain configurations, can highlight important structural characteristics. For example, adults who lack power in setting limits on child behavior may be asked to sit closely together so that they can provide support to each other. Likewise, two estranged siblings might be instructed to sit next to and even face each other, as a means of encouraging their interaction. Space manipulation, also known as *sculpting*, can also be used to visually highlight family structural characteristics. This technique was developed by social worker Virginia Satir (1964). The plight of a child who feels ignored by his parents, for example, can be "illustrated" by the social worker turning the child's chair around while his parents talk among themselves about the child. The goal of these activities is always to promote the development of more functional structural arrangements.

In *communication skills training,* the social worker instructs families in methods of clear speaking and listening to communicate their needs, ideas, and feelings. It was stated earlier that the quality of communication is a primary determinant of family functioning. Functional families are characterized by a shared understanding of messages between senders and receivers and rules about communication that are consistently observed (the range of topics that are appropriate to discuss,

when they can be discussed, and who can participate). Communication intervention includes the following activities:

- Pointing out confusing messages ("I don't understand something. You tell
  your son that he should spend time with his friends, but then you won't let
  him go out on weekends.")
- Teaching members to make clear requests of one another
- Teaching members how nonverbal behaviors (expressions, tone of voice,
  and physical distance) may enhance or disrupt communication
- Disallowing interruptions, so that all members have the opportunity to be
  heard
- Helping clients learn to disengage from unproductive conflict (to stop its
  escalation before reaching the point of negativity)

Directing *role-plays*, simulations of actual or possible family situations, is a means
of adjusting family interactions. During role-plays, the social worker asks the entire
family, or certain members, to act out a specific episode that has relevance to the
participants. For example, if a parent has difficulty setting limits with an adolescent
child, the social worker may ask the two members to role-play a conversation in
which the parent tries to establish a curfew agreement. Afterward, the social worker
and family members evaluate the exchange and make suggestions about how the
members might behave differently to be more consistent with the family's goals.
Role-plays may be brief (less than a minute) or more lengthy (10 to 15 minutes).
In *role reversals*, members are asked to play the roles of other persons in the family
to sensitize them to the feelings of others with whom they may be in conflict.

A major practice strategy in structural family theory is to *assign tasks* for
members to complete between sessions. These tasks are always intended to
strengthen or loosen alliances and subsystems in accordance with the family's
goals. The practice ensures that the family works actively toward its goals in the
natural environment. As examples, two spouses who have become disengaged
may be asked to spend one evening together each week without other family
members. A sibling who is enmeshed with an adult may be asked to undertake
a household maintenance task with another sibling or adult. There is much room
for social worker and family creativity in devising such tasks. The social worker
should leave it to the family members to decide on the specific elements of tasks
so that they will be suitable to the persons involved. At some point during the
follow-up meeting, the social worker should assess whether the tasks have been
completed, whether they were helpful, and what other tasks might be useful.

Ending Structural Family Interventions   Structural interventions focus on
behavioral change, and thus indicators that the process should end can be ascer-
tained through formal change measures, family member behaviors in sessions,
and family self-reports of activities between sessions.

Formal Instruments   Several instruments have been designed to assess and measure
change in structural family therapy. One example of an established instrument that is

partially suitable as a change measure within this theory is the *Family Assessment Device* (FAD) (Franklin, Hopson, & Barge, 2003). This instrument includes six subscales, four of which (problem solving, communication, roles, and behavior control) are consistent with the focus of structural intervention. These four subscales, composed of between 6 and 11 items that are rated on a Likert scale, can be used independently of the other two subscales. A social worker can ask family members to complete the FAD at intervals during the intervention process as a measure of structural changes regarding the four variables. The instrument is brief, practical, and valid. Other instruments that may help to assess the quality of family interactions include the *Structural Family Systems Ratings Scale* (Mitrani, Feaster, McCabe, Czaja, & Szapocznik, 2005), which has been adapted for use with Alzheimer's caregivers, and the *Boundary Violations Scale* (Madden-Derdich, Estrada, Updegraff, & Leonard, 2002), which assesses children's perceptions of intergenerational boundary violations.

Time Measures   The social worker can use time measures to see how alliances change among family members. For example, toward the goal of developing rules for appropriate boundaries, a child may be asked to monitor how much time she is permitted to spend alone in her room or out of the house with friends without parental interruption. The issue of permanence of change can be addressed by evaluating the consistency of these measures over some specified length of time. At the end of the intervention the practitioner can summarize in concrete terms (time, frequency, and content) the manner in which various subsystems have changed.

Quality of Role-Plays   As a family's functioning improves, the social worker can use role-plays more flexibly to help members anticipate possible future challenges. He or she can ask family members to respond to difficult situations they have not yet faced. Their ability to do so flexibly indicates that the family has acquired the ability to respond to new challenges.

Monitoring External Interactions   Throughout the intervention, the social worker and family will be sharing impressions of how well they are managing their target behaviors related to task activities in the natural environment. When there is consensus among the participants that they have mastered these behaviors, the intervention can end unless the family sets additional goals.

SPIRITUALITY IN STRUCTURAL FAMILY THEORY

Structural family theory is not as rich as family emotional systems theory with regard to incorporating members' spiritual issues because it is focused on organization rather than emotional life. Concepts such as authority, boundaries, rules, power, subsystems, and roles do not encourage an exploration of the belief systems of members, except as they relate to structural operations. For example, one member's decision to pursue a career in human services in a family of businesspeople may create conflict related to this perceived values difference, which may result in the "outside" member being restricted from certain roles and alliances. However, in structural family intervention, the *content* of such a conflict would be less important than the effects it has on the family structure. As far as considering the spirituality of individual family members, the perspective described for cognitive theory in Chapter 7 is consistent with structural theory.

ATTENTION TO SOCIAL JUSTICE ISSUES

Structural family theory is clearly consistent with the professional value of social justice. In fact, Minuchin (1984) wrote that its interventions have little value without the practitioner's attention to macro-social issues that affect the family's life. Although the theory is useful with many presenting problems, the families for whom it was initially developed included vulnerable and oppressed people. With the principles of structural intervention, social workers can focus change efforts on issues related to poverty, unemployment, discrimination, and other forms of social injustice. The earlier discussion about LGBT families provides one illustration of this point.

Some structural theorists have systematically enlarged the theory to include attention to social structures so that families can gain access to external information, services, and resources. For example, one community mental health center implemented a structural family therapy program that features a two-tiered, home-based intervention (Aponte, Zarski, Bixenstine, & Cibik, 1991). The home-based therapy provides a viable means of intervention for families that are not receptive to office-based counseling, either for cultural reasons or because they do not have transportation resources. Families suited to this model of intervention tend to be poor and *underorganized*, meaning that member roles are ill-defined and parental authority is either diffuse or overbearing. These families often become involved with social agencies and thus lose some control over their own destiny. With the two-tiered approach, social workers help families resolve their internal problems, and then help them address community problems that they share with other families. The intervention persists for 12 to 16 weeks.

The first and primary focus in this program is the provision of structural family intervention, so that family members can develop consensus about their roles and responsibilities within the unit. The adults are helped to develop and enforce appropriate controls over the younger members. The social workers attempt to provide practical solutions to the family's concrete problems, which tend to be initially centered on one child's problem behavior, but are eventually accepted as systemic problems. If the structural interventions are successful, the second tier of intervention is introduced, and the family is invited to participate in a multiple-family support group composed of other families who have completed the structural therapy. This open-ended group is conducted in a public community setting by different staff members. The goals of the ongoing group are for participants to increase their awareness of community factors that influence their lives and to empower themselves to take action toward enhancing their community lives.

CASE ILLUSTRATIONS

The Dalton Family

Nita Dalton was a 42-year-old Caucasian married mother of three children living in the rural outskirts of a large city. She was referred to the family agency by a case manager at the county human services department who had been managing her requests for financial assistance. The referring worker was concerned about Nita's reports of family conflict that included emotional detachment from her husband and acting-out behaviors from her two sons. The social worker met with Nita once and decided that the client's concerns could be best addressed if the entire family came for a second appointment. All of the household members agreed to do so except for Nita's husband, who remained uninvolved throughout the five-session intervention. The members who did participate included Nita, her two sons (ages 22 and 20), their new wives (ages 20 and 19, respectively), and her eight-year-old daughter (see Figure 9.1).

The social worker quickly observed that the family was highly conflicted. Nita's husband was employed part-time as an auto mechanic, but was estranged from the others, living several miles from the house and maintaining minimal contact with them. He was also said to have a drinking problem. Nita was over-functioning as the de facto head of the household, trying to manage it on the limited income her husband provided. As a result she was continuously stressed, anxious, and depressed. She complained that her two sons were irresponsible, working sporadically and always trying to "borrow" money from her. It was hard for Nita to set limits with them; they were able to "wear her down" with persistent cajoling. The social worker noticed that the older children were cheerful in the session, seeming to feel entitled to the family resources, and having little sensitivity to their mother's distress. Nita felt close to her young daughter, and spent most of her free time with her. She wanted to work outside the home (and had done so in the past) but felt that she had no time to do so. She said that if her sons would leave home and take care of themselves, she could get a job.

Nita and her family came from an Appalachian cultural background. In that culture, women are expected to assume the role of household manager and

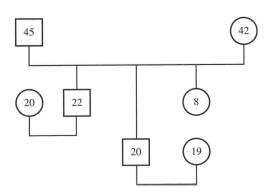

FIGURE 9.1 The Dalton Family Genogram

survive with little material support, all for the good of the family. Men maintained primary power, but were less involved in day-to-day family interactions. Marital infidelity was common among members of their community. In fact, women often came to view themselves as "martyrs" (as Nita did), accepting that it was their fate to "suffer" for the sake of the family.

The sons, feeling a need to defend themselves against their mother's criticisms, agreed to several sessions of family counseling. The social worker decided that the Daltons were suitable for structural family intervention, and assessed them as outlined below.

Locus of Power   Dad maintained absent, passive control over the family. He maintained the authority to do what he wanted, which was usually to stay away. He took the money he wanted out of his paycheck and gave the rest to his wife. Nita could not predict how much of his pay would come into the household each week, but she maintained it was "too little." She was ambivalent about whether she wanted the marriage to continue (they had been separated several times in the past), and felt it was "up to him." In dad's absence the boys were able to "team up" to exert power over mom.

Problematic Boundaries   Nita and her husband were disengaged. Nita and her sons were enmeshed; that is, despite their conflicts they seemed to need each other. Nita's relationship with her daughter was positive, but there was a potential for enmeshment because of mom's reliance on the daughter for emotional support. Living in a semi-rural area, the family was moderately isolated from its external environment. This was typical of families in the region with Appalachian roots. The children all had friends, but Nita was close only to a sister who lived nearby.

Relevant Subsystems   There was an absence of an adult "couple" system and a related lack of partnership regarding parental authority. The brother subsystem was strong, and the mother/daughter subsystem was also strong. Only the latter seemed to be functional with regard to family structure. There did not seem to be a "daughter-in-law" subsystem—these young women appeared to have a congenial but not close relationship. Nita's own daughter seemed to be an "outsider" sibling because of her age, although she enjoyed the others. The social worker felt that Nita needed support from another adult (husband, close friend, or other extended-family member) to strengthen the adult subsystem.

Relevant Triangles   Three problematic triangles within the family were: *mom/dad/daughter* (Nita relied on her daughter to meet her needs for companionship that she did not get from her husband); *mom/dad/oldest son* (mom tried to rely on this son for assistance with family management, although this was frustrating for her); and *new spouse/son/mom* (the older son's spouse encouraged her husband to make demands on mom for money and other material resources).

Context   This was an Appalachian family in which women were expected to fill certain traditional roles. Nita accepted her caregiver role, and, despite her stress level, got attention from her sons with the current arrangement. Additionally, dad was attempting to recover from alcoholism, which may have accounted for his desire to avoid internal family stresses. Another important issue was the family's poverty, as there were insufficient resources for maintaining the household. Even if dad had invested his entire paycheck into the family, it would have been difficult to cover the basic financial needs.

Family Stage   As young adults, the sons "should" have been working and leaving home, particularly to support their new wives. Nita and her husband wished to begin relinquishing their day-to-day parenting roles so that they could attend to some of their own interests.

Function of Nita's Symptoms   In her current role, in which the others blamed her for being the "unstable" member, Nita served to absorb the family's chaos. She served a function for her husband as well by keeping the rest of the family's focus away from him.

Overall Nature of the Family Structure   The social worker concluded that the Dalton family had become chaotic, characterized by an absence of appropriate executive authority, subsystem functions, and boundaries.

The social worker had moderate success with helping the Dalton family restructure itself into a more functional unit. Whereas the father's refusal to participate was an initial concern, the social worker was encouraged by the motivation of the other members. Several of them were angry with each other, but they shared an interest in resolving their conflicts, if only for selfish reasons. Nita was in conflict with everyone but her daughter; the sons and older wife were in conflict with Nita; and the daughter was angry with her brothers (for monopolizing mom's attention) and her sisters-in-law (for not spending enough time with her). With this assessment the social worker provided the following interventions.

Reframing   The social worker summarized Nita's symptoms of anxiety and depression, and her feelings of anger, as evidence that she was working "too hard" to be a good parent, and perhaps caring "too much" about her adult children. Nita accepted the reframe, which helped her feel affirmed, and also suggested to the others that their mother was interested in their well-being. None of the children challenged this perspective.

Developing a Shared Definition of "Family Challenges"   After hearing each member's point of view about the family situation, the social worker summarized the problem as a lack of sufficient *emotional* and *material* resources to go around the family. He shared his belief that the family members had the capacity to work toward expanding those resources. Those members who had few material resources might make up for this with task contributions to the family unit. This problem definition was relatively nonthreatening to the children so they agreed with it.

Practicing Clear Communication Skills with All Family Members   The Daltons (except for Nita) shared a habit of arguing with and interrupting each other. Even the social worker had trouble containing their interruptions, so he formalized their interactions during the first two visits. He called on members to speak in turn, silenced any interruptions that occurred, and assured everyone that they would have the opportunity to respond to others' comments. The social worker was authoritative but not abrupt in this task, and he was careful to repeatedly explain his rationale for this controlling behavior. After a while the Dalton children's interactions became more peaceful.

Positioning Family Members to Highlight Appropriate Alliances   As examples, the sons were separated from their wives at times (to break up a problematic alliance or triangle), and the daughter (who idolized her sisters-in-law) was seated next to them, to encourage their relationship development. Nita was seated next to various of her sons and daughters-in-law at times when the social worker wanted them to carry on conversations to establish new household rules about money and personal responsibilities. The social worker supported the parental subsystem by sitting next to Nita at times and taking her side (joining) in conversations about family authority, roles, and rules. This was important because Nita was the only adult member without an ally in the household. At these times the social worker shared his concern that Nita was still on her own at home. Nita had mentioned that her sister and two other friends always tried to be helpful to her. The social worker encouraged her to collaborate with any of them when making household decisions.

Role-Playing to Practice New Styles of Family Interaction   For example, Nita role-played a hypothetical situation with her son (in which he was requesting money she could not afford to give) so that the social worker could assess their behavior and help them to improve their abilities to control anger and bring discussions to constructive closure. During all role-plays, the social worker assigned the uninvolved members to pay attention and comment on the participants' behaviors. This tactic brought all members into the process of problem solving and promoted their sense of mutual participation in family activities. In *role reversals*, certain members were instructed to take the role of another family member in discussions of specific problem situations so that they could perceive their own behavior more clearly and better understand the point of view of the other person. As one example, Nita was asked to portray her son and ask him (playing the role of mom) for money. Her son (as Nita) was assigned to reject her request and articulate the reasons why she should not get any more of the family's limited funds.

Task Assignments   Between family meetings, task assignments were intended to support the development of appropriate alliances and clarify boundaries between family members and subsystems. The social worker assigned Nita (with her approval) to spend two hours away from the family, two times during the coming week, doing whatever she wanted. He assigned her this same task each week, because it proved difficult for her to disengage from the household. The sons were asked to spend a certain amount of time alone with their spouses each week talking about future plans. The social worker hoped that this activity would help the young couples to realize that they might benefit from greater self-reliance. The daughters-in-law were asked to include the daughter in one social activity each week, to strengthen that bond and to reduce the potential enmeshment of Nita and her daughter.

The family made significant gains. Their communications became less conflicted, some new household rules were developed, and the roles of the children expanded. Nita spent more time with her friends, the sons were looking for work more regularly, and the daughters-in-law assumed some responsibility for taking care of the daughter. The level of tension was lower in the social worker's office and in the Dalton home. The social worker would have liked to see the family for several more sessions, but the family (primarily the sons) wanted to terminate because, in the social worker's view, their motivation and interest had waned. He was disappointed, but felt that they had made some progress.

The Family Drawings

Cynthia's agency provided in-home intervention services to families identified as being "at risk" for child emotional and behavioral problems. These were generally single-parent families living in poverty. The families tended to lack strong authority and consistency in the behavior of parent figures and have poor limit setting on the behavior of the children. Cynthia worked with the Paulson family for six months. The family included Kendra, a 20-year-old single mother of seven-year-old, five-year-old, and newborn boys. Her mother had moved in with Kendra when the new baby was born, and the two adults often argued. Grandmother tried to take on the traditional parent role because Kendra was away working, sometimes at odd hours. Kendra was a strict parent when she was home, but grandmother was permissive and set few limits with the kids. The two women could not agree on how to manage the kids. Damon, the five-year-old, began to develop behavior problems of aggression in the home, neighborhood, and school.

After the assessment Cynthia decided to work with Kendra and her mother on improving their relationship. She infrequently included the two older children in the process. She felt that if the adults could get along better and agree on appropriate parenting strategies, the children would respond with improved behavior. Cynthia met with Kendra and her mother weekly for three months, and then twice monthly when the situation began to improve. Her goal was system restructuring, as evidenced by both adults assuming appropriate roles of authority in the family. She taught them how to communicate clearly, directly, and frequently with each other. Cynthia also helped Kendra resolve the lingering anger she felt toward her mother. Kendra was bitter about the lack of supportive parenting she had received as a child. The pair was able to learn and practice a process for resolving their differences and agreeing on household and child-rearing rules. Cynthia developed role-plays based on possible conflict situations that the adults practiced during her visits. Occasionally the social worker brought in the older boys to talk about what they were doing and to let the adults practice what they had learned with them.

One day when Cynthia was visiting, the children were behaving rambunctiously. To calm them down she suggested that the older boys draw a picture of the family. To Cynthia's surprise, the pictures portrayed the family's problems. They indicated where each child saw himself in relation to the others in the size of the figures, their expressions, and their positions. Because the boys seemed to enjoy drawing, it occurred to Cynthia that this might be a good way to monitor the family's changes over time. Every month or so she asked the boys to draw family pictures, and then discussed with them and the adults what the drawings showed. As the weeks went by, the pictures demonstrated that the family system was stabilizing. The figures of the family members, including the baby, became more equal in size and closer to each other.

When Kendra and her mother became able to solve problems consistently without the social worker's assistance, and Damon's behavior improved as well, it was time to end the intervention. As a closing activity, Cynthia asked each of the four family members (excluding the infant) to draw a picture of what he or she wanted the family to be like. Afterward she used the pictures to review the work they had done together during the previous six months. All of them had made changes that the social worker felt were likely to persist. Cynthia took the pictures and had them mounted together on a mat board. The family members all agreed that the board should hang on the wall of their home.

EVIDENCE OF EFFECTIVENESS

The results of a PsycINFO® literature search on structural family intervention included articles describing its applicability to families characterized by divorce, single fatherhood, mental illness, multigenerational parenting, violence, and incest. It is also used with families with children who experience autism, chronic pain, enuresis and encopresis, chronic illness, cancer, learning disabilities, depression, anorexia, brain injury, substance abuse, and school behavior problems. There are undoubtedly many other types of presenting problems for which this theory has been used.

There is limited empirical evidence beyond single case studies, however, that structural family interventions are more effective than other clinical modalities. Described here are multi-client or comparison group studies that have been conducted on the topic. Minuchin himself carried out several of these. The theory's founder and his colleagues tested the new structural approach with 11 families at Wiltwyck School, and compared outcomes to the standard 50% success rate recorded at the facility (Minuchin, Montalvo, Guerney, Rosman, & Schumer, 1967). Pre- and posttest measures on variables including leadership, behavior control, and guidance statements indicated that seven of the 11 families improved (63.6%) after 6 to 12 months of intervention. The authors noted that the families assessed as enmeshed developed clearer boundaries, whereas the disengaged families showed no improvement.

Ten years later, Minuchin, Rosman, Baker, and Liebman (1978) summarized the findings from a variety of their studies of families that included children with anorexia, diabetes, and asthma. Forty-five of 53 anorexic children (85%) were improved or greatly improved regarding target symptoms and social functioning after a course of treatment including hospitalization and outpatient family therapy. These positive results persisted after follow-ups over several years. Their studies of 20 clients with psychosomatic diabetes (in which an emotional condition worsened the medical symptoms) indicated that *all* clients (100%) were fully or moderately improved following family intervention. Of 17 families that included a child with psychosomatic asthma, 14 (84%) were said to recover or improve moderately. The researchers concluded from these latter two projects that a child's psychosomatic symptoms may serve to moderate stress between parents.

An unusual process study of structural family intervention demonstrated that the effectiveness of the modality was dependent on the practitioner's use of theoretically appropriate intervention strategies (Walsh, 2004). The author of this 100-participant study hypothesized that when the practitioner focused on increasing parental power in at least half of all sessions, more positive change in family organization would be observed than if the practitioner did not maintain this focus in at least half the sessions. The hypothesis was supported based on scores from the Control and Organization subscales of the Family Environment Scale.

Two studies have focused on children with attention deficit/hyperactivity disorder (ADHD). Aman (2001) conducted a nonequivalent pretest/posttest control group study (62 families in each group) to determine whether a multiple-family group model that included structural interventions could produce positive outcomes regarding parenting stress level and family satisfaction. Results indicated that the experimental families experienced fewer home conflicts and reported improved family relationships. Barkley, Guevremont, Anastopoulos, and Fletcher (1992) randomly assigned 61 adolescents (ages 12 to 18) to four intervention modalities, one of which was structural family therapy for 8 to 20 sessions. Families were assessed at pre-treatment, posttreatment, and three months later. All four interventions (also including behavior management, communications training, and problem solving) resulted in significant reductions in negative communications, conflict, and anger. Improvements were noted in school adjustment, ADHD symptoms, and the mother's depressive symptoms, but there were no significant differences in outcomes among the four modalities. Most outcomes remained stable between posttreatment and the follow-up measure.

A number of intervention studies have been conducted on the problem of substance abuse. One qualitative study of families from ethnically diverse backgrounds investigated whether structural family interventions would reduce or eliminate alcohol abuse. The intervention was organized to focus on adaptive capacity and boundary change (Hunter, 1998). Three families (African-American, Caucasian, and Hispanic) received structural family therapy for 6 to 10 weeks after completing pre- and posttreatment measures of family stress and relationships. All three families made changes in the two target domains, which resulted in improved communication, age-appropriate child behavior, and decreased parental stress. In another study, with a pre- and posttreatment follow-up design, structural interventions were provided to 122 African American and Hispanic youth, aged 12 to 14 years, as a preventive factor against drug use (Santisteban, Coatsworth, Perez-Vidal, Mitrani, Jean-Gilles, et al., 1997). The interventions were intended to reduce behavior problems and enhance family functioning. It was found that the interventions were effective in significantly modifying both high-risk factors. Further, both high-risk factors were predictive of drug initiation nine months later. Drug use was also reduced for the few study participants who were already using.

Cancrini, Cingolani, Compagnoni, Costantini, and Mazzoni (1988) studied outcomes for 131 heroin addicts (aged 16 to 33) who were treated with either structural or paradoxical family therapy in one agency during the same year. Structural family therapy was found to be most effective with addicts who had additional psychological problems. Zeigler-Driscoll (1979) compared the effectiveness of structural family therapy with an inpatient drug treatment program for individuals. No differences were found in abstinence or recidivism rates, but the structural interventions improved the families' coping abilities when an addicted member returned to drug use. Stanton and Todd (1979) provided 65 families with a heroin-addicted son with a family intervention that included structural methods and compared outcomes with a control group of 25 non-addict families. After intervention the structural families were more expressive than the controls and better able to resolve disagreements, maintain solidarity during task completion, and maintain clear subsystem boundaries.

Several empirical studies have focused on adolescents with behavior problems. In one study the outcomes of structural and psychodynamic interventions (with a control group) were compared for 69 6 to 12-year-old Hispanic boys with behavioral and emotional problems (Szapocznik, Arturo, & Cohen, 1989). The two treatment conditions were similarly effective in reducing the presenting problems and in improving psychodynamic ratings of child functioning. Structural family therapy was more effective, however, in maintaining family cohesion at one-year follow-up. Chamberlain and Rosicky (1995) conducted a literature review of seven studies between 1989 and 1994 on the effects of structural family intervention. Generally, the results were supportive of family interventions for adolescent conduct disorders. Structural family intervention was used as the basis for a prevention program for African-American and Hispanic youth who were deemed at risk for initiating drug use (Santisteban, Coatsworth, Perez-Vidal, Mitrani, Jean-Gilles, et al., 1997). More than 100 young adolescents were provided with structural family intervention with a one-group, pretest, posttest follow-up design. The program was effective in modifying the two risk factors of behavior problems and quality of family functioning. The effects persisted nine months later.

Finally, an interesting control group study of 30 families of persons suffering recent loss of sight found that structural family intervention was useful as a component of the rehabilitation process (Radochonski, 1998). The experimental families demonstrated positive changes in the internal structure and functioning of the families, with significant improvements in the personal functioning of the members who had lost their sight.

CRITICISMS OF THE THEORY

Structural family theory has been a popular approach to family intervention for 40 years, but, like every theory, it can be criticized. First, in its focus on the "external architecture" of a family system, the theory de-emphasizes people's emotional lives. Structural practitioners believe that functional family structure will result in an improved quality of life, including emotional life, for all members. Still, it does not directly attend to this aspect of the human experience, and thus some practitioners may overlook the nuances of family relationships that influence structural characteristics. Family emotional systems theory (Chapter 5) is more concerned with that aspect of human functioning.

Second, practitioners may mistakenly hold biases about "appropriate" family structure. Structural theory was based on its founder's recognition that many multiproblem families lacked strong executive authority and rules. In the twenty-first century, with diverse family forms emerging in this country and around the world, more egalitarian family structures may be appropriate. For example, some feminists criticize structural theory for promoting patriarchal ideas about family life (Dziegielewski & Montgomery, 1999).

Structural practitioners must be careful not to begin with specific assumptions about family structure prior to assessing a system and how well it works for members. The practitioner must also engage in cross-cultural family study to ensure that he or she does not impose a rigid perspective of appropriate family structure. With these precautions in mind, structural family theory can be used with diverse family forms. In fact, there are case studies in the literature indicating that it has been useful with Hispanic, Chinese, Vietnamese, Jewish, West African, Native American, Mexican-American, and Italian-American families.

SUMMARY

Structural family theory provides a useful perspective for clinical social work practice with diverse family forms. It is focused on the external "architecture" of families—including their rules, boundaries, and subsystems—rather than on the inner psychology of members and their interactions. A functional family structure will result in a system that meets members' basic material and emotional needs. Structural family interventions were specifically developed to help the kinds of families encountered by social work practitioners—those experiencing multiple problems such as poverty, illness, unemployment, physical abuse, substance abuse, absent members, and acting out. With this theoretical approach social workers can also continue to provide the environmental interventions (through case management) that make the profession so distinctive. In fact, the theory is outstanding in its promotion of social justice activities.

TOPICS FOR DISCUSSION

1. Structural theorists believe that an appropriate family structure will result in positive emotional relationships among the members. Do you agree? If so, can a social worker de-emphasize emotional issues in family assessment and intervention?

2. Observing member interactions can provide a great deal of information about a family's structure. Describe from your own clinical or personal experience examples of important elements of a family's structure being manifested in the members' behavior.

3. Select one type of racial or ethnic group that for you would be an example of family diversity. Consider three major concepts of structural family theory, and describe how they might be different from that which is common in your own ethnic/racial group, but still functional.

4. It is said in structural theory that "action precedes understanding." What does this mean? Do you agree? How does it compare with the intervention stance in family emotional systems theory?

5. Consider a single female parent of two adolescent children who is experiencing high stress because of pressing family responsibilities (work, childcare, budgeting). Her children, in a normal way, have become less interactive with her, not communicating as they once did. They are also beginning to get into trouble at school for disruptive behavior. Discuss some possible intervention strategies from structural theory that might enhance the family's quality of communication.

IDEAS FOR ROLE-PLAYS

(The roles of social worker, client, and observer should all be represented, and each role may include more than one person.)

1. Consider a family unit that includes a maternal grandfather (58), mother (37), daughter (18), and male cousin (17). The mother and daughter experience angry outbursts, and sometimes physically fight with one another. The school made a family referral to the social worker after the mother and daughter, in the presence of the grandfather, got into a public shouting match during a school activity. Select and implement intervention strategies that might interrupt this family's negative patterns of interaction.

2. Stan and Mike are gay men who recently moved in together, along with Mike's seven-year-old son (the boy's mother died five years ago). They are

both concerned about the well-being of Mike's son, and seek the social worker's assistance in helping them organize a "healthy household." Select and implement intervention strategies that might help them to accomplish this goal.

3. A Latino father has been physically abusing the two older of his three children (ages 11, 9, and 7), partly because he knows no other way to discipline them. His wife is angry with him for ignoring her objections to his behavior. He has been mandated to see the social worker alone to receive parenting assistance. Select and implement intervention strategies that might help to stop the abuse.

APPENDIX: Structural Family Theory Outline

Focus	Functional family structure (the organized patterns in which members interact)
	Executive authority in the family unit
Major Proponents	Minuchin, Satir, Aponte, Colapinto, Szapocnik, Nichols
Origins and Social Context	Expansion of family intervention to multiproblem families
	Need for brief interventions
	Rise in prominence of social learning, cognitive, and behavior theories
Nature of the Individual	Not specifically addressed, but concepts from cognitive and behavior theory are consistent with it
Structural Concepts	Structure (an invisible set of rules that organizes how members interact)
	Executive authority
	Power
	Member roles
	Subsystems
	Boundaries (internal and external)
	Transactional patterns
	Rules
	Flexibility
Family Development Themes	Accommodation and boundary-making
	Adult, adult/child, and sibling subsystems
	Structural adaptations to life transitions
Nature of Problems	Disengaged family members or subsystems
	Ineffective hierarchies
	Rigid or diffuse boundaries
	Excessive emotional distance
	Enmeshed family members or subsystems

APPENDIX: Structural Family Theory Outline (Continued)

	Triangles
	System interference with normal development
	Conflict avoidance
	Failure to realign after stress
Nature of Change	Action precedes understanding
	Learning and practicing can result in more effective problem-solving, decision-making, and communication skills
Goals of Intervention	Create structural change
	Alter boundaries
	Realign subsystems
	Resolve immediate symptoms (short-term)
	Increase/preserve mutual support of members
Nature of Worker/ Client Relationship	Worker as "stage director" (high level of worker activity)
	Worker assumes a position of "shaping competence"
	Clients are conceptualized as victims of circumstances
	Worker joins with individuals or subsystems as needed (adjusts personal style)
Intervention Principles	Normalize symptoms
	Join alliances as appropriate
	In-session enactments
	Structural mapping
	Educate about structure
	Manipulate space
	Encourage problem behavior tracking
	Highlight and modify interactions*
	Support strengths
	Shape competence (build on strengths)*
	Enhance self-control of members via relaxation and stress management
	Affirm sympathetic responses, nonjudgmental observations of members
	Realign boundaries*
	Unbalance subsystems* (change behaviors within subsystems)
	Challenge unproductive member assumptions

APPENDIX: Structural Family Theory Outline (Continued)

	*These strategies can be implemented through:
	Teaching communication skills (speaking, listening skills, managing conflicts)
	Assigning tasks for implementation in the natural environment
	Role-plays, role reversals
Assessment Questions	What are the family's patterns of interacting?
	How does the family present itself structurally?
	Where does the power lie in this family? In what contexts?
	What subsystems appear to be prominent?
	Does the presenting problem serve a function for the family?
	What are this family's patterns of managing stress?
	How sensitive are family members to each other?
	What kinds of behavior do members seem to expect of each other?
	Do they accommodate each other's needs?
	Is the family involved with external systems?

10

Solution-Focused Therapy

I find my feet have further Goals –
I smile upon the Aims
That felt so ample – Yesterday –
Today's – have vaster claims –

I do not doubt the self I was
Was competent to me –
But something awkward in the fit –
Proves that – outgrown – I see★

Solution-focused practice is a short-term approach to clinical intervention in which the social worker and client attend to solutions or exceptions to problems more than to problems themselves (DeJong & Berg, 2008; Corcoran, 2005; O'Hanlon & Weiner-Davis, 1989). Its focus is on helping clients identify and amplify their strengths and resources toward the goal of finding solutions to presenting problems. *Solution-focused therapy* (SFT) does not represent a single theoretical perspective, but is a model of practice that draws from theories in clinical practice and sociology. This model is clearly oriented toward the future, much more so than most of the practice theories discussed so far. From a practice perspective, this shift in emphasis from problems to solutions is more radical than it might first appear.

ORIGINS AND SOCIAL CONTEXT

The principles underlying solution-focused therapy reflect a synthesis of ideas drawn from the systems, cognitive, communication, and crisis intervention theories; the

---

principles of brief therapy; and the social theory of constructivism. We will review each of these influences except for the last one, which is described in the context of narrative theory in Chapter 12.

Family systems theory, already discussed in Chapter 5, is a cornerstone of the social work profession, and has great relevance to the solution-focused approach to practice (Andreae, 1996). It assumes that human behavior is less a function of the characteristics of individuals than of the patterns of behavior they learn in their families of origin. General systems theory takes an even broader view, emphasizing the reciprocal influences between people and the environmental circumstances they encounter (Von Bertalanffy, 1968). Activity in any area of a system affects all other areas. The thoughts, feelings, and behaviors of individuals in a given system, then, are malleable and influenced by the behavior of other elements in the system. This is, of course, consistent with social work's person-in-environment perspective.

One important implication of systems thinking in clinical practice is that a client's change efforts do not need to be directly related to a presenting problem. Because any change will affect the entire system, new actions will influence its elements in ways that cannot be predicted or contained. The social worker may thus consider many creative strategies for change when working with a client system.

SFT was largely influenced by systems thinking as developed at the Mental Research Institute (MRI) in Palo Alto, California (Weakland & Jordan, 1992). The MRI brief therapy model views clinical problems as developing because people by nature develop a limited range of patterns of interaction in relation to their life problems that do not always resolve them. These patterns may include under-reacting, overreacting, avoiding, denying, and even taking actions that worsen the situation. In a sense, the problem becomes the sum of the failed solution efforts. MRI interventions represent efforts to identify and explore a client's vicious cycles and find new ways of interrupting the problem cycle. The focus of this work is on presenting problems, not underlying issues.

Cognitive theory has contributed to the development of solution focused practice principles with its accounts of how people create unique meaning in their lives. The concept of schemas, described in Chapter 6, describes how we develop habits of thinking that should ideally be flexible, but can at times become rigid, preventing us from assimilating new information that might enhance our creative adaptability to life challenges.

Communications theory and the study of language was of interest to the developers of solution-focused therapy with regard to the impact of the words people use about their attitudes toward the self and the world (de Shazer, 1994). SFT proceeds from the assumption that language shapes reality, and thus it emphasizes the importance of word clarity in clinical intervention. Solution-focused practitioners maintain a distrust of the abstractions found in many other practice theories. Such preoccupations are nonsensical and, worse, unproductive toward the goals of furthering a client's welfare. The social worker tries hard to understand the specific nature of a client's concerns and goals, and supports client initiatives toward change that are concrete as well.

Crisis theory (described more fully in Chapter 13) developed as human service professionals in many settings faced demands to provide focused, effective interventions for people in need of immediate relief. Crises may be developmental (leaving home, retirement), situational (natural disasters, death of a loved one, loss of a job), or existential (meaning-of-life issues). Caplan (1990, 1989) developed one widely respected model of crisis theory. He defined a crisis as a disruption in a person's physical or emotional equilibrium due to a hazardous event that poses an obstacle to the fulfillment of important needs or life goals. Crises are characterized by a person's need to resolve problems while feeling overwhelmed.

Crisis intervention must be short-term because, with its associated debilitating physical effects, a crisis can only persist for four to eight weeks. All interventions are time-limited, have a here-and-now focus, rely on tasks to facilitate change, and feature a high level of practitioner activity (Gilliland & James, 2005). Initial interventions include the social worker's attempts to alleviate the client's distress through reassurance, support, stress-reduction exercises, and social support linkages. As the symptoms begin to subside, later interventions include enhancing the client's awareness of precipitating events, teaching how current stresses connect with patterns of past functioning, and helping clients develop improved modes of coping to avoid future crisis episodes. Like systems theory, crisis theory recognizes that the environmental context influences the severity of distress as well as the availability of resources to meet its demands.

A final, more general influence on the development of solution-focused practice was the proliferation of brief therapy models that emerged within the human service professions in the 1980s (Corwin, 2002). Some of these approaches did not result from an evolution of ideas about appropriate practice but were a reaction to external pressures, including the need to manage long waiting lists in agencies and reduced insurance coverage for clinical services. Still, it was discovered that these methods were effective, sometimes more so than longer-term interventions. Brief treatment models have emerged within most practice theoretical frameworks and tend to share the following elements:

- A narrow focus on the client's most pressing concerns
- A belief that not all of a client's presenting concerns need to be addressed
- A focus on change, not "cure"
- An assumption that the origins of a client's problems need not be understood in order to help the client
- Clients should lead the process of problem formulation, goal setting, and intervention
- Intervention should have a strengths orientation

Solution-focused therapy is distinct from some brief therapies in its strategies for assessment, goal setting, and intervention, as we will see.

MAJOR CONCEPTS

Despite its roots in other theories, solution-focused therapy has become recognized as a unique approach to clinical practice. Its major principles are described below.

"Grand theories" of human development and the nature of problems—those that emphasize similarity across populations and cultures—are no longer relevant to the world of social work practice. For example, not all children and adolescents progress through the same stages of cognitive, moral, and social development. This principle is shared with most other practice approaches that have emerged in the past several decades.

Language is powerful in shaping one's sense of reality. The words we use to define ourselves and our situations are influential in the conclusions we draw about those situations. A drug abuser who "buys into" the language of addiction may define himself as "diseased," and thus less functional by nature than many other people. Social workers need to be attuned to how clients use language to define their challenges and their functioning. Is their language constructive or destructive? Interestingly, social workers themselves may be tied to a professional language that stigmatizes clients. If I use the language of the DSM ("major depression"), for example, I may conclude that my client has a limited capacity to alleviate her depression without medications.

Social workers must *de-emphasize problem talk* in an effort to shift the clinical focus away from a search for the causes of a client's difficulties. An emphasis on *solution talk* represents an effective means of helping clients focus on solutions to problems and to act or think differently than they normally do. This includes the social worker's cultivating an atmosphere in which strengths and resources will be highlighted. It is important to emphasize again that solutions do not need to be directly related to a client's presenting problem. Just as the causes of problems do not need to be understood for significant change to occur, a client's decisions to act differently in the future may emerge independently of any problem talk. This idea is consistent with the systems perspective that any change reverberates through a system, affecting every other element. The social worker thus does not need to feel constrained by "linear" thinking about problems and solutions.

This non-linear perspective is quite different from that espoused in other practice theories and models, where it is assumed that there is a logical, systematic relationship between problems and solutions, and that a solution should be directly related to the nature of a problem. For example, a cognitive practitioner might conclude that a client's ongoing depression was a consequence of negative self-talk, and that the solution to this problem should include changes in specific types of self-talk. A solution-focused practitioner would be more open to a range of client-generated solutions.

Problems are real, but often not so ubiquitous in the lives of clients as they may assume. It is through habits of selective attention that clients become preoccupied with the negative aspects of their lives. An adolescent girl who feels hopeless about her ongoing social rejection at school may benefit from recognizing more clearly when this problem is not happening in her life—for example, when she is participating in youth groups at church.

The social worker's role in a client's goal achievement is made more constructive with an exploration of problem exceptions rather than a focus on problems.

THE NATURE OF PROBLEMS AND CHANGE

As we have seen, the solution-focused perspective includes few assumptions about human nature. This supports its focus on the future and its de-emphasis of lengthy assessment protocols. The perspective does assume, however, that people want to change, are suggestible, and have the capability to develop new and existing resources to solve their problems.

The nature of problems in SFT can be summarized through several principles (O'Connell, 1998). Many problems result from patterns of behavior that have been reinforced. Our rigid beliefs, assumptions, and attitudes prevent us from noticing new information in the environment that can provide solutions to our problems. That is, we are often constrained from change by our habitual, narrow views of situations. There is in fact no "correct" way to view any problem or solution.

Significant change can be achieved for most problems that clients present to social workers in a relatively brief period of time (O'Hanlon & Weiner-Davis, 1989). This is largely because change is constant in our lives—it is always happening, whether we recognize it or not. There is no difference in SFT between symptomatic and underlying change—all change is equally significant. Small changes are important because they set ongoing change processes in motion in any system. The process of change is facilitated in our favor by our learning to reinterpret existing challenging situations and acquire new ideas and information about them.

The goals of intervention in solution-focused therapy are for clients to focus on solutions to their problems or challenges, discover exceptions to their problems (times when they are not happening), become more aware of their strengths and resources, and learn to act and think differently. Examples of the kinds of questions that the social worker might ask that illustrate this difference in focus are included in Figure 10.1.

Problem Focus	Solution Focus
How can I help you?	How will you know if the intervention has been helpful?
Is the problem a symptom of something deeper?	Have we clarified the central issue that you want to address?
Can you tell me more about the problem?	Can we discover exceptions to the problem?
How can we understand the problem in light of the past?	What will the future look like without the problem?
What defense mechanisms or cognitive distortions are operating?	How can you better utilize your skills and qualities?
In what way does the relationship between us reflect your problems?	How can we collaborate?
How many sessions may we need?	Have we achieved enough to end?

FIGURE 10.1 Problem-Focused versus Solution-Focused Approaches to Intervention

SOURCE: Reproduced by permission of SAGE publications, London, Los Angeles, New Delhi, and Singapore, from Bill O'Connell, *Solution Focused Therapy*, Fig 3.1, p. 21. © 1998 Sage Publications, Ltd., by Sage Publications, Ltd.

ASSESSMENT AND INTERVENTION

The Social Worker/Client Relationship

During the engagement stage, the social worker attempts to build an alliance by accepting, without interpreting or reformulating, the client's perspective on the presenting problem, in the client's own language. The worker promotes a collaborative approach to intervention by communicating that he or she does not possess "special" knowledge about problem solving, but is eager to work with the client on desired solutions. The practitioner builds positive feelings and hope within the client with *future-oriented questions*, such as "What will be different for you when our time here has been successful?"

With its emphasis on short-term intervention and a rapid focus on client goals, solution-focused therapy is sometimes criticized for not adequately attending to the initial development of a positive worker/client relationship. That is, the rapid application of techniques may prohibit the development of a sound working relationship, which in turn might decrease the effectiveness of the therapy (Coyne, 1994). In response to this concern, one study compared client perceptions of the "working alliance" at a university counseling center when receiving either solution-focused or brief interpersonal therapy (Wettersten, Lichtenberg, & Mallinckrodt, 2005). The working alliance was assessed after each session with respect to the client's sense of bonding, shared tasks, and shared goals. With approximately 30 clients in each treatment group, it was found that the quality of the early working alliance was significantly related to client outcomes in the interpersonal therapy group, but not in the solution-focused therapy group. On the other hand, overall ratings of the working alliance (from beginning to end of the intervention) were not different between the therapies, and clients from both groups benefited from the interventions about equally. The researchers concluded that in spite of SFT's de-emphasis on the importance of the clinical relationship, such practitioners do develop a working alliance with their clients, although it is not perceived as such by clients early in treatment.

One of the unique characteristics of solution-focused therapy is the lack of a major distinction between the assessment and intervention stages. Although a client's presenting issue does need to be investigated, many of the social worker's questions and comments made during that stage are intended to initiate change processes. The reader should keep in mind, then, that distinctions between "stages" of therapy are somewhat artificial. Further, the social worker de-emphasizes the need to develop a working alliance with the client by moving rather quickly into the intervention process. All of the techniques presented below are drawn from DeJong and Berg (2008), Corcoran (2005), de Shazer (1994, 1985), O'Hanlon and Weiner-Davis (1989), and Selekman (1993).

Assessment and Intervention Strategies

The assessment (or engagement) stage is intended to gather information directly related to the client's presenting problem. During assessment, the social worker evaluates the client's level of motivation by discussing the value of resolving the presenting situation. This can be done informally with a *scaling exercise*, whereby the social worker asks the client to rate his or her willingness to invest effort into problem resolution on a 1-to-10 scale. If the client's motivation is low, the social worker raises the dilemma with the client of how the problem situation can improve in that context. Raising the client's motivation may even become the initial goal of intervention. Of course, there are several ways to formulate or partialize any problem, and the client may be motivated to address some aspects more than others. Parents of an acting-out adolescent, for example, may be more highly motivated to change his school behavior than his related playground behavior.

Through *reframing* comments and actions, the social worker gives the client credit for the positive aspects of his or her behavior relative to the presenting problem. This strategy also introduces clients to new ways of looking at some aspect of themselves or the problem. For example, a client who feels so stressed about a family issue that he is unable to sleep or work can be credited with caring so much that he is willing to sacrifice his own well-being. The social worker might also suggest that the client is working too hard on the problem, and might consider sharing responsibility for problem resolution with other family members. The social worker's goal is not to be deceptive, but to help the client feel less overwhelmed and more capable of managing the issue. The practitioner must never falsify the client's reality through the use of compliments and reframes. The social worker does not fabricate strengths or distort situations in order to make the client feel better. Rather, he or she identifies genuine qualities of which the client may be unaware but can realistically bring to bear on the problem situation.

The social worker asks *strengths-reinforcing coping questions*, such as "How have you been able to manage the problem thus far?" or "What have you done recently that has been helpful?" These same types of questions are asked at the beginning of subsequent sessions to evaluate client activities, and are sometimes called *pre-session change* questions. Questions designed for clients who seem to be stuck in a pessimistic stance might be formulated thus: "It sounds like the problem is serious. How come it is not even worse? What are you (or your family) doing to keep things from getting worse?"

If appropriate, the social worker asks questions about the desired behavior of other persons in the client's life who are connected to the problem, such as: "What will your son be doing when you are no longer concerned about his behavior on the weekends?" If the client is reluctant to interact, the social worker asks questions that serve to promote collaboration, such as: "Whose idea was it that you come here? What do they need to see to know that you don't have to come anymore? How can we work together to bring this about? Can you describe yourself from the perspective of the person who referred you here?" The social worker thus attempts to engage the client by joining with him or her against the external coercive source.

During exploration the practitioner *externalizes* the client's problem, making it something apart from, rather than within, the person. This gives the client a reduced sense of victimization or pathology, and a greater sense of control. For example, with depression, the practitioner focuses on aspects of the environment that create or sustain the client's negative feelings. In situations in which the client must cope with a physical illness or disability, the worker focuses on aspects of the environment that inhibit his or her ability to cope. The social worker often personifies the problem ("How closely does depression follow you around? Does depression stay with you all day long? Does it ever leave you alone?"), reinforcing the idea that it is an entity separate from the essence of the person.

The practitioner explores *exceptions* to the client's presenting problems. This is in keeping with the assumption in solution-focused practice that problems are not so ubiquitous as clients tend to assume. These questions initiate the intervention stage as they bring ideas for solutions to the client's attention. The questions help clients identify their strengths, and the practitioner will often prescribe that the client do more of what he or she does during these "exception" periods. The following types of questions seek exceptions:

- "What was different in the past when the problem wasn't a problem?"
- "Are there times when you have been able to stand up to, or not be dominated by, the problem? How did you make that happen? What were you thinking? When did it happen? Where did it happen? Who was there? How did they have a part in creating that? What did you think and feel as a result of doing that?"
- "Pay attention to what you are doing when the symptom isn't happening."
- "What do you want to continue to happen?"

The client is encouraged to define his or her goals, and from that starting point the practitioner collaborates with the client to select goals that are achievable. The social worker may present alternative perspectives regarding goals that are intended to free the client from habitual patterns of thinking and consider new ideas. For example, if a client wishes to "feel less depressed" or "experience more happy moods," the social worker might clarify that the client "wants to spend more time with his interests" (if these have been identified as strengths) or "join the civic association" (if that has been articulated as a possibility). All goals must be articulated in ways that are concrete so that the client and practitioner will know when they have been met. It is important for the social worker to partialize goals, or break them down into discrete units that can be actively and specifically addressed. For each goal that is identified, the client is asked to scale its importance with regard to his or her well-being in general and relative to the other goals.

After goals are developed and exceptions are identified, intervention tasks may be developed following responses to the *miracle question* (DeJong & Berg, 2008). The client is asked to imagine that, during the night while asleep, the presenting problem went away, but he or she did not know that it had. What, then, would the client notice as he or she got up and went through the next day that would provide evidence of problem resolution? The social worker helps the client report specific observations of what would be different, not settling for such global comments as "I would be happy" or "My wife would love me again." The client might reply that his wife greeted him warmly, and that he got through breakfast without an argument with his spouse and child.

It is important to emphasize here that at no time does the social work suggest specific tasks for the client to enact between sessions. The client always has the responsibility for doing so. The social worker helps the client formulate task ideas and alternatives, and supports certain tasks as appropriate, but it is always left to the client to choose a task. This is an empowering process for the client and is a core principle of the model.

The client's answers to the "miracle question" provide indicators of change that can be incorporated into tasks intended to bring about those indicators in real life. These tasks can relate to the client's personal functioning, interactions with others, or interactions with resource systems. They are based on existing strengths, or new strengths and resources that the client can develop. Often, the client is encouraged to do more of what he or she was doing when the problem was not happening. In every task assignment, the social worker predicts potential failures and setbacks because these are always possible, are a part of life in the best of circumstances, and should not be taken as indications of total client failure.

All task interventions are intended to *encourage the client to think and behave differently* with regard to the presenting problem than has been typical in the past. Clients may still rely on their existing resources to a large degree, but they will be using them in new ways. It may seem paradoxical to note that in many cases the social worker encourages easier alternatives to prior attempts at problem resolution. This is not to minimize the seriousness of the problems people face, but to emphasize that people commonly react to failed problem resolution ideas by applying the same (failed) ideas more intensively. For example, a couple who argues each evening at home may decide, with the social worker's support, to take a walk through the neighborhood after supper, with no expectation that they address their family concerns. Their rationale may be that spending quiet time alone doing something new will reconnect them in an important way.

Before ending this overview of intervention strategies, two other techniques need to be highlighted. First, *the surprise task* is an assignment whereby a client is asked to do something between this session and the next that will "surprise" another person connected with the problem (spouse, friend, child, other relative, employer, teacher, etc.) in a positive way. The social worker leaves the nature of the surprise up to the client. The rationale behind this technique is that whatever the client does will "shake up" the client system from its routine, and perhaps initiate new, more positive behavior patterns within the system. Second, the *formula first-session task* is an assignment given to the client at the end of the initial visit. The social worker states: "Between now and the next time we meet, I'd like you to observe things happening in your life that you would like to see continue, and then tell me about them." This is an invitation to clients to act in a forward-looking manner, and the task may also influence the client's thinking about solutions.

Each session includes a segment in which the practitioner and client review therapy developments and task outcomes. The client's progress toward goal achievement is measured by scaling changes on a 1-to-10 continuum. During goal setting, the social worker asks what point on the scale will indicate that the client's goal has been satisfactorily achieved. The practitioner asks the client during each subsequent meeting to indicate where he or she is on the scale, and what needs to happen for the client to advance to higher points on the scale.

It should be evident from the above description of assessment and intervention strategies that solution-focused therapy is concerned with systems activity, client strengths, quick intervention, a variety of task-oriented change activities, and short-term work. It also encourages creative thinking on the part of social workers—a challenge for some of us. Social workers have the opportunity to develop unique, situation-relevant intervention activities with their clients.

Ending the Intervention

In solution-focused therapy, the practitioner focuses on the ending almost from the beginning of intervention, as goal setting and solution finding orient the client toward change within a brief time period. Progress is monitored each time the social worker and client meet. In fact, the social worker should approach each session as though it might be the last, and ask the client each time to think about one thing he or she can do during the following week to continue progress toward goals.

Once a client has achieved his or her goals, new goals are set, or the intervention ends. The ending focuses on helping clients identify strategies to maintain changes and the momentum to continue enacting solutions. The social worker introduces a language of possibility to replace earlier language of the certainty of change. Listed below are examples of questions the practitioner may use during the end stage of intervention (O'Connell, 1998).

"What will you do to make sure you do not need to come back and see me?"

"How confident do you feel about following the plan of action? What help will you need to persist with the plan?"

"What do you expect your hardest challenge to be?"

"What do you think the possible obstacles might be, and how will you overcome them?"

"What do you need to remember if things get difficult for you again?"

"What will be the benefits for you that will make the effort worth it?"

"Who is going to be able to help you? Who do you feel will remain a problem?"

"How will you remind yourself about the things that you know help?"

"With all the changes you are making, what will you tell me about yourself if I run into you at a supermarket six months from now?"

The practitioner must be careful to end the intervention collaboratively, because clients do not always perceive the process as such. In one study of couples who had completed SFT, clients and practitioners gave different perspectives on the status of the presenting problem (Metcalf & Thomas, 1994). Some clients felt that the intervention ended too soon, and that the practitioner forced the process. The researchers concluded that practitioners should be less quick to assume collaboration, and ask routinely whether clients are getting what they want. Social workers should also take care to present a comfortable enough environment that clients will genuinely share their feelings about the process, including the desire for a lengthier intervention.

SPIRITUALITY AND SOLUTION-FOCUSED INTERVENTION

Keeping in mind that solution-focused therapy does not subscribe to particular concepts of human development, it should not be surprising that a client's spiritual or existential concerns are not a focus of the social worker's intervention unless they are raised as such by the client. That is, a client's appropriate goals may include these concerns, just as they might include any others in this future-oriented practice approach. In following the lead of the client, the social worker should be prepared to address spiritual goals and help the client to generate tasks for goal achievement relative to them. For example, a client of Methodist faith may feel depressed because she has been "sinful," and wish to reconnect with God. The social worker should, as always, accept the problem from the perspective of the client, and help the client set goals that will result in her feeling more worthy of God's grace and the church's fellowship. These goals might involve new, different, or increased activities with people associated with the church, or different solitary behaviors to enhance the client's religious or existential well-being, such as prayer and service work.

ATTENTION TO SOCIAL JUSTICE ISSUES

An outstanding characteristic of solution-focused therapy is its client-centered nature, which has positive implications for the social worker's potential social justice activity with clients. SFT highlights client strengths and the client's potential to access resources and enact change. Intervention is always composed of tasks, tailored to the client's particular situation, and these tasks may address a client's social justice goals. The social worker must be prepared to help clients gain access to needed information, services, and resources, and to pursue social change activities if those activities constitute the client's goals. The practitioner will not initiate related activities, but will be responsive to the client's leads in that respect. The therapy has applicability for a broad range of presenting issues that could include poverty, unemployment, discrimination, and other forms of social injustice. Finally, with its emphasis on understanding clients' perspectives on themselves and their world, SFT interventions mandate that the social worker become knowledgeable about issues of oppression and cultural and ethnic diversity as they relate to a client's problem presentation.

CASE ILLUSTRATIONS

The Journalist

Felicia was a 23-year-old single female recreation therapist who came to see the social worker through her Employee Assistance Program. She had a pressing request: She needed to overcome her inability to express her feelings toward men. Felicia reported that her current boyfriend had asked to see her during the coming weekend (four days away), and she suspected that he was going to break up with her. He had been complaining recently that she did not seem to care about him when, in fact, Felicia was deeply invested in the relationship.

Felicia explained that she had had a lifelong problem of being unable to express feelings of affection to men. This had often ruined her chances for relationships with young men. Whenever she cared about a man she became tongue-tied to the point of avoiding intimate conversations altogether. Because she was so quiet by nature, the men interpreted her reticence as indifference, and did not pursue the relationship. Felicia was devastated in these situations, but had never been able to make any progress with the problem. On the other hand, Felicia had many close female friends, and had no trouble communicating with them. The social worker perceived nothing in Felicia's appearance or manner that would repel men or women. She was bright, interesting, nice-looking, and communicated her feelings clearly.

The social worker asked Felicia if she had experienced any exceptions over the years to her inability to communicate with potential boyfriends. She could not think of any, but she described what she considered the source of her problem. Her father was a domineering, non-expressive individual who punished his two daughters for any displays of emotion. Felicia had learned to be more expressive with women through the example of her mother. The social worker appreciated Felicia's willingness to disclose this information, but stated that it would have limited relevance to their work together. Her current strengths and resources should be sufficient for her goal achievement.

Continuing on the theme of seeking exceptions, the social worker reminded Felicia that verbal communication was not the only way to express feelings to others, and asked if she was able to be effectively expressive in other ways. After thinking about it, Felicia responded that she was a pretty good writer. She could express herself well in writing because she was alone at those times, and could think carefully about what she wanted to say. In fact, she had kept a journal for several years. The social worker asked if Felicia ever sent letters or shared any of her writings with men. She had not done so, but the idea furthered her thinking about her strengths as a writer.

Felicia decided that she might be able to discuss her feelings with her boyfriend verbally if he learned in advance what they were. She could arrange this by first writing her boyfriend a letter in which she expressed what she wanted to say. She would end the letter by saying she wanted to keep their date on Friday to discuss what was in the letter. The social worker supported Felicia's plan and praised her creativity in formulating this strategy. They agreed to meet one week later to talk about the process. The social worker reminded Felicia that the letter may or may not help achieve her goal, and that she should not consider the plan a "sure thing." There might be other ways to tap Felicia's strengths to achieve her goal.

A week later Felicia reported that the letter had worked perfectly. She had felt comfortable writing the five-page document and only mildly anxious about putting it in the mailbox. Her boyfriend called her after reading the letter to say how much he appreciated it, and that he would be excited to see her the following day. The date went well, and their relationship was continuing. Felicia added that since the ice had been broken with her boyfriend it had become easier to share her feelings verbally.

This was an excellent outcome for that task, and what Felicia said next surprised the social worker. Feeling good about the incident with her boyfriend, she had decided to write a letter to her father as well, expressing anger at how he had treated her and her sister over the years, and asking that he talk with her about this in person. He had agreed, and Felicia spent an afternoon with him. Her father was quite upset by what Felicia had to say, but had responded with empathy. Felicia said she planned to continue talking about family issues with her dad. It seemed that within one week she had tapped into an existing personal strength to become an effective communicator.

The social worker gave Felicia the option of coming back a few more times so that they could monitor her progress, but she turned down the offer, saying she had achieved her goals. As part of the ending process, the social worker asked Felicia a series of questions to help her look ahead toward ways of sustaining her achievements. Felicia was asked how confident she felt about continuing with her strategy for improving her verbal expressiveness. The client responded that, because the strategy had been effective, she would continue to use it when she felt unable to communicate verbally. She also planned to regularly reflect in her journal on her capacity for clear communication with men and women.

The social worker next asked Felicia to consider any obstacles she might experience relative to her ongoing interpersonal success, and how she might manage them. Felicia quickly admitted that she was not sure how her "verbal confidence" would hold up during and after arguments with her boyfriend and her father. She planned to use letters in these instances because those had proven successful, and she would also consult more openly with her good friends about these concerns. Felicia also planned to read more books about relationships. She framed verbal communication as a skill requiring practice.

The social worker's final question was: "With the changes you are making, what will you tell me about yourself if I run into you on the street in six months?" Felicia would tell the social worker that she was continuing to work on her communication skills, had more male friends (besides a boyfriend), and was in regular contact with her parents. She would no longer be feeling inadequate in her relationships, and would be able to resolve disagreements with friends. The social worker congratulated Felicia on her success.

The Adolescent Mother

Brenda had first come to the attention of her school social worker two years ago. At that time she was a 15-year-old high school freshman who was frequently truant. Her social worker learned then that Brenda was also in trouble with the police for several misdemeanor violations, and was an occasional runaway. Her mother, Doris, a single 33-year-old who worked in computer programming, noted that Brenda would not follow minimal household rules, had parties when her mother was away, lacked a sense of personal responsibility, and spent her time with a "bad crowd." The whereabouts of Brenda's father were unknown. The social worker had limited success with engaging the young woman in a relationship, but her mother had been interested in working to resolve their problems. The social worker's involvement ended when Brenda began attending school more consistently.

At the time of this intervention, Brenda was the 17-year-old single mother of a newborn girl. Once pregnant, she again developed a truancy problem, and now she was also under the supervision of the county children's services agency. Brenda had lived at home through her pregnancy, but since the birth of the infant, Doris had become increasingly exasperated with her. Brenda loved her baby, but showed little consistent concern about meeting the child's basic needs. She expected her mother to take care of the baby while Brenda maintained a social life. Doris believed that Brenda was again in danger of getting into trouble with the law, although she wasn't sure how her daughter spent her time. Doris was so distressed about the situation that she lost her job due to absenteeism and poor performance, and she now survived on public assistance benefits. A member of the family's church who had observed the deteriorating home situation made the referral to the children's services agency.

Despite being concerned about the infant's welfare, Doris lacked the energy to provide complete care for her. Further, she had thrown Brenda and the infant out of the house four times in the past two months. She believed that mothers need to care for their young children, and she would not provide a setting in which Brenda could avoid responsibility for her own child. There was an extended family in the neighborhood, and Brenda and the baby stayed at the homes of her aunts, uncles, cousins, and friends for brief periods. Doris eventually allowed Brenda to return home, but the cycle continued. Some members of the church were pressuring Doris to keep Brenda at home until other suitable arrangements could be made.

Doris was willing to participate in the interventions offered by the school and children's services agency, but was less enthusiastic than before because of her depression and ongoing frustration with her daughter. Brenda showed minimal willingness to invest in any interventions. She relied on her circle of friends and relatives for most of her emotional and material support.

Brenda agreed to a family meeting only after the school threatened legal action for her not attending school. At the first meeting, the social worker spent much time empathizing with the perspectives of each client. She pointed out each person's strengths, including Doris's resilience as a single mother, her concern for her daughter and granddaughter, a solid work history and desire to work, and her good judgment about appropriate parenting. She added that Doris had good coping skills, but was perhaps trying to do too much, more than one person could reasonably manage. She seemed to be ignoring her own needs. In turn, the social worker noted that Brenda cared for her child, had good social skills, was healthy, a good learner, and welcomed some assistance in getting her life better organized. Brenda also seemed to have good judgment about her baby's needs when she was at home. The social worker shared her good feelings about the social network of the family, including their friends at church and in the neighborhood.

The social worker externalized the presenting problem by formulating a theme that two new elements had entered their lives: a new baby and "chaos." She framed the new baby as the exciting change, and chaos as the draining one. They all wanted to keep the baby, but needed to think of ways to use their resources to get rid of "chaos." When they discussed goals, the social worker asked Brenda how she might be of help in getting the other agencies "off her back," and improving how she and her mother "got along," which were Brenda's priorities. Doris's goals for Brenda were more extensive, focusing on her assuming more household and parenting responsibilities. Regarding her own goals, Doris wanted to work and have some leisure time on the weekends.

The social worker's request that Brenda and Doris "scale" their motivation to work on their issues resulted in moderate to high scores. The social worker concluded the assessment by asking Doris and Brenda what their lives would be like when a social worker was no longer required to be a part of it. Doris said that she would be working, always knowing where Brenda was, and having Brenda home for part of each day. Brenda said that she would not have to deal with agencies, not have to go to school, have a part-time job, and be able to see her friends several evenings per week. Brenda added that she would also be getting along better with her mother. The social worker did not ask the miracle question in this case, because the clients' answers to the above question already laid out many ideas for solution-oriented tasks. The social worker told Doris and Brenda that, after this and all subsequent sessions, she would ask them to identify a number of existing life situations in which they did not experience their presenting problems. These conversations helped them to focus on their capacities to interact without argument, Brenda organizing her time around childcare more carefully, and Doris taking time for herself.

During the third meeting, Brenda mentioned that she was interested in attending a vocational school in preparation for a job as an alternative to attending her high school. The client mentioned that she was interested in being a dental assistant, but wasn't sure if that was an attainable goal. Doris agreed to support this goal if Brenda would agree to continue spending all weekday evenings at home with the baby. The social worker offered to get information about vocational education in the area to share with the family. On another topic, Doris reflected on the possibility of her cousins and sisters helping with Brenda's transition to parenthood so that she could look for work more regularly. The social worker suggested that they might be willing to help if it could be done in a proactive rather than a reactive way. Doris agreed, and also said that they might also help connect her (Doris) with job opportunities. Among Doris's ideas for tasks was to seek out several friends and her pastor to solicit their guidance in initiating job searches and also some weekend social activities.

During the next several weeks, the clients attended to these and other tasks developed during the counseling sessions. The social worker asked the clients each week to perform a "surprise task"—something unexpected that would please the other person. The social worker's assessment was that the pair shared a positive bond beneath their anger, and that the surprise tasks might strengthen their bond. This strategy proved useful. As examples, Brenda served her mother breakfast in bed one day; Doris made Brenda a sweater.

The intervention ended after six meetings. Brenda was applying to vocational schools in the area and attending high school regularly. She was assuming some household tasks in return for her mother's blessing in seeing her friends. Her attention to parenting tasks was increasing. Doris was still not employed, but was interacting more with her friends and looking for work. Brenda was staying with relatives at times, but these visits, arranged in advance, did not include "chaos," and thus were welcomed. Both clients expressed satisfaction with their level of goal achievement.

EVIDENCE OF EFFECTIVENESS

Because solution-focused therapy is relatively new, its effectiveness has not been extensively researched. A number of experimental, quasi-experimental, single-subject, and pre-experimental designs, however, provide evidence of its utility with a variety of client populations at the individual, couple, family, and group levels.

In an Australian child and adolescent mental health clinic, practitioners experimented with a two-hour, single-session SFT intervention model (Perkins, 2006). The 216 5- to 15-year-olds were diagnosed with parent-child relational problems (26.6%), oppositional defiant disorder (17.9%), anxiety disorder (8.7%), ADHD (8.2%), adjustment disorders (8.2%), disruptive behavior disorder NOS (6.8%), and separation anxiety disorder (3.9%). The clients received SFT featuring assessment, family education, an examination of previously attempted problem solutions, and an array of new tasks and strategies. All outcome measures demonstrated a statistically and clinically significant improvement in clients four weeks after treatment compared to the control group (wait-list) condition. The researchers concluded that single-session SFT provided a prompt, minimal-dose, low-intrusion, client-centered assessment and intervention strategy that was effective for young clients and their families.

Data from one SFT private practitioner's 277 clients, analyzed by an outside researcher, indicated that clients presenting with mood disorders attended an average of 4.14 solution-focused therapy sessions, with 60.9% partially or mostly resolving their presenting problems (Reimer & Chatwin, 2006). Those clients who presented with relationship problems attended an average of 2.34 sessions with 76% partially or mostly resolving their presenting problems. While a limitation of this study is the use of one practitioner's caseload, the authors concluded that the results support the utility of SFT with these kinds of clients.

Gingerich & Eisengart (2000) conducted a major literature review of SFT outcome studies, reviewing all 15 controlled studies available at the time. The five "well-controlled" studies on depression, parent-child conflict, orthopedic injury rehabilitation, prison recidivism, and antisocial adolescent offenders all showed positive outcomes, with SFT being more effective than a comparative intervention or no intervention in four studies, and equal to a comparison intervention in the other study. The four "moderately controlled" studies, on counseling high school students with academic, personal, and social problems; groups for elementary and high school students; depression and oppositional behavior; and intervention with couples, included methodological limitations, but produced results consistent with the utility of SFT. The other six "poorly controlled" studies (on problem drinking, family environment with schizophrenia, parent-child conflict, child welfare, school-age children with behavioral problems, and depression/substance abuse) also reported positive results. The authors concluded that while the existing research supported the effectiveness of SFT, more high-quality research is necessary to establish this claim.

Three studies have focused on general adult outpatient populations, without specifying the nature of the presenting problems. In a pretest/posttest study of 83 clients treated with SFT at a university counseling center, 82% reported problem resolution, based on personalized scaling measures, with a mean number of 5.6 sessions (excluding dropouts) (Beyebach, Sanchez, de Miguel, de Vega, Hernandez, et al., 2000). A one-year follow-up of 36 mental health agency clients at another site revealed sustained positive outcomes for 64% of participants (Macdonald, 1997). Researchers in another outpatient setting reported that 80% of 129 clients treated with solution-focused therapy reported between-session progress, which is a major goal of the model (Reuterlov, Lofgren, Nordstrom, Ternston, & Miller, 2000).

Interventions have been effective with couples and families in groups. A quasi-experimental study of a psychoeducational group for 12 HIV serodiscordant couples that included solution-focused therapy as part of a broader intervention package resulted in significantly less depression, less anxiety, and greater marital satisfaction among participants (Pomeroy, Green, & Van Lanningham, 2002). A single-subject design with multiple baseline measures for an SFT group of five couples experiencing marital problems reported that eight of the ten participants achieved greater marital satisfaction and various other individual goals (Nelson & Kelley, 2001). A quasi-experimental control group study of 23 couples who participated in a six-week SFT group focused on marital concerns found significant improvements in members' adjustments in a variety of problem areas, but not in their likelihood of divorce (Zimmerman, Prest, & Wetzel, 1997). An experimental study (pretest/posttest control group design) of a six-week SFT group for parents of adolescents ($N = 530$) found significant participant gains in parenting skills (Zimmerman, Jacobsen, MacIntyre, & Watson, 1996).

The following two studies included families seen outside of group modalities. A study of a ten-session family therapy intervention (including 45 families randomly assigned to three treatment groups) demonstrated the effectiveness of solution-focused therapy's "formula first-session task" in subsequent measures of family compliance, clarity of treatment goals, and resolution of presenting problems (Adams, Piercy, & Jurich, 1991). There were no differences among the groups after the intervention, however, on family outcome or optimism. Another experimental study of 22 clients with schizophrenia and their families, which included solution-focused interventions provided in five sessions over a ten-week period, reported significant differences between groups on measures of expressiveness, active-recreational orientation, moral-religious emphasis, and family congruence (Eakes, Walsh, Markowski, & Cain, 1997).

Several studies have focused on children and adolescents. Using a single-subject design, one group of researchers found that 5 to 10 sessions of solution-focused intervention with seven children aged 10 to 13 with learning disabilities and classroom behavior problems were effective in resolving their major behavior problems (Franklin, Biever, Moore, Clemons, & Scamardo, 2001). A larger pre-test/posttest study of 136 children (aged 5 to 17 years) referred from a school system due to behavioral problems indicated that solution-focused interventions produced improvements in learning, appropriate levels of activity, and self-image (Corcoran & Stephenson, 2000). Results were mixed with regard to the clients' conduct problems.

Two studies have been done with youths in protective settings. An experimental study of 21 offenders in a detention center demonstrated that ten sessions of individual solution-focused intervention resulted in a lessening of clients' chemical abuse and antisocial tendencies, and increases in their levels of empathy, appropriate guilt, and problem-solving abilities (Seagram, 1998). SFT was introduced in a residential center for 39 youths aged 7 to 18 years with mental and emotional impairments, and those receiving the interventions demonstrated increases in adaptive behaviors and a decrease in maladaptive behaviors (Gensterblum, 2002).

Interesting results have also been found in studies of various special populations. Pre- and posttest data were collected on 74 older adults, aged 65 to 89 years, who received solution-focused outpatient mental health services for problems including depression, anxiety, marital distress, and stress related to chronic illness. The compiled results showed significant improvements among clients with regard to their self-ratings and global assessment of functioning scores (Dahl, Bathel, & Carreon, 2000). A seven-stage crisis-intervention model that included SFT was effective in working with three substance-dependent individuals in another setting (Yeager & Gregoire, 2000). A pretest/posttest control group study of 52 mental health agency clients with depression indicated that the experimental clients acquired significantly greater levels of hope, but there were no differences between groups in depression inventory scores (Bozeman, 2000). In an orthopedic work adjustment program for adolescents, 48 clients were divided into two groups, one of which was provided with solution-focused interventions. Client in both groups demonstrated an enhanced adjustment to their condition (Cockburn, Thomas, & Cockburn, 1997).

As noted earlier, additional research is required to fully test the effectiveness of solution-focused therapy with various types of clients, but existing research does support its utility.

CRITICISMS OF THE THERAPY

The major criticisms of solution-focused therapy imply that the practice is superficial, denying clients the opportunity to explore their presenting problems and related emotions in greater depth (Lipchik, 2002). For example, its encouragement of clients to "think positively" may induce a client's denial or minimization of problems. Clients who perceive the social worker's de-emphasis of problems may feel discouraged from sharing important information or negative feelings about the presenting issue. Some clients may also feel strongly about working on problems in ways that are not compatible with SFT (such as exploring their family backgrounds and developing insight). Of course, proponents of SFT always encourage clients to consider alternative perspectives about human behavior and the nature of change. Finally, some critics have concerns that the principles of the approach may create a false impression in beginning practitioners that intervention is "easier" than in fact it may be.

Many practitioners who do not subscribe to the SFT model nevertheless see value in adopting some of its principles, suggesting that they can be incorporated into, and not necessarily exist apart from, other modalities. Principles from solution-focused therapy can prompt the social worker to reconsider the time spent discussing the client's past, present, and future; encourage the use of scaling techniques when "stuck" in problem exploration; attend to the client's coping strategies as a corrective against a problem bias; and be careful not to foster client dependency.

SUMMARY

Solution-focused therapy is a practice model that has steadily grown in popularity since the 1980s. Its principles derive from the crisis, cognitive, systems, and communications theories, as well as those of short-term practice. Much work is being done at present to test the effectiveness of SFT; in the future, its major concepts may become more fully refined, and its range of applications more clearly articulated. Solution-focused therapy seems ideally suited to the current economics of direct practice as one of a handful of approaches that are task focused and use short-term methods. Although SFT is an effective intervention model for many types of clients, the social worker using it must also possess the knowledge and skills to be able to connect with clients, assess their motivation, streamline goals that are appropriate to the presenting situation, and apply sound clinical judgment in bringing about lasting solutions.

TOPICS FOR DISCUSSION

1. Solution-focused practitioners believe that a client's solutions need not be directly tied to his or her problems. Do you agree? Are interventions that are tied to specific presenting problems more likely to be effective?

2. When externalizing a problem, does a social worker risk helping a client avoid taking responsibility for it?

3. How does the SFT skill of "not knowing" fit with the notion that social workers should have expertise in understanding the nature of problems and how they develop?

4. Why is there such an emphasis on "giving compliments" in SFT? Present three "new" compliments that you could have "genuinely" given to a client on your caseload prior to learning about SFT. Would these have enhanced your intervention?

5. Discuss various strategies that a practitioner might use to help clients find (a) exceptions to their presenting problems, and (b) solutions that are based on continuing certain behaviors. Use types of clients of interest to you and your classmates as examples.

IDEAS FOR CLASSROOM ACTIVITIES/ROLE-PLAYS

1. Students should pair off, with one playing a social worker, and the other portraying a client. Each "client" should be assigned a different presenting problem. After the social worker clearly ascertains the nature of the problem, he or she asks the "miracle question," and helps the client concretize the response as much as possible. After the role-play, students can share what was helpful in completing the task, and what goals the client articulated as a result.

2. Describe how SFT might be used with a ten-year-old child (boy or girl) who refuses to attend school (fourth grade) because she is worried about her newly divorced single mother, who stays home to care for a younger (two-year-old) child.

3. Using any type of client and presenting problem, ask students to role-play a termination session in which the client is feeling uncertain about his or her chances of avoiding a problem recurrence. The social worker should use future-oriented questions to help the client resolve the uncertainty.

APPENDIX: Solution-focused Therapy Outline

Focus	A short-term approach to intervention that focuses on solutions or exceptions to problems rather than problems themselves
Major Proponents	Berg, Corcoran, de Shazer, Lipchik, O'Hanlon, Weiner-Davis
Origins and Social Context	Developments in brief therapy
	Crisis theory
	Systems theory in social work
	Communications theory (the uses of language)
	A rise in the strengths perspectives
	Social constructivism
Nature of the Individual	People create meaning out of their experiences
	People want to change
	People are suggestible
	People have sufficient resources to solve their problems
Structural Concepts	The power of language in shaping one's reality
	A de-emphasis on problem talk (what has happened and why)
	An emphasis on solution talk (what can happen)
Developmental Concepts	None
Nature of Problems	Problems result from cycles of behavior that have been reinforced
	People are constrained by narrow, pessimistic views of problems
	There is no "right" way to view any problem or solution
	Problems are not so ubiquitous as assumed
	Problems can be resolved without understanding causes
	Problems do not serve a function in a system
	Rigid beliefs and attitudes prevent people from noticing new information
Nature of Change	Change is constant
	Change occurs by reinterpreting situations and filling information gaps
	Change may be behavioral or perceptual
	There is no distinction between symptomatic and structural change
	Change is subject to the self-fulfilling prophecy (what one expects is what one gets)

APPENDIX: Solution-focused Therapy Outline (Continued)

	Small change can snowball
	Rapid change is possible
Goals of Intervention	Focus on solutions to problems
	Help clients to act or think differently than they usually do
	Highlight client strengths and resources
	Recognize when a problem is not happening
Nature of Worker/Client Relationship	Social worker is a collaborator
	Clients define goals; the social worker helps clients select goals and strategies that are achievable
	Worker affirms clients' rights to their perspectives on problems and solutions
	Worker communicates the possibility of change
Intervention Principles	Normalize problems
	Compliment (focus on positives)
	Offer alternative perspectives on typical patterns of thinking, feeling, and behaving
	Externalize the problem (reframe)
	Gives the client a greater sense of control
	Promotes teamwork
	"Relative influence" scales
	Establish the worth of challenging the problem (to enhance motivation)
	The miracle question
	Task interventions—to do more of what the client is doing when the problem is not happening
	Encourage the client to think and behave differently
	Complaint patterns
	Context patterns
	The "surprise task"
	The formula first-session task
	Suggest easier alternatives to prior solution attempts
	Predict setbacks
Assessment Questions (May be used as interventions)	How has the client tried to manage his or her concerns thus far?
	What are the client's overall survival strategies?
	How much, or how often, has the client been able to stand up to, or not be dominated by, the problem?

APPENDIX: Solution-focused Therapy Outline (Continued)

How will the client know when the problem
has resolved?

What was different in the past when the problem
did not exist?

What is the client doing when the symptom
isn't happening?

What does the client want to continue to happen?

What has changed since the client scheduled the
first appointment?

11

Motivational Interviewing

JOSEPH WALSH AND JACQUELINE CORCORAN

> Somewhat, to hope for,
> Be it ne'er so far
> Is Capital against Despair –
>
> Somewhat, to suffer,
> Be it ne'er so keen –
> If terminable, may be borne*

*M*otivational interviewing is a client-centered, directive method for enhancing motivation to change by exploring and resolving the client's ambivalence (Miller & Rollnick, 2002). Like the interpersonal and solution-focused therapies discussed earlier, motivational interviewing does not represent a particular theoretical perspective, but uses concepts from a variety of theories. It has become quite popular in the past 25 years as a means of engaging clients who are either reluctant or unmotivated to address problems that are considered serious by significant others, if not by the clients themselves. These types of clients have presented clinical practitioners with special challenges for generations (e.g., Rooney, 1992). Initially developed for the treatment of substance abuse, motivational interviewing is now being applied to other types of problems, such as eating disorders, behavioral problems of adolescence, general health care issues, physical exercise, cigarette smoking, diabetes, HIV high-risk behavior, medication adherence, family preservation, sex offenses, and pain management. Typically a brief intervention (four sessions or less), motivational interviewing has been employed

---

*Reprinted by permission of the publishers and the Trustees of Amherst College from *The Poems of Emily Dickinson*, Thomas H. Johnson, ed., Cambridge, Mass.: The Belknap Press of Harvard University Press, Copyright © 1951, 1955, 1979, 1983 by the President and Fellows of Harvard College.

both as a stand-alone treatment and as an initial step toward engaging clients in other intervention approaches (Walitzer, Dermen, & Conners, 1999).

ORIGINS AND SOCIAL CONTEXT

Motivational interviewing was developed by William Miller and his colleagues in response to the frustrations experienced by substance abuse practitioners who could not motivate many of their clients to change or to see the seriousness of their problems (Miller & Rollnick, 2002). At that time (the 1980s), intervention in the field tended to be highly confrontational. Practitioners relied on a medical model for problem formulation and took authoritative stances, arguing that the client had a problem and needed to change, offering direct advice, and using punitive measures for noncompliance. Confrontation was said to be necessary to break through the clients' denial, which is pervasive in substance abuse. Even so, many clients did not benefit from these interventions.

Collaboration, rather than confrontation, became a hallmark of motivational interviewing. Indeed, within this model, confrontation is viewed as a tactic that only escalates client resistance. Motivational interviewing "sidesteps" denial, and instead emphasizes listening reflectively to clients' concerns, and selectively emphasizing "change talk." Motivational interviewing also contrasts with the principles of Alcoholics Anonymous (AA), a dominant treatment paradigm, which demands that people label themselves as alcoholic, and admit their powerlessness over alcohol. Motivational interviewing downplays the use of labels in general. It stresses more of a non-hierarchical collaboration between the client and practitioner, as well as the development of self-efficacy, so the client can develop confidence that he or she is able to change.

One prominent social worker who has written about motivational interviewing is Jacqueline Corcoran (2005) who, in response to a perceived lack of strengths-based practice models in the profession, developed an intervention model incorporating solution-focused therapy, motivational interviewing, and cognitive-behavioral therapy. Other elements of the origin and context of motivational interviewing will be evident in the description of its major concepts.

MAJOR CONCEPTS

The principles of motivational interviewing are drawn from Miller's personal style of counseling (Draycott & Dabbs, 1998), Rogerian therapy (1951), the theory of cognitive dissonance (Festinger, 1962), and the Transtheoretical Stages of Change model (Martino, Carroll, Kostas, Perkins, & Rounsaville, 2002). Although both Rogerian therapy and motivational interviewing are client-centered approaches that rely on the worker's use of empathy, there are key differences between the two. Unlike Rogerian therapy, which is non-directive and employs empathy throughout the process, motivational interviewing seeks to enhance the client's motivation to change, and uses empathy in a selective way to achieve this goal (Miller & Rollnick, 1991). Rogerian therapy explores the client's feelings and conflicts "in the moment," while motivational interviewing creates and amplifies the client's experience of dissonance so that motivation for change is tapped.

Cognitive dissonance is a theory maintaining that a person is not capable of holding two incompatible beliefs at one time. When we are presented with environmental input that contradicts a firmly held belief, we need to somehow reconcile that discrepancy in order to avoid anxiety. For example, the pedophile who cannot resist the urge to fondle a young child, but who also believes that children should never be victimized, may resolve this dissonance by deciding that the particular child "needs love." This process usually occurs outside of the person's awareness, although an "objective" outsider (such as a clinical practitioner) may be able to identify it. Ambivalence can be understood as a mild form of cognitive dissonance, in that we are unable to choose between two beliefs or goals that are in contrast to one another. Many clients with mental illnesses want to get jobs, but they also want to avoid the work-related stress that might exacerbate their symptoms. In motivational interviewing, the practitioner helps the client to resolve this ambivalence, hopefully in a direction that strengthens the client's desire to change (for example, to get a certain kind of job). If this goal becomes a dominant cognition, other thoughts and behaviors will be more easily brought into compliance with it.

Another major influence on motivational interviewing is the Transtheoretical Stages of Change (TSOC) model, developed to recognize and address the reluctance of many people with substance use disorders to change their behaviors (Connors, Donovan, & DiClemente, 2001; Prochaska & Norcross, 1994). In this model, the following six stages of change have been formulated:

- Precontemplation—The alcohol-dependent (for example) person does not believe he or she has a problem and is unwilling to change.

- Contemplation—The person is contemplating change, seeing that there are significant benefits to be gained by stopping alcohol use, even as he or she continues to drink.

- Preparation—The person is poised to change within the next month, and works on a strategy to do so.

- Action—The person begins to take action (for example, attending AA meetings).

- Maintenance—Sustained change has occurred for six months.

- Relapse—In the event that the person slips back into old behaviors, the steps are revisited.

The Stages of Change model may seem simple, but as a guide to approaching intervention it has advanced the process of treating substance abuse remarkably. One attractive feature of the model is that intervention techniques from different theoretical orientations can be used when addressing the final four stages of change.

Within the TSOC model, motivational interviewing is designed to work with those who are either in precontemplation, denying that change is needed, or those in contemplation, who believe there might be a problem, but are only considering change. The clinical perspective in motivational interviewing can be summarized as follows:

- Motivation to change is elicited from the client, not imposed from the outside.
- A client's motivation for enacting change relative to some problem behavior is often impeded by ambivalence.
- It is the client's task to articulate and resolve his or her ambivalence.
- Readiness to change is a product of interpersonal interaction.
- Direct persuasion is not an effective method for resolving ambivalence.
- Practitioner directives are useful, however, in examining ambivalence.

Although the major concepts of motivational interviewing (motivation, ambivalence, and stages of change) have been described, several merit additional discussion. The first is ambivalence toward change, which is viewed as a natural process in many people (Killick & Allen, 1997). Few decisions that we make, major and minor, are completely free of conflicted thoughts. We might experience agonizing ambivalence when deciding whether to accept a particular job offer, but this sense of uncertainty may also be present as we decide whether to accept an invitation to a party with people we don't know well. Motivational interviewing works with the ambivalence of the client, in that the advantages and disadvantages of the problem behavior, as well as the advantages and disadvantages of changing, are openly considered. In this process, the social worker selectively reflects and affirms change talk, and asks the client to elaborate on statements about change. The social worker seeks to create dissonance between a person's values and goals (in terms of health, future well-being, success, and family relationships) and the problem behavior, so that the desire to change is bolstered. Another major focus of motivational interviewing involves a client's confidence that he or she can succeed at change efforts. The practitioner assesses not only a client's willingness to change, but also the confidence that he or she can make changes if desired (Miller & Rollnick, 2002).

THE NATURE OF PROBLEMS AND CHANGE

Motivational interviewing does not incorporate unique ideas about how problems develop. Because the approach does not emphasize unconscious mental processes, however, its ideas about the nature of problems are consistent with those of the cognitive, behavioral, and solution-focused theories. Attention is focused on how change occurs. The prevalent reason why change happens is that the client perceives that the disadvantages of a problem behavior outweigh its advantages and, simultaneously, that the advantages of changing behavior outweigh the disadvantages. The person whose wife complains about his smoking marijuana every weekend may decide that his marriage is more valuable than his need to relieve his stress in that particular way. Interviewing techniques employ practitioner empathy in a strategic manner so that motivation to change is enhanced. Also critical to change is that clients build a sense of self-efficacy so that they will believe they have the resources to carry out a change effort. The above client may need to be shown that there are other ways to effectively manage his anxiety. This self-efficacy is encouraged by an emphasis on client strengths.

In motivational interviewing, the initial intervention goal is to build clients' motivation when they are not willing to change, rather than focusing on actual behavior change. A client's perception of the (alleged) problem is thus the focus of the early part of the social worker's contacts. As the work moves into the action stage of the TSOC model, actual client behavior becomes a target for intervention (Treasure & Ward, 1997). At this point the practitioner may utilize interventions based on any theoretical perspective. Corcoran's (2005) model was described earlier, and Fassler (2008) has developed a practice model combining motivational interviewing and task-centered practice.

ASSESSMENT AND INTERVENTION

The Social Worker/Client Relationship

Motivation is not a stable, internal quality of an individual, but is affected by the interaction between the practitioner and the client (Killick & Allen, 1997). The context of the helping relationship is therefore emphasized. The social worker initially seeks to understand the client's frame of reference about the presenting issue with reflective listening. He or she affirms the validity of the client's perspective and the client's freedom of choice in dealing with the situation. The practitioner then elicits and selectively reinforces the client's own self-motivational statements about the problem issue. The motivational interviewer seeks to engage clients at their current place in the stages of change model to build their motivation, and to enlarge upon the concerns and strengths they demonstrate. Given this emphasis, client resistance is an invalid concept. A more appropriate term is client *reactance*, which is intended to describe a client's normal, expectable reactions to uncertainties about the purposes of the client/worker interaction (Hepworth, Rooney, Rooney, Strom-Gottfried, & Larsen, 2005). The presence of reactance is a problem for the practitioner rather than the client, signifying that the practitioner needs to adjust change strategies to match the client's position toward change. The responsibility for how behavior change occurs is left to the client.

Assessment

The developers of motivational interviewing have not delineated formal procedures for client assessment. In fact, some adherents state that it is possible to offer motivational interviewing without a formal assessment at all (Agostinelli, Brown, & Miller, 1995). This is not an oversight, but a reflection of the nature of the approach, which does not make a clear distinction between assessment and intervention. It is important to emphasize, however, that when the social worker becomes aware of a client's reason for referral, he or she should not presume that the client will wish to address that issue during the initial meeting. The practitioner should allow the client to choose topics for exploration. This principle should be evident in the intervention approaches described below.

Intervention

Four intervention principles underlie motivational interviewing, including *expressing empathy, developing a discrepancy between goals and behaviors, rolling with resistance,* and *supporting self-efficacy* (Miller & Rollnick, 2002; Killick & Allen, 1997; Treasure & Ward, 1997). The following guidelines help the practitioner to enact these principles.

- Begin where the client is. The social worker should not assume that the client is ready to engage in change. Neither should the social worker conclude that the client is "totally resistant."

- Explore clients' problem behaviors, and reflect clients' perceptions. The social worker listens with empathy to clients' concerns. In this way, the social worker can more accurately assess the person's relationship to the process of change.

- Reinforce client statements about wanting to change. The social worker attends selectively to client expressions about change. Here, strategic interviewing is interwoven with the practice of empathy. The social worker also seeks to point out discrepancies between the client's values and goals, such as long-term health, and how the problem stands in the way. Advice and feedback are postponed until sufficient motivation to change has been built.

- Affirm clients' statements about their ability to change. In this way, confidence is built, and the individual feels empowered to take the first steps toward change.

Specific techniques of motivational interviewing *include eliciting self-motivational statements, strategies to handle resistance, the decisional balance,* and *building self-efficacy* (Miller & Rollnick, 1991).

Eliciting Self-Motivational Statements   Self-motivational statements are statements made by clients that indicate a desire to bring about a change. They emerge from the client's decision to change, but also his or her sense of competence, confidence, and awareness of resources that will support change efforts. The social worker elicits self-motivational statements by posing a series of questions that the client might answer in a way that favors change. The conversation will lead into exploring the disadvantages of the status quo situation through:

- Problem-recognition questions. "What things make you think that this is a problem? In what ways do you think you or other people have been harmed?"

- Concern questions. "What worries you about your behavior? What can you imagine happening to you? What do you think will happen if you don't make a change?"
- Questions about extremes. "What concerns you the most about this in the long run? How much do you know about what can happen if you continue with this behavior, even if you don't see this happening to you?"

Other types of questions encourage the client to explore the advantages of changing. These questions involve:

- Intention to change. "The fact that you're here indicates that at least a part of you thinks it's time to do something. What are the reasons you see for making a change? What would you like your life to be like five years from now?"
- Optimism about change. "What makes you think that, if you decided to make a change, you could do it? What do you think would work for you, if you decided to change? When else in your life have you made a significant change like this? How did you do it? What personal strengths do you have that will help you succeed? Who could offer you support in making this change?"
- Questions about extremes. "What might be the best results you could imagine if you make a change? If you were completely successful in making the changes you want, how would things be different?"

These types of questions provoke the individual to consider change by examining and contrasting views of the future (both with and without the problem), the functions the behavior serves, and its harmful consequences. The social worker then asks the client to elaborate further on his or her comments that favor change. Still, the motivational interviewer is encouraged to use questions sparingly, selecting a few that will begin the conversation about change, and then move on to statements that require the client to elaborate further on statements that affirm and reinforce a client's consideration of change.

Handling "Resistance" (or Reactance)   As discussed earlier, signs of "resistance," such as the client's arguing, interrupting, denying, and ignoring certain issues, alert the social worker to the need to switch intervention strategies. In general, the new strategies should involve reflective responses that diffuse potential power struggles and mobilize the side of the client's ambivalence that is geared toward change (Moyers & Rollnick, 2002). Strategies include *simple reflection, amplified reflection, double-sided reflection, shifting focus, agreement with a twist, reframing, clarifying free choice,* and *using paradox*. Each of these is summarized below.

   Simple reflection is acknowledging a client's feeling, thought, or opinion so that the client continues to explore the presenting problem rather than become defensive ("You have a lot of stress going on in your life right now. Do you think this may not be the best time to change your behavior?"). The client, given the freedom to decide where to go with the topic, might respond, "I don't know. Maybe it's not a good time, but I'm not sure." (Carroll, 1998).

Amplified reflection goes beyond simple reflection in that the client's statement is acknowledged, but in an extreme fashion. The purpose of such a statement is to bring out the side of the client that wants to change. An amplified reflection, such as the statement, "You say that you're fine the way you are, so maybe there is nothing that you should change," typically has the effect of getting the client to back down from an entrenched position and allow for the possibility of negotiation about change. This strategy is similar to that of paradoxical intention. Paradox involves siding with the client's defensiveness, which then causes the client to take the other side of the argument for change ("You've convinced me that you're not ready to do anything about this issue right now. It's not the right time for you."). Sometimes, clients who have been entrenched in a negative position regarding change will start to argue from the other side of their ambivalence, the part that wants to change, when the practitioner joins with their position. (For example, "Well, I don't want to say there's nothing I can do to make my life better.")

Double-sided reflection taps into both aspects of the client's ambivalence. It acknowledges that when people are exploring the possibility of change, they are divided between wanting to change and wanting to hold onto the behavior that has become problematic (Carroll, 1998). Examples of this kind of comment are: "You're not sure your drinking is a big deal, yet your girlfriend left you because of how you acted when you were drinking, and you're really upset she's gone," and "Your relationship was very important to you, and your alcohol use caused problems in the relationship." Double-sided reflection can pull the client's attention to the inconsistency between the problem behavior and his or her goals and values.

Shifting focus is when the social worker moves the client's attention from a potential impasse to avoid becoming polarized from the client's position. When the client begins to argue against what the practitioner might feel is the best course of action, the practitioner should immediately shift his or her position, and redirect the focus ("I think you're jumping ahead here. We're not talking at this point about you quitting drinking for the rest of your life. Let's talk some more about what the best goal is for you right now, and how to go about making it happen."). A guideline for shifting focus is to first defuse the initial concern, and then direct attention to a more workable issue.

Agreement with a twist involves agreeing with some of the client's message, but in a way that orients the client in a change direction ("I agree there's no need for you to say you're an alcoholic. I am hearing that there are certain aspects of drinking that you enjoy, and that it's also causing you some problems.").

Reframing, a concept described in several other chapters of this book, involves taking arguments that clients use against change and altering the meaning of the information to instead promote change. A common example involves the tendency of drinkers to consume large quantities without experiencing ill effects and loss of control. This tendency is sometimes used as an excuse for why the drinking is not a problem. This excuse can be reframed by the social worker as tolerance of alcohol, which is actually symptomatic of problem drinking

("You're right, you don't notice any effects from the alcohol. But that's because you've been drinking so long your body is used to it. The alcohol is affecting your body but not your mind.")

Clarifying free choice involves communicating to the client that it is up to him or her to make a change, rather than getting embroiled in a debate about what the client should or must do ("You can decide to take this on now or wait until another time."). This is a useful intervention because when people perceive that their freedom of choice is being threatened, they tend to react by asserting their liberty. A good antidote for this reaction is to assure the client that in the end it is he or she who determines what happens.

Decisional Balance   A decisional balance is another motivational technique that involves weighing the costs and benefits of the client's problem behavior, and the costs and benefits of change. The advantages and disadvantages of change are a continual focus of motivational interviewing, but in this intervention they are gathered together more formally in a "balance sheet." The client can perceive the root of the problem in a visual and concrete way and the aspects of it that are pushing him or her to make the change. This intervention is similar to the "cost/benefit" strategy used in cognitive therapy.

Supporting Self-Efficacy and Developing a Change Plan Techniques involved in building self-efficacy, with examples that illustrate the technique, include:

- Evocative questions. "How might you go about making this change? What would be a good first step? What obstacles do you foresee, and how might you deal with them?"

- Ruler assessment. "How confident are you that you could stop your purging behavior? On a scale from 0 to 10, where 0 is not at all confident and 10 is extremely confident, where would you say you are? Why are you at 2 and not 0? What would it take for you to go from 2 to [a higher number]?"

- Reviewing past successes. "When in your life have you made up your mind to do something challenging, and did it? It might be something new you learned, or a habit that you quit, or some other significant change that you made. When have you done something like that? What did you do that worked?"

- Discussing personal strengths and supports. "What is there about you, what strong points do you have, that could help you succeed in making this change? What sources of social support do you have? Are there others you could call on for support?"

- Asking questions about hypothetical change. "Suppose you did succeed in stopping your drug use, and are looking back on how that happened. What most likely is it that worked? How did it happen? Suppose that this one big obstacle weren't there. If that obstacle were removed, then how might you go about making this change?"

- Brainstorming. This involves freely generating as many ideas as possible for how a change might be accomplished, and as a result perceiving one or two ideas that might work.

- Giving information and advice. Social workers should be reluctant to give advice to clients, because doing so takes responsibility for behavior away from the client. Whenever advice is given, it should be done reluctantly, tentatively, and on matters that are not likely to have negative consequences. For example, if a client had success with maintaining sobriety in the past because of involvement with Alcoholics Anonymous, but relapsed after terminating that involvement, a social worker may suggest that the client consider resuming that program as one part of his or her desire to resume sobriety.

These interventions may result in a person's readiness to negotiate a change plan in which goals are set, options for change are considered, a plan is formulated, and a commitment is made to the plan. Notice that several of these techniques are consistent with some principles of behavior theory, cognitive theory, and ego psychology.

SPIRITUALITY IN MOTIVATIONAL INTERVIEWING

Motivational interviewing is client-centered, focused on helping clients resolve ambivalence about their goals. It is quite possible that clients will raise issues of spirituality as they struggle with difficult life decisions. The questions used with motivational interviewing are consistent with a spiritual focus, as the social worker may ask about clients' life goals and what is most important and meaningful to them. Like solution-focused therapy, however, motivational interviewing does not assume any particular spiritual aspects of human nature. To the extent that issues of meaning are motivating for, or enhance the ambivalence of, a client, the social worker should ask questions about them, just as he or she would any other topic, to help the client expand on his or her thinking. For example, if a substance abuser wants to stop getting drunk because doing so "goes against my values as a parent—I'm supposed to be with my family on the weekends, and take my children to temple," the social worker should help the client reflect on this value as a basis for deciding to change the drinking behavior. On the other hand, the social worker should not raise the possibility of spirituality as a motivating force; this must be left to the client.

ATTENTION TO SOCIAL JUSTICE ISSUES

Motivational interviewing works primarily at the individual level of change, but can encompass a broad range of client concerns. Social workers should always be alert to macro issues that might be noted by the client as factors affecting motivation and self-efficacy. At the same time, motivational interviewing is respectful

of people's ability to make choices that are right for them. Clients are often ambivalent about initiating change efforts that involve confronting other people or
systems they perceive to be more powerful than they are. For example, an employee may be considering bringing charges of discriminatory practice against an
employer, but fears that such an effort will result in failure or long-term retribu-
tion. The social worker can certainly use motivational interviewing questions to
help the client resolve this dilemma. Of course, it must be left to the client to
decide whether to proceed and, if so, how a change plan can be developed. That
is, methods of change that might involve fighting against an oppressive force are not
suggested to the client in a predetermined way. The social worker assumes that
there may be some good reasons for the client to maintain the problem behavior,
and instills hope in the client's ability, if change is warranted, to design a change
plan that incorporates his or her best interests and unique strengths.

CASE ILLUSTRATIONS

Two cases are presented below, one about a client with a substance abuse problem, and the other featuring an adolescent girl with behavior problems. They
demonstrate how motivational interviewing can be used with different types of
clinical issues.

The Man at the Medical Shelter

Philippe was a 50-year-old Argentinean male recently admitted to a Virginia
hospital due to liver failure from a history of alcohol and drug abuse. He was
hospitalized after discharging himself from a medical shelter before the staff there
felt he was ready to leave. Philippe no longer had a place to live because he had
lost his apartment six months previously.

The client, born in Argentina, had lived in the United States for 30 years
and was an American citizen. He had attended college briefly. His family of origin lived in New York State. Philippe's wife was deceased, and his two children,
who lived in Tennessee, were not on speaking terms with him.

The medical shelter would not allow Philippe to return. The social worker's
role now was to help him find a place to stay where staff would also take care of
his medical needs. Rather than being focused on her agenda, though, the social
worker started the interview on more tentative terms, inviting the client to share
his concerns. For example, after introducing herself, the social worker stated,
"My job is to talk with you about how you're doing right now, and to help
you figure out where you can go after you're discharged, so that you can continue to recover. You've been through surgery, and that takes some time and
rest to get over. But that might not be what's on your mind right now, so we
can also talk about what concerns you most at the moment." This opening statement initiated a collaborative process in which the client had an equal say in
what was discussed.

In this case, the priority for the client was his physical pain. Philippe alluded to the fact that he had a "nasty" scar, and he even showed it to the worker. The social worker did some simple reflection about the way he felt physically, to which Philippe responded by sharing details about his emotional state: "I just can't believe I let my life get like this, and I have no one, and I have nothing." The social worker, at this point, responded with the simple reflection, "You're feeling lonely and sad because of all you have lost from alcohol," which encouraged Philippe to explore the losses he had sustained from alcohol use. Among other statements, Philippe said he had no one to stay with, and his family wanted him "to get better here first" before he went to them. The social worker responded with another simple reflection: "You seem to understand why they're taking this position." With this, Philippe centered on the damage that had been caused to his family relationships from his alcohol abuse. He said, "Where I come from, family is everything."

The social worker followed with an exploration of the discrepancy between his values—the importance of family—and his alcohol use: "Family is everything to you, and you have alienated a lot of your family members with your alcohol use." The social worker discovered in the ensuing discussion that Philippe was feeling particularly alone since he had made the choice six months ago to no longer associate with people who used drugs. The social worker complimented him on his ability to take such a bold step to beat his addiction.

At this point, Philippe said he "wasn't doing so good," admitting that he had left the shelter to "have a beer." The rule at the shelter was abstinence from alcohol and drugs; as a result, he had not been allowed to return. His physical condition had deteriorated, and he had returned to the emergency room. The social worker reflected, "You have taken some steps to beat the alcohol—you have stopped hanging around some people you used with—and you found it hard to resist drinking when you were at the shelter." He said he had done a good job in stopping his drug use, but alcohol was still hard for him. She asked what might happen if he continued on the path he was on now. He said he would probably die soon, which he adamantly did not want to do before he was able to reconcile with his family. He concluded that he would have to make a change to get this to happen.

The social worker mentioned another medical shelter in the city, but the rules were even stricter against substance use than the first shelter he had stayed in. Philippe said he thought he "could do it this time." The social worker asked, "What makes you think you can make a change right now?" Philippe responded that he didn't want to keep on the way he had; he couldn't keep cycling in and out of the hospital; otherwise, he would never get better.

She asked him if he had thought about a plan. He said he would do what he had done for drugs; he would stay away from people who drank and places that sold alcohol. He said praying helped, although he didn't like AA—he had been made to go before, and preferred his own Catholic God, rather than a "higher power." He admitted he wasn't sure how long he could go without drinking, that maybe after he was better physically, he might think about treatment. He had been mandated to do so; this time, he would go because he wanted to.

To summarize the social worker's method of interviewing, she used a collaborative approach, reflecting Philippe's statements and getting him to argue for his own change, rather than confronting him about possible alcohol use and telling him what he must do. This allowed Philippe to open up slowly rather than remain guarded and defensive. As he revealed more, she elaborated on the discrepancy between his desire to reconcile with his family and the impossibility of this if he was still drinking. She worked toward building his self-efficacy by complimenting him on his ability to quit drugs and stay away from people who used. Rather than lecturing him about how to stay sober, she asked him for his own plan. She allowed him to take some referrals for treatment in the future, knowing that it would be his choice whether to follow through with such a plan.

The School Brawler

This intervention took place in a school setting where the social worker saw a 12-year-old African-American girl named Bettina who had been in trouble for frequent fighting. Following a few minutes of introductions the social worker began with setting a brief agenda: "Bettina, you've been sent to me to talk about some problems at school and what we can do about those, but we can also talk about whatever else you think is important." In this way, the social worker directed the focus of the meeting, but allowed for flexibility so that any or all of the client's concerns could be given attention. Still, Bettina chose to focus on the presenting problem.

The social worker listened with empathy as she tried to elicit statements about change from the client. She asked Bettina, "What are some of the good things about fighting?" and "What are some of the not-so-good things about fighting?" Like many clients, Bettina was surprised at the former line of questioning. The social worker explained, "There must be some good things about it, otherwise you wouldn't keep doing it, right?"

As Bettina responded, the social worker probed for more information and selectively reinforced the client's statements about change. On why she liked to fight, Bettina said that it made her feel proud when she won. It also ensured that her peers "respected" her. On the other hand, Bettina said she didn't want to get expelled from school or end up in juvenile hall. She was also afraid of the hurt she might cause people. For instance, she found herself during one fight pounding another girl's head against the sidewalk, and she didn't want to do that kind of thing. The social worker, rather than just allowing Bettina to list these reasons for not fighting, explored with her the disadvantages of the status quo. For instance, the social worker asked, "What worries you about getting expelled for fighting? How will getting expelled for fighting stop you from doing what you want in life?" Thus the social worker helped the client talk herself into changing rather than using direct persuasion.

The social worker avoided challenging the client's statements because direct confrontation was likely to escalate resistance rather than reduce it. Any resistance to change was sidestepped. For instance, when Bettina said, "If I don't fight, I'll get disrespected," the social worker used the technique of amplified reflection: "So the only way to get people's respect is to fight them." Amplified reflection often results in verbal backpedaling from the client, who attempts to soften the extreme position reflected by the social worker. In this case, Bettina said, "No, sometimes I just give them a look. I can give some pretty mean looks."

As part of motivational interviewing, the social worker picks up on what the client holds as important in her life. She then works to enlarge the discrepancy between the client's values and her present problem behavior. Bettina valued her friendships at the school, but her fighting was endangering those relationships: "So on one hand, those friends are important to you, and on the other, if you get expelled for fighting and get transferred to another school, you won't be able to see your friends like you do now."

As the conversation continued the social worker focused on instilling in Bettina some optimism about change. For instance, when the social worker asked the question, "What makes you think that if you decided to make a change, you could do it?" Bettina said, "I can do it if I set my mind to it. I only wanted to cut my fighting down a little bit before. But now I want it to stop." The social worker asked, "What personal strengths do you have that will help you succeed?" The client answered, "I can talk. I know how to talk to people so they don't mess with me. I just lay them straight. No need to fight most of the time." The social worker further inquired about who could help Bettina make these changes. She identified her friends as a support system: "I can say to them, 'you-all, talk me down, because I can't fight no more. I don't want to get kicked out of school.' So when I'm in an argument, they'd probably say something like, 'forget her—she ain't worth it.' And they'd be right—she ain't."

The social worker assessed the client's commitment to change, as well as her confidence that she could make changes. To begin, the social worker used the commitment ruler technique: "If there was a scale to measure your commitment, and it went from 0 to 10, with 10 being totally committed—nothing could make you fight—where would you say you are right now?" Bettina identified herself at a "seven," and the social worker asked her to account for this value. Bettina said, "One more fight, and I'm kicked out of school. They already told me that. They might mean it this time."

The social worker then asked Bettina to rate herself on a similar ruler involving her confidence that she could change. Bettina said about her "five" ranking, "I already changed some. Like last year I got in trouble every day, but this year I don't get in trouble very often. I try to stay away from people I got a problem with. Before, I wouldn't think about it, and I would just fight people and not think about what would happen. But now I think about it."

Because Bettina's confidence that she could change was lower than her commitment, the social worker turned to a technique that would enhance the client's self-efficacy, asking evocative questions: "How might you go about continuing to make change? What would be a good first step?" Bettina answered that she would continue to avoid people who bother her. She would also talk to her friends about helping her "calm down."

When asked about possible obstacles, Bettina admitted it could be difficult if someone "got up in her face." The social worker and client began brainstorming about how to handle this obstacle. With some prompting and suggestions, Bettina produced three options: making threats but not necessarily following through; staying in public settings so that other people could intervene; and telling the instigator, over and over again if need be, "You're not worth it."

In motivational interviewing, when the social worker offers information and advice, it is phrased tentatively ("If it's okay, I'm going to make a suggestion. I don't know if it will work for you or not. It's worked for others who have struggled with the same things you have."). The social worker avoids struggle with the client about what she must do. Instead, the social worker strategically applies techniques so that the client's motivation to change is bolstered. In this way, during the course of a single session, Bettina decided that she was ready to commit to a change plan. She met with the social worker for several more weeks, reporting on her progress in staying out of fights, and getting feedback that helped to maintain her positive direction.

EVIDENCE OF EFFECTIVENESS

Empirical research has been conducted on motivational interviewing for the past 25 years. Dunn, Deroo, and Rivara (2001) reviewed 29 studies that focused mainly on substance-abuse issues, but also included problems related to smoking, HIV risk reduction, and diet and exercise. They found generally moderate to large effects for the intervention's reduction of both substance abuse and substance dependence, with maintenance of effects over time. Motivational interviewing was also found to promote client engagement in more intensive substance abuse programs. Although studies to date have largely been conducted on adults, adolescent substance use has also shown positive results from motivational interviewing (Burke, Arkowitz, & Dunn, 2002). Some of these effects are modest, however, and not necessarily superior to alternative interventions, as found in one major review (Gates, McCambridge, Smith, & Foxcroft, 2006). There is some indication that motivation intervention is most effective with heavy substance abusers in moderating their substance use (McCambridge & Strang, 2004).

In the Project Match Research Group (PMRG) study (1997, 1998), 952 individuals with alcohol problems from outpatient clinics and 774 from aftercare treatment were provided with twelve-step facilitation (12 sessions), cognitive/behavioral coping skills therapy (12 sessions), or motivational enhancement therapy (4 sessions). Motivational enhancement fared as well as the other two interventions that were three times as long, both at posttest and three years later. Motivational interviewing has also shown to be beneficial in reducing substance abuse among college students (Michael, Curtin, Kirkley, Jones, & Harris, 2006), persons with dual (mental health/substance abuse) diagnoses (Martino, Carroll, Nich, & Rounsavillle, 2006), homeless adolescents (Peterson, Baer, Wells, Ginzler, & Garrett, 2006), regular amphetamine users (Baker, Lee, Claire, Lewin, Grant, et al., 2005), psychiatric inpatients (Santa Ana, Wulfert, & Nietert, 2007), and gay men (Morgenstern, Irwin, Wainberg, Parsons, Muench, et al., 2007). It must be noted again, however, that in a majority of these studies the intervention was not superior to alternative interventions.

In addition to problems related to substance abuse and drug addiction, motivational interviewing has been found effective for health-related behaviors related to diabetes and hypertension and eating disorders such as binge eating (Dunn, Neighbors, & Larimer, 2006; Treasure, Katzman, Schmidt, Troop, Todd, et al., 1999). Only mixed findings, however, have been reported with the use of motivational interviewing for quitting cigarette smoking (Persson & Hjalmarson, 2006; Steinberg, Ziedonis, Krejci, & Brandon, 2004) increasing physical exercise (Jackson, Asimakopoulou, & Scammel, 2007; Butterworth, Linden, McClay, & Leo, 2006; Brodie, 2005), and reducing HIV risk behaviors (Burke, Arkowitz, & Dunn, 2002).

Some studies have shown that while motivational interviewing has a greater short-term effects on clients' change behaviors on reducing drug consumption than some alternative interventions, these differences may not persist over time (Morgenstern, Irwin, Wainberg, Parsons, Muench, et al., 2007; McCambridge & Strang, 2005). While these findings still demonstrate overall positive effects for motivational interviewing, they call into question the preferability of that approach.

These reviews indicate that motivational interviewing can be helpful for a number of types of problems that social workers encounter, but more needs to be learned regarding the scope of its utility.

CRITICISMS OF MOTIVATIONAL INTERVIEWING

Motivational interviewing focuses on one aspect of the individual: motivation. It does not take into account other important aspects of client functioning, such as emotions, intelligence, and skill levels. Neither does it encourage a proactive attendance to the influence of larger social influences such as discrimination and oppression that may contribute to problem situations. To put this criticism into a larger context, motivational interviewing is a practical approach to intervention, but lacks a clear theoretical basis that might generate broader thinking about its applications. Since the model is primarily an interviewing strategy, however, this criticism may not be justified.

Two other criticisms of motivational interviewing are worth mentioning. First, by selectively reinforcing reasons the client wants to change, practitioners may allow some possibly powerful reasons for the client's holding onto the behavior to go unchallenged. For instance, if a client mentions that drinking makes her better able to manage social situations, attention should perhaps be paid to ways that she could develop skills to improve her ability to manage "trigger" situations. The social worker might be more effective if he or she spent time discussing these advantages, and challenging the client's beliefs around them. This broader strategy might enhance the client's motivation and self-efficacy. A final criticism is that motivational interviewing is manipulative of clients. Though client choice is respected, the social worker will often favor one alternative to an extent that his or her questioning may be biased to help that result come

about. This issue may or may not be controversial in the area of substance dependence, where basic survival may be at stake, but in other clinical areas (for example,
some types of relationship conflict) client self-determination may be compromised.

SUMMARY

Motivational interviewing is a directive, client-centered intervention style that
enhances motivation for change by helping clients to clarify and resolve their
ambivalence about behavior change associated with some presenting problem.
Its goal is to clarify discrepancies between clients' present behavior and broader
goals. The intervention has proven useful with clients who demonstrate little
outward motivation to change behaviors identified by others as problematic.
Social workers may already be familiar with some of the principles of motivational
interviewing, such as the emphasis on collaboration and strengths, beginning
where the client is, and self-determination. The particular strategies associated
with the technique are worth learning because social workers are often engaged
with clients who are reluctant to change, especially those who have been man
dated to seek assistance from social service agencies. Further, the use of motivational interviewing techniques does not preclude the social worker from using
other intervention methods as well. That is, it may be used as a stand-alone treatment, but also as a way to prepare clients for other intervention approaches once
the client's motivation is galvanized.

TOPICS FOR DISCUSSION

1. Share some of the difficult decisions you have made in life about which you
    needed to resolve a great deal of ambivalence. Discuss the factors that helped
    you make a decision, and how you moved through the Transtheoretical
    Stages of Change (given that you were not aware of the model at the time).
2. What other strategies do you use, or know about, that can help clients develop
    motivation to confront some problem issue? How successful are they?
3. Motivational interviewing discourages the social worker's confrontation of
    clients. In what situations do you now confront clients? Is it appropriate in
    those situations? Can motivational interviewing offer a realistic alternative to
    confrontation?
4. Is motivational interviewing a manipulative intervention strategy? That is,
    does it tend to push clients toward particular goals? In what situations, if any,
    is this appropriate?
5. Discuss some "macro" or social justice issues, such as perceived age, gender,
    or class discrimination, that clients may lack the motivation to address. Can
    motivational interviewing be helpful for resolving their ambivalence?

IDEAS FOR CLASS ROLE-PLAYS

1–4. Identify several types of clients or clinical situations that may be appropriate for motivational interviewing. Conduct a series of role-plays in which students focus on each of the four major intervention strategies (elicit self-motivational statements, handle "resistance," promote decisional balance, and support self-efficacy and develop a change plan). Use the questions and comments presented in this chapter when implementing the strategies. After the role-plays, discuss what was helpful and what was difficult.

APPENDIX: Motivational Interviewing Outline

Focus	Enhancing clients' motivation to change by exploring and resolving ambivalence about change
Major Proponents	Allen, Carroll, Killick, Miller, Moyers, Rollnick, Treasure, Ward, Corcoran
Origins and Social Context	Changing philosophy of substance abuse intervention
	Rogerian therapy
	Cognitive dissonance theory
	Transtheoretical Stages of Change model
Nature of the Individual	None specified, except that ambivalence about change is a normal human condition
Major Concepts	Motivation
	Appropriate motivation to change is within the client, not imposed from the outside
	A client's motivation for enacting change relative to some problem is often impeded by ambivalence
	Ambivalence
	It is the client's responsibility to articulate and resolve his or her ambivalence
	Readiness to change is a product of interpersonal interaction
	Direct persuasion is ineffective for resolving ambivalence
	Practitioner directives are useful for examining ambivalence
	Client confidence to enact change
Developmental Concepts	None specified
Nature of Problems	Not specified; they are accepted as formulated by the client. Problem perspectives are consistent with those in the cognitive, behavioral, and solution-focused theories

APPENDIX: Motivational Interviewing Outline (Continued)

Nature of Change	Transtheoretical Stages of Change model
	Precontemplation
	Contemplation
	Preparation
	Action
	Maintenance
	Relapse
	Focus is on the precontemplation and contemplation stages
Goals of Intervention	To point out and amplify discrepancies between clients' present behavior and broader goals
Nature of Worker/ Client Relationship	Collaboration
	Empathy
	Reflective listening
	Worker elicits self-motivational statements
	Worker engages clients when in the state of change
	Resistance is a problem of the practitioner, not the client
Intervention Principles	Explore clients' problem behaviors and reflect clients' perceptions
	Reinforce clients' statements about wanting to change
	Affirm clients' statements about their ability to change
	Elicit self-motivational statements
	Problem recognition questions
	Concern questions
	Intention to change
	Optimism about change
	Questions about extremes
	Handle "resistance"
	Simple reflection
	Amplified reflection
	Double-sided reflection
	Shift focus
	Agreement with a twist
	Reframing
	Clarify free choice
	Paradox
	Decisional balance

APPENDIX: Motivational Interviewing Outline (Continued)

	Support self-efficacy and develop a change plan
	Evocative questions
	Ruler assessment
	Review past successes
	Discuss personal strengths and supports
	Ask questions about hypothetical change
	Brainstorm
	Give information and advice cautiously
Assessment Questions	Do you think that this might be a problem? Are there ways in which you or other people may have been harmed by this behavior?
	What worries you about your behavior? What can you imagine happening if you don't make a change?
	How much do you know about what can happen if you continue with this behavior—even if you don't see this happening to you?
	What are the reasons you see for making a change? What would you like your life to be like five years from now?
	What makes you think that if you decided to change, you could do it?
	What are the best results you could imagine if you make a change?

12

Narrative Theory

> A word is dead
> When it is said,
> Some say
> I say it just
> Begins to live
> That day.*

*N*arrative theory is the newest approach to clinical practice presented in this book. Its major premise is that all people are engaged in an ongoing process of constructing a life story, or *personal narrative,* that determines their understanding of themselves and their position in the world (Kelley, 1996; Monk, Winslade, Crocket, & Epston, 1997; White & Epston, 1990). It holds that human development is inherently fluid, that there are no developmental "milestones" that people *should* experience to maximize their chances for a satisfying life. Instead it is the *words* we use, and the *stories* we learn to tell about ourselves and about others, that create our psychological and social realities. These life narratives are co-constructed with the narratives of significant other people in one's family, community, and culture.

According to narrative theory, all personal experience is fundamentally ambiguous, and thus we must arrange our lives into stories to give them coherence and meaning. These stories do not merely reflect our lives—they *shape* them! As we develop a dominant "story line" (and self-concept), our new experiences are filtered in or out, depending on whether they are consistent with the ongoing

---

life narrative. Many problems in living that we experience are related to life narratives that exclude certain possibilities for future action.

An ultimate value of narrative practice is *empowering* clients, or helping them to gain
greater control over their lives and destinies. Narrative theory is unique in its conceptualization of problems as (at least in part) by-products of cultural practices that are oppressive
to the development of functional life narratives. In this sense it is a "therapy of advocacy"
and is highly consistent with social work's emphasis on social justice. While some argue
that narrative interventions may not be well-suited for client problems related to basic
needs such as food, shelter, safety, and physical health, they are certainly suitable for issues
related to self-concept, interpersonal relationships, and personal growth.

ORIGINS AND SOCIAL CONTEXT

Narrative theory integrates a variety of philosophical and sociological theories
into a perspective for clinical social work practice. Some of its ideas are drawn
from the traditions of *existentialism* and *symbolic interactionism* (the latter of which
is described in Chapter 10). It also incorporates ideas from *multiculturalism* (see
Chapter 2) and the solution-focused and cognitive theories. Most immediately,
narrative theory has emerged from the broad social theories of *postmodernism* and
social constructivism. These represent different approaches to the understanding of
human behavior and the nature of change than we have considered thus far.

Existentialism

Existentialism is not a coherent philosophical system, but rather a term that describes
a refusal to subscribe to any particular system of thought that attempts to summarize
human experience (May, Angel, & Ellenberger, 1958). Existentialism celebrates the
absolute uniqueness of each individual. The early existential writers influenced
developments in art, music, and psychology throughout the twentieth century.
Postmodernism itself incorporates much of what is central to existential thinking.

Several themes characterize existential thought. One is the uniqueness of the
individual (Kierkegaard, 1954). People discover their uniqueness in the ways
they relate to their subjective experiences of life, and they should be careful
about identifying too closely with other persons and groups. Concepts about human nature that postulate connections between individuals and larger social systems (found in almost every chapter of this book) tend to delude people into
accepting stereotypes about themselves that serve to limit their unique potentials.
The essence of one's existence can in fact never be fully apprehended by another, because perception is internal to the perceiver rather than representing
an "objective" state of affairs. By extension, efforts to make generalizations about
people (which social scientists often do) reflect the subjective belief systems of
the architects of those statements. To the existentialist they are dehumanizing.

Among existential thinkers, the possibility of choice is central to human nature (Sartre, 1956). Choice is ubiquitous: All of a person's actions imply choices.

We are always free to make choices, and there are no truly "rational" grounds for choice, because any criteria that we use to make choices are themselves chosen. People do tend to adopt criteria for making choices in their lives, just as in this book the author has made choices about which theories to include and how to evaluate them. Existentialist thinkers want us to understand that, though we can choose to align ourselves with other people and ideas, there is nothing necessary about those choices.

Whatever one's view about the nature of individuals in the context of the society, existential thinkers remind us that clients' views of themselves and their problems may be contaminated by an acceptance of external standards that could be changed. The task of the existentialist social worker is to apprehend the essence of each client's life, and help him or her to create or discover new purposes for living that may be more suitable to the client's unique nature.

Postmodernism

Postmodernism is not a uniform social or philosophical theory either, but represents various developments in the social sciences, the arts, and even architecture (Ritzer, 2000). It provides new ways of theorizing about the social world and the people within it. It is a "top-down" perspective that analyzes how prevailing ideologies affect people's perceptions of their worlds. Postmodernism takes the position that it is not possible to find broad, rational solutions to society's problems. This is different from many other social theories that advance themes of universalism and systematic problem solving. Postmodernists assert, following the ideas of Foucault (1966), that *any* generalizations about people and societies serve to reinforce positions of power among groups rather than represent objective truth. The prevailing ways in which a society is "understood" or explained give some groups privilege at the expense of others.

For these reasons, postmodernists reject the idea of a "grand narrative." They are instead attracted to the perspectives of individuals and small groups, particularly those that have been marginalized by privileged members of society. These perspectives are considered as valid as those of other social groups. Postmodernism is clearly a manner of thinking that focuses on the "small." It is sometimes criticized by social activists for ignoring social problems and de-emphasizing collective action (Lengermann & Niebrugge-Brantley, 2000).

The following aspects of postmodernism have influenced the development of narrative theory (Anderson & Levin, 1998; Weingarten, 1998):

- "Knowledge" represents beliefs that are rooted in social contexts (time, place, and culture) and influence what people understand, see, and say. Knowledge is not objective, but reflects the values of certain people at a certain place in time.

- Discourse, or conversations about ideas, tends to be based on prevailing ideologies. There are many *possible* discourses; some ideologies are dominant and others are subjugated. Some social workers argue, for example, that the fields of psychiatry and medicine dominate the public discourse about mental health and illness, and subjugate the alternative perspectives of other professional and social groups who may, for example, strive to work with people more holistically.

- Knowledge is power, and those who control the nature of knowledge preserve their situations of influence in a culture. For example, as men occupy most positions of political power, their values tend to be prioritized and perpetuated.
- Personal narratives are reflections of a culture as much as of the lives of individuals.
- With its emphasis on individuals and small groups, postmodernism encourages social workers to help clients understand how their narratives, or beliefs about themselves, may be rooted in societal oppression.

Postmodernism is criticized by some theorists as lacking any coherent agenda that might build consensus in a society around such issues as transcendent values and shared priorities. In fact, its emphasis on the relativism of knowledge is antithetical to the social work profession's drive to establish generalizations in research (Wakefield, 1995). Many practicing social workers may take issue with postmodernism's rejection of the possibility of people sharing common experiences related to psychosocial development.

Social Constructivism

The theory of social constructivism maintains that there is no objective reality that people might all apprehend and agree on (Rodwell, 1998). In comparison to postmodernism, this is a "bottom-up" perspective that considers how individuals and groups "create" their social worlds. All of us experience an objective *physical* reality (our bodies and the material world), but what that reality means to us (including our perspectives on relationships, social situations, and ourselves) is a mental creation. We apply our beliefs acquired from prior experiences to new input received from the environment. This perspective is largely consistent with cognitive theory (Chapter 7), although social constructivism incorporates fewer assumptions about human nature.

All of us are born with biological and temperamental qualities that influence our abilities to integrate sensory perceptions, but we become active participants in the process of making sense of the world early in life. It is the interaction of what we bring to social situations and what those situations present that produces our evolving view of "reality." These subjective processes shape our sense of self, competence, and contentment. Whereas satisfactory interpersonal functioning depends on maintaining many patterns of shared meaning with others, it is often useful for us (and our clients) to remember that these perceptions do not reflect absolute truths.

A major implication of social constructivism is that one's presumed knowledge about the self and others is wholly subjective. Social workers cannot make generalizable assertions about the nature of the self and an "appropriate" social world. In contrast, psychodynamic theories assume the existence of common psychosexual or psychosocial stages, and clinical social workers use that knowledge to assess the "normalcy" of their clients' social functioning. Cognitive theorists maintain that there are stages of cognitive and moral development that are relevant to assessment and intervention. In social constructivism, the notion of a common human nature is de-emphasized. Of course, these implications are the source of some critiques of social constructivism (Nichols, 2009). With this perspective, narrative practitioners do not rely on developmental stages as significant to problem development or intervention. Not relying on any such universals may be very difficult, however, for social workers who are educated to see all people as sharing certain characteristics, such as identifiable life stages.

Michael White and David Epston

The originators of narrative theory for clinical practice are Michael White and David Epston, who live in Australia and New Zealand, respectively. They began collaborating in the 1980s. Their best-known book is *Narrative Means to Therapeutic Ends,* published in 1990. Michael White worked as an electrical and mechanical draftsman in his early adulthood, but he became disenchanted with that career, and with systems thinking in general. He became a social worker in 1967. Early in his human-service career, he became frustrated with the traditional modes of intervention that he believed to be ineffective and dehumanizing. White was drawn to the work of sociologists Michel Foucault and Erving Goffman and the anthropologist (and communications theorist) Gregory Bateson. He developed an interest in how people come to understand their worlds, and his major ideas for narrative therapy evolved from this theme. White went on to serve as co-director of a clinic in South Australia.

David Epston was a family therapist who, like White, had longstanding interests in anthropology (and its concept of the narrative metaphor) and literature. Epston was an excellent storyteller and is also known for the innovative narrative techniques of *letter writing* (which he felt had more lasting influence than conversations), *resource collections* (letters and tapes) that could be passed from one client to another, and the development of *supportive communities* for persons who are rewriting their personal narratives. Epston now serves as co-director of a family therapy center in New Zealand.

MAJOR CONCEPTS

Narrative theory is premised on the idea that people's lives and relationships are shaped by their life stories and the ways of life they develop based on those stories (Nichols & Schwartz, 2001). Their stories are always unique, but are shared to some degree with others in their communities, and they reflect the value systems of those communities. Interestingly, narrative theory ignores the concept of systems in its prioritizing of the life story told from the perspective of the individual.

Each person's notion of identity, or the "self," is inherently fluid. That is, identity is how we define ourselves at particular points in time. Who we are, however, is a matter of ongoing contradiction, change, and struggle, a dynamic process of "being" rather than something continuous. This is a very different position from many other theories in this book that assume a changeable but more or less cohesive and continuous "self." From the narrative perspective, all people are capable of developing new, empowering stories that include new senses of the self. There is a great deal of variety in how practitioners operationalize narrative theory. What follows is an effort to summarize its major ideas.

The Personal Narrative

The concept of the personal narrative, so central to this theory, was described earlier. To elaborate, any personal narrative includes a process of selective perception. Some story lines are dominant, establishing primary themes in the person's mind, and interpretations of experience that do not fit the dominant story line may be suppressed. Thus, a narrative is always biased and selective. The case of Martin provides an example of this process.

Martin was a 30-year-old single white male with a good job in a furniture company sales department, referred to the social worker by his probation officer to get help with controlling his violent temper. Martin had recently been convicted of assault after fighting with and seriously injuring a neighbor at a holiday barbecue. Martin had been arrested on several other occasions for disturbing the peace and fighting in bars. A former girlfriend once invoked a restraining order against him for alleged abusive behavior. Martin admitted that he was quick to become upset and resort to fighting rather than using other methods of working out conflicts. He actually resisted any observations from others that he could be "soft" and "emotional" at times. Martin was an effective salesman but his supervisors had told him that his presentation was sometimes too aggressive. They had advised him to learn to relax more with customers.

Martin met with the social worker ten times over the course of one year. The social worker was interested in Martin's telling the story of his life and where he saw himself at present with regard to his personal goals. The social worker asked Martin how satisfied he was with himself. As he began this process the social worker could see that Martin's identity was tied up with images of the strong, athletic, dominant male. These seemed to have been learned from and patterned after his father (an assembly line worker) and older brothers, all of whom had similar perspectives on life. The social worker engaged Martin in a process of analyzing his assumptions about himself and the role of men in families and society. Martin admitted that he was not altogether comfortable with his persona, but that he had always avoided his other inclinations because he thought they would not be acceptable within his family and community.

Martin's example demonstrates how cultural values influence one's personal narrative, and how they can contribute to problem behavior. As another example, women in American society from certain socioeconomic classes were once—and often still are—expected to be submissive to men. This cultural norm contributes to the depression of many women (Kelley, 1996). More generally, people with low self-esteem may maintain that characteristic because their thoughts and conversations feature themes of self-degradation (perhaps with the language of "mental illness"). They continue to unwittingly construct life narratives that portray themselves as having certain limitations. These stories tend to be self-perpetuating because of their habits of language, and also because of the influence of cultural values that may impede alternative modes of thinking.

Deconstruction

Another central concept in narrative theory is that of *deconstruction*, a term derived from postmodernism. It refers to the social worker and client's analysis of the client's claims to knowledge and understanding in order to see the underlying assumptions that are manifested in surface complaints. It is similar to the ego psychology concept of insight, except that it refers more broadly to the client's awareness of social conditions and power relationships that contribute to his or her personal beliefs. Deconstruction involves exploring ingrained cultural assumptions that contribute to the occurrence of a problem. It is a process of uncovering and challenging assumptions about the way the world "should" be, and thereby opening up new possibilities. This concept will be elaborated later in this chapter.

Reconstruction, or Reauthoring

In essence, *re-authoring* is the term that summarizes the work of narrative intervention. Sometimes called *reconstruction*, it refers to the process by which the client, with the assistance of the social worker, develops a new personal narrative that is consistent with his or her personal goals. The process is based on the client's enhanced awareness of, and liberation from, limiting cultural influences, exploration of unique outcomes (aspects of one's narrative that are not consistent with the dominant problem-saturated story), exploration of "sparkling moments" (the awareness of new personal truths that highlight strengths), and the consideration of new possibilities for the new story line. It is important to note that a re-authored personal narrative affects not only the client's present and future sense of identity, but also the client's past, as events from the past are now seen from a new and different perspective.

THE NATURE OF PROBLEMS AND CHANGE

From the perspective of narrative theory, problems that bring clients to seek professional help are conditions of emotional or material suffering that result from personal narratives saturated with self-denigrating beliefs. Through a process of refocusing, social workers can help clients to construct different life narratives, or stories, that portray them in a different light. Clients can formulate alternative past and future stories, and devise unique outcomes for themselves. In this process the practitioner places great emphasis on the client's use of language. He or she is always alert to the elements of experience that a client chooses to express, and the language or meaning that is given to that experience. It is important to emphasize that narrative practitioners do not help clients ignore or wish away problems by creating new "fictions." Many problems that clients identify are concrete and must be dealt with by concrete action. A family with insufficient money to support itself must be helped to regain necessary resources. But life narratives *always* influence the experiences that clients label as challenges, and how they address them. A final point on this issue is that the practitioner makes sure that the client understands that the person is never the problem—it is the problem that is the problem! ˙

Returning to Martin, the client soon admitted that he was not satisfied with himself. He was often getting into trouble and losing friends. The social worker asked Martin to examine his lifelong relationship with anger—where it had come from and why it was persistent in his day-to-day life. Martin eventually realized that anger was not a necessary component of his life and he could develop alternative lifestyles, and attend to other aspects of himself and his world. Martin was a reflective man and with the social worker's encouragement could see that he might make other choices and consider broader possibilities for his future. Martin saw that he was locked into a rigid but not necessary pattern of living. He could reauthor his life narrative.

In summary, the goals of narrative therapy are not so much to solve problems as to:

- Awaken the client from a problematic pattern of living
- Liberate the client from externally imposed constraints
- Help the client author stories of dignity and competence
- Recruit supportive others to serve as audiences to the client's new life story

The nature of narrative therapy makes it appropriate for a variety of client populations, but there are also some clients whose situations make them less likely to benefit from the approach. What follows is a listing of clients from both categories, compiled by graduate social work students. Clients who are appropriate for narrative therapy include:

- Survivors of all types (trauma, illness, abuse) because of their frequent desire to engage in life reassessment
- Gay, lesbian, and transgendered clients who struggle with identity issues related to social oppression
- Members of all oppressed groups, and self-described "outsiders"
- Persons who carry "labels" (such as diagnoses) that are imposed from the outside
- Immigrant and migrant families, as they struggle to meld their original and new cultures

- People experiencing life transitions of any type, as those events require adjustments and lead to reflection and decision-making about life goals and values
- Juvenile sex offenders (who are faced with the challenge of developing new identities)
- Any client with a troubled sense of self, since this approach is focused on personal identity
- People with low self-esteem, who can be helped to re-interpret events in their life stories toward a sense of greater competence
- Older adults, who may wish to engage in life review, including terminally ill and hospice clients
- Caregivers of cancer (and other long-term illness) patients
- Children in foster care, who are in a process of authoring new stories of identity and family
- Children dealing with traumas, including those related to natural disasters

Narrative interventions by themselves may not be as useful for:

- Persons for whom behavioral controls or monitoring are required, or who are at-risk for re-offending (such as pedophiles)
- Single-issue clients, such as persons who are seeking assistance with budgeting or time management
- Persons in immediate crisis who require personal and material supports for stabilization
- Any client whose presenting issues are problematic to the social worker; that is, the social worker's own discourses (values) interfere with the ability to engage in the narrative process (examples may include certain types of criminals, but could really include any type of client, since all social workers have biases)

Practice *settings* where the relatively informal process of narrative therapy may be used include schools, hospice agencies, college counseling centers, in-home counseling programs, residential settings, mentor/peer programs, prisons, substance abuse rehabilitation facilities, and other in-patient settings.

ASSESSMENT AND INTERVENTION

The Social Worker/Client Relationship

The role of the clinical social worker is to help clients construct new life narratives that portray them in a different, more positive or productive, light. The social worker adopts an "archaeological" position, not to study the details of the client's history so much as to understand the "building blocks" of the client's life stories (beliefs, assumptions, and values).

The social worker/client relationship is different from that found in more conventional theories because the practitioner relinquishes the role of expert and functions as a collaborator. Toward this end the social work must reflect on his or her own "preferred self-description" as a practitioner, and the ways in which this might set up a power differential with the client (Richert, 2003). The social worker further demystifies the relationship by orienting clients to the narrative therapy process and inviting them to ask questions or make comments about the intervention as it unfolds. In this way, the client is given a shared responsibility for the shaping of the counseling conversation. The client may be given the freedom to meet with the social worker as often or as seldom as desired, within realistic limits of the social worker's availability. The social worker further rejects labeling the client as normal or abnormal, or "disordered," as this is an oppressive practice.

In one study of six pairs of clients and practitioners, Grafanaki and McLeod (1999) identified three appropriate categories of practitioner participation from the narrative perspective. These included the practitioner as *audience* for the client's telling of his or her life story, *negotiator* of a new story line, and *co-constructor* of a new story line. In the examples provided below, the ways in which these roles are operationalized will become clearer.

Narrative therapy is a process of understanding and deconstructing a client's stories through listening and reflection, and then constructing alternative stories. The client tells and explores his or her story along with the practitioner, describes a preferred reality, develops goals, develops an alternate story, and evaluates the outcomes of the process. The interventions are far less structured than in most other clinical approaches.

Assessment

Because narrative interventions are considered consultative rather than therapeutic, the assessment stage is relatively brief. The client is initially invited to share his or her presenting concerns. To learn how they see themselves, the social worker asks clients to describe their concerns and how they generally spend their time and deal with challenges. The social worker asks clients about strengths, talents, and accomplishments as a means of setting the stage for a constructive emphasis. There are no standard diagnostic procedures (except as mandated by the social worker's agency). Instead, the practitioner perceives clients as having individual, lived experiences to share and build upon. Clients are encouraged to think of themselves as protagonists in their life stories rather than as victims. Elements of the assessment can be summarized as follows:

- Use externalizing conversations (the person is not the problem)
- Map the effects of the problem on the person
- Map the effects of the person on the problem (strengths, exceptions, competence)
- Determine whether the client favors the present situation

The social worker tends to move quickly into the intervention phase. Discussion topics are varied and not easy to categorize (Monk, Winslade, Crocket, & Epston, 1997). We will consider intervention as falling into the four stages described below.

Normalizing and Strengthening

This first intervention overlaps with client assessment. The social worker encourages the client to describe how she understands and approaches the problem situation. In a manner similar to solution-focused intervention, the social worker helps the client to externalize the problem so that her entire self-image is not affected by it. (Again, the client is not the problem; the problem is the problem.) This helps the client avoid identifying herself as a victim or feeling "consumed" by the problem issue. The social worker avoids engaging with the client in a linear problem-solving process.

The practitioner next invites the client to describe other related challenges in her life and how she is managing them. Using active listening skills, the social worker asks the client about her most important life priorities and values. The social worker encourages the client to conceptualize the problem as only one aspect of her life, one that may be more contingent on external than internal factors—some of which may be unknown to the client at the moment. Throughout their conversations the social worker is careful to validate the significance of the presenting issue from the client's perspective. As one example of the variety of perspectives that people may have about a common issue, Dalton (1997) studied the narratives of 23 new mothers and found that they were all in a process of redefining mothering from their own points of view, separate from traditional social roles assigned to women.

Reflecting (Deconstructing)

The social worker helps the client to analyze her assumptions about the self and the world in order to uncover the fundamental ideas and social relationships represented by the presenting problem. The practitioner helps the client challenge assumptions about the way the world *should* be, and thereby open up new possibilities. This is similar to the concept of insight development, except that it emphasizes the client's awareness of social conditions and power relationships that contribute to assumptions about the self. The social worker helps the client to identify values and biases that underlie her construction of problems. This is done with questions about what the client's behaviors and beliefs seem to say about her as a person, and questions about what is most important in her life. As the client's narrative unfolds, the social worker encourages the client to consider any social forces that might influence her thinking, and to separate her life and relationships from knowledge and stories that the client judges to be oppressive. These therapeutic interactions do not fit with the client's "preferred" story because the social worker refuses, so to speak, to act as a receptive audience for the client's typical story. The social worker's actions offer the client new ways of dialoguing and the client's story begins to change.

Using the example of the violent client presented earlier, the social worker suggested that Martin consider that one of the stressful aspects of his world might be societal expectations of male dominance. This idea confused Martin at first, but he eventually came to accept it as a part of his cultural learning.

Enhancing Changes (Reauthoring or Reconstructing)

The social worker helps the client to give up stories that are the result of rigid narratives, and encourages the client to "envision," or consider, alternate stories about both the past and the future. This is sometimes termed "reconstruction," because the client makes decisions about the person he or she wants to be based on values that are more true to the self than those derived from arbitrary external factors such as traditional gender norms. The social worker helps the client recognize parts of the life story that represent "exceptions" to the problem-saturated story, and to identify "preferred outcomes" for the personal narrative.

This furthers the process of reflection begun in the previous stage, but the social worker may help the client to recognize resources he or she can utilize to promote her broader thinking. These resources (such as people, events, and practices) may exist in the client's environment but may also be recognized by watching videos or movies of persons who have faced similar challenges, personal journaling, and letter writing to significant others who might add to the client's self-understanding. Each of these practices can help clients reflect on their situations in novel ways. As one example, Diamond (1997) found that for persons in treatment for substance addiction, letter writing to friends, relatives, and even to the self (journaling) about the recovery process helped them change their attitudes about the problem and their relationships to others. Another study of 30 individuals who received general psychotherapy services found that journaling produced their primary impetus for change (McClellan, Schneider, & Perney, 1998).

Through discussion and these other techniques, the social worker encourages the client to reauthor her life story according to alternative and preferred stories of identity. The client is helped to consider life perspectives that may be in conflict with the expectations of significant others. Spectator questions, in which the social worker asks the client to consider how his or her changes may be perceived and evaluated by others, are useful in this regard. There is no expectation that the client will terminate involvement with these people, but she may want to let them know about the changes she has undergone. The client may also want to expand her social interactions to include new groups of people. This leads into the final stage of intervention.

Celebrating and Connecting

The social worker helps the client plan to sustain the new narrative, or the new sense of self. This "new" person may be similar to the one who entered intervention, but she may have made changes that she wants others to learn about. This final stage of narrative therapy is one in which the client connects with others in a familiar social world and perhaps recruits others in the celebration and acknowledgment of her arrival at a new status in life (Epston, White, & "Ben," 1995). This is different from how endings are approached in other theories because the focus is not on the maintenance of problem resolution. This emphasis on inclusion is different from the analytic conceptualization of ending as a loss. There are three ways to implement this strategy.

In *consultation,* the social worker leads the client through reflective conversations and tasks that help her place her new life narratives into a broad context. The client is helped to recognize her development of strengths and resources, and to retrace her steps to new knowledge through a review of "historical accounts," such as therapy notes, videotapes and audiotapes of sessions, or journals that were written during the intervention. The social worker challenges the client to consider what new directions her life may take with this new knowledge. The practitioner may invite the client to indirectly help other clients by permitting the use of her story as an example in future clinical interventions. Clients are often gratified to know that their journeys may be helpful to others.

Personal declarations involve the client's circulation of pertinent written information with significant others about her arrival at a new status. The client may choose to write individual letters to certain people for this purpose. In the spirit of identifying audiences that bear witness to the client's new self-understanding, the client may join clubs or organizations that will be supportive of her new position in life. Epston and White (1995) cite the example of some clients with "mental illnesses" who choose to affirm their dignity by joining advocacy organizations to combat the public stigmas associated with their labels. *Joining* activities may also include something as simple as a client who develops an interest in literature (appreciating the stories of others) and becomes a member of a book club.

Celebrations are any special commemorations of a client's development of new life narratives. These can take many forms, depending on the client's particular circumstances. They may include prizes or awards given in ceremonies attended by significant others. These commemoratives work especially well with children and adolescents. The practitioner may or may not be a direct participant in a celebration —his role may most prominently include assisting clients to devise suitable celebrations. For example, Martin's social worker suggested that he try to think of ways to celebrate his accomplishments. The client gave the issue some thought for a few weeks. He recalled seeing a football player after the Super Bowl walking across the television screen and announcing, "I'm going to Disney World." Martin enjoyed the self-mocking idea of taking on the image of that "macho" athlete and actually taking his parents and two brothers on a trip to Disney World. He thought it would provide him with a pleasant way to enhance his relationship with his family. He also wanted to use the time to let his family get to see his new, more "patient" self.

Because narrative therapy is relatively structured, its ending is considered a natural process of completing a consultation. Often, clients and practitioners do not make a definitive decision to end their work. They may leave the door open for occasional consultations without boundaries on time frames (Freedman & Combs, 1996).

SPIRITUALITY AND NARRATIVE THEORY

Narrative theory is particularly open to exploring issues of spirituality in clients' lives. Recalling that spirituality is a person's search for ultimate values, meanings, and commitments, narrative theory's desire to help people author life stories that are consistent with their most personal aspirations almost always touches on spiritual issues. In relating their life stories, clients are encouraged to talk about and explore the nature of their religious or secular belief systems as well as their social concerns (including commitments to causes or social groups). Some existential thinkers assert that meaning can also be found in creative pursuits such as art, music, literature, and novel approaches to one's work. A client's spirituality generally becomes a focus of that person's thinking at times of self-doubt or despair, and the narrative social worker's questions and comments encourage the client to become more aware of, or consider how well his or her life is manifesting, these personal ideals. The social worker does not attempt to direct the client's thinking in any particular direction, but is prepared to help the client come to terms with his or her most basic beliefs about the self and its place in the world.

ATTENTION TO SOCIAL JUSTICE ISSUES

More than any other theory in this book, narrative theory can be classified as a "theory of social justice." The social worker always considers how the client system may be vulnerable to cultural narratives that include forces of oppression, such as racism, ageism, and sexism. That is, practitioners help clients to consider problem-saturated stories as they relate to social conditions. In this way, they may encourage the client to address social conditions and change through access to new information, services, resources, equal opportunities, and greater participation in collective decision-making.

To effectively provide narrative therapy, the social worker must be knowledgeable about oppression and cultural and ethnic diversity. When considering the source of problems, the social worker can then attempt to give clients the opportunity to liberate themselves from certain cultural assumptions. This helps clients identify and challenge commonly unexamined "life prescriptions" that permeate their societies. The social justice aspects of narrative theory are further seen in its effort to promote communities of support for clients.

One example of a social justice issue that can be addressed with narrative therapy is that of working with the children of Japanese-Americans who experienced internment during World War II (Nagata, 1991). Over 60% of those incarcerated at the time were United States citizens, many of whom were given less than a week's notice of their removal and had to give up businesses, property, and personal possessions. These Japanese-Americans lived an average of two to three years in the camps, enclosed by barbed wire and watched by armed guards. These people felt especially victimized, having been rejected by their own country of citizenship. Such massive trauma came to serve as an unconscious organizing principle for later generations of Japanese-Americans. Virtually all of their children report that their parents maintained a silence about their experiences in the camps, a silence that inhibited communication within the family and created a sense of foreboding and secrecy. Their children also felt a significantly greater sense of vulnerability than those whose parents had not been interned.

The children of interned Japanese-Americans tend to report deficits in family communication, problems with self-esteem (as they are pressured to prove their "worth" after their parents had been demeaned), limited vocational choices (again, having internalizing a need to "prove" themselves to their parents and to the broader American culture), problems with assertiveness (with their parents modeling a self-protective passivity in the larger culture), and, finally, identity problems. The children were raised to "stick with" their Japanese-American peers rather than move into the mainstream American culture.

In narrative therapy, exploring the above internment themes can be useful with members of subsequent generations, as not all of them recognize the relevance of their parents' internment on their own life stories. These clients may in fact either openly deny such a relationship or present a restricted life narrative that omits this aspect of their cultural past. Social workers can help clients make the latent themes of internment manifest by drawing attention to events and attributes in the client's lives not accounted for by their present narratives, or challenging the completeness of their stories as initially shared.

Now we will consider three examples of narrative intervention, two with specific clients and a third with a specific type of presenting problem.

CASE ILLUSTRATIONS

The Hospice Client

Narrative theory, with its emphasis on reflection and the search for meaning, is well-suited to hospice patients seeking to construct their own end-of-life stories. Additionally, it is suited to using relatively few sessions spread over a longer period of time. For a hospice patient, the death-inducing illness may unfortunately become the dominant story line. As family and professional caregivers become increasingly involved with the patient, the co-created reality is that the patient is the illness rather than the one afflicted by illness. Interventions that reduce threat and enhance the individual's sense of control over the process positively affect mental and physical health (Aldwin, 1994).

Mrs. Kelly, aged 86, was dying of ovarian cancer. She had been ill for seven months, and was living at home with her husband of 60 years. The couple had two daughters, one of whom lived in town and was often with her parents; the other, who had a history of conflict with the family, lived farther away and was a less frequent visitor. Mr. Kelly, also 86, was a caring but domineering provider who was accustomed to making all major family decisions and taking care of his wife and daughters. As the social worker came to know the family, she became aware that Mrs. Kelly wanted to take more charge of her life during the final

weeks. She wanted time to "prepare" and her husband, despite his good intentions, was somewhat intrusive in that process. The social worker mediated this
issue between the couple and helped diffuse Mr. Kelly's feelings of helplessness
and fear.

Through listening and reflective questioning, the social worker wanted to
help Mrs. Kelly assess her life and the "realities" of her situation, and mobilize
her underlying strengths to challenge the power of the illness. Rather than
teaching coping strategies, the social worker planned to listen for and identify
examples of Mrs. Kelly's creative coping. The social worker began the narrative
process by asking the client to "Tell me the story of your name." This led to
Mrs. Kelly's lengthy reminiscence of her family of origin. The social worker
asked the client to reflect on the special talents and qualities possessed by her
family members. Mrs. Kelly was quite verbal and became increasingly animated
as she recalled the important people and events in her life. The social worker
later asked Mrs. Kelly for a list of three things that once gave meaning and purpose to her life. This led to a dialogue about work, love, art, nature, and other
topics that were quite personal to Mrs. Kelly. Later, the social worker asked,
"How has your illness changed what's meaningful in your life?" and again requested Mrs. Kelly to name three things that were still beautiful and three things
that still inspired her laughter.

At first, Mrs. Kelly had not seemed sure of the value of talking with anyone.
"Talk therapy" is not easily embraced by members of her generation. Before
long, however, the client was consistently interactive and appeared to enjoy the
invitation to reflect. With her description of each older family member, all of
whom had died, Mrs. Kelly seemed to become clearer about her identity and
more validated as a unique individual. One of nine children, she reported being
spoiled by her sisters and growing up timid and quiet. She had continued these
patterns when she was married by allowing her husband, and later her daughters,
to manage all decision making. Mrs. Kelly did not regret this but was now aware
that she had been more capable of self-care than she was given credit for.

The social worker agreed that women of Mrs. Kelly's generation were not
generally encouraged to function independently. She shared with Mrs. Kelly a
pattern she had noticed in women in their seventies and eighties. Their acceptance of being cared for by their spouses seemed to carry over into their assumptions of how they coped with life's challenges. They acknowledge that difficult
events have occurred in their lives but mistakenly conclude that they were shel-
tered from them. They do not recognize their own part in surviving stressful
times. This theme became apparent to Mrs. Kelly in her review of the past.

During the reconstruction phase, the social worker asked Mrs. Kelly about
her hopes for the future. Even when hope for a cure has been lost, many critically important hopes remain, including the hope to live whatever time is left
with joy and purpose, and perhaps the hope to be remembered. Mrs. Kelly
wanted to become more active during her final months on earth. Her daughters
had almost no contact with each other, and she wanted to meet with them together; to ask them to reconcile and recognize the importance of family ties. She
wanted to communicate with confidence to her husband that he would survive

her death and continue making a good life for himself and their daughters. The social worker affirmed these priorities and helped Mrs. Kelly arrange to have sufficient private time with her family members. She congratulated Mrs. Kelly for making these efforts, and the client said, "I like the way I feel when I do new things. It makes me feel important."

Following through with these tasks, Mrs. Kelly experienced a greater sense of connection to other people and, perhaps more important, to something greater than herself. She began to request more time alone; to think about her spiritual nature as her illness worsened. Mrs. Kelly passed away five weeks after her relationship with the social worker had begun. They had six meetings for time periods ranging from 30 minutes to 2 hours. By the time of her death, Mrs. Kelly had revised her life story to include episodes of strength and quiet wisdom, and she had successfully brought the other three members of her family closer together.

Although it did not pertain to this case, narrative therapy can empower clients to partner with the entire hospice team in fighting the effects of the illness. There is often a disconnection between the main drivers of treatment (physicians) and the recipients of treatment. Families and clients long for communication that is honest and provided with empathy, and that recognizes their unique qualities (Farber, 1999). Physicians, in part because of time constraints and their training, may appear insensitive and authoritarian, focused on survival rather than on quality of life. They may find it difficult to promote the benefits of dying well over living poorly. Narrative therapy can serve as a complement to traditional medical services while providing the reciprocity and individualized attention desired by patients and families.

The next illustration demonstrates how narrative therapy can effectively be used with clients in need of a much more structured, problem-solving intervention approach.

The Bag Lady

Lexie was a 43-year-old unemployed widow who came to the mental health agency and stated that she wanted to retain custody of her two adolescent children. After her husband's death from cancer eight years ago, her parents-in-law had accused her of being an unfit mother and acquired temporary custody of the children through the county children's service bureau. Lexie wanted the children to be with her and, after many appeals, the children's bureau was preparing to return them. At this time, an acquaintance suggested to Lexie that getting counseling would further impress the bureau of her determination to be a good parent. Strangely, however, Lexie chose to keep her counseling experience a secret from everyone.

Lexie had been diagnosed at a previous agency with schizotypal personality disorder. During her initial meetings with the social worker she was suspicious, quiet, ill at ease, and vague. She shared no particular counseling agenda except to note vaguely that she wanted to "get out to the pool." Her affect was constricted, her communications were terse and obscure, and her vocabulary was primitive. Her grooming was haphazard; on some summer days she came dressed in a fur coat, mini-skirt, and hiking boots. Most of her sessions lasted only 15 to 20 minutes. Following a pleasant but rambling conversation, Lexie would abruptly announce that she had to leave, sometimes to "get to work," and walk out, although she always made a point of scheduling a meeting for the following week. Eventually, Lexie disclosed to the social worker that her work involved collecting aluminum cans for recycling. Otherwise, she spent her time taking long walks through the city. She reported having a positive relationship with her mother but no one else.

Despite Lexie's odd presentation, the social worker realized that she had some remarkable strengths. She was a college graduate with an impressive athletic background. She had married shortly after finishing college, after becoming pregnant, but had done little since then outside of the house. She raised her children as best she could while tolerating what she described as a neglectful husband who had many affairs. Lexie actually felt relieved when he died, saying, "being married never did me any good." She had functioned marginally, with no relationships outside her extended family. The social worker liked Lexie, and once he got used to her idiosyncratic conversational style he learned that she wanted to ease her loneliness, prevent further social isolation, be a good parent, and develop a more satisfying daily routine. She did *not* want to find a regular job or participate in any formal social activities.

"Odd" people like Lexie are often considered misfits with limited potential to become part of a conventional social network. They are given diagnostic labels, even though they do no harm and can make positive contributions to their communities. The social worker adopted a narrative intervention approach with Lexie because it suited both her need to be affirmed and her natural style of interaction. He assessed her as a confused but strong woman, a single parent who lived independently with minimal support. The social worker wanted to affirm her personal value, which it seemed that no one else was doing, and help her find a comfortable place in the world with access to the material and social supports she desired. He hoped that, given the chance to tell her story and consider her options, Lexie might refine and feel more secure in her chosen roles, or perhaps choose new roles.

Their short (15- to 20-minute) weekly meetings (Lexie's preference) consisted of conversations about the client's activities, goals, and options for organizing her time. Her narratives were filled with themes of incompetence based on the judgments of others about her. The social worker mostly listened but also gave Lexie input about how others might perceive her in various situations. He asked questions about how she might plan her days to be consistent with her personal goals, and ways to interact with her children. Although Lexie was not inclined toward sustained reflection, the social worker helped to deconstruct some of her assumptions about her position in the world. He reminded Lexie that she seemed to feel pressure to adapt conventional roles that her in-laws and others prescribed for her even though these were contrary to her preferred lifestyle. He once said to her, "Your in-laws refer to you as a bag lady. But I think you see yourself differently. How would you describe yourself?" The client thought for a few moments, and responded, "I'm Lexie, that's all."

Much of what the social worker provided to Lexie, or allowed her to express, seemed helpful. Lexie already had an independent spirit but had not received any support for her lifestyle. She had few social skills, a suspicious view of the world, an ongoing state of mild confusion, and nothing from which to draw pleasure but her solitary sports activities such as swimming and basketball. But she cared about her kids, and wanted to give them a good home.

After six months of intervention (but only 12 hours of direct contact), Lexie's attitudes about herself and her environment changed significantly. She seemed to regard herself as a free spirit with the capability of taking care of her children and herself. Her manner of dress became more conventional. She discussed her childcare concerns with the social worker, and always tried to follow through with parenting decisions she made in collaboration with him. Her efforts at child discipline were not always successful. The social worker learned that Lexie could not generalize parenting or social skills practices from one situation to another. They reviewed the same basic topics frequently, all of them focused on increasing Lexie's sense of competence in her home and helping relieve her anxieties by learning to take time out for herself. This is what Lexie wanted to do.

After one year of intervention, Lexie felt much better. Her changes were not radical and to her neighbors she probably remained the eccentric lady on the block who was best left alone. But there were no further complaints about her parenting from her extended family or neighbors. She made one good friend from her neighborhood and even joined the woman in a weekly volunteer group at the local hospital. Lexie gradually asked to meet with the social worker less often, and eventually they were out of contact. She seemed to have developed a new life story that featured herself as an independent middle-aged woman with survival skills who could manage two children.

Juvenile Sex Offenders

Daybreak is a residential juvenile sex offender treatment program that serves adolescents aged 11 to 17. Interventions focus on issues related to the clients' past traumas, past victimizations, behavior problems, cognitive distortions, and defenses that are common among sex offenders. Treatments include individual and group therapy, family therapy, life skills instruction and activities, educational groups, music and drama therapy, academic educational programs, and structured recreational activities.

Narrative therapy, which is one part of the intervention, helps the adolescents separate themselves from their problem-saturated stories and open up avenues by which they can bypass the problems that have plagued them. This approach allows the clients to reconstruct meanings and experiences in their lives to produce a more constructive view of themselves and their futures. This is especially important for youths who perceive only the negative aspects of their life stories. Many of the clients at Daybreak have difficulty seeing past their offending behaviors and the abuses they have suffered. Clients often point out that they were abused because they are "bad" people. By exploring their unique outcomes (evidence of "good" behavior), social workers can provide the adolescents with opportunities to develop an alternative story, one not dominated by abuse.

Although Daybreak uses a largely cognitive-behavioral based treatment method, the narrative approach is present in a 14-objective treatment module that begins with "My Life Story." Completing the Life Story objective provides an opportunity for offenders and their social workers to gain greater insight into the offender's past experiences and his interpretation of those experiences. The Life Story objective serves as a non-threatening means of supporting the client during his introductions to his peers and the staff. It helps the client identify significant life events that may have contributed to his offending, and it helps the professionals understand the offender's worldview, view of self, self-concept, use of time, and coping styles. It acts as a beginning stage for the development of a therapeutic relationship between the client and his therapist.

The treatment objectives that follow incorporate the narrative approach as well. Juvenile sex offenders often exhibit qualities such as resilience, resourcefulness, and intelligence that they are unable to see in themselves due to society's dominant negative constructs about their behaviors. Through the narrative approach, clients are confronted with their own self-assumptions and are encouraged to more fully explore their beliefs and feelings with the social worker who, in turn, works to break down those cultural assumptions and the negative feelings related to them.

One 15-year-old male client in the program named Jacob complained about feeling depressed, having trouble sleeping and not being able to focus in school and on his treatment. He stated that no one on the unit liked him and that he felt worthless. He also stated that those feelings move him into his cycle of abuse because it reminds him of the emotional abuse he suffered at the hands of his mother.

Jacob presented in the first session as lethargic and withdrawn, not wanting to talk. The social worker asked what he was feeling and he stated that he was sad and tired. The social worker asked him why he was feeling tired and Jacob replied that he was up all night reading. He related that one of the characters in his book died and he "feels pain in his chest" because of it. They explored how passionate Jacob is about his reading. Jacob stated that he loves to read to escape from his "hell." He appeared to be in a better mood when talking about the content of his readings.

Through the use of metaphors, the social worker attempted to open Jacob up to explore some of his emotions. He explained that the characters in the book possessed certain powers and were able to fly. He wished he could be like them. The social worker questioned why he would want that and Jacob replied that with special powers he could change things that have happened in the past, and flying would make him feel free.

Jacob and the social worker talked about some of the things that made him feel that he could not fly, such as his sexual abuse, his abuse of his sister, and the impact of his offending on his family. They used the metaphor of flying to help Jacob talk about how he can change things in the present that will help him to grow wings and fly. Jacob stated that completing his treatment successfully would enable him to return home and make his father happy. They agreed that this would be his first step to growing wings and decided to work on a list of "special powers" that Jacob might already possess to keep him focused on his treatment. He appeared to enjoy the idea of the metaphors.

In a subsequent session Jacob stated that he had used some of his "special powers," which consisted of processing with his peers and staff the angry feelings that perpetuate his feelings of sadness or incompetence, and going to bed early instead of staying up reading all night, which causes him to think of sad things. Jacob stated that these actions put him in a better mood, resulting in him being approachable to his peers. The course of his intervention at Daybreak began to improve from this point.

EVIDENCE OF EFFECTIVENESS

There are many descriptions in the literature of the types of problems for which narrative therapy has been found useful. Though narrative practitioners resist labeling clients, the results of a PsycINFO® literature search included articles describing the theory's applicability to clients who experience attachment disorders, eating disorders, body image disorders, post-traumatic stress disorder, depression, stuttering, substance abuse, panic disorder, adolescent behavior problems, childhood adjustment issues (as a component of play therapy), life with violent partners, general relationship problems, and mental illnesses. The interventions are useful with families and groups as well as individuals. Much existing research on narrative therapy is qualitative, featuring case studies and small convenience samples. In fact, much of the research, which is admittedly in the early stages of development, focuses on the intervention process rather than its outcomes. We will consider both types of research here.

Outcome Studies

Quantitative research methods are not completely incompatible with narrative theory, and several examples are described here. One researcher applied a set of narrative techniques (including externalization, relative influence questioning, identifying unique outcomes and accounts, facilitating the circulation of new narratives, and assigning between-session tasks) to six families experiencing parent–child conflicts (Besa, 1994). Five of the six families reported improved relationships. In a follow-up study of 49 clients discharged from a substance use treatment facility who had been treated with narrative therapy, it was found that the clients' new life narratives had been integrated into their post-discharge lives (Kuehnlein, 1999). Researchers studied the narratives of 20 clients with post-traumatic stress disorder after they had completed intervention, attempting to find differences in narrative style between the 8 clients who improved and the 12 who did not improve (van Minnen, Wessel, Dijkstra, & Roelofs, 2002). The clients who improved showed a significantly greater decrease in "disorganizing thoughts" and an increase in sensitivity to their internal events.

female adolescents seeking reproductive health services and considered . for pregnancy were provided with narrative therapy, with the goal of aging them to consider a trial of contraception (Cowley, Farley, & iis, 2002). Over an unspecified length of time, one-third of the clients did so, and attributed their decisions to a variety of personal concerns that emerged during their story telling. Another pilot study of 14 depressed older adults demonstrated that such clients could be helped to reduce their depression after only two to three home visits with the use of a strengths–focused, narrative approach (Sharman, 1998). This study is noteworthy in its use of a control group and pre- and posttest scores.

In an early study of narrative-related therapy, Seymour and Epston (1989) evaluated a program for children (aged 7 to 15 years) who were engaged in stealing. The semi-structured program included the steps of understanding the child, engaging the child and parents, defining the stealing behavior, eliciting the child's response to his or her stealing activities, and "regrading" the child to the status of an honest person. Follow-ups conducted between 6 and 22 months after the intervention indicated that 81% of the children had not stolen at all or stole less often.

Process Studies

Presented next are examples of research on the narrative intervention process, all of which included more than one client. Two authors have written about the significance of narrative interventions in the context of play therapy with children. One study of six videotapes from play therapy sessions indicated that children symbolize themes of traumatic events in play therapy, alternating happy/ neutral and angry stories (Kanters, 2002). In a study of ten children receiving "sand" therapy, Cockle (1993) notes that the five "coping" children viewed their world as balanced and showed resourcefulness in dealing with adversity. The five "difficult coping" children described their worlds as barren and dangerous, and their stories lacked elements of resourcefulness.

"Anger" narratives were investigated by Andrew and McMullen (2000), who reviewed audiotapes of 109 stories of anger experiences told by 19 adult clients in one psychotherapy center. The researchers identified five common anger themes, and asserted that this confirmed earlier research about common scripts in the lives of people with similar backgrounds. Regarding themes that may be common to eating disorders, Von Wyl (2000) analyzed stories told during interviews with seven anorexic and eight bulimic clients from inpatient psychiatric centers, and concluded that the major conflicts represented in the two disorders are different.

Barber, Foltz, DeRubeis, and Landis (2002) investigated the hypothesis that psychiatric clients display consistent narrative themes in narratives when describing relationships with mothers, fathers, same-sex best friends, and romantic partners. Ninety-three clients were asked to give narratives about each of those people, and independent judges rated these with respect to intensity of wishes, responses of others, and responses from self. They found substantial variability in interpersonal themes across narratives, which implies that client narratives are less predictable than the researchers had imagined. This unpredictability in client presentation is consistent with the assumptions of narrative theory.

The "process" studies described above illustrates how narrative theorists have become interested in understanding within-session narrative activity by clients. Several researchers have developed instruments to help practitioners review their own narrative processes with clients. The *Narrative Process Coding System* is one example of a method for studying the narrative sequences of intervention with individual clients (Angus, Levitt, & Hardtke, 1999). This is a manual that guides researchers through a study of session transcripts to document topic shifts and three types of narrative process, including references to a client's external events, internal events, and reflections. At a micro level, the coding system helps to outline social worker/client interactions around narration, plot, and narrative process style. At a macro level, it helps to show how specific narratives become linked to a client's life story. The structured understanding of within-session client behaviors might eventually result in knowledge about the types of practitioner comments that promote client storytelling and the types of narratives that tend to be presented by different types of clients.

CRITICISMS OF THE THEORY

Narrative theory is attractive to many social workers because of its focus on client empowerment and social change activities. However, it has been subject to several criticisms. First, narrative therapy may not be suitable as a primary intervention with persons whose problems are related to basic needs acquisition (Williams & Kurtz, 2003). These types of clients represent a large segment of the social work profession's traditional client populations. Narrative theory's relative lack of structure and emphasis on subjective impressions may not be helpful with clients who face, for example, problems related to unemployment, lack of health care, or inadequate housing. It might be used with these clients once the initial problem is resolved to help them reconsider their life courses.

Other criticisms stem from narrative theory's rejection of general theories of physical, psychological, cognitive, and moral development. Some argue that it is not possible for practitioners to help people change without such a guiding set of principles (Nichols, 2009). Put another way, can a clinical social worker really avoid any assumptions about the nature of people and how they change? Most other theories in this book offer extensive ideas about human nature and the change process.

Narrative theory rejects labeling clients because such labels arbitrarily impose the narratives of outside social groups. Many social workers are trained to conceptualize some client problems as "illnesses." Narrative theory has been criticized for encouraging practitioners to ignore these serious conditions. When working with a client who has schizophrenia, for example, a narrative practitioner might be less likely to encourage medication use and challenge "delusional" ideas.

The therapeutic neutrality of any practitioner may not be possible, and the narrative practitioner risks imposing his or her own values, perhaps unwittingly, to influence how the client shapes his or her story (Gottlieb & Lasser, 2001). The social worker may tend to promote a story that represents one particular discourse and marginalizes the client's inner voices that don't fit the story. A feminist practitioner, working with a client who has experienced repeated domestic violence, may hope that the client reshapes her personal narrative in a way that highlights lifestyle alternatives other than returning to the abusive spouse, and in subtle ways act accordingly. Wyche (1999) further notes that the validity of a social worker's interpretations of client narratives may be limited in situations in which the practitioner is a member of a different race, class, or gender. Bias is a potential problem with any practice approach, but narrative theory may be particularly open to it without principles that might serve as checks on the social worker's activities.

Narrative theory de-emphasizes systems thinking (White & Epston, 1990). This minimization of the role of systems is particularly glaring in the profession of social work, where the person-in-environment perspective gives great weight to the reciprocal impact of families, groups, organizations, and communities.

A final criticism of narrative therapy is that its processes are at odds with the emergence of managed care in clinical social work practice—a development that occurred at the same time that narrative theory was emerging (Kelley, 1998). Managed care demands DSM-IV-TR diagnoses and pre-approved intervention plans based on empirically proven methods, while in narrative therapy the emphasis is on the social worker and client's co-creating new realities through dialogue.

SUMMARY

The ideas that underlie narrative theory represent outgrowths of developments in postmodern social thought, although they are also related to other, longer-standing developments in the human service professions such as multiculturalism, the strengths perspective, and client empowerment. The impact of narrative theory on professionals engaged in clinical practice has been great, as it provides a useful alternative for intervention with many types of presenting problems. Narrative therapy is even moving into the field of medicine. Goodrich (2006) writes that by listening more closely to the stories of patients and reflecting more deeply on their clinical experiences, physicians can more clearly understand each patient's situation, adopt the patient and family's perspectives on an illness, and, as a result, provide more individualized and comprehensive care.

A practitioner's full embracing of narrative theory is not always possible, however, because its relatively unstructured methods are incompatible with the strict policies about structured service provision present in many agency settings. A challenge for social workers in the future will be to identify the types of clients for whom the approach may be beneficial, consider ways of flexibly implementing the theory into a variety of agencies, and establishing further evidence of its effectiveness through both qualitative and quantitative methods.

TOPICS FOR DISCUSSION

1. Narrative therapy is said to be consultative and informal in nature. Can it be adapted for use in agencies that demand structure from practitioners with regard to such matters as length of sessions and duration of intervention?

2. Think about the kinds of clients seen by social workers for whom narrative interventions would and would not be appropriate. What is the difference? Can narrative interventions be incorporated into other clinical interventions without violating the essence of the approach?

3. Share examples of clients from field placement agencies whose problems may be related to culturally oppressive values and practices. Discuss how the social worker might proceed to help a client explore (deconstruct) these influences.

4. Related to the above point, discuss how these clients might be helped to construct new life stories that do not reflect cultural oppression, and the role of the social worker in that process.

5. What are some ways that various types of clients can be helped to "celebrate" their new life stories at the end of narrative intervention?

IDEAS FOR ROLE-PLAYS

1. Divide the class into pairs. One member of each pair (the client) thinks of a personal belief that has been highly influential in his or her development of an identity. Choices may include race, education, religion, sexuality, social class, lineage, or culture. The student portraying the social worker provides the client with an opportunity to talk about the belief and it influence on the client's life. The social worker should listen with interest and curiosity, and encourage the client to explore the effects of the belief on his or her life. The student practitioner helps the client to focus on family, work, spirituality, relationships, history, the future, and life position. In a follow-up class discussion, the client should discuss the effects of the conversation on his sense of identity, and what the social worker did that was useful to the process.

2. Practice the informal, nondirective type of assessment favored by narrative practitioners with clients who have specific presenting problems, but are willing to explore them in detail with the social worker.

3. Practice ways of externalizing clients' problems without absolving them of responsibility for their behavior, especially with client populations who tend to blame others (such as adolescent legal offenders, substance abusers, and spouse batterers).

4. Practice deconstruction interventions with a variety of types of clients. Two examples that might provide interesting contrasts for follow-up class discussion are women who have been battered and men who have been batterers.

5. In separate role-play activities, practice reconstruction interventions with the same clients as in the above exercise.

APPENDIX: Narrative Theory Outline

Focus	Personal narratives that determine one's understanding of the self and the world
Major Proponents	Crockett, Dickerson, Epston, Freedman, Monk, Kelley, White, Winslade, Zimmerman
Origins and Social Context	Existentialism
	Postmodernism
	Social constructivism
	Multiculturalism
Nature of the Individual	Personal experience is fundamentally ambiguous
	People arrange their lives into stories to give them meaning
	New experiences are filtered in or out of a story line depending on whether they are consistent with the ongoing life narrative
	Life narratives are co-constructed with significant others
	Cultural norms contribute significantly to life narratives
	Some story lines are dominant and others are suppressed
	People are capable of developing new, empowering stories
Major Concepts	The narrative: a story that is authored by a person about his or her life, including the past, present, and future, in which objective and subjective experiences are selectively arranged
	Deconstruction: the analysis of one's perspectives about the self, relationships, and the world to see what cultural ideas and personal assumptions lie beneath the surface
	Reauthoring/Reconstruction: A process of developing a new personal narrative that includes moving away from problematic beliefs and social constraints and toward new possibilities
Nature of Problems	Problems are conditions of emotional or material suffering that result from narratives saturated with negative assumptions
	Problems are in part by-products of cultural practices that are oppressive to the development of functional life narratives
	People are separate from their problems

APPENDIX: Narrative Theory Outline (Continued)

Nature of Change	Awareness of arbitrary beliefs and assumptions about the self and world
	Examination of culturally reinforced assumptions that may be limiting (deconstruction)
	Consideration of alternative life narratives
	Reauthoring one's life and relationships
Goals of Intervention	Awaken the client from a problematic pattern of living
	Free the client from externally imposed constraints
	Help the client author stories of dignity and competence
	Recruit supportive others as audiences (and supports) for the client's new life story
Nature of Worker/ Client Relationship	A collaborative atmosphere
	Social worker relinquishes "expert" position
	The social worker as archaeologist
	Worker communicates to clients that they are protagonists in their life stories
	Labels and divisions of behavior into normal and abnormal are rejected
	Client is welcome to ask questions and make comments about the intervention process
Intervention Principles	Acknowledge the problem
	Normalize and strengthen
	Externalize the problem
	Encourage the client to tell and explore his or her life story
	Ask questions about personal meaning in the client's life
	Reflecting (deconstruction)
	Enhance client's understanding of the life story through reflective discussion
	Identify values and biases that underlie problem construction
	Enable the client to separate his or her life from knowledge and stories judged to be oppressive
	Help the client give up problem-saturated stories that result from rigid narratives
	Encourage the client to reauthor the life story with a preferred identity
	Enhance and change (reconstruction)
	Open up new possibilities with exceptions questions
	Envision (discuss alternate futures)
	Encourage the client to consider life perspectives that may be in conflict with the expectations of significant others
	Celebrating and connecting

APPENDIX: Narrative Theory Outline (Continued)

	Help the client make plans to sustain the new narrative
	Help the client connect with others in a familiar social world who will celebrate and acknowledge the new narrative
	Leave the door open for occasional future consultations without boundaries on time frames
Assessment Questions	Ask questions about how the client spends his or her time in an effort to learn how he or she sees himself or herself
	Ask about strengths, talents, and accomplishments as a means of setting the stage for a constructive emphasis

13

Crisis Theory and Intervention

'Twas Crisis – All the length had passed –
That dull – benumbing time
There is in Fever or Event –
And now the Chance had come –
The instant holding in its claw
The privilege to live
Or warrant to report the Soul
The other side the Grave.★

S tudying *crisis theory* provides a means for us to integrate many of the theoretical perspectives described throughout this book. Crisis theory is sometimes
described as a *theory of human behavior*, and sometimes as a *theory for clinical practice*.
It can alternately pertain to the study of human reactions to highly stressful situations, or to the principles of intervention that can be used with clients experiencing crises. In this final chapter, we will consider both aspects of crisis theory, but
focus more closely on intervention. These topics are important to study because
social workers of all theoretical backgrounds often work with people in crisis,
regardless of agency setting.

A *crisis* can be defined as the *perception* or *experience* of an event (genuine
harm, the threat of harm, or a challenge) as an intolerable difficulty (James &
Gilliland, 2001). The crisis is an aberration from the person's typical pattern of
functioning, and he or she cannot manage the event through usual coping methods. The person either lacks knowledge about how to manage the situation or,
because of feeling overwhelmed, lacks the ability to focus his or her energies on
it. All of us experience crises at times in their lives. A crisis often results when we

---

★Reprinted by permission of the publishers and the Trustees of Amherst College from *The Poems of Emily Dickinson*,
Thomas H. Johnson, ed., Cambridge, Mass.: The Belknap Press of Harvard University Press, Copyright © 1951, 1955,
1979, 1983 by the President and Fellows of Harvard College.

face a serious stressor with which we have no prior experience. The stressor may be biological (a major illness), interpersonal (the sudden loss of a loved one), environmental (unemployment or a natural disaster), or existential (inner conflicts regarding values and purpose in life).

Crisis intervention can be used with a range of presenting problems, such as sexual assault, medical illness, combat stress, post-traumatic stress, migration, suicidal ideation, chemical dependence, personal loss, school violence, partner violence, and family stress (James & Gilliland, 2001; Lantz & Walsh, 2007). It represents a strengths approach because it underscores the possibility of client growth, even in horrible situations. The social worker must build upon clients' strengths in order to help them adapt to, and grow from, the experience.

A strengths-based approach to crisis intervention is founded on the following practice assumptions (Chazin, Kaplan, & Terio, 2000).

1. In a crisis event, each individual's response is unique, and the helping process should be individualized.
2. Each individual is the "expert" in his or her own recovery process. Social workers facilitate what is already there—strengths and copings skills, and connecting with supports and resources.
3. The natural recovery process needs to occur without artificial interventions disrupting the process as much as possible. "Help," whether psychological first aid or practical assistance, should fit seamlessly into the natural process.

ORIGINS AND SOCIAL CONTEXT

Social workers have practiced crisis intervention since the profession's earliest years (Golan, 1987). In fact, the social work profession emerged in response to socially identified needs to help growing numbers of citizens who experienced high-stress situations. Smith College offered its first summer program in 1918 to train workers in skills for rehabilitating shell-shocked soldiers. Social workers also provided services in the first suicide prevention center, the National Save-a-Life League in New York City in 1906. Through the years caseworkers assisted families experiencing disruption during the Great Depression; homeless, runaway, and impoverished people (through the Traveler's Aid Societies); and people dealing with life disruptions during World War II (though family service agencies). Social workers generally preferred long-term interventions during those years, but, as caseloads and waiting lists increased, they effectively adopted short-term approaches as well (Parad, 1965).

Formal crisis theory was developed in the fields of psychiatry, psychology, and sociology. It first emerged during the 1940s, primarily through the work of psychiatrists Erich Lindemann and Gerald Caplan, both of whom had been affiliated with Massachusetts General Hospital (Roberts, 2000). Lindemann and his associates developed concepts of crisis intervention in the aftermath of Boston's Coconut Grove nightclub fire, in which 493 people died. Their ideas were based on observations of the grief reactions of survivors and the friends and relatives of those who died. Lindemann identified common crisis (grief) reactions of somatic distress, guilt, anger, disrupted patterns of conduct, and preoccupation with images of the deceased. He concluded that the length and outcome of a grief reaction were dependent on the person's having time to mourn, adjust to the changed environment, and eventually develop new relationships.

Military psychiatrists have always tried to predict the behavior of soldiers in field situations, and to quickly rehabilitate those who become overwhelmed. Lindemann's ideas were adapted to military intervention methods during World War II. Crisis outcomes were found to be most positive when soldiers were treated close to the setting of the precipitating event (the front lines), when the psychiatrist focused only on the immediate situation, and when the soldier was returned to the combat situation in a relatively short time (Golan, 1987).

Caplan (1990) expanded on Lindemann's work of the 1940s and 1950s. His ideas were influenced by his work with immigrant mothers and children. Among his major contributions to crisis theory was the idea that all people are vulnerable to crisis reactions during developmental transitions, such as moving into adolescence and adulthood. Caplan specified two types of crises: normal life transitions and hazardous events. He was the first to relate the concept of homeostasis to crisis intervention and to describe stages of a crisis reaction, which will be presented later. It is noteworthy that developmental theorists, such as Erikson (1968), also postulated the normalcy of psychosocial crises in human development during the 1950s and 1960s. Further, the field of sociology made important contributions to crisis theory with studies on the effects of stressful family events such as marriage, parenthood, and old age on family structure and member interaction.

In the 1960s, the social worker Lydia Rapoport wrote about the importance of adapting various clinical intervention modalities, such as ego psychology, learning theory, and others, to crisis intervention. She emphasized the importance of rapid assessment, and the practitioner's ready access to the victim. Later, Naomi Golan (1978) emphasized that people were most receptive to receiving help during the most difficult period of a crisis, and that intensive, brief interventions were more successful when the client was motivated in this way.

The suicide prevention movement expanded greatly during the 1960s, initially with telephone hotlines. Between 1966 and 1972, the number of these centers grew nationally from 28 to almost 200. The greatest boost to crisis intervention programs came with the community mental health movement, for which 24-hour crisis programs were a required component. The number of centers that included these units grew to almost 800 by 1980.

Social interest in providing crisis intervention services exploded during the 1970s for two major reasons (Myer, 2001). One was the increase in geographic mobility in the United States and other modern countries, and many people's consequent lack of ties to nuclear families and other primary supports. Myer cites evidence of 130 million situational crisis episodes occurring annually in the United States. A second reason is the awareness in science of links between psychological trauma and long-term neurological disorders (Nelson & Carver, 1998). Today, crisis programs continue to be found in mental health centers and hospitals.

Most social workers receive training in crisis intervention in schools or their agencies, as it is recognized that clients of all types may experience crises.

MAJOR CONCEPTS

Stress

Stress can be defined as an event in which environmental or internal demands tax or exceed a person's coping resources (Lazarus & Lazarus, 1994). The event may be *biological* (a disturbance in body systems, such as the experience of a disease), *psychological* (cognitive and emotional factors involved in the evaluation of a stressor, such as the fear of an important relationship ending), or *social* (the disruption of a social unit; for example, the closing of a town's major industrial plant). Psychological stress, about which we are primarily concerned in this chapter, can be summarized into three categories:

- *Harm* refers to the effects of a damaging event that has already occurred.

- *Threat* is probably the most common form of psychological stress. The person perceives a potential for harm in an event that has not yet happened.

- *Challenge* consists of events that a person appraises as opportunities, rather than occasions for alarm. The person is mobilized to struggle against the obstacle, as with a threat, but with a different attitude. Faced with a threat, a person is likely to act defensively. In a state of challenge the person is excited and confident about the task to be undertaken. The challenge may be perceived as a productive experience.

The nature of a person's experience of stress is related to biological constitution and previous experiences in managing stress (Aldwin, 1994). Vulnerability to stress is also related to one's position in the social structure; some social positions (including poverty, racism, and blocked opportunities) are exposed to a greater number of adverse situations than others (Lupien, King, Meaney, & McEwen, 2000). Although a single event may pose a crisis for one person but not another, some stressors are so severe that they are almost universally experienced as crises.

Traumatic stress refers to events that involve actual or threatened severe injury or death to oneself or to significant others (APA, 2000). These include *natural* (such as flood, tornado, earthquake) and *technological* (such as nuclear) disasters; *war and related problems;* and *individual* trauma, such as being raped or assaulted (Aldwin, 1994). Many trauma survivors experience a set of symptoms known as *post-traumatic stress disorder* (APA, 2000). These symptoms include persistent reliving of the traumatic event, persistent avoidance of stimuli associated with the traumatic event, and a persistently high state of arousal. The symptoms of post-traumatic stress disorder may occur as soon as one week after the event, or as long as 30 years after! Complete or partial recovery from symptoms is possible, but not certain (almost 50% of survivors continue to experience some long-term symptoms), which supports the importance of timely professional intervention (Sadock & Sadock, 2007).

Crisis

The term *crisis* was defined earlier. To elaborate, the experience of crisis occurs in three stages (Caplan, 1990). First, there is a sharp and sudden increase in the person's level of tension. Second, the person tries but fails to cope with the stress, which further increases tension, and contributes to the sense of being overwhelmed. At this point the person is highly receptive to accepting help. Third, within approximately four weeks, the crisis resolves, either negatively (with an unhealthy coping solution) or positively (with successful management of the crisis and perhaps an enhanced sense of personal competence). The emotions most likely to emerge in a person's experience of crisis include anxiety, guilt, shame, sadness, envy, jealousy, and disgust (Lazarus, 1993).

Types of Crises   Crises can be classified into three types (Lantz & Walsh, 2007). *Developmental* crises occur as events in the normal flow of life create dramatic changes that produce extreme responses. Examples include college graduation, the birth of one's child, a midlife career change, and retirement from primary occupations in later life. People may experience crises at these times if they have difficulty negotiating the typical challenges outlined by Erikson (1968) and Germain and Gitterman (1996). *Situational* crises refer to uncommon and extraordinary events that a person has no way of forecasting or controlling. Examples include physical injuries, sexual assault, loss of a job, illness, and the death of a loved one. *Existential* crises are characterized by escalating inner conflicts related to issues of purpose in life, responsibility, independence, freedom, and commitment. Examples include remorse over past life choices, a feelings that one's life has no meaning, and a questioning of one's basic values or spiritual beliefs.

A Person's Response to a Crisis   A client in crisis may follow three general courses (James & Gilliland, 2001). In the *growth* pattern, the client recovers from the event and then, often with the help of a practitioner, develops new skills and strengths. In the *equilibrium* pattern, the client returns to the pre-crisis level of functioning, but does not experience enhanced social functioning. In the *frozen crisis* pattern, the client does not improve, but makes adjustments that involve harmful strategies (such as substance abuse) that keep him or her in a chronically troubled state.

Whether a stress experience becomes a crisis depends on the person's coping capacities, so we now turn to a discussion of that concept.

Coping and Adaptation   Coping is a person's efforts to master the demands of stress (Lazarus, 1993). It includes the thoughts, feelings, and actions that constitute those efforts. Adaptation involves related adjustments the person makes in biological responses, perceptions, or lifestyle.

Biological Coping   The biological view of stress and coping emphasizes the body's attempts to maintain physical equilibrium, or a steady state of functioning (Seyle, 1991). Stress results from any demand on the body, specifically the nervous and hormonal systems, during perceived emergencies. The body's response to a stressor is called the *general adaptation syndrome*. It occurs in three stages. In the state of *alarm*, the body becomes aware of a threat. During *resistance*, the body attempts to maintain or restore homeostasis. This is an active response of the body in which endorphins and specialized cells of the immune system fight off stress and infection. In the third stage, *exhaustion*, the body terminates coping efforts because of its inability to physically sustain the state of disequilibrium. The immune system is constructed for adaptation to stress, but the cumulative wear and tear of stress episodes can gradually deplete its resources. Common outcomes of chronic stress include stomach and intestinal disorders, high blood pressure, heart problems, and some emotional disorders.

Psychological Coping   The psychological aspect of managing stress can be viewed in two different ways. Some theorists consider coping ability as a stable personality characteristic, or *trait;* others see it instead as a transient *state*—a process that changes over time, depending on the context (Lazarus, 1993). Those who consider coping a trait see it as an acquired defensive style, a set of automatic responses that enable us to minimize perceived threats. Those who see coping as a state, or process, observe that coping strategies change depending on our perceptions of the threats. The context has an impact on our perceived and actual abilities to apply effective coping mechanisms. The trait and state approaches can be integrated. That is, coping can be conceptualized as a general pattern of managing stress that incorporates flexibility across diverse contexts.

A person's coping efforts may be *problem-focused* or *emotion-focused* (Lazarus, 1993). The function of problem-focused coping, which includes confrontation and problem-solving strategies, is to change the stressful situation. This method tends to dominate when we view the situation as controllable by action. In emotion-focused coping (distancing, avoidance, and reappraisal of the threat) the external situation does not change, but our behavior or attitudes change with respect to it. When we view stressful conditions as unchangeable, emotion-focused coping may dominate. People may productively use either of these general approaches at different times.

American culture tends to venerate problem-focused coping and the independently functioning self, and to distrust emotion-focused coping and what may be called relational coping. Relational coping takes into account actions that maximize the survival of others—such as families, children, and friends—as well as the self (Banyard & Graham-Bermann, 1993). Feminist theorists propose that women are more likely than men to employ the relational coping strategies of negotiation and forbearance. Further, power imbalances and social forces such as racism and sexism affect the coping strategies of individuals. Social workers must be careful not to assume that one type of coping is superior to the other.

People exhibit some similarities in the ways they cope with crises and the ways they cope with everyday stress, but there are several differences (Aldwin, 1994). Because people tend to have less control in crisis situations, a primary coping strategy is emotional numbing, or the constriction of emotional expression. They also make greater use of the defense mechanism of denial. Confiding in others takes on greater importance. The process of coping takes a longer time, and reactions may be delayed for months. The search for ultimate values and life meanings takes on greater importance, and personal identity transformations are more common. Despite the many negative consequences of traumatic stress, however, it is important to recognize that survivors sometimes report the experience as positive. In this "growth" pattern (Lantz & Walsh, 2007), clients utilize their experience to discover new strengths, skills, behavioral patterns, insights, and meaning potentials in their lives.

As described below, a strong system of social support helps a person to avoid or recover from crises.

Social Support Social support can be defined as the interpersonal interactions and relationships that provide people with assistance or positive feelings of attachment (Hobfoll, Freedy, Lane, & Geller, 1990). A key function of crisis intervention should involve the client's linkage with formal or natural social support resources. The utilization of natural supports by clients is important because of limits in the scope and availability of formal services. Most important, natural supports promote normalcy in clients' lives.

Many people perceive their support networks to be inadequate. McPherson, Brashears, and Smith-Lovin (2006) found that 43.6% of their 2004 sample reported that they have either no one or only one person with whom they discuss important matters in their lives, in contrast to an average of three such persons reported in a 1985 sample. People who experience "marginalizing" problems, such as chronic mental and physical disorders, tend to have smaller networks that people whose challenges are more universal.

There are many possible sources of social support. Examples include the client's subjective perceptions of support from family and friends (Procidano & Heller, 1983), and the availability of others who can provide listening, task appreciation, task challenge, emotional support, emotional challenge, reality confirmation, and personal assistance (Richman, Rosenfeld, & Hardy, 1993). One relatively simple system with utility for crisis intervention focuses on the availability of *material* support (food, clothing, shelter, and other concrete items), *emotional* support (all interpersonal supports), and *instrumental* support (services provided by casual contacts, such as grocers, hairstylists, and landlords) (Walsh & Connelly, 1996). Supportive relationships often occur in *clusters,* distinct categories of interaction such as the nuclear family, extended family, friends, neighbors, formal community relationships, school peers, work peers, church associates, recreational groups, and professional associations (Vaux, 1990). Having contacts in a variety of clusters is desirable, as it indicates that a person is supported in many areas of life.

How Social Support AIDS Coping The experience of crisis creates an emotional arousal in a person that reduces the efficiency of his or her cognitive functioning (Caplan, 1990). When under stress, a person becomes less effective at focusing attention and negotiating the environment. Social supports help to compensate for these deficits in the following ten ways:

- Promotes an ordered worldview
- Promotes hope

- Promotes timely withdrawal and initiative
- Provides guidance
- Provides a communication channel with the social world
- Affirms one's personal identity
- Provides material help
- Contains distress through reassurance and affirmation
- Ensures adequate rest
- Mobilizes other personal supports

There is no consensus about how social workers can evaluate a client's level of social support, but one useful model suggests gathering four types of information (Vaux, 1988). The social worker asks the client to list all persons with whom he or she has interacted in the past one or two weeks. Next, the social worker asks the client to draw from that list the persons he or she perceives to be supportive in significant ways. The client is then asked to describe specific recent acts of support provided by those significant others. Finally, the social worker asks the client to evaluate the adequacy of the support received from each source. Based on this assessment the social worker can identify the client's supports and target certain cluster areas for development.

ASSESSMENT AND INTERVENTION

Overview

Crisis intervention requires the social worker's attention to structured stages, as listed below and adapted from Corwin (2002) and Dixon (1987).

Rapid establishment of a constructive social worker/client relationship. The social worker must connect quickly with the overwhelmed client through demonstrations of acceptance, empathy, and verbal reassurance. The social worker must convey a sense of optimism and hope to the client, as well as his or her competence to assist in the resolution of the crisis. The social worker must be active in helping the client focus and make decisions, and the practitioner may also establish relationships in person or by phone with the client's significant others, if appropriate and available.

Eliciting and encouraging the client's expression of painful feelings toward the goal of helping the client feel calmer, gain greater mastery of his or her emotions, and become better able to focus on immediate challenges.

Assessment must be rapid but thorough enough to result in a well-crafted intervention plan. The social worker investigates the full range of precipitating factors, the meaning to the client of the hazardous event (considering cultural factors), the client's existing capacities for adaptive functioning, and the client's potential and actual support systems. A formal assessment protocol is described later. Notice, however, that assessment is not the first stage in crisis intervention. The client's other needs are initially more pressing.

Restoration of cognitive functioning. After assessment, the social worker shares his or her (possibly tentative) conclusions with the client about the causes of the crisis and the meaning of the client's reactions. This normalizes the experience somewhat for the client and helps him or her to assume a proactive problem-solving attitude in contrast to the initial avoidance strategies.

Planning and implementing interventions. Depending on the situation, the social worker can draw from many intervention options. All of these must incorporate time limits, structure, a here-and-now orientation, and a high level of practitioner activity. They must include the social worker's continued reassurance and encouragement of the client, enhancement of his or her ability to connect current stress with patterns of past functioning, and promotion of improved coping methods. A review of major developments in the field of trauma provides encouraging evidence regarding the efficacy of exposure-based treatments for victims (Kamphuis & Emmelkamp, 2005). As the client regains a sense of safety, control, and support, the social worker's level of activity diminishes.

Environmental work secures and develops material and social supports for the client, as needed. This involves referral and linkage and, if needed, the practitioner's advocacy for the client with other systems.

Ending and follow-up. To assist with anticipatory guidance, the social worker may review the crisis episode and what the client learned from it as a means of preventing future crisis episodes. There is some discouraging evidence, however, regarding the efficacy of debriefing following trauma, based on the rationale that such activity sensitizes the victim to the possibility of pathology (Rose, Bisson, Churchill, & Wessely, 2002). In contrast to this evidence, one recent study found that "high-avoidance copers" appear to benefit from post-trauma information provision, so, for at least some trauma survivors, debriefing appears to be a useful strategy (Gist & Devilly, 2002).

Assessment

The purpose of crisis assessment is to gather information from the client and perhaps his or her significant others about the crisis in order to help the client mobilize resources as quickly as possible. Because it must be completed quickly and retain a focus, it is less in-depth than assessments in other types of practice. The social worker learns more about the client as the intervention proceeds, and the client's mental status stabilizes. The social worker initially attempts to get information from the client about safety options, the dynamics of the crisis situation, prior attempts to resolve the problem, and information about support systems. The following questions should be a part of that assessment:

- What factors can the client identify relative to the onset of the crisis?
- What is the current quality of the client's affective, cognitive, and behavioral functioning? Which areas appear to be the most adversely affected?
- Is the client self-destructive?

- Does the client require immediate medical or psychiatric attention?
- How does the client's current level of functioning compare with pre-crisis functioning?
- Has there been significant trauma, illness, pathology, or substance abuse in the client's past?
- What are the client's strengths? Areas of life stability?
- What are the client's realistic alternatives for managing the distress?
- What are the client's formal, informal, and potential support systems?
- Are there financial, social, or personal impediments to the client's progress?

One example of a structured assessment process is the *triage assessment model* (Myer, 2001). It assesses crisis reactions in the domains of affect, cognition, and behavior. Each of these domains includes three types of possibly problematic responses. In the affective domain these include anger/hostility, anxiety/fear, and sadness/melancholy. The cognitive domain includes the client's perception of the event as a transgression, threat, or loss. Reactions in the behavioral domain include the client's patterns of approach, avoidance, or immobility. The *Triage Assessment Form* attaches severity scores to each of these domains (Myer, Williams, Ottens, & Schmidt, 1992). The greater the severity of the client's reaction, the more directive the social worker should be.

A Word About Suicide Assessment

Before moving into a discussion of crisis intervention, it is worth identifying some special issues that surround the topic of suicide prevention. Suicide is estimated to be the tenth leading cause of death in the United States (Strasser & Strasser, 1997). It has also been reported that 1 in 20 adolescents meets the criteria for Major Depressive Disorder (March, Franklin, & Foa 2005). Depression is considered a leading factor in suicidal behavior, and suicide is the third leading cause of death for adolescents ages 15 to 19 (Bertera, 2007).

There are numerous factors associated with an increased risk of suicidal behavior in people of all ages (Bertera, 2007; James & Gilliland, 2001; Miller & Glinski, 2000). Women are more likely than men to attempt suicide, but men are more likely to successfully complete suicide. Elderly people and adolescents are more likely to attempt suicide than other age groups. Separated or divorced people are more likely to attempt suicide than people who are married. People suffering from serious medical illnesses, such as cancer, are more likely to attempt suicide than healthy people. People who experience chronic pain are frequently at risk for suicide. People suffering from chronic mental illness are at an increased risk for suicide. People who have previously attempted suicide are at greater risk than people with no previous attempts. People suffering with depression often wish to commit suicide in order to "end their pain." Finally, people who are experiencing a crisis of any type are often at risk to commit suicide.

A risk and protective factor model for suicide assessment includes the social worker's attention to the following five areas (Högberg & Hällström, 2008):

- Historical information about the client—demographic, developmental, mental health, and medical information

- Personal information—the client's general cognitive, emotional, and ego functioning

- Clinical information—the specific symptoms of the client's depression

- Person-environmental interactions—the significance to the client of any life transitions, loss episodes, developing isolation, or breakdowns in social support

- Protective factors—the client's present social supports, occupational supports, sense of purpose in living, social skills, and children

The social worker's presentation to the client is key to a successful suicide intervention process (Högberg & Hällström, 2008). The social worker's relationship with the client is a powerful, respectful collaboration in which the social worker acknowledges that some topics, like suicide, are overwhelming to deal with. The social worker conveys an empathic understanding of the client and the client's meaning of suicide, and does not initially take a judgmental stance about the possibility of suicide. The social worker assures the client that he or she will not take any actions against the client's will unless an impasse is reached and the situation is such that the social worker has no other choice. That is, the social worker affirms the client's feelings, but at the same time helps the client separate these valid feelings from the link to self-destructive behavior. The social worker's conversational mode conveys safety and respect, inviting the client to move the discussion in certain directions, and allowing the client to proceed at his or her own pace.

Intervention

Crisis intervention is a unique practice modality, but the social worker's specific intervention strategies must be adapted from other practice theories. That is, crisis theory does not suggest unique interventions. The remainder of this section considers the social worker's intervention options, all of them drawn from theories presented earlier in the book.

Two unique features of crisis intervention are the social worker's short-term but sometimes intensive involvement with the client and his or her significant others, and the social worker's active use of the environment in establishing linkages and supports. For this reason it is important for us to review a commonly recognized but underappreciated professional role: that of the clinical case manager.

Clinical Case Management   Case management is an approach to service delivery that focuses on developing growth-enhancing environmental supports for clients, using resources that are spread across agency systems (Rubin, 1992). In *clinical* case management, the social worker combines the interpersonal skill of the clinical practitioner with the action orientation of the environmental architect (Walsh, 2000). It includes the following 13 activities in four areas of focus (Kanter, 1996):

- *Initial phase*—Engagement, assessment, and planning
- *Environmental focus*—Linking clients with community resources, consulting with families and caregivers, maintaining and expanding social networks, collaborating with physicians and hospitals, and advocacy
- *Client focus*—Intermittent psychotherapy, living skill development, and psychoeducation
- *Client-environment focus*—Monitoring the client's activities and progress within the service system.

There are three therapeutic tasks for the social worker in clinical case management practice (Harris & Bergman, 1988). First is to forge a relationship, or make a positive connection, with the client. This may unfold in a variety of ways depending on a particular client's characteristics, and may range from high levels of interaction to maintaining formality and distance. Second is to model healthy behavior in ways that may facilitate the client's movement from a position of dependence to greater self-efficacy during the crisis period. Finally, the social worker must alter the client's physical environment, as needed, to facilitate his or her improved adjustment to the crisis situation.

In addition to relationship-building skills, the clinical skills needed for case management include the social worker's ability to do the following (Kanter, 1996, 1995):

- Recognize a client's fluctuating competence and changing needs
- Develop a realistic view of the client's strengths, limitations, and symptoms
- Make ongoing judgments about the intensity of involvement with a client
- Titrate support to maximize a client's capacity for self-directed behavior
- Differentiate the biological and psychological aspects of reaction to a crisis
- Help the client's significant others cope with the crisis situation
- Appreciate the effects of social factors on a client's sense of competence
- Appreciate a client's conscious and unconscious motivations for behavior
- Maintain appropriate relationship boundaries during this often-intensive work

With the assumption that the social worker will almost always provide case management interventions in crisis work, we now consider a variety of specific clinical interventions, drawn from six theories presented in this book, which may be used as a part of that process. These interventions are not tied to specific types of crises, as their use may reflect, at least in part, the practitioner's preferences.

From Ego Psychology   *Ego-sustaining* techniques (Woods & Hollis, 2000) can help clients become mobilized to resolve their crises and to understand their motivations and actions more clearly. These strategies are particularly useful for clients who require a supportive relationship and an opportunity to process their distress through ventilation and reflection. Specific strategies for the social worker include *sustainment* (to develop and maintain a positive relationship), *exploration/description/ventilation* (to encourage the client's emotional expressions for stress relief and for gaining objectivity about problems), and *person-situation reflection* (toward solutions to present difficulties). The practitioner may also provide *education* to the client, often about environmental resources, and *direct influence,* particularly when the client is temporarily unable to exercise good judgment about self-care. The practitioner will almost certainly use the technique of *structuring* as a means of breaking down the client's concerns into manageable units.

The Sexual Assault Mary Ellen, a 21-year-old emergency medical technician, had a history of conflicted relationships with men. She had a low opinion of herself and, despite her best intentions, often entered into relationships with neglectful, verbally abusive men. At this time Mary Ellen was living with a female roommate and had been seeing a young man, Dale, for several weeks. The relationship was pleasant but superficial. One evening, however, Dale showed up at her apartment drunk. He was loud and threatening, and after a brief argument Mary Ellen told him to leave. Instead, he became angrier. Dale forced Mary Ellen to have sex with him after making threats that he would physically harm her otherwise. Afterward he abruptly left. Mary Ellen's roommate returned home soon, learned what had happened, and drove her distraught friend to the hospital.

Following a brief medical exam Mary Ellen saw Laura, a social worker, for a mental health assessment. In rape crisis situations Laura always intervened with the ego psychology techniques of sustainment and exploration/description/ventilation. She felt that it was important to initially communicate acceptance and empathy to rape victims, who usually felt degraded after the event. The social worker also used the structuring techniques to narrow the focus of the client's thoughts if the ventilation of feelings proved overwhelming. Later on in her interviews, Laura always educated clients about their options for self-care and (possibly) prosecution, and used direct influence to guide them toward resources (such as supportive friends, and medical and counseling professionals). Laura gave each client up to several hours of her time, and always made arrangements for them to leave with a close friend or family member.

Mary Ellen was by nature a quiet person who had learned to suppress her negative feelings as a coping strategy. Respecting this, Laura sat with her client and made calm, affirming statements about her innocence in the event. Mary Ellen gradually began to share feelings of fear and anxiety, but emphasized her capacity to "deal with it." The social worker acknowledged the client's strengths, but reminded her of some of the short- and long-term effects of rape that many women face. She educated the client about the resources available to her. Mary Ellen began to talk more freely, sensing Laura's acceptance, and eventually admitted to her anger at Dale and at all men. The client cried as she described her frustration with relationships in general, and her fears of going back home. Laura engaged in person-situation reflection with the client, who wanted to explore her pattern of destructive relationships with men. After Mary Ellen became quiet again, Laura helped her focus on precautions she could take to be safe. She helped the client make plans to have friends and family near, and to prevent future contact with Dale. Mary Ellen left with her roommate, agreeing to return to the outpatient clinic in a few days for a more extended counseling session.

From Behavior Theory   Behavioral interventions can be useful with clients whose crises are related to problematic reinforcement patterns (rewards and punishments) in their lives (Thyer & Wodarski, 2007). The techniques are useful when specific client (or significant others') behaviors are contributing to the crisis episode, and thus need to be adjusted for problem resolution. The social worker's target behaviors may relate to *life skills* training, *relaxation* training, *coping skills* training, *assertion* training, or *desensitization*. All behavioral interventions are highly structured, which is helpful for people who feel overwhelmed and out of control.

The Seizure Disorder   One winter morning, fifth-grade student Scott Owens had a seizure during math class. The teacher and other students watched in horror as the grand mal episode left the 11-year-old boy writhing on the floor for several minutes. Afterward, Scott was taken to the nurse's station, where he rested, recovered, and then went home with his mother. That first episode signaled the onset of a seizure disorder that would require ongoing monitoring and medication for Scott. While waiting for the results of the initial medical testing, Scott had a second seizure at school two weeks later. Medical treatment would soon eliminate seizures from Scott's life. The onset of the disorder, however, precipitated a crisis for him.

Scott felt humiliated about having the seizures at school. He was concerned that his classmates considered him a freak, or a frail, dangerous kid. He was also frightened about his health, wondering (despite what the medical tests revealed) if he had a brain tumor or disorder. His family and teachers were supportive, but Scott became depressed, isolative (not even going to basketball practice), and preoccupied. His fears were evident in his new tendency to become easily agitated about everyday frustrations. Some of Scott's peers did, of course, avoid and stigmatize him. Like many 11-year-old boys, Scott did not talk about his feelings, but the adults around him were concerned about the abrupt changes in his behavior.

Chandra, the school social worker, promptly organized a behaviorally based crisis intervention plan with Scott's teachers and parents. Chandra felt that Scott could be helped through this crisis if his engagement in healthy behaviors was gently and consistently encouraged. These behaviors, as identified by the adults, included talking (at least a bit) about his condition, participating in routine activities including schoolwork and sports, spending time with friends, and participating in family meals (a major shared activity in the household) and weekly church. The social worker had previously asked Scott about his own priorities, but he had declined to respond. Chandra asked Scott's parents and teachers to document "target" (pre–seizure disorder) levels of these activities, and also the level and quality of those behaviors since the seizures occurred. Chandra then helped the parties determine how they might reinforce Scott's efforts to resume his previous activities. She emphasized that they should avoid punishing Scott's problem behaviors because that might worsen his feelings.

During the meeting, they all agreed to: (a) provide Scott with information about seizure disorder and its controllable nature; (b) ask the physician to provide Scott with examples of patients with the disorder who lead normal lives; (c) monitor his use of anti-seizure medications; (d) encourage Scott to resume his sports activities; (e) enforce the importance of academic success, and expect that he perform well in that regard; and (f) speak to the parents of Scott's best friends to inform them of Scott's condition. Scott's teachers and parents would probably have focused on these activities without the social worker's help, but this structured approach helped their efforts be more quickly and consistently applied. Afterward, Scott was invited into the room so that they could share the plan with him. This was intended to confirm for Scott that they cared about him and were confident that he could adjust to his medical condition.

Scott was a resilient child who responded positively to the behavioral interventions within several weeks. He felt cared about, and the information he received about his disorder helped him develop a more balanced perspective. He never shared many feelings about the condition but did resume his normal activities. He had no further seizures, and his classmates eventually seemed to forget about the few episodes from the fifth grade.

From Cognitive Theory   Crises may be characterized by strong emotional reactions that are precipitated by a client's subjective, negative appraisals of a life situation. Examples of such developmental crises include moving out of the parental home, the loss of a close relationship, or the onset of post-college life. Even when a crisis is clearly due to some material deprivation, a client's core beliefs about the self and the world will influence his or her capacity to cope with the crisis. For these reasons, cognitive interventions may be effective in helping clients resolve crises. The steps involved in this type of cognitive intervention are as follows (Beck, 1995):

- Assess the client's cognitive assumptions, and identify any distortions that may contribute to the onset and persistence of the crisis
- When a client demonstrates clear thinking patterns, educate the overwhelmed client about ways of managing the crisis, and implement a problem-solving process (the social worker will need to be more directive than with clients who are not in crisis)
- When the client exhibits significant cognitive distortions, identify situations that trigger the critical misconceptions, determine how they can be most efficiently replaced with new thinking patterns, and implement corrective tasks

The social worker assesses the validity of a client's assumptions associated with the crisis issue through focused questions, such as "What is the *logic* behind the client's beliefs regarding the significance of the crisis situation?" "What is the *evidence* to support the client's views?" "What *other explanations* for the client's perceptions are possible?" "How do particular *beliefs* influence the client's attachment of significance to events, emotions, or behaviors related to the crisis?"

Strategies that may be used in cognitive intervention fit into three general categories. The first is *cognitive restructuring,* used when the client's thinking patterns are distorted and contribute to problem development and persistence. Some techniques include *education,* the *ABC (event/thought/feeling) review,* and the *point/counterpoint* technique. The second category is *problem solving,* a structured means for helping clients who do not experience distortions, but nevertheless struggle with certain life challenges. The third is *cognitive coping.* The practitioner helps the client learn and practice new or more effective ways of dealing with stress and negative moods. Some techniques include *self-instruction training* and *communication skills development.*

Many social workers combine intervention approaches from cognitive theory and behavior theory when working with clients in crisis. Cognitive interventions help clients to develop new ways of thinking, and behavioral approaches help reinforce clients' new thought patterns with effective new behaviors.

Woman with a Gun   Becky, a member of a mobile crisis intervention team, accompanied four police to the home of Kate Carter, a 30-year-old woman who was threatening to shoot herself. Kate had been abandoned earlier that day by her fiancé after an argument and physical altercation. She had called the mental health center's emergency number and said her fiancé was gone for good. Kate felt desperate. She stated that she was weak, unattractive, and unlovable. Becky, who had talked to Kate, assessed that the client was in danger of self-harm, but that her call was a constructive reaching out for help. Becky further assumed, with her clinical experience, that people in such crises focus only on their negative self-beliefs. Becky used cognitive intervention in these situations, gently pointing out the clients' distortions and helping them recall positive aspects of their lives.

Kate was inside the small house with a gun. She had taken several shots into the air while on the phone with Becky, and took one more such shot when the police first arrived. She commanded all of them to stay outdoors, but was willing to talk through the closed door. Becky kept a safe distance as she talked with the client. The social worker was patient, calm, and conversational. She got acquainted with Kate as much as the client would allow. She learned that Kate had been in and out of several intensive relationships in her adult life and, in her view, had always been abandoned. Becky also perceived that the client was somewhat dependent and histrionic, but she did not attempt to make any formal diagnosis.

Becky made comments and asked questions throughout the conversation to challenge the distortions that underlay the client's suicidal thoughts and feelings. Examples included: "Your relationship has not worked out, Kate. That doesn't mean that your entire life is a failure" (overgeneralization). "You seem to believe all the critical comments your fiancé made about you. But you were together for two years. I'm sure he saw good qualities in you as well. Can you identify any of them?" (selective abstraction). "Why do you assume that the breakup is all your fault? Don't you think he had anything to do with the problems?" (personalization). "I don't know anyone whose life is all good or all bad. You seem to think it is all bad now" (dichotomous thinking).

The client eventually calmed down, and agreed to go to a regional psychiatric unit for an assessment. She was hospitalized for four days, and then released to live with her older sister. Becky counseled Kate for several weeks until her mood stabilized and she was able to make some short-term plans. The social worker continued to support the client's initiatives, and to challenge her distortions. Some of these had surfaced in reaction to the situation, but others seemed to be rooted in core beliefs.

From Structural Family Theory   Families can experience crises as well as individuals with regard to such issues as housing, income, food, crime, violence, and medical care, among others. *Structural* family interventions are often appropriate in these cases. Structural theory assumes that the establishment and maintenance of appropriate authority, rules, roles, and subsystems within families facilitates productive behaviors among the members (Minuchin, Nichols, & Lee, 2007). The social worker is concerned with strengthening the basic organization of the family unit so that its members can constructively address their pressing concerns. Structural theory generally works well for families in crisis because it focuses on concrete goals that can be pursued even in a context of emotional turmoil.

During family assessment, the social worker must (in addition to providing case management services) identify any problematic structural characteristics, such as weak bonds between spouses or others, conflicts between family subsystems, the alienation or enmeshments of any members, and alliances outside the family that may be contributing to the crisis. Subsequent interventions may include any of the following:

- *Normalizing* some aspects of the crisis so that family members can develop a more confident attitude about the situation
- *Communication skills development,* in which the social worker instructs family members in methods of clear speaking and listening to better communicate their needs, ideas, and feelings about the situation
- *Supporting the family system's strengths*—providing compliments about aspects of family functioning that are going well during the crisis
- Encouraging family members to *enact* (through role-plays) rather than describe their old and new approaches to managing the crisis
- Helping the family to *modify its rules* through discussion and mutual decision making, to better adapt to the crisis situation
- *Clarifying each member's appropriate roles* within the family
- *Assigning tasks* for members to complete between meetings, to "practice" making adjustments in family organization in response to the crisis.

The Emergency Shelter   The Holton family faced immediate eviction from their apartment because of failing to pay rent over a period of several months. The family, consisting of mother Debra (31), children Sasha and Scott (8 and 6), and father Donald (27), had nowhere to go. Under increasing financial and marital stress during the preceding few months, Donald had been escaping to the company of his friends, leaving Debra to manage the household as best she could. Donald was drinking heavily, and Debra was becoming verbally abusive of the children. The children, in turn, were doing poorly in school, and getting into fights in the neighborhood. In a panic about the eviction, Debra called 911, and was quickly linked by phone with the Emergency Shelter (ES).

That same day, the shelter's social worker, Valerie, met with the Holtons. The shelter had an opening, and the family was offered placement there. Relative to structural family intervention, conditions of the placement were that both parents would: (a) attend ES parenting classes to learn more effective means of establishing appropriate expectations of their children; (b) participate in couples counseling with Valerie, to make decisions about their relationship and roles within the family; (c) participate in job-search activities (the shelter offered childcare); (d) ensure that their children were ready for school each day; and (e) use appropriate discipline with their children. Additional expectations of the agency were that the family would visit the department of social services for a financial benefits and housing assessment, not use any substances, observe curfew, and use psychiatric services if deemed appropriate by agency staff.

The Holton family was greatly relieved to secure the ES placement. Once the material crisis situation was relieved, all of them calmed somewhat, although family tensions were still evident. Donald and Debra frequently argued, and, though the children were well-behaved, they seemed to avoid both parents. Valerie noticed, as she often did, that, once the family became materially comfortable, their motivation to participate in growth activities at the shelter diminished. She needed to be firm with Donald and Debra about attending their classes and counseling. The family stayed at the center for 60 days, at which time a subsidized apartment became available for them. The relationship between Donald and Debra was still conflicted, but Donald had found a job and become more organized about budgeting income for the family. The couple had made some important agreements about childcare strategies that did not involve physical discipline. When the Holtons moved out of the shelter, Valerie was concerned that major responsibility for the family's cohesion would again fall to Debra, but all of them had nonetheless made important gains.

From Solution-Focused Therapy   In solution-focused crisis intervention the social worker and client attend to *solutions* or *exceptions* to problems, more so than to the problems themselves (Corcoran, 2000b). Its focus is on helping clients identify and amplify their strengths, so that available resources can be better utilized as solutions to the crisis. This approach is useful in crises when the client has the capacity to organize and direct his or her thinking and behavior. In solution-focused crisis intervention the social worker:

- *Accepts the client's perspective* on the crisis
- *Builds positive feelings and hope* within the client with future-oriented questions, such as "What will be different for you when our time here has been successful?"

- Collaborates with the client to *select specific, concrete, and prioritized goals*
- *Credits the client* for the positive elements of his or her behavior relative to the crisis
- *Asks strengths-reinforcing coping questions* ("How have you been able to manage the situation this well so far?")
- *Asks questions about the desired behavior of other people* in the client's life who are connected to the crisis situation
- Explores *exceptions* to the client's feelings and behaviors in the crisis situation ("Are there times when you think you can stand up the problem? How so?")
- Asks the *miracle question* to determine indicators of change that can be incorporated into solution tasks
- *Elicits solution-focused tasks* from the client in which he or she applies strengths to new and existing resources to test solutions to the crisis

The client's progress toward crisis resolution may be measured by scaling changes on a numerical continuum.

A Pregnancy Crisis   Gordon and Adrienne, a married couple in their 20s, were expecting their first child in three months. Although their marriage was strong, Adrienne had schizoaffective disorder and was, in the words of her husband, "psychologically fragile." There had been two episodes in which Adrienne became so anxious with paranoid delusions that she was unable to go outside their apartment on her own. She usually responded well to medications, but even so tried to minimize stress in her life by depending on her husband for support and spending much time at home. The couple had recently relocated near Gordon's family. Adrienne had not yet received mental health services in the new city.

The pregnancy had gone well until the seventh month, when Adrienne again began to develop psychotic symptoms. Gordon brought her to the local mental health agency for help, but after their assessment the doctor and social worker faced a dilemma. It would be dangerous to the child to medicate Adrienne prior to delivery. Yet Adrienne's symptoms worsened, and she begged for relief. She talked about being frightened for her life; she said that there were intruders trying to break into her house each afternoon while her husband was at work. She had called the police for help, but they were no longer willing to respond to the "crazy" calls. Gordon was trying to be supportive, but was stressed about his need to continue working. Sandy, the social worker, called for a meeting of the couple, the physician, and the client's mother-in-law to work out an alternative intervention plan.

Sandy felt that an intervention strategy was needed whereby the family and agency staff could provide Adrienne with enough support that she could get through the remaining months of her pregnancy without medication. Because the couple had been able to successfully contain Adrienne's symptoms in the past (although with medication), Sandy developed a solution-focused approach to the present crisis. He first reframed Adrienne's anxiety, remarking that pregnancy was a difficult time, and all women need extra help when they get close to delivery. He credited Adrienne and her family with having been able to manage her symptoms in the past, and then asked coping questions such as "What did you do to help Adrienne feel more secure in the past? What have you done recently that has been helpful?"

Sandy and the physician learned that Gordon had been staying home every evening, and he came home for lunch every day. Adrienne's in-laws had been visiting her each afternoon. The family acknowledged that this level of contact was excessive, and they were all becoming emotionally drained. Sandy credited Adrienne with having good judgment about when she needed help. He instilled positive feelings in the distressed client with such comments as "Your family cares, and wants to continue helping. We just need to figure out the best way to do this." The social worker asked about exceptions to the client's feelings of stress in the crisis situation, asking "Are there times when you have been able to stand up to your anxieties? How did you make that happen?" Adrienne and Gordon agreed that she was most comfortable in the afternoons when she was watching certain television programs or, on pleasant days, when she could walk in the park.

Sandy acknowledged that it might not be feasible for her husband, sister-in-law, mother-in-law, and counselor to be with her at all times. He led a discussion, however, in which the family eventually agreed on a schedule of contacts. The in-laws would take Adrienne along when they ran household errands (thereby accomplishing tasks while providing her with support), Gordon would call home at lunchtime each day, and the social worker would visit Adrienne at home twice weekly and call her once per week. The physician agreed to take Gordon's calls if he had questions about symptoms or felt the need to reconsider the medication option. Adrienne agreed to go for walks on sunny days if she felt enough energy to do so. These were all solution-focused tasks in which the family utilized existing resources to manage the crisis. Sandy agreed to meet with Gordon and Adrienne weekly to review task implementation.

The plan was successful in that Adrienne delivered her child (a daughter) without having to take psychotropic medication. It was a difficult process for all involved, however, as Adrienne pushed the limits of the plan, particularly by making many phone calls per day to the agency and to family members. As her delusions persisted, Adrienne became more demanding, but with mutual support the "team" maintained their situation. Adrienne was given appropriate medications immediately after delivery.

From Narrative Theory   Narrative theory asserts that people arrange their lives into stories to give them coherence and meaning (Monk, Winslade, Crocket, & Epston, 1997). As each person develops a dominant "story line," new experiences are filtered in or out, depending on whether they are consistent with the ongoing life narrative. Many crises that people experience during life transitions (divorce, children leaving home, death of loved ones, etc.) may be complicated by life narratives that exclude certain possibilities for self-understanding and future action. Narrative interventions, though not practical in most crisis situations because of its unstructured, slow-paced format, can help people gain greater control over their lives during difficult transitions.

Narrative therapy is a process of a client's coming to understand his or her life story through reflection, and then broadening that story to include new possibilities. Interventions generally adhere to the following stages:

Normalizing and strengthening. The social worker encourages the client to describe how he or she understands and approaches the crisis situation, and affirms the client's resources for dealing with it.

Reflecting (deconstructing). The social worker helps the client to analyze his or her assumptions about the self and the world in order to uncover the fundamental ideas and social relationships that are represented by the crisis. The social worker helps the client to identify values that underlie his or her construction of the crisis and the social conditions that contribute to the client's assumptions about the self.

Enhancing changes (reconstructing). The social worker helps the client to "give up" stories that result from rigid narratives and consider alternate stories about the past, present, and future, and to make decisions about the person he or she now wants to be.

Celebrating and connecting. The social worker helps the client make plans to sustain the new narrative, or the new sense of self, after crisis resolution.

The Empty Nest Wesley was a 42-year-old divorced man who lived in a small house with his only child, Ben, age 21. Wesley had been divorced for ten years. His wife had developed a serious substance abuse problem at that time, and moved across the country to escape her interpersonal problems with family, friends, and employers. Wes was given custody of their son, and he was a devoted father. The watch repairman had always felt guilty about the conflicted domestic situation during his son's youth, and became highly involved in Ben's life after the divorce. Ben had been a good high school and college student, majoring in engineering. Now he had accepted a job with a prestigious engineering firm in another part of the country. Wes was proud of his son, and gave him a new car as a gift.

Wes had been dreading the day his son moved away. He had organized his life around the young man, and ignored his own needs for other companionship and activities. The day his son flew off to his new situation, Wes became depressed. He cried every day for a week, and could not sleep well. He did continue working, and it was a customer who referred him for counseling at a local mental health agency. A social worker, Brad, was assigned to work with Wesley, and he quickly assessed that the client was in crisis. Wesley was not suicidal, but felt empty and lacking direction. Brad assumed a narrative stance with the client, inviting Wes to relate and explore the story of his marriage and parenting up to the present time. Wesley seemed to connect well with Brad, who was not much younger than he was. Brad encouraged Wesley to describe the person he was and wanted to be. He encouraged the client to talk about a variety of areas of his life. Wesley acknowledged that he had given up a number of personal interests after his marriage, and he eventually decided to resume some of them. Brad helped Wesley to understand that his age did not preclude him from developing relationships with women, something that Wesley had avoided after his marriage ended. Over a period of weeks, Wesley began to define himself as more than a parent. He was also a craftsman and outdoors enthusiast who had a greater interest in people than he had realized for a while. He continued to miss his son terribly, but felt more productively occupied, joining a hiking club and offering watch repair classes at a local community college.

Intervention Summary   Each social worker must adopt one or several theoretical perspectives and intervention strategies that will be useful for his or her client, depending on the nature of the crisis situation. The examples above have attempted to show how various interventions might be applied.

SPIRITUALITY AND CRISIS THEORY

It should not be surprising that, in times of crisis, people tend to draw upon their religious resources (if they have such beliefs and affiliations) or, in a more general sense, reflect on their most deeply held values and commitments. Indeed, a crisis may be spiritual (or existential) in nature, characterized by inner conflicts related to issues of purpose in life and commitment (remorse over past life choices, feeling that life has no meaning, and questioning basic values or spiritual beliefs). In every case, clients' worlds are turned inside out, and they may be either soothed or confused as they face the implications of the crisis for their spiritual lives.

The social worker must be prepared to help clients in crisis articulate their spiritual concerns, provide active listening, and perhaps link clients with appropriate resources to help them though the situation. For clients who have formal religious affiliations, the social worker should provide empathic listening, but also help the client connect with religious professionals for more formal assistance. The social worker can help clients who struggle with existential values face the facts of the spiritual dilemma, but also maintain hope for resolution. Periods of active crisis are not the time to engage clients in a critical reflection about their spirituality *unless* the crisis is spiritual in nature. Such an intervention may be appropriate following the client's stabilization.

As noted by Caplan (1990), the purposes of crisis support include the promotion of hope, reassurance and an affirmation of the client's sense of identity, and the mobilization of support from others. The first two of these directly touch on the social worker's ability to mobilize aspects of spirituality that will promote crisis resolution. Most of the intervention strategies included in this book can promote that goal.

ATTENTION TO SOCIAL JUSTICE ISSUES

The clinical social worker's development of crisis intervention skills is very much in keeping with the profession's value of promoting social justice. This is because all people, and all types of clients, are vulnerable to material and emotional crises throughout their lives. In that sense, crisis intervention skills may be the only set of clinical skills with equal applicability to all client populations. Further, through the linkage, referral, and advocacy activities that are common to crisis intervention, social workers can initiate change activities on behalf of vulnerable clients who experience crises related to such issues as poverty, unemployment, and discrimination. These activities can enhance clients' access to relevant information, services, resources, and opportunities about events critical to their lives. Social workers have a responsibility to develop knowledge about cultural and ethnic diversity, so that they can better understand the unique ways in which clients from special populations experience and recover from crises.

EVIDENCE OF EFFECTIVENESS

The effectiveness of crisis intervention across programs and types of clients is difficult to evaluate. Every crisis is different, and the nature of a crisis (the event, the client's perception of that event, and the client's resources) is significant in determining its course and outcome. Evaluating crisis intervention is further complicated by the absence of consistent theoretical or philosophical bases across programs. Perhaps for these reasons, little large-scale outcome research has been conducted on the topic. Some recent literature reviews have found that crisis intervention is effective for stabilizing people with severe mental illnesses (Joy, Adams, & Rice, 2006), and enhancing medication adherence (Haynes, Ackloo, Sahota, McDonald, & Yao, 2008).

Corcoran and Roberts (2000) have conducted a meta-analysis of the literature and acknowledge that, though clients consistently express satisfaction with crisis intervention services, other outcome measures might better determine the long-range impact of these services as well as their curative factors. Only four areas of crisis intervention are represented in the evaluation literature more than anecdotally: crime victimization, suicide prevention, psychiatric emergencies, and child abuse (Corcoran & Roberts, 2000). These are briefly summarized here. Two studies of victim assistance for child sexual abuse (including counseling and material assistance) found that parents were satisfied with those services and reported positive family changes. Three evaluations of police crisis teams (including officers and mental health workers) responding to domestic violence calls determined that the officers were able to make more arrests, and a majority of victims expressed that the intervention was helpful to their adjustments. Fourteen studies found a consistently negative correlation between the presence of suicide prevention centers and suicide attempts in a variety of cities, particularly among persons aged 15 to 24 years.

In ten studies psychiatric emergency services were found effective with regard to reduced client hospitalizations and perceived mental health benefits from clients. The services were effective for depressed persons, especially those who did not have co-morbid personality disorders. They further appeared to be more beneficial for females, older persons, and those from higher socioeconomic groups. A four-year follow-up of one crisis program determined that the only clients who required further intervention were those with previous treatment histories (Mezzina & Vidoni, 1996). In programs targeted to clients with severe mental illnesses (schizophrenia, bipolar disorder, and major depression), fewer clients were rehospitalized and a majority expressed service satisfaction. A short-term (three-day) inpatient crisis intervention program effectively relieved symptoms, and prevented longer-term hospitalizations for clients with mental illnesses (Ligon & Thyer, 2000). Programs for children and adolescents at mental health centers have also resulted in fewer hospital admissions. Treatment compliance and the presence of family support are often stated as important factors in positive outcome.

Family preservation services are intensive in-home programs of counseling and case management for children who are at risk of abuse or neglect. The goals of such services are to prevent out-of-home placements and improve family functioning. In 11 evaluation studies of these programs, all of which included a crisis intervention component, it was consistently found that fewer out-of-home placements occur. Interestingly, it does not appear that the quality of family functioning improved in all cases, and there is not always a positive correlation between parent attitudes about the program and placement outcomes. Parents often find these programs intrusive. A study of a related type of program found that community-based crisis intervention for children was successful in maintaining children in the home and increasing family adaptability and cohesion, but only in the short term (Evans, Boothroyd, Armstrong, Greenbaum, Brown, et al., 2003).

Because of the many uncontrollable factors involved in crisis intervention, evaluating their relative effectiveness requires creative use of various research designs (Dziegielewski & Powers, 2000). One set of researchers, writing about mobile crisis psychiatric programs, urges the development of evaluation strategies that can control for program variability, types of referrals, and program philosophy (Ferris, Shulman, & Williams, 2001). A more extensive use of service recipients in the evaluation process might also be helpful in clarifying impact factors.

CRITICISMS OF THE THEORY

Crisis intervention is composed of elements from many practice theories. It is not a coherent practice theory unto itself, and thus cannot be subject to the "thematic" criticisms raised with other theories in this book. No practitioner disputes that crisis intervention is an essential practice modality. What can be criticized, however, is crisis theory as a human behavior theory, with its emphasis on uniform stages in the experience of crisis for all people. What is needed is a greater application of cross-cultural knowledge to issues of crisis experience and recovery. Four related attributes that can productively guide the work of the crisis practitioner (and other practitioners) include knowledge about the status and experiences of different cultural groups, skills for implementing culturally appropriate crisis interventions, and experience in crisis intervention with different types of clients (Kiselica, 1998). Among the common assumptions that crisis practitioners must always question are that individuals (rather than the family or social group) should be the focus of crisis intervention, that a client's dependence on others is an undesirable trait, and that formal services are superior to a client's natural supports (Pedersen, 1987). The processes of assessment and planning in crisis intervention will become more appropriately client-centered as social workers develop broader guidelines for understanding the crisis experiences of different cultural groups.

SUMMARY

All clinical social workers must be prepared to provide crisis intervention services, regardless of their client population or practice setting. Although some agencies have special crisis programs, any client can experience a developmental, situational, or existential crisis. The social worker's specific methods of crisis intervention can be quite varied, but they must always fit the context of the client's level of distress and be characterized by rapid assessment, brief time span, focus on few issues, and a high level of practitioner activity. Crisis intervention is also unique for some social workers in that it often requires cooperative and intensive work with other professionals and the client's significant others. In this chapter, the nature of stress, crisis, and coping have been discussed, as well as a variety of strategies for crisis intervention, all of them drawn from the book's earlier chapters.

TOPICS FOR DISCUSSION

1. Share examples of crises that you or people you know (not clients) have experienced. What was the nature of the crisis? How did the person (or group) respond, and what factors seemed to influence the response?
2. Psychological stresses can be categorized as involving harm, threats, or challenges. Identify examples of each of these stress perceptions as they are seen in clinical practice. How does the way in which the situations are perceived influence clients' reactions? Are client perceptions generally realistic in this regard?
3. In this chapter, crisis intervention strategies are described from the perspective of six clinical practice theories. Consider other examples of client presentations that would be suited to each of these intervention perspectives.
4. All crisis interventions feature rapid assessment, time limits, a focus on few issues, and a high level of practitioner activity. Review the case illustrations included in this chapter and identify each of these features.

5. Discuss some ways that a social worker can help a client in crisis process issues of spirituality (when the client wishes to do so) while maintaining a position of spiritual "neutrality."

IDEAS FOR ROLE-PLAYS

Organize role-plays for each of the following scenarios in two parts. First, the social worker and client are meeting for the first time. Second, the social worker and client have met twice already, and are now engaging in their final conversation (the client may be terminating or being referred to another provider for ongoing assistance). As usual, use the roles of social worker, client, and observer/assistant, and include other details as desired.

1. A 52-year-old working mother with a spouse and two children (aged 25 and 20) learns that she has pancreatic cancer, and will probably not live through another year.
2. A family of four (father, 46; mother, 45; and two daughters, 16 and 11) has lost its home due to hurricane damage. They must break up temporarily to occupy other living quarters (the homes of a friend and a relative, and a shelter).
3. An adolescent learns that his single father is going to prison. He will be living with an aunt in another city whom he knows, but is not close to.

After each role-play, discuss the actions of the social worker, the rationales, and the apparent effectiveness.

APPENDIX: Crisis Theory Outline

Focus	The nature and types of crises experienced in human life
	Characteristics of crisis intervention
Major Proponents	Lindemann, Caplan, Parad, Rapoport, Golan
Origins and Social Context	The effects of stress in urban environments
	Formal studies of social disasters
	Studies of the behavior of soldiers in combat situations
	Suicide prevention movement
	Community Mental Health Centers Act
	Geographic mobility (separation from natural supports)
	Awareness of links between trauma and long-term neurological functioning
Nature of the Individual	Universality of crisis stages (event, failed coping, positive or negative adjustment)
Major Concepts	Crisis (developmental, situational, existential)
	Stress (including the general adaptation syndrome)

APPENDIX: Crisis Theory Outline (Continued)

	Crisis response (growth, equilibrium, frozen)
	Coping and adaptation (biological and psychological)
	Problem-focused
	Emotion-focused
	Social support (material, emotional, instrumental)
Developmental Concepts	Stress experiences
	Acquired coping patterns
Nature of Problems	Physical, psychological, and social events, the perceptions of which exceed coping capacities
Nature of Change	Growth, equilibrium, "frozen crisis"
Goals of Intervention	Restore the client to the pre-crisis level of functioning
	Enhance the client's pre-crisis coping skills
	Assist the client's personal transformation
Nature of Social Worker/Client Relationship	Intensive (client is vulnerable, receptive to help, dependent)
	Worker is active
	Client and worker focus on concrete tasks
	Worker may develop relationships with client's significant others, other professionals
Intervention Principles	Clinical case management
	Ego psychology
	Behavioral
	Cognitive
	Structural
	Solution-focused
	Narrative
Assessment Questions	What factors can the client identify related to the onset of the crisis?
	What is the current quality of the client's affective, cognitive, and behavioral functioning? Which areas appear to be the most adversely affected?
	Is the client suicidal?
	Does the client require immediate medical or psychiatric attention?
	How does the client's current functioning compare with his or her pre-crisis functioning?
	Has there been significant trauma, illness, pathology, or substance abuse in the client's past?
	What are the client's strengths? Areas of stability?

APPENDIX: Crisis Theory Outline (Continued)

What are the client's present alternatives for managing the stress?

What are the client's available support systems (both formal and informal)? Potential supports?

Are there financial, social, or personal impediments to the client's progress?

References

Abbott, A. (1999). *Department and discipline: Chicago sociology at one hundred.* Chicago: University of Chicago Press.

Ackerson, B. J., & Harrison, W. D. (2000). Practitioners' perceptions of empowerment. *Families in Society, 81*(3), 238–244.

Adams, J. F., Piercy, F. P., & Jurich, J. A. (1991). Effects of solution-focused therapy's "formula first-session task" on compliance and outcome in family therapy. *Journal of Marriage and Family Therapy, 17*(3), 277–290.

Adams, R. (1996). *Social work and empowerment.* London: Macmillan.

Addams, J. (1910). *Twenty years at Hull House.* New York: Macmillan.

Agostinelli, G., Brown, J. M., & Miller, W. R. (1995). Effects of normative feedback on consumption among heavy drinking college students. *Journal of Drug Education, 25,* 31–40.

Agras, W. S., Telch, C. F., Arnow, B., & Eldridge, K. (1995). Does interpersonal therapy help patients with binge eating disorder who fail to respond to cognitive-behavioral therapy? *Journal of Consulting & Clinical Psychology, 63*(3), 356–360.

Ainsworth, M. S., Blehar, M. C., & Waters, E. (1978). *Patterns of attachment: A psychological study of the strange situation.* Oxford, England: Lawrence Erlbaum.

Albarracín, D., Gillette, J. C., Earl, A. N., Glasman, L. R., Durantini, M. R., & Ho, M-H. (2005). A test of major assumptions about behavior change: A comprehensive look at the effects of passive and active HIV-prevention interventions since the beginning of the epidemic. *Psychological Bulletin, 131*(6), 856–897.

Aldwin, C. M. (1994). *Stress, coping, and development: An integrative perspective.* New York: Guilford.

Allen-Meares, P. (1995). *Social work with children and adolescents.* White Plains, NY: Longman.

Aman, L. A. (2001). Family systems multigroup therapy for ADHD children and their families. *Dissertation Abstracts International, 61*(10-B), 5548.

American Psychiatric Association (2000). *Diagnostic and statistical manual of mental disorders* (4th ed.). Washington, DC: Author.

Anderson, H., & Levin, S. B. (1998). Generative conversations: A postmodern approach to conceptualizing and working with human systems. In M. F. Hoyt (Ed.), *The handbook of constructive therapies: Innovative approaches from leading practitioners* (pp. 46–67). San Francisco: Jossey-Bass.

Andreae, D. (1996). Systems theory and social work treatment. In F. J. Turner (Ed.), *Social work treatment* (4th ed.) (pp. 601–616). New York: Free Press.

Andrew, G., & McMullen, L. M. (2000). Interpersonal scripts in the anger narratives told by clients in psychotherapy. *Motivation & Emotion, 24*(4), 271–284.

Angus, L., Levitt, H., & Hardtke, K. (1999). The Narrative Process Coding System: Research applications and implications for psychotherapy practice. *Journal of Clinical Psychology, 55*(10), 1255–1270.

Aponte, H. J., & DiCesare, E. J. (2002). Structural family therapy. In J. Carlson & D. Kjos (Eds.), *Theories and strategies of family therapy* (pp. 1–18). Boston: Allyn & Bacon.

Aponte, H. J., Zarski, J. J., Bixenstine, C., & Cibik, P. (1991). Home/community-based services: A two-tier approach. *American Journal of Orthopsychiatry, 61* (3), 403–408.

Apple, R. F. (1999). Interpersonal therapy for bulimia nervosa. *Journal of Clinical Psychology, 55*(6), 715–725.

Applegate, J. S. (1990). Theory, culture, and behavior: Object relations in context. *Child and Adolescent Social Work Journal, 7*(2), 85–100.

Appleyard, K., Egeland, B., van Dulmen, M. H., & Sroufe, L. A. (2005). When more is not better: the role of cumulative risk in child behavior outcomes. *Journal of Child Psychology and Psychiatry, 46*(3), 235–245.

Arean, P. A., & Cook, B. L. (2002). Psychotherapy and combined psychotherapy/pharmacotherapy for late

life depression. *Biological Psychiatry, 52,* 293–303.

Avnir, Y., & Shor, R. (1998). A systematic qualitative evaluation of levels of differentiation in families with children at risk. *Families in Society, 79*(5), 504–514.

Baker, A., Lee, N. K., Claire, M., Lewin, T. J., Grant, T., Pohlman, S., Saunders, J. B., Kay-Lambkin, F., Constable, P., Jenner, L., & Carr, V. J. (2005). Brief cognitive behavioural interventions for regular amphetamine users: A step in the right direction. *Addiction, 100*(3), 367–378.

Bandura, A. (1977). *Social learning theory.* Englewood Cliffs, NJ: Prentice-Hall.

Banyard, V. L., & Graham-Bermann, S. A. (1993). A gender analysis of theories of coping with stress. *Psychology of Women Quarterly, 17,* 303–318.

Bara, B. G. (1995). *Cognitive science: A developmental approach to the simulation of the mind.* Hove, UK: Lawrence Erlbaum.

Barber, J. P., Foltz, C., DeRubeis, R. J., & Landis, J. R. (2002). Consistency of interpersonal themes in narratives about relationships. *Psychotherapy Research, 12*(2), 139–158.

Barber, J. P., & Muenz, L. R. (1996). The role of avoidance and obsessiveness in matching patients to cognitive and interpersonal psychotherapy: Empirical findings from the Treatment for Depression Collaborative Research Program. *Journal of Consulting & Clinical Psychology, 64*(5), 951–958.

Barkley, R. A. (2000). Commentary: Issues in training parents to manage children with behavior problems. *Journal of the American Academy of Child & Adolescent Psychiatry, 39*(8), 1004–1007.

Barkley, R. A., Guevremont, D. C., Anastopoulos, A. D., & Fletcher, K. E.

(1992). A comparison of three family therapy programs for treating family conflicts in adolescents with attention-deficit hyperactivity disorder. *Journal of Consulting and Clinical Psychology, 60*(3), 450–462.

Barlow, C. A., Blythe, J. A., & Edmonds, M. (1999). *A handbook of interactive exercises for groups.* Needham Heights, MA: Allyn & Bacon.

Bartle-Haring, S. (1997). The relationships among parent-child-adolescent differentiation, sex role orientation and identity development in late adolescence and early adulthood. *Journal of Adolescence, 20*(5), 553–565.

Basham, K. K. (1999). Therapy with a lesbian couple: The art of balancing lenses. In J. Laird (Ed.), *Lesbians and lesbian families* (pp. 143–177). New York: Columbia University Press.

Baucom, D. H., Epstein, N., Rankin, L. A., & Burnett, C. K. (1996). Understanding and treating marital distress from a cognitive-behavioral orientation. In K. Dobson & K. Craig (Eds.), *Advances in cognitive-behavioral therapy* (pp. 210–236). Thousand Oaks, CA: Sage.

Beck, A. T. (1967). *Depression: Clinical, experimental, and theoretical aspects.* New York: Hoeber.

Beck, A. T. (1976). *Cognitive therapy and the emotional disorders.* New York: International Universities Press.

Beck, A. T. (1988). *Love is never enough.* New York: Harper and Row.

Beck, A. T., Steer, R. A., Bell, R., & Ramieri, W. F. (1996). Comparison of the Beck Depression Inventory IA and II in psychiatric outpatients. *Journal of Personality Assessment, 67*(3), 588–597.

Beck, J. S. (1995). *Cognitive therapy: Basics and beyond.* New York: Guilford.

Bell, L. G., Bell, D. C., & Nakata, Y. (2001). Triangulation and adolescent development in the U.S. and Japan. *Family Process, 40*(2), 173–186.

Bellak, L., & Goldsmith, L. A. (1984). *The broad scope of ego function assessment.* New York: Wiley.

Bellino, S., Zizza, M., Rinaldi, C., & Bogetto, F. (2007). Combined therapy of major depression with concomitant borderline personality disorder: Comparison of interpersonal and cognitive psychotherapy. *The Canadian Journal of Psychiatry, 52*(11), 718–725.

Benjamin, J. (1990). An outline of intersubjectivity: The development of recognition. *Psychoanalytic Psychology, 7*(suppl.), 33–46.

Beresford, P., & Evans, C. (1999). Research note: Research and empowerment. *British Journal of Social Work, 29,* 671–677.

Berlin, S. B. (2002). *Clinical social work practice: A cognitive-integrative perspective.* New York: Oxford.

Berlin, S. B. (1982). Cognitive behavioral interventions for social work practice. *Social Work, 27*(3), 218–226.

Bertera, E. M. (2007). The role of positive and negative social exchanges between adolescents, their peers and family as predictors of suicide ideation. *Child & Adolescent Social Work Journal, 24*(6), 523–538.

Bertolino, B., & O'Hanlon, B. (2002). *Collaborative, competency-based counseling and therapy.* Boston: Allyn and Bacon.

Besa, D. (1994). Evaluating narrative family therapy using single-system research designs. *Research on Social Work Practice, 4*(3), 309–325.

Beutler, L. E., & Baker, M. (1998). The movement toward empirical validation: At what level should we analyze, and who are the consumers? In K. S. Dobson & K. D. Craig (Eds.), *Empirically supported therapies: Best practice in professional psychology* (pp. 43–65). Thousand Oaks, CA: Sage.

Beyebach, M., Sanchez, M. S. R., de Miguel, J. A., de Vega, M. H., Hernandez, C., & Morejon, A. R. (2000). Outcome of solution-focused therapy at a university family therapy center. *Journal of Systemic Therapies, 19*(1), 116–128.

Binks, C. A., Fenton, M., McCarthy, L., Lee, T., Adams, C. E., & Duggan, C. (2006). Psychological therapies for people with borderline personality disorder. *Cochrane Database of Systematic Reviews 2006, Issue 1.* Art. No.: CD005652. DOI: 10.1002/14651858.CD005652.

Bisman, C. D., & Hardcastle, D. A. (1999). *Integrating research into practice: A model for effective social work.* Belmont, CA: Wadsworth.

Blagys, M. D., & Hilsenroth, M. J. (2000). Distinctive features of short-term psychodynamic-interpersonal psychotherapy: A review of the comparative psychotherapy process literature. *Clinical Psychology—Science & Practice, 7*(2), 167–188.

Blanck, G., & Blanck, R. (1979). *Ego psychology II: Psychoanalytic developmental psychology.* New York: Columbia University Press.

Blanco, C., Clougherty, K. F., Lipsitz, W. J., Mufson, L., & Weissman, M. M. (2006). Homework in interpersonal psychotherapy (IPT): Rationale and practice. *Journal of Psychotherapy Integration, 16*(2), 201–218.

Blanco, C., Lipsitz, W. J., & Caligor, E. (2001). Treatment of chronic depression with a 12-week program of interpersonal psychotherapy. *American Journal of Psychiatry, 158,* 371–375.

Blatt, S. J., & Felsen, I. (1993). Different kinds of folks may need different kinds of strokes: The effects of patients' characteristics on therapeutic process and outcome. *Psychotherapy Research, 3*(4), 245–259.

Blatt, S. J., & Ford, R. Q. (1999). The effectiveness of long-term, intensive inpatient treatment of seriously disturbed, treatment-resistant young adults. In H. Kaley & M. Eagle (Eds.), *Psychoanalytic theory as health care: Effectiveness and economics in the 21st century* (pp. 221–238).

Blatt, S. J., Ford, R. Q., Berman, W. H., Cook, B., Cramer, P., & Robins, C. E. (1994). *Therapeutic change: An object relations perspective.* New York: Plenum.

Bloom, M., Fischer, J., & Orme, J. G. (1995). *Evaluating practice: Guidelines for the accountable professional* (2nd ed.). Needham Heights, MA: Allyn & Bacon.

Blumer, H. (1969). *Symbolic interactionism: Perspective and method.* Englewood Cliffs, NJ: Prentice-Hall.

Boehm, A., & Staples, L. H. (2002). The functions of the social worker in empowering: The voices of consumers and professionals. *Social Work, 47*(4), 449–460.

Boog, B., Coenen, H., & Keune, L. (Eds.) (2001). *Action research: Empowerment and reflection.* Oisterwijk: Dutch University Press.

Borden, W. (2009). *Contemporary psychodynamic theory and practice.* Chicago: Lyceum.

Bowen, M. (1959). The family as the unit and study of treatment: I. Family psychotherapy. *American Journal of Orthopsychiatry, 31,* 40–60.

Bowen, M. (1978). *Family therapy in clinical practice.* Northvale, NJ: Jason Aronson.

Bowen, M. (1991a). Alcoholism as viewed through family systems theory and family psychotherapy. *Family Dynamics of Addiction Quarterly, 1*(1), 94–102.

Bowen, M. (1991b). Family reaction to death. In F. Walsh & M. McGoldrick

(Eds.), *Living beyond loss: Death in the family* (pp. 79–92). New York: Norton.

Bowlby, J. (1979). *The making and breaking of affectional bonds*. London: Tavistock.

Bozeman, B. N. (2000). The efficacy of solution-focused therapy techniques on perceptions of hope in clients with depressive symptoms. *Dissertation Abstracts International*, *61*(2-B), 1117.

Bredy, T., Weaver, I., Champagne, F. C., & Meaney, M. J. (2001). Stress, maternal care, and neural development in the rat. In C. A. Shaw & J. C. McEachern (Eds.), *Toward a theory of neural plasticity* (pp. 288–300). Philadelphia: Psychology Press/Taylor & Francis.

Brierley, E., Guthrie, F. A., Busby, C., Marino-Francis, F., Byrne, J., & Burns, A. (2003). Psychodynamic interpersonal therapy for early Alzheimer's disease. *British Journal of Psychotherapy*, *19*(4), 435–446.

Brodie, D. A. (2005). Motivational interviewing to promote physical activity for people with chronic heart failure. *Journal of Advanced Nursing*, *50*(5), 518–527.

Brownell, J. (1986). *Building active listening skills*. Englewood Cliffs, NJ: Prentice-Hall.

Buckley, W. (1967). *Sociology and modern systems theory*. Englewood Cliffs, NJ: Prentice-Hall.

Burke, B., Arkowitz, H., & Dunn, C. (2002). The efficacy of motivational interviewing and its adaptations: What we know so far. In W. R. Miller & S. Rollnick (Eds.), *Motivational interviewing* (2nd ed.). (pp. 217–250). New York: Guilford.

Burns, M. J. (1997). The effectiveness of a brief, inpatient group therapy program with sexually abused women. *Dissertation Abstracts International*, *57*(9–B), 5908.

Butler, A. C., & Beck, J. S. (2001). Cognitive therapy outcomes: A review of meta-analyses. *Journal of the Norwegian Psychological Association*, *37*, 698–706.

Butler, G., Fennell, M., Robson, P., & Gelder, M. (1991). Comparison of behavior therapy and cognitive behavior therapy in the treatment of generalized anxiety disorder. *Journal of Consulting and Clinical Psychology*, *59*, 167–175.

Butterworth, S., Linden, A., McClay, W., & Leo, M. C. (2006). Effect of motivational interviewing-based health coaching on employees' physical and mental health status. *Journal of Occupational Health Psychology*, *11*(4), 358–365.

Cacioppo, J. T., Berntson, G. G., Sheridan, J. F., & McClintock, M. K. (2000). Multilevel integrative analyses of human behavior: Social neuroscience and the complementing nature of social and biological approaches. *Psychological Bulletin*, *126*(6), 829–843.

Cancrini, L., Cingolani, S., Compagnoni, F., Costantini, D., & Mazzoni. (1988). Juvenile drug addiction: A typology of heroin addicts and their families. *Family Process*, *27*(3), 261–271.

Caplan, G. (1990). Loss, stress, and mental health. *Community Mental Health Journal*, *26*(1), 27–48.

Caplan, G. (1989). Recent developments in crisis intervention and the promotion of support services. *Journal of Primary Prevention*, *10*(1), 3–25.

Carlson, E. A. (1998). A prospective longitudinal study of attachment disorganization/disorientation. *Child Development*, *69*(4), 1107–1128.

Carroll, K. (1998). *A cognitive-behavioral approach: Treating cocaine addiction.* http://www.drugabuse.gov/TXManuals/CBT/CBT1.html. Downloaded on August 28, 2001.

Carroll, K. M. (1995). Methodological issues and problems in the assessment of substance use. *Psychological Assessment,* 7(3), 349–358.

Carroll, M. A. (1994). Empowerment theory: Philosophical and practical difficulties. *Canadian Psychology,* 35(4), 376–381.

Carter, B., & McGoldrick, M. (Eds.) (1999). *The expanded family life cycle: Individual, family, and social perspectives.* Boston: Allyn and Bacon.

Chamberlain, P., & Rosicky, J. G. (1995). The effectiveness of family therapy in the treatment of adolescents with conduct disorders and delinquency. *Journal of Marital and Family Therapy,* 21(4), 441–459.

Chambless, D. L., & Ollendick, T. H. (2001). Empirically supported psychological interventions: Controversies and evidence. *American Review of Psychology, 52,* 685–716.

Chambless, D. L. (1998). Empirically validated treatments. In G. P. Koocher, J. C. Norcross, & S. S. Hill (Eds.), *Psychologists' Desk Reference* (pp. 209–219). New York: Oxford.

Chazin, R., Kaplan, K., & Terio, S. (2000). The strengths perspective in brief treatment with culturally diverse clients. *Crisis Intervention & Time-Limited Treatment,* 6(1), 41–50.

Clark, C. L. (2000). *Social work ethics: Politics, principles, and practice.* Houndmills, Basingstoke, Hampshire: MacMillan Press.

Clarkin, J. F., Foelsch, P. A., Levy, K. N., Hull, J. W., Delaney, J. C., & Kernberg, O. F. (2001). The development of a psychodynamic treatment for patients with borderline personality disorder: A preliminary study of behavior change. *Journal of Personality Disorders,* 15(6), 487–495.

Coates, J., & Sullivan, R. (2006). Achieving competent family practice with same-sex parents: Some promising

directions. In J. J. Bigner (Ed.), *An Introduction to GLBT Family Studies* (pp. 245–270). New York: Haworth Press.

Cockburn, J. T., Thomas, F. N., & Cockburn, O. J. (1997). Solution-focused therapy and psychosocial adjustment to orthopedic rehabilitation in a work hardening program. *Journal of Occupational Rehabilitation,* 7(2), 97–106.

Cockle, S. (1993). Sandplay: A comparative study. *International Journal of Play Therapy,* 2(2), 1–17.

Coco, E. L., & Courtney, L. J. (1998). A family systems approach for preventing adolescent runaway behavior. *Adolescence,* 33(130), 485–497.

Cocoli, E. (2006). Attachment dimensions, differentiation of self, and social interest: A structured equations modeling investigation of an interpersonal-maturational model. *Dissertation Abstracts International, Section B: The Sciences and Engineering,* 67(6-B), 3343.

Coe, J. E. (1999). Developmental perspectives on women's experiences of loneliness. *Dissertation Abstracts International,* 59(8-A), 3206.

Coleman, D. (2006). Interpersonal psychotherapy for depressed adolescents. *Child & Adolescent Social Work Journal,* 23(1), 127–130.

Coleman, S. B., Avis, J. M., & Turin, M. (1990). A study of the role of gender in family therapy training. *Family Process,* 29(4), 365–374.

Coman, L. G. (1995). Family factors associated with the rearing of children of dysfunctional mothers by the maternal grandparents. *Dissertation Abstracts International,* 55(11-B), 5062.

Comes-Diaz, L., & Jacobsen, F. M. (1991). Ethnocultural transference and countertransference in the therapeutic cyad. *American Journal of Orthopsychiatry, 61*(3), 392–402.

Connolly, C. M. (2004). Clinical issues with same-sex couples: A review of the literature. In J. J. Bigner & J. L. Wetchler (Eds.), *Relationship therapy with same-sex couples* (pp. 3–12). New York: Haworth Press.

Connors, G., Donovan, D., & DiClemente, C. (2001). *Substance abuse treatment and stages of change: Selecting and planning interventions.* New York: Guilford.

Conte, H. R. (1997). The evolving nature of psychotherapy outcome research. *American Journal of Psychotherapy, 51*(3), 445–448.

Coombs, M. M., Coleman, D., & Jones, E. E. (2003). Working with feelings: The importance of emotion in both cognitive-behavioral and interpersonal therapy in the NIMH Treatment of Depression Collaboration Research program. *Psychotherapy: Theory, Research, Practice, Training, 39*(3), 233–244.

Cooper, M. G., & Lesser, J. G. (2002). *Clinical social work practice: An integrated approach.* Boston: Allyn & Bacon.

Corcoran, J. (2005). *Building strengths and skills: A collaborative approach to working with clients.* New York: Oxford.

Corcoran, J. (2000). Brief solution-focused therapy. In N. Coady & P. Lehman (Eds.), *Theoretical perspectives in direct social work practice: An eclectic-generalist approach* (pp. 326–343). New York: Springer.

Corcoran, J., & Roberts, A. R. (2000). Research on crisis intervention and recommendations for future research. In A. R. Roberts (Ed.), *Crisis intervention handbook: Assessment, treatment, and research* (2nd ed.) (pp. 453–486). New York: Oxford.

Corcoran, J., & Stephenson, M. (2000). The effectiveness of solution-focused therapy with child behavior problems:

A preliminary report. *Families in Society, 18*(5), 468–474.

Corcoran, K. & Videka-Sherman, L. (1992). Some things we know about effective social work. In K. Corcoran (Ed.), *Effective practice for common client problems* (pp. 15–27). Chicago: Lyceum.

Cournoyer, B., & Powers, G. (2002). Evidence-based social work: The quiet revolution continues. In A. R. Roberts & G. J. Greene (Eds.), *Social workers' desk reference* (pp. 798–807). New York: Oxford University Press.

Corwin, M. (2002). *Brief treatment in clinical social work practice.* Pacific Grove, CA: Brooks/Cole.

Cowley, C. B., Farley, T., & Beamis, K. (2002). "Well, maybe I'll try the pill for just a few months...": Brief motivational and narrative-based interventions to encourage contraceptive use among adolescents at high risk for early childbearing. *Families, Systems, & Health, 20*(2), 183–204.

Coyne, J. C. (1994). Possible contributions of 'cognitive science' to the integration of psychotherapy. *Journal of Psychotherapy Integration, 4*(4) 401–416.

Crepaz, N., Passin, W. F., & Herbst, J. H. (2008). Meta-analysis of cognitive-behavioral interventions on HIV-positive persons' mental health and immune functioning. *Health Psychology, 27*(1), 4–14.

Crits-Cristoph, P. (1998). Training in empirically validated treatments: The division 12 APA task force recommendations. In K. S. Dobson & K. D. Craig (Eds.), *Empirically supported therapies: Best practice in professional psychology* (pp. 3–25). Thousand Oaks, CA: Sage.

Crits–Christoph, P., Connolly, M. B., Shappell, S., Elkin, I., Krupnick, J., & Sotsky, S. (1999). Interpersonal narratives in cognitive and interpersonal psychotherapies. *Psychotherapy Research, 9*(1), 22–35.

Dahl, R., Bathel, D., & Carreon, C. (2000). The use of solution-focused therapy with an elderly population. *Journal of Systemic Therapies, 19*(4), 45–55.

Dalton, T. A. (1997). Listening to maternal stories: Reconstructing maternal-child relations to include the voices of mothers. *Dissertation Abstracts International, 58*(1-A), 0290.

Daniels, A. A. (1994). Reminiscence, object relations and depression in the elderly. *Dissertation Abstracts International, 54*(9-A), 3542.

Davis, M., Eshelman, E. R., & McKay, M. (2000). *The relaxation and stress workbook* (5th ed.). New York: MJF Books.

Day, P. J. (2000). *A new history of social welfare* (3rd ed.). Boston: Allyn & Bacon.

DeJong, P., & Berg, I. K. (2008). *Interviewing for solutions* (3rd ed.). Pacific Grove, CA: Brooks/Cole.

Dekovic, M. (1999). Parent-adolescent conflict: Possible determinants and consequences. *International Journal of Behavioral Development, 23*(4), 977–1000.

de Mello, M. F., de Jesus Mari, J., Bacaltchuk, J., Verdeli, H., & Neugebauer, R. (2005). A systematic review of research findings on the efficacy of interpersonal therapy for depressive disorders. *European Archives of Psychiatry and Clinical Neuroscience, 255*(2), 75–82.

Dennis, C. L., & Hodnett, E. (2007). Psychosocial and psychological interventions for treating postpartum depression. *Cochrane Database of Systematic Reviews*, Issue 4: Art. No.: CD00616.

DeRubeis, R. J., & Crits-Christoph, P. (1998). Empirically supported individual and group psychological treatments for adult mental disorders. *Journal of Consulting and Clinical Psychology, 66*(1), 37–52.

de Shazer, S. (1994). *Words were originally magic*. New York: Norton.

de Shazer, S. (1985). *Keys to solution in brief therapy*. New York: Norton.

Dewey, J. (1938). *Logic: The theory of inquiry*. New York: Holt.

DeYoung, P. A. (2003). *Relational psychotherapy: A primer*. New York: Brunner-Routledge.

Diamond, J. P. (1997). Narrative means to sober ends: Language, interpretation, and letter writing. *Dissertation Abstracts International, 57*(10-A), 4542.

Dingledine, D. W. (2000). Standing in the shadows: Adult daughters of alcoholic mothers. *Dissertation Abstracts International, 61*(5-A), 2037.

Dixon, S. L. (1987). *Working with people in crisis: Theory and practice* (2nd ed.). Columbus, OH: Merrill.

Dobson, K. S. (1989). A meta-analysis of the efficacy of cognitive therapy for depression. *Journal of Consulting and Clinical Psychology, 57*, 414–419.

Dodge, T. D. (2001). An investigation of the relationship between the family of origin and selected career development outcomes. *Dissertation Abstracts International, 62*(2-B), 1140.

Dolgoff, R., Loewenberg, F. M., & Harrington, D. (2005). *Ethical decisions for social work practice* (7th ed.). Itasca, IL: F. E. Peacock.

Dorfman, R. A. (1996). *Clinical social work: Definition, practice, and vision*. New York: Brunner/Mazell.

Draycott, S., & Dabbs, A. (1998). Cognitive dissonance 2: A theoretical grounding of motivational interviewing. *British Journal of Clinical Psychology, 37*, 335–364.

Dunn, C., Deroo, L., & Rivara, F. (2001). The use of brief interventions adapted from motivational interviewing across behavioral domains: A systematic review. *Addiction, 96,* 1725–1742.

Dunn, E. C., Neighbors, C., & Larimer, M. E. (2006). Motivational enhancement therapy and self-help treatment for binge eaters. *Psychology of Addictive Behaviors, 20*(1), 44–52.

Dymetryszyn, H., Bouchard, M. A., Bienvenu, J. P., de Carufel, F., & Gaston, L. (1997). Overall maturity of object relations as assessed by the McGill Object Relations Scale. *Bulletin of the Menninger Clinic, 61*(1), 44–72.

Dysinger, R. H., & Bowen, M. (1959). Problems for medical practice presented by families with a schizophrenic member. *American Journal of Psychiatry, 116,* 514–517.

Dziegielewski, S. F., & Montgomery, D. II. (1999). Gender issues in family therapy. In C. Franklin & C. Jordan (Eds.), *Family practice: Brief systems methods for social work* (pp. 321–340). Pacific Grove, CA: Brooks/Cole.

Dziegielewski, S. F., & Powers, G. T. (2000). Designs and procedures for evaluating crisis intervention. In A. R. Roberts (Ed.), *Crisis intervention handbook: Assessment, treatment, and research* (2nd ed.) (pp. 487–511). New York: Oxford.

Eakes, G., Walsh, S., Markowski, M., & Cain, H. (1997). Family-centered brief solution-focused therapy with chronic schizophrenia: A pilot study. *Journal of Family Therapy, 19*(2), 145–158.

Edmonson, C. R. (2002). Differentiation of self and patterns of grief following the death of a parent. *Dissertation Abstracts International, Section B: The Sciences and Engineering, 62*(12-B), 5960.

Ehrenberg, D. B. (1995). Self-disclosure: Therapeutic tool or indulgence? *Contemporary Psychoanalysis, 31,* 213–228.

Ehrenreich, J. H. (1985). *The altruistic imagination: A history of social work and social policy in the United States.* Ithaca, NY: Cornell University Press.

Elkin, I., Shea, M. T., Watkins, J. T., Imber, S. D., Sotsky, S. M., Collins, J. F., et al. (1989). National Institute of Mental Health Treatment of Depression Collaborative Research Program: General effectiveness of treatments. *Archives of General Psychiatry, 46,* 971–982.

Ellis, A. (1962). *Reason and emotion in psychotherapy.* New York: Stuart.

Ellis, A., & McLaren, C. (1998). *Rational emotive behavior therapy: A therapist's guide,* vol. 2. Atascadero, CA: Impact Publishers, Inc.

Ellis, P. M., Hickie, I. B., & Smith, D. A. R. (2003). Summary of guidelines for the treatment of depression. *Australasian Psychiatry, 11*(1), 34–38.

Emerson, R. W. (1958). *Emerson: A modern anthology.* Boston: Houghton Mifflin.

Emery, G. (1985). Cognitive therapy: Techniques and applications. In A. T. Beck & G. Emery (Eds.). *Anxiety disorders and phobias: A cognitive perspective* (pp. 167–313). New York: Basic Books.

Entin, A. D. (2001). Pets in the family. *Issues in Interdisciplinary Care, 3*(3), 219–222.

Epps, S., & Jackson, B. (2000). *Empowered families, successful children.* Washington, DC: APA.

Epston, D., White, M., & "Ben." (1995). Consulting your consultants: A means to the co-construction of alternative knowledges. In S. Friedman (Ed.), *The reflecting team in action* (pp. 277–313). New York: Guilford.

Erikson, E. (1968). *Identity: Youth and crisis.* New York: W. W. Norton.

Evans, M. E., Boothroyd, R. A., Armstrong, M. I., Greenbaum, P. E., Brown, E. C., & Kuppinger, A. D.

(2003). An experimental study of the effectiveness of intensive in-home crisis services for children and their families: Program outcomes. *Journal of Emotional and Behavioral Disorders, 11*(2), 93–104.

Everett, J. E., Homstead, K., & Drisko, J. (2007). Frontline worker perceptions of the empowerment process in community-based agencies. *Social Work, 52*(2), 161–170.

Eysenck, H. J., & Rachman, S. (1965). *The causes and cures of neurosis: An intro- duction to modern behavior therapy based on learning theories and the principles of conditioning.* London: Routledge & Kegan Paul.

Fairburn, C. G., Jones, R., Peveler, R. C., Hope, R. A., & O'Connor, M. (1993). Psychotherapy and bulimia nervosa: The longer term effects of interpersonal psychotherapy, behav- iour therapy and cognitive behaviour therapy. *Archives of General Psychiatry, 50*, 419–428.

Farber, S. (with Romer, A.). (1999). An interview with Dr. Stuart Farber: Living with a serious illness: A workbook for patients and families [Electronic version]. *Innovations in End-of-Life Care, 1*, 2–13.

Fassler, A. (2008). Merging task-centered social work and motivational inter- viewing in outpatient medication assisted substance abuse treatment: model development for social work practice. Unpublished doctoral dis- sertation, Virginia Commonwealth University, Richmond.

Feldman, E. L. (1998). Loneliness and physician utilization in a primary care population. *Dissertation Abstracts International, 59*(1-A), 0322.

Fenichel, G. H. (Ed.) (1994). *Psychoanalysis at 100: An issues in ego psychology book.* Lanham, MD: University Press of America.

Ferris, L. E., Shulman, K. L., & Williams, J. I. (2001). Methodological

challenges in evaluating mobile crisis psychiatric programs. *The Canadian Journal of Program Evaluation, 16*(2), 27–40.

Festinger, L. (1962). *A theory of cognitive dissonance.* Palo Alto, CA: Stanford University Press.

Fischer, J. (1976). *The effectiveness of social casework.* Springfield, IL: Charles C. Thomas.

Fischer, J. (1973). Is casework effective? A review. *Social Work, 18*, 5–20.

Flanagan, L. M. (2007). The theory of self psychology. In J. Berzoff (Ed.), *Inside out and outside in* (pp. 173–198). Lanham, MD: Jason Aronson.

Fleischer, L. M. (1998). Dimensions of personality functioning: Implications for clinical social work assessment. *Dissertation Abstracts International, 59*(8-A), 3208.

Fong, R., & Furuto, S. (Eds.) (2001). *Culturally competent practice: Skills, in- terventions, and evaluations.* Boston: Allyn & Bacon.

Foucault, M. (1966). *The order of things: An archaeology of the human sciences.* New York: Vintage.

Frank, E. (2005). *Treating bipolar disorder: A clinician's guide to interpersonal and social rhythm therapy.* New York: Gilford.

Frank, E., Kupfer, D. J., & Perel, J. M. (1990). Three-year outcomes for maintenance therapies in recurrent depression. *Archives of General Psychiatry, 47*, 1093–1099.

Frank, J. D., & Frank, J. B. (1993). *Persuasion and healing: A comparative study of psy- chotherapy* (3rd ed.). Baltimore: Johns Hopkins University Press.

Frankl, V. E. (1988). *The will to meaning: Foundations and applications of logother- apy.* New York: Meridian.

Franklin, C., Biever, J., Moore, K., Clemons, D., & Scamardo, M. (2001). The effectiveness of solution- focused therapy with children in a school setting. *Research on Social Work Practice*, *11*(4), 411–434.

Franklin, C., Hopson, L., & Barge, C. T. (2003). Family systems. In C. Jordan & C. Franklin (Eds.), *Clinical assessment for social workers: Quantitative and qualitative methods* (2nd ed.) (pp. 255–311). Chicago: Lyceum.

Fraser, M. W. (2004) Intervention research in social work: Recent advances and continuing challenges. *Research on Social Work Practice*, *14*(3), 210–222.

Fraser, M. W. (1997). *Risk and resilience in childhood: An ecological perspective.* Washington, DC: NASW Press.

Freedberg, S. (2007). Re-examining empathy: A relational-feminist point of view. *Social Work*, *52*(3), 251–259.

Freedman, J., & Combs, J. (1996). *Narrative therapy: The social construction of preferred realities.* New York: W. W. Norton.

Friesen, P. J. (2003). Emotional cutoff and the brain. (pp. 83–108)

Furman, R. (2002). Jessie Taft and the functional school: The impact of our history. *Canadian Journal of Social Work*, *4*(1), 7–13.

Gabbard, G. O. (1995). Countertransference: The emerging common ground. *International Journal of Psychoanalysis*, *76*, 475–485.

Gambrill, E. D. (2006). *Social work practice: A critical thinker's guide* (2nd ed.). New York: Oxford University Press.

Gambrill, E. D. (1994). Concept and methods of behavioral treatment. In D. K. Granvold (Ed.), *Cognitive and behavioral treatment: Methods and applications* (pp. 32–62). Pacific Grove, CA: Brooks/Cole.

Gates, S., McCambridge, J., Smith, L. A., & Foxcroft, D. R. (2006). Interventions for programs for prevention of drug use by young people delivered in nonschool settings. *Cochrane Database of Systematic Reviews*, *1*, Art. No.: CD005030.

Gensterblum, A. E. (2002). Solution-focused therapy in residential settings. *Dissertation Abstracts International*, *62*(7-B), 3377.

Georgetown Family Center (2008). http://www.georgetownfamily center.org/index.html.

Gerhardt, S. (2004). Why love matters: How affection shapes a baby's brain. Philadelphia: Routledge/Taylor and Francis.

Germain, C. B., & Gitterman, A. (1996). *The life model of social work practice: Advances in theory and practice* (2nd ed.). New York: Columbia University Press.

Gibbs, J. T. (1998). African American adolescents. In J. T. Taylor & L. N. Huang (Eds.), *Children of color: Psychological interventions with culturally diverse youth* (pp. 171–214). San Francisco: Jossey-Bass.

Gilligan, C. (1982). *In a different voice.* Cambridge, MA: Harvard University Press.

Gilliland, B. E., & James, R. K. (2005). *Crisis intervention strategies* (5th ed.). Belmont, CA: Brooks/Cole.

Gingerich, W. J., & Eisengart, S. (2000). Solution-focused brief therapy: A review of the outcome research. *Family Process*, *39*(4), 477–498.

Gist, R., & Devilly, G. J. (2002). Post-trauma debriefing: The road too frequently traveled. Lancet, 360(9335), 741–742.

Glade, A. C. (2005). Differentiation, marital satisfaction, and depressive symptoms: An application of Bowen theory. *Dissertation Abstracts International, Section B: The Sciences and Engineering*, *66*(6-B), 3408.

Golan, N. (1987). Crisis intervention. In A. Minahan (Ed.), *Encyclopedia of social work* (pp. 360–372). Silver Spring, MD: NASW.

Golan, N. (1978). *Treatment in crisis situations.* New York: Free Press.

Goldberg, E. H. (1989). Severity of depression and developmental levels of psychosocial functioning in 8–16-year-old girls. *American Journal of Orthopsychiatry, 59*(2), 167–178.

Goldfried, M. R., & Wolfe, B. E. (1998). Toward a more clinically valid approach to therapy research. *Journal of Consulting and Clinical Psychology, 66*(1), 143–150.

Goldstein, E. G. (2001). *Object relations theory and self psychology in social work practice.* New York: Free Press.

Goldstein, E. G. (1995). *Ego psychology and social work practice* (2nd ed.). New York: Free Press.

Goldstein, E. G., & Noonan, M. (1999). *Short-term treatment and social work practice.* New York: Free Press.

Goldstein, H. (1990). The knowledge base of social work practice: Theory wisdom, analogue, or art? *Families in Society, 71,* 32–43.

Goodrich, T. J. (2006). A new department. *Family Systems & Health, 24*(2), 218–219.

Gonzalez, J. E., Nelson, J. R., & Gutkin, T. B. (2004). Rational emotive therapy with children and adolescents: A meta-analysis. *Journal of Emotional and Behavioral Disorders, 12*(4), 222–235.

Gorey, K., Thyer, B. A., & Pawluck, D. (1998). The differential effectiveness of social work interventions: A meta-analysis. *Social Work, 43*(3), 269–278.

Gottlieb, M. C., & Lasser, J. (2001). Competing values: A respectful critique of narrative research. *Ethics and Behavior, 11*(2), 191–194.

Grafanaki, S., & McLeod, J. (1999). Narrative processes in the construction of helpful and hindering events in experiential psychotherapy. *Psychotherapy Research, 9*(3), 289–303.

Granvold, D. K. (1994). Concepts and methods of cognitive treatment. In D. K. Granvold (Ed.), *Cognitive and behavioral treatment: Methods and applications* (pp. 3–31). Pacific Grove, CA: Brooks/Cole.

Gray, P. (1994). *The ego and analysis of defense.* Northvale, NJ: Jason Aronson.

Green, B., & Boyd-Franklin, N. (1996). African American lesbians: Issues in couples therapy. In J. Laird & R. J. Green (Eds.), *Lesbians and gays in couples and families: A handbook for therapists* (pp. 251–271). San Francisco: Jossey-Bass.

Green, R. J. (2007). Gay and lesbian couples in therapy: A social justice perspective. In E. Aldarondo (Ed.), *Advancing social justice through clinical practice* (pp. 119–149). Mahwah, NJ Lawrence Erlbaum.

Green, R. J., & Mitchell, V. (2002). Gay and lesbian couples in therapy: Homophobia, relational ambiguity, and social support. In A. S. Gurman & N. S. Jacobson (Eds.), *Clinical handbook of couple therapy* (3rd ed.). (pp. 546–568). New York: Guilford Press.

Greenan, D. E., & Tunnell, G. (2003). *Couple therapy with gay men.* New York: Gilford Press.

Greenberg, M., Speltz, M., DeKlyen, M., Jones, K. (2001). Correlates of clinic referral for early conduct problems: Variable- and person-oriented approaches. *Development & Psychopathology, 13,* 255–276.

Gregory, R. J., Canning, S. S., & Lee, T. W. (2004). Cognitive bibliotherapy for depression: A meta-analysis. *Professional Psychology: Research and Practice, 35*(3), 275–280.

Grenyer, B. F. S., & Laborsky, L. (1996). Dynamic change in psychotherapy: Mastery of interpersonal conflicts. *Journal of Consulting and Clinical Psychology, 64*(2), 411–416.

Gresham, F. M., (2005). Methodological issues in evaluating cognitive-behavioral treatments for students with behavioral disorders. *Behavioral Disorders, 30*(3), 213–225.

Guerin, P. J., Fogarty, T. F., Fay, L. F., & Kautto, J. G. (1996). *Working with relationship triangles: The one-two-three of psychotherapy.* New York: Guilford.

Guerin, P. J., & Guerin, K. (2002). Bowenian family therapy. In J. Carlson & D. Kjos (Eds.), *Theories and strategies of family therapy* (pp. 126–156). Boston: Allyn & Bacon.

Gunnar, M. R., Broderson, L., Nachimas, M., Buss, K., & Rigatuso, J. (1996). Stress reactivity and attachment security. *Developmental Psychobiology, 29*(3), 191–204.

Guthrie, E. A., Kapur, N., Mackway-Jones, K., Chew-Graham, C., Moorey, J., Mendel, E., Francis, F. M., Sanderson, S., Turpin, C., & Boddy, G. (2003). Predictors of outcome following brief psychodynamic-interpersonal therapy for deliberate self-poisoning. *Australian & New Zealand Journal of Psychiatry, 37*(5), 532–536.

Guthrie, E. A., Moorey, J., Margison, F., Barker, H., Palmer, S., McGrath, G., Tomenson, B., & Creed, F. (1999). Cost-effectiveness of brief psychodynamic-interpersonal therapy in high utilizers of psychiatric services. *Archives of General Psychiatry, 56*(6), 519–526.

Haby, M. M., Donnelly, M., & Corry, J. (2006). Cognitive behavioral therapy for depression, panic disorder, and generalized anxiety disorder: A meta-regression of factors that may predict outcome. *Australian and New Zealand Journal of Psychiatry, 40*(1), 9–19.

Haby, M. M., Tonge, B., Littlefield, L., Carter, R., & Vos, T. (2004). Cost-effectiveness of cognitive behavioural therapy and selective serotonin reuptake inhibitors for major depression in children and adolescents. *Australian and New Zealand Journal of Psychiatry, 38*(8), 579–591.

Haddock, G., Tarrier, N., Spaulding, W., Yusupoff, L., Kinney, C., & McCarthy, E. (1998). Individual cognitive-behavior therapy in the treatment of hallucinations and delusions: A review. *Clinical Psychology Review, 18*(7), 821–838.

Hale, N. G. (1995). *The rise and crisis of psychoanalysis in the United States: Freud and the Americans, 1917–1985.* London: Oxford University Press.

Hamilton, G. (1951). *Theory and practice of social case work* (2nd ed) New York: Columbia University Press.

Hammond, R. T., & Nichols, M. P. (2008). How collaborative is structural family therapy? *The Family Journal, 16*(2), 118–124.

Hanna, E. A. (1993). The implications of shifting perspectives in countertransference on the therapeutic action of clinical social work. Part II: The recent-totalist and intersubjective position. *Journal of Analytic Social Work, 1*(3), 53–79.

Hargie, O. D. W. (Ed.) (1997). *The handbook of communication skills.* New York: Routledge.

Harper, K. V., & Lantz, J. (2007). *Cross-cultural practice: Social work with diverse populations* (2nd ed.) Chicago: Lyceum.

Harris, M., & Bergman, H. C. (1988). Clinical case management for the chronically mentally ill: A conceptual analysis. In M. Harris & L. Bachrach (Eds.), *Clinical case management* (pp. 5–13). New Directions for Mental Health Services, 40, San Francisco: Jossey-Bass.

Hartmann, H. (1958). *Ego psychology and the problem of adaptation.* New York: International Universities Press.

Hartstein, J. A. (1990). Object relations, social supports, and coronary artery disease. *Dissertation Abstracts International,* `50(7-A), 2244.

Hauser, S. T., & Safyer, A. W. (1995). The contribution of ego psychology to developmental psychopathology. In D. Cicchetti & D. J. Cohen (Eds.), *Developmental psychopathology, Volume 1: Theory and methods* (pp. 555–580). New York: Wiley.

Haynes, R. B., Ackloo, E., Sahota, N., McDonald, H. P., & Yao, X. (2008). Interventions for enhancing medication adherence. *Cochrane Database of Systematic Reviews, 2,* Art. No.: CD000011.

Helgeson, V., Reynolds, K., & Tomich, P. (2006). A meta-analytic review of benefit finding and growth. *Journal of Consulting and Clinical Psychology, 74,* 797–816.

Hepworth, D., Rooney, R., Rooney, G. D., Strom-Gottfried, K., & Larsen, J. (2005). *Direct social work practice: Theory and skills* (7th ed.). Belmont, CA: Brooks/Cole.

Hertlein, K. M., & Killmer, J. M. (2004). Toward differential decision-making: Family systems theory with the homeless clinical population. *American Journal of Family Therapy, 32*(3), 255–270.

Himle, J. A., Rassi, S., Haghighatgou, H., Krone, K. P., Nesse, R. M., & Abelson, J. (2001). Group behavioral therapy of obsessive-compulsive disorder: Seven vs. twelve-week outcomes. *Depression and Anxiety, 13*(4), 161–165.

Hinshaw, S. P., Klein, R. G., & Abikoff, H. B. (2002). Childhood attention deficit hyperactivity disorder: Nonpharmacological treatments and their combination with medication. In P. E. Nathan & J. M. Gordon (Eds.), *A guide to treatments that work* (2nd ed.) (pp. 3–23). London: Oxford University Press.

Hobfoll, S., Freedy, R., Lane, C., & Geller, P. (1990). Conservation of social resources: Social support resource theory. *Journal of Social and Personal Relationships, 7,* 465–478.

Hodges, V. G. (1994). Home-based behavioral intervention with children and families. In D. K. Granvold (Ed.), *Cognitive and behavioral treatment: Methods and applications* (pp. 90–107). Pacific Grove, CA: Brooks/Cole.

Högberg, G. & Hällström, T. (2008). Active multimodal psychotherapy in children and adolescents with suicidality: Description, evaluation and clinical profile. *Clinical Child Psychology and Psychiatry, 13*(3), 435–448.

Hollis, F. H. (1964). *Casework: A psychosocial therapy.* New York: Random House.

Horvath, A. O. (1994). Research on the alliance. In A. O. Horvath & L. S. Greenberg (Eds.), *The working alliance: Theory, research, and practice* (pp. 259–286). New York: Wiley.

Horvath, A. O., & Greenberg, L. S. (Eds.) (1994). *The working alliance: Theory, research, and practice.* New York: Wiley.

Howe, L. T. (1998). Self-differentiation in Christian perspective. *Pastoral Psychology, 46*(5), 347–362.

Howells, J. G., & Guirguis, W. R. (1985). *The family and schizophrenia.* New York: International Universities Press.

Hull, C. (1943). *Principles of behavior.* New York: Appleton-Century-Crofts.

Hunter, T. J. (1998). Naturalistic inquiry of alcoholic families from ethnically diverse backgrounds. *Dissertation Abstracts International, 59*(1-B), 0418.

Illick, S. D., Hilbert-McAllister, G., Jefferies, S. E., & White, C. M. (2003). Toward Understanding and Measuring Emotional Cutoff. In P. Titelman (Ed.), *Emotional cutoff: Bowen family systems theory perspectives* (pp. 199–217). New York: Haworth Press.

Ingram, R. E. (Ed.) (1986). *Information processing approaches to clinical psychology.* Orlando, FL: Academic Press.

Institute for the Advancement of Social Work Research (2008). *Evidence based practice.* Washington, DC: National Association of Social Workers.

Irwin, M. R., Cole, J. C., & Nicassio, P. M. (2006). Comparative meta-analysis of behavioral interventions for insomnia and their efficacy in middle-aged adults and in older adults 55+ years of age. *Health Psychology, 25*(1), 3–14.

Jackson, R., Asimakopoulou, K., & Scammel, A. (2007). Assessment of the transtheoretical model as used by dieticians in promoting physical activity in people with type 2 diabetes. *Journal of Human Nutrition and Dietetics, 20*(1), 27–36.

Jacobs, T. J. (1999). Countertransference past and present: A review of the concept. *International Journal of Psychoanalysis, 80*, 575–594.

James, R. K., & Gilliland, B. E. (2001). *Crisis intervention strategies* (4th ed.). Pacific Grove, CA: Brooks/Cole.

Johnson, H. C. (1991). Theories of Kernberg and Kohut: Issues of scientific validation. *Social Service Review, 65*(3), 403–433.

Johnson, T. W. & Keren, M. S. (1998). The families of lesbian women and gay men. In M. McGoldrick (Ed.), *Re-visioning family therapy: Race, culture, and gender in clinical practice* (pp. 320–329). New York: Guilford Press.

Josephson, L. (1997). Clinical social work practice with young inner-city children who have been sexually abused: An object relations approach. *Dissertation Abstracts International, 58*(1-A), 0291.

Joy, C. B., Adams, C. E., & Rice, K. (2006). Crisis intervention for people with severe mental illnesses. *Cochrane Database of Systematic Reviews, 4*, Art. No.: CD001087.

Kamphuis, J. H., & Emmelkamp, P. M. G. (2005). 20 years of research into violence and trauma: Past and future developments. *Journal of Interpersonal Violence, 20*(2), 167–174.

Kanter, J. (1996). Case management with long-term patients. In S. M. Soreff (Ed.), *Handbook for the treatment of the seriously mentally ill* (pp. 259–275). Seattle, WA: Hogrefe & Huber.

Kanter, J. (1995) (Ed.). *Clinical issues in case management.* San Francisco: Jossey-Bass.

Kanters, A. L. (2002). Resolution of symbolic play therapy narratives of traumatic events: Exposure play therapy. *Dissertation Abstracts International, 62*(10-B), 4790.

Kassop, M. (1987). Salvador Minuchin: A sociological analysis of his family therapy theory. *Clinical Sociology Review, 5*, 158–167.

Kazdin, A. (2000). *Behavior modification in applied settings* (6th ed.). Pacific Grove, CA: Brooks/Cole.

Keller, B. D. (2007). Beyond individual differences: The role of differentiation of self in predicting the career exploration of college students. *Dissertation Abstracts International, Section B: The Sciences and Engineering, 68*(1-B), 649.

Kelley, P. (1998). Narrative therapy in a managed care world. *Crisis Intervention, 4*(2-3), 113–123.

Kelley, P. (1996). Narrative theory and social work practice. In F. Turner (Ed.), *Social work treatment* (4th ed.) (pp. 461–479). New York: Free Press.

Kernberg, P. F., & Chazan, S. E. (1991). *Children with conduct disorders: A psychotherapy manual.* New York: Basic.

Kerr, K. B. (1984). Issues in aging from a family theory perspective. In *The best of the family 1978–1983* (pp. 243–247). New Rochelle, NY: Center for Family Learning.

Kerr, M. E., & Bowen, M. (1988). *Family evaluation: An approach based on Bowen theory*. New York: W. W. Norton.

Kerr, S., Goldfried, M. R., Hayes, A. M., Castonguay, L. G., & Goldsamt, L. (1992). Interpersonal and intrapersonal focus in cognitive-behavioral and psychodynamic-interpersonal therapies: A preliminary analysis of the Sheffield project. *Psychotherapy Research, 2*(4), 266–276.

Kierkegaard, S. (1954). *Fear and trembling and the sickness unto death*. Garden City, NY: Doubleday.

Killick, S., & Allen, C. (1997). 'Shifting the balance': Motivational interviewing to help behaviour change in people with bulimia nervosa. *European Eating Disorders Review, 5*(1), 35–41.

Kim, J. M. (2003). Structural family therapy and its implications for the Asian American family. *The Family Journal, 11*(4), 388–392.

Kim-Appel, D. (2003). The relationship between Bowen's concept of differentiation of self and psychological symptom status in individuals age 62 years and older. *Dissertation Abstracts International, 63*(7-A), 2467.

Kipps-Vaughan, D. (2000). The integration of object relations family therapy and cognitive behavior therapy: The development of a treatment protocol for increasing anger control in male adolescents with externalizing behavior difficulties. *Dissertation Abstracts International, 61*(3-B), 1639.

Kiselica, M. S. (1998). Preparing Anglos for the challenges and joys of multiculturalism. *The Counseling Psychologist, 26*, 5–21.

Klein, D. M., & White, J. M. (1996). *Family theories: An introduction*. Thousand Oaks, CA: Sage.

Klerman, G., & Weissman, M. M. (1993). *New applications in interpersonal psychotherapy*. Washington, DC: American Psychiatric Press.

Klerman, G., Weissman, M. M., Rounsaville, B., & Chevron, E. (1984). *Interpersonal psychotherapy of depression*. New York: Basic Books.

Knauth, D. G., Skowron, E. A., & Escobar, M. (2006). Effects of differentiation of self on adolescent risk behavior. *Nursing Research, 55*(5), 336–345.

Knudson-Martin, C. (2004). Gender and biology: A recursive framework for clinical practice. *Journal of Feminist Family Therapy, 15*(2–3), 1–21.

Knudson-Martin, C. (2002). Expanding Bowen's legacy to family therapy: A response to Horne and Hicks. *Journal of Marital and Family Therapy, 28*(1), 115–118.

Kobak, K. A., Griest, J. H., Jefferson, J. W., Katzelnick, D. J., & Henk, H. J. (1998). Behavioral versus pharmacological treatment of obsessive-compulsive disorder: A meta-analysis. *Psychopharmacology, 136*(3), 205–216.

Kocan, M. (1988). *Transference and countertransference in clinical work*. Dayton, MD: American Healthcare Institute. Distributed at Columbus, Ohio, workshop.

Kohlberg, L. (1969). *Stages in the development of moral thought and action*. New York: Holt, Rinehart, & Winston.

Krabbendam, L., & Aleman, A. (2003). Cognitive rehabilitation in schizophrenia: A quantitative analysis of controlled studies. *Psychopharmacology, 169*(3-4), 376–382.

Kramer, S., & Akhtar, S. (Eds.) (1991). *The trauma of transgression: Psychotherapy of incest victims*. Northvale, NJ: Jason Aronson.

Kramer, S., & Akhtar, S. (Eds.) (1991). *The trauma of transgression: Psychotherapy of incest victims*. Northvale, NJ: Jason Aronson.

Krill, D. F. (1996). Existential social work. In F. J. Turner (Ed.), *Social work treatment* (4th ed.) (pp. 250–281). New York: Free Press.

Kuehnlein, I. (1999). Psychotherapy as a process of transformation: Analysis of posttherapeutic autobiographical narrations. *Psychotherapy Research, 9*(3), 274–288.

Kupfer, D. J., Frank, E., Perel, J. M., Cores, C., Mallinger, A. G., et al. (1992). Five-year outcomes for maintenance therapies in recurrent depression. *Archives of General Psychiatry, 49*, 769–773.

Kurtz, P. D. (1972). American philosophy. In P. Edwards (Ed.), *The encyclopedia of philosophy*, Volume 1 (pp. 83–93). New York: Macmillan.

Kvarfordt, C. L., & Sheridan, M. J. (2007). The role of religion and spirituality in working with children and adolescents: Results of a national survey. *Journal of Religion & Spirituality in Social Work, 26*(3), 1–23.

Laird, J. (1993). Lesbian and gay families. In F. Walsh (Ed.), *Normal family processes* (2nd ed.) (pp. 282–328). New York: Guilford Press.

Lantz, J., & Walsh, J. (2007). *Short-term existential intervention in clinical practice.* Chicago: Lyceum.

Lantz, J. (1996). Cognitive theory and social work treatment. In F. J. Turner (Ed.), *Social work treatment* (4th ed.) (pp. 94–115). New York: Free Press.

Lantz, J. (1978). Cognitive theory and social casework. *Social Work, 37*, 361–366.

Larson, J. H., Benson, M. J., Wilson, S. M., & Medora, N. (1998). Family of origin influences on marital attitudes and readiness for marriage in late adolescents. *Journal of Family Issues, 19*(6), 750–769.

Larson, J. H., & Wilson, S. M. (1998). Family of origin influences on young adult career decision problems: A test of Bowenian theory. *American Journal of Family Therapy, 26*(1), 39–53.

Lastoria, M. D. (1990). A family systems approach to adolescent depression. *Journal of Psychology and Christianity, 9*(4), 44–54.

Lazarus, R. S., & Lazarus, B. N. (1994). *Passion and reason: Making sense of our emotions.* New York: Oxford.

Lazarus, R. S. (1993). Coping theory and research: Past, present, and future. *Psychosomatic Medicine, 55*, 234–247.

Leahy, R. L. (1996). *Cognitive therapy: Basic principles and applications.* Northvale, NJ: Jason Aronson.

Lee, J. A. B. (2001). *The empowerment approach to social work practice: Building the beloved community* (2nd ed.). New York: Columbia University Press.

Lee, M. (2002). *Working with Asian American populations: A treatment guide.* Columbus, OH: Asian American Community Services.

Leffel, R. J. (2000). Psychotherapy of schizophrenia. *Dissertation Abstracts International, 60*(8-B), 4232.

Leichsenring, F. (2005). Are psychodynamic and psychoanalytic therapies effective?: A review of empirical data. *International Journal of Psychoanalysis, 86*(3), 841–868.

Leichsenring, F. (2001). Comparative effects of short-term psychodynamic psychotherapy and cognitive-behavioral therapy in depression: A meta-analytic approach. *Clinical Psychology Review, 21*(3), 401–419.

Leichsenring, F., & Leibing, E. (2007). Psychodynamic psychotherapy: A systematic review of techniques, indications and empirical evidence. *Psychology and Psychotherapy: Theory, Research and Practice, 80*(2), 217–228.

Leichsenring, F., Rabung, S., & Leibing, E. (2004), The Efficacy of short-term psychodynamic psychotherapy in specific psychiatric disorders: A meta-analysis. *Archives of General Psychiatry*, *61*(12), 1208–1216.

Lengermann, P. M., & Niebrugge-Brantley, J. (2000). Contemporary feminist theory. In G. Ritzer (Ed.), *Modern sociological theory* (6th ed.) (pp. 307–355). Boston: McGraw-Hill.

Leonardsen, D., (2007). Empowerment in social work: An individual vs. a relational perspective. *International Journal of Social Welfare*, *16*(1), 3–11.

Levant, R. F., & Silverstein, L. B. (2001). Integrating gender and family systems theories: The "both/and" approach to treating a postmodern couple. In S. H. McDaniel & D. D. Lusterman (Eds.), *Casebook for integrating family therapy: An ecosystem approach* (pp. 245–252). Washington, DC: American Psychological Association.

Levine, H. A. (2002). Intrapsychic and symptomatic change in patients with borderline psychopathology. *Dissertation Abstracts International*, *62*(12-B), 5969.

Levine, L. V., & Tuber, S. B. (1993). Measures of mental representation: Clinical and theoretical considerations. *Bulletin of the Menninger Clinic*, *57*(1), 69–87.

Levinsky, L. (2002). Integrative group treatment for bulimia nervosa. *Social Work with Groups*, *25*(4), 97–100.

Levinson, D. J. (1978). *The seasons of a man's life*. New York: Knopf.

Ligon, J., & Thyer, B. A. (2000). Community inpatient crisis stabilization in an urban setting: Evaluation of changes in psychiatric symptoms. *Crisis Intervention and Time-Limited Treatment*, *5*(3), 163–169.

Lipchik, E. (2002). *Beyond technique in solution-focused therapy: Working with emotions and the therapeutic relationship*. New York: Guilford.

Loftis, R. H. (1997). A comparison of delinquents and nondelinquents on Rorschach measures of object relationships and attachment: Implications for conduct disorder, antisocial personality disorder, and psychopathology. *Dissertation Abstracts International*, *58*(5-B), 2720.

Long, J. (2004). Review of couple therapy with gay men. *Journal of Feminist Family Therapy*, *16*(2), 83–84.

Luborsky, L., & Crits-Christoph, P. (1990). *Understanding transference: The CCRT method (the core conflictual relationship theme)*. New York: Basic Books.

Lubove, R. (1965). *The professional altruist: The emergence of social work as a career 1880–1930*. Cambridge, MA: Harvard University Press.

Lupien, S. J., King, S., Meaney, M. J., & McEwen, B. S. (2000). Child's stress hormone levels correlate with mother's socioeconomic status and depressive state. *Biological Psychiatry*, *48*(10), 976–980.

Lussier, J. P., Heil, S. H., Mongeon, J. A., Badger, G. J., & Higgins, S. T. (2006). A meta-analysis of voucher-based reinforcement therapy for substance use disorders. *Addiction*, *101*, 192–203.

Lynch, T. R., Chapman, A. L., Rosenthal, M. Z., Kuo, J. R., & Linehan, M. M. (2006). Mechanisms of change in dialectical behavior therapy: Theoretical and empirical observations. *Journal of Clinical Psychology*, *62*(4), 459–480.

Macdonald, A. J. (1997). Brief therapy in adult psychiatry: Further outcomes. *Journal of Family Therapy*, *19*(2), 213–222.

Mackay, H. C., Barkham, M., Stiles, W. B., & Goldfried, M. R. (2002). Patterns of client emotion in helpful sessions of cognitive-behavioral and psychodynamic-interpersonal therapy. *Journal of Counseling Psychology, 49*(3), 376–380.

Madden-Derdich, D. A., Estrada, A. U., Updegraff, K. A., & Leonard, S. A. (2002). The boundary violations scale: An empirical measure of intergenerational boundary violations in families. *Journal of Marital & Family Therapy, 28*(2), 241–254.

Maddi, S. R. (1996). *Personality theories: A comparative analysis* (6th ed.). Pacific Grove, CA: Brooks/Cole.

Magai, C. (1996). Personality theory: Birth, death, and transfiguration. In R. D. Kavanaugh, B. Zimmerberg, & S. Fein (Eds.), *Emotion: Interdisciplinary perspectives* (pp. 171–202). Mahwah, NJ: Lawrence Erlbaum.

Mahler, M. S., Pine, F., & Bergman, A. S. (1975). *The psychological birth of the human infant.* New York: Basic Books.

Main, M. (1996) Introduction to the special section on attachment and psychopathology: 2. Overview of the field of attachment. *Journal of Consulting and Clinical Psychology, 64*(2), 237–243.

Maloney-Schara, A. (1990). Biofeedback and family systems psychotherapy in the treatment of HIV infection. *Biofeedback and Self-Regulation, 15*(1), 70–71.

March, J. S., Franklin, M., & Foa, E. (2005). Cognitive-behavioral psychotherapy for pediatric obsessive-compulsive disorder. In E. D. Hibbs & P. S. Jensen (Eds.), *Psychosocial treatments for child and adolescent disorders: Empirically based strategies for clinical practice* (2nd ed.) (pp. 121–142). Washington, DC: American Psychological Association.

Margles, D. (1995). The application of family systems theory to geriatric hospital social work. *Journal of Gerontological Social Work, 24*, 45–54.

Markowitz, J. C. (2001). Learning the new psychotherapies. In M. M. Weissman (Ed.), *Treatment of depression: Bridging the 21st century* (pp. 281–300). Washington, DC: American Psychiatric Press.

Markowitz, J. C. (1997). *Interpersonal psychotherapy for dysthymic disorder.* Washington DC: American Psychiatric Press.

Markowitz, J. C., Klerman, G. L., & Perry, S. W. (1993). Interpersonal psychotherapy of depressed HIV-positive outpatients. *Hospital and Community Psychiatry, 43*(9), 885–890.

Marks, I. M. (1987). *Fears, phobias, and rituals: Panic, anxiety, and their disorders.* New York: Oxford University Press.

Martino, S., Carroll, K. M., Kostas, D., Perkins, J., & Rounsaville, B. J. (2002). Dual diagnosis motivational interviewing: A modification of motivational interviewing for substance-abusing patients with psychotic disorders. *Journal of Substance Abuse Treatment, 23*, 297–308.

Martino, S., Carroll, K. M., Nich, C., & Rounsaville, B. J. (2006). A randomized controlled pilot study of motivational interviewing for patients with psychotic and drug use disorders. *Addiction, 101*(10), 1479–1492.

Mattaini, M. (1997). *Clinical practice with individuals.* Washington, DC: NASW Press.

Masterson, J. F. (1972). *Treatment of the borderline adolescent.* New York: Wiley-Interscience.

May, R., Angel, E., & Ellenberger, H. (Eds.) (1958). *Existence: A new dimension in psychiatry and psychology.* New York: Basic.

May, R. & Yalom, I. D. (2000). Existential psychotherapy. In R. J. Corsini & D. Wedding (Eds.), *Current psychotherapies* (6th ed.) (pp. 273–302). Itasca, IL: F. E. Peacock.

McCambridge, J., & Strang, J. (2005). Deterioration over time in effect of Motivational Interviewing in reducing drug consumption and related risk among young people. *Addiction*, *100*(4), 470–478.

McCambridge, J., & Strang, J. (2004). The efficacy of single-session motivational interviewing in reducing drug consumption and perceptions of drug-related risk and harm among young people: Results from a multi-site cluster randomized trial. *Addiction*, *99*(1), 39–52.

McClam, T., & Woodside, M. (1994). *Problem solving in the helping professions*. Pacific Grove, CA: Brooks/Cole.

McClellan, M. L., Schneider, M. F., & Perney, J. (1998). Rating (life task action) change in journal excerpts and narratives using Prochaska, DiClemente, and Norcross's Five Stages of Change. *Journal of Individual Psychology*, *54*(4), 546–559.

McGoldrick, M., & Carter, B. (2001). Advances in coaching: Family therapy with one person. *Journal of Marital & Family Therapy*, *27*(3), 281–300.

McGoldrick, M., Gerson, R., & Petry, S. (2008). *Genograms: Assessment and intervention (3rd ed.)*. New York: W. W. Norton.

McGoldrick, M. (Ed.) (1998). *Re-visioning family therapy*. New York: Guilford.

McGoldrick, M. (1996). *The legacy of unresolved loss: A family systems approach*. New York: Newbridge Communications.

McGrath, M. L., Mellon, M. W., & Murphy, L. (2000). Empirically supported treatments in pediatric psychology: Constipation and enuresis. *Journal of Pediatric Psychology*, *25*(4), 225–254.

McKnight, A. S. (2003). The impact of cutoff in families raising adolescents.

In P. Titelman (Ed). *Emotional cutoff: Bowen family systems theory perspectives*. New York: Haworth. (pp. 273–287).

McPherson, M., Brashears, M. E., & Smith-Lovin, L. (2006). Social isolation in America: Changes in core discussion networks over two decades. *American Sociological Review*, *71*(3), 353–375.

Mead, G. H. (1934). *Mind, self, and society*. Chicago: University of Chicago Press.

Meichenbaum, D. (1999). *Cognitive-behavior modification: An integrative approach*. Cambridge, MA: Perseus Publishing.

Meichenbaum, D. (1977). *Cognitive-behavior modification: An integrative approach*. New York: Plenum.

Meichenbaum, D., & Deffenbacher, J. (1988). Stress inoculation training. *Counseling Psychologist*, *16*, 69–90.

Metcalf, L., & Thomas, F. (1994). Client and therapist perceptions of solution-focused brief therapy: A qualitative analysis. *Journal of Family Psychotherapy*, *5*(4), 49–66.

Metzger, J. W. (1997). The role of social support in mediating the well-being of children placed in kinship foster care and traditional foster care. *Dissertation Abstracts International*, *58*(6-A), 2394.

Meuser, T. M. (1997). An integrative model of personality, coping, and appraisal for the prediction of grief involvement in adults: A dissertation study. *Dissertation Abstracts International*, *57*(8-B), 5336.

Meyer, C. H. (1970). *Social work practice: The urban crisis*. New York: The Free Press.

Mezzina, R., & Vidoni, D. (1996). Beyond the mental hospital: Crisis intervention and continuity of care in Trieste: A four-year follow-up study in a community mental health centre. *International Journal of Social Psychiatry*, *41*, 1–20.

Michael, K. D., Curtin, L., Kirkley, D. E., Jones, D. L., & Harris, R. (2006). Group based motivational interviewing for alcohol use among college students: An exploratory study. *Professional Psychology: Research and Practice, 37*(6), 629–634.

Miller, A.L., & Glinski, J. (2000). Youth Suicidal Behavior: Assessment and Intervention. *Journal of Clinical Psychology, 56*(9), 1132–1152.

Miller, R. B., Anderson, S., & Keala, D. K. (2004). Is Bowen theory valid? A review of basic research. *Journal of Marital & Family Therapy, 30*(4), 453–466.

Miller, S. D., Duncan, B. L., & Hubble, M. A. (2005). Outcome-informed clinical work. In J. C. Norcross & M. R. Goldfried (Eds.), *Handbook of psychotherapy integration* (2nd ed.) (pp. 84–102). New York: Oxford University Press, 2005.

Miller, W., & Rollnick, S. (1991). *Motivational interviewing* (1st ed.). New York: Guilford.

Miller, W., & Rollnick, S. (2002). *Motivational interviewing: Preparing people to change addictive behavior* (2nd ed.). New York: Guilford.

Mindell, J. A. (1999). Empirically supported treatments in pediatric psychology: Bedtime refusal and night waking in young children. *Journal of Pediatric Psychology, 24*(6), 465–481.

Minuchin, S. (1984). *Family kaleidoscope.* Cambridge, MA: Harvard University Press.

Minuchin, S. (1974). *Families and family therapy.* Cambridge, MA: Harvard University Press.

Minuchin, S., Lee, W., & Simon, G. M. (1996). *Mastering family therapy: Journeys of growth and transformation.* New York: Wiley.

Minuchin, S., Montalvo, B., Guerney, B., Rosman, B., & Schumer, F. (1967). *Families of the slums.* Cambridge, MA: Harvard University Press.

Minuchin, S., Nichols, M. P., & Lee, W. Y. (2007). *Assessing families and couples: From symptom to system.* Boston: Allyn & Bacon.

Minuchin, S., Rosman, B. L., Baker, L., & Liebman, R. (1978). *Psychosomatic families: Anorexia nervosa in context.* Cambridge, MA: Harvard University Press.

Mitchell, S. A. (1988). *Relational concepts in psychoanalysis.* Cambridge, MA: Harvard University Press.

Mitrani, V. B., Feaster, D. J., McCabe, B. E., Czaja, S. J., & Szapocznik, J. (2005). Adapting the structural family systems rating to assess the patterns of interaction on families of dementia caregivers. *The Gerontologist, 45*(4), 445–455.

Mitte, K. (2005). Meta-Analysis of Cognitive Behavioral Treatments for Generalized Anxiety Disorder: A Comparison With Pharmacotherapy. *Psychological Bulletin, 131*(5), 785–795.

Moerk, K., & Klein, D. (2000). The development of major depressive episodes during the course of dysthymic and episodic major depressive disorders: A retrospective examination of life events. *Journal of Affective Disorders, 58*, 117–123.

Monk, G., Winslade, J., Crocket, K., & Epston, D. (Eds.). (1997). *Narrative therapy in practice.* San Francisco: Jossey-Bass.

Montgomery, A. (2002). Converging perspectives of dynamic theory and evolving neurobiological knowledge. *Smith College Studies in Social Work, 72*(2), 178–196.

Moore, S. T. (1990). Family systems theory and family care: An examination of the implications of Bowen theory. *Community Alternatives: International Journal of Family Care, 22*(2), 75–86.

Morgenstern, J., Irwin, T., Wainberg, M. L., Parsons, J. T., Muench, F., Bux, D. A.,

Kahler, C. W., Marcus, S., & Schulz-Heik, J. (2007). A randomized controlled trial of goal choice interventions for alcohol use disorders among men who have sex with men. *Journal of Counseling and Clinical Psychology*, *75*(1), 72–84.

Moyers, T., & Rollnick, S. (2002). A motivational interviewing perspective on resistance in psychotherapy. *JCLP/In Session: Psychotherapy in Practice*, *58*, 185–193.

Mufson, L., Dorta, K. P., Moreau, D., & Weissman, M. M. (2004). *Interpersonal psychotherapy for depressed adolescents* (2nd ed.). New York: Guilford.

Mufson, L., Weissman, M. M., Moreau, D., & Garfinkel, R. (1999). The efficacy of interpersonal psychotherapy for depressed adolescents. *Archives of General Psychiatry*, *56*, 573–579.

Mullahy, P. (1970). *The beginnings of modern American psychiatry: The ideas of Harry Stack Sullivan*. Boston: Houghton Mifflin.

Murphy, S. L., & Khantzian, E. J. (1996). Addiction as a "self-medication" disorder: Application of ego psychology to the treatment of substance abuse. In A. M. Washton (Ed.), *Psychotherapy and substance abuse: A practitioner's handbook* (pp. 161–175). New York: Guilford.

Murray, T. L., Daniels, M. H., & Murray, C. E. (2006). Differentiation of self, perceived stress, and symptoms severity among patients with fibromyalgia syndrome. *Families, Systems, & Health*, *24*(2), 147–159.

Myer, R. A. (2001). *Assessment for crisis intervention: A triage assessment model*. Belmont, CA: Wadsworth.

Myer, R. A., Williams, R. C., Ottens, A. J., & Schmidt, A. E. (1992). Crisis assessment: A three-dimensional model for triage. *Journal of Mental Health Counseling*, *14*, 137–148.

Myers, L. L., & Thyer, B. A. (1997). Should social work clients have the right to effective treatment? *Social Work*, *42*(3), 288–298.

Nagata, D. K. (1991). Transgenerational impact of Japanese-American internment: Clinical issues in working with children of former internees. *Psychotherapy: Theory, Research, Practice, Training*, *28*(1), 121–128.

National Association of Social Workers (1996). *Code of Ethics*. Washington, DC: Author.

Nelson, C. A. (2000). The neurobiological basis of early intervention. In J. P. Shonkoff & S. J. Meisels (Eds.), *Handbook of early childhood intervention* (2nd ed.) (pp. 204–227). New York: Cambridge University Press.

Nelson, C. A. (1999). How important are the first three years of life? *Applied Developmental Science*, *3*(4), 235–238.

Nelson, C. A., & Carver, L. J. (1998). The effects of stress and trauma on brain and memory: A view from developmental cognitive neuroscience. *Development & Psychopathology*, *10*(4), 793–809.

Nelson, T. S., & Kelley, L. (2001). Solution-focused couples group. *Journal of Systemic Therapies*, *20*(4), 47–66.

Nichols, M. P. (2009). *The essentials of family therapy* (4th ed.). Boston: Allyn and Bacon.

Nichols, M. P., & Schwartz, R. C. (2007). *Family therapy: Concepts and methods* (5th ed.). Boston: Allyn & Bacon.

Nichols, M. P., & Schwartz, R. C. (2001). *Family therapy: Concepts and methods* (5th ed.). Boston: Allyn & Bacon.

Nims, D. R. (1998). Searching for self: A theoretical model for applying family systems to adolescent group work. *Journal for Specialists in Group Work*, *23*(2), 133–144.

Nolan, P. (1994). Therapeutic response in improvisational music therapy: What goes on inside? *Music Therapy Perspectives, 12*(2), 84–91.

Nugent, W. R. (1987). Use and evaluation of theories. *Social Work Research and Abstracts, 23,* 14–19.

O'Connell, B. (1998). *Solution-focused therapy.* Thousand Oaks, CA: Sage.

O'Connor, M. K. (2002). Using qualitative research in practice evaluation. In A. R. Roberts & G. J. Greene (Eds.), *Social workers' desk reference* (pp. 777–781). New York: Oxford University Press.

O'Hanlon, W. H., & Weiner-Davis, M. (1989). *In search of solutions: A new direction in psychotherapy.* New York: Norton.

Ornduff, S. R. (1997). TAT assessment of assessment of object relations: Implications for child abuse. *Bulletin of the Menninger Clinic, 61*(1), 1–15.

Oxman, T. E., Barrett, J. F., Sengupta, A., Katon, W., Williams, J. W., Frank, E., et al. (2001). Status of minor depression or dysthymia in primary care following a randomized controlled treatment. *General Hospital Psychiatry, 23*(6), 301–310.

Pallesen, S., Nordhux, I. H., & Kvale, G. (1999). Nonpharmacological interventions for insomnia in older adults: A meta-analysis of treatment efficacy. *Psychotherapy: Theory, Research, Practice, Training, 35*(4), 472–482.

Parad, H. J. (Ed.) (1965). *Crisis intervention: Selected readings.* New York: Family Services Association of America.

Parsons, R. J. (1991). Empowerment: Purpose and practice principles in social work. *Social Work with Groups, 14*(2), 7–21.

Parsons, T. (1977). On building social system theory: A personal history. In T. Parsons (Ed.), *Social systems and the evolution of action theory.* New York: Free Press.

Pavlov, I. P. (1927). *Conditioned reflexes.* London: Oxford.

Payne, M. (2005). *Modern social work theory* (3rd ed.). Chicago: Lyceum.

Pedersen, P. (1987). Ten frequent assumptions of cultural bias in counseling. *Journal of Multicultural Counseling and Development, 15,* 16–24.

Perkins, R. (2006). The effectiveness of one session of therapy using a single-session therapy approach for children and adolescents with mental health problems. *Psychology and Psychotherapy: Theory, Research, and Practice, 79*(2), 215–227.

Perlman, H. H. (1979). *Relationship: The heart of helping people.* Chicago: University of Chicago Press.

Perris, C. (1992). Integrating psychotherapeutic strategies in the treatment of young severely disturbed patients. *Journal of Cognitive Psychotherapy, 6*(3), 205–219.

Persson, L-G., & Hjalmarson, A. (2006). Smoking cessation in patients with diabetes mellitus: Results from a controlled study of an intervention programme in primary healthcare in Sweden. *Scandanavian Journal of Primary Health Care, 24*(2), 75–80.

Peterson, P. L., Baer, J. S., Wells, E. A., Ginzler, J. A., & Garett, S. B. (2006). Short-term effects of a brief motivational intervention to reduce alcohol and drug risk among homeless youth. *Bulletin of the Society of Psychologists in Addictive Behaviors, 20*(3), 254–264.

Pham, M. (2006). Differentiation and life change events in a chemical dependent population. *Dissertation Abstracts International, Section B: The Sciences and Engineering, 67*(4-B), 2237.

Piaget, J. (1977). *The development of thought: Equilibration of cognitive structures.* New York: Viking Press.

Pionek-Stone, B., Kratochwill, T. R., Sladezcek, I., & Serlin, R. C. (2002).

Treatment of selective mutism: A best-evidence synthesis. *School Psychology Quarterly, 17*(2), 168–190.

Piper, W. E., McCallum, M., Joyce, A. S., Azim, H. F., & Ogrodniczuk, J. S. (1999). Follow-up findings for interpretive and supportive forms of psychotherapy and patient personality variables. *Journal of Counseling and Clinical Psychology, 67*(2), 267–273.

Polansky, N. A. (1986). "There is nothing so practical as a good theory." *Child Welfare, 65*, 3–15.

Pollard, J., Hawkins, D., Arthur, M. (1999). Risk and protection: Are both necessary to understand diverse behavioral outcomes in adolescence? *Social Work Research, 23*, 145–158.

Pomeroy, E. C., Green, D. L., & Van Lanningham, L. (2002). Couples who care: The effectiveness of a psychoeducational group intervention for HIV seriodiscordant couples. *Research on Social Work Practice, 12*(2), 238–252.

Popper, K. R. (1968). *Conjectures and refutations: The growth of scientific knowledge.* New York: Harper and Row.

Prazeres, A. M., de Souza, W. F., & Fontenelle, L. F. (2007). Cognitive-behavior therapy for obsessive-compulsive disorder: A systematic review of the 1st decade. *Revista Brasilieria de Psiquiaatria, 29*(3).

Prest, L. A., Benson, M. J., & Protinsky, H. O. (1998). Family of origin and current relationship influences on codependency. *Family Process, 37*(4), 513–528.

Prochaska, J., & Norcross, J. (1994). *Systems of psychotherapy: A transtheoretical analysis* (3rd ed.). Pacific Grove, CA: Brooks/Cole.

Procidano, M., & Heller, K. (1983). Measures of perceived social support from friends and family: Three validation studies. *American Journal of Community Psychology, 11*, 1–24.

Project MATCH Research Group. (1998). Matching alcoholism treatments to client heterogeneity: Project MATCH three-year drinking outcomes. *Alcoholism: Clinical & Experimental Research, 22*, 1300–1311.

Project MATCH Research Group. (1997). Matching alcoholism treatments to client heterogeneity: Project MATCH posttreatment drinking outcomes. *Journal of Studies on Alcohol, 58*, 7–29.

Racite, J. A. (2001). Marital satisfaction and level of differentiation in distressed and non-distressed couples. *Dissertation Abstracts International, Section A: Humanities and Social Sciences, 62*(2-A), 792.

Radochonski, M. (1998). Family therapy following loss of sight in an adult member. *Polish Psychological Bulletin, 19*(2), 167–171.

Redondo, S., Sanchez-Meca, J., & Garrido, V. (1999). The influence of treatment programmes on the recidivism of juvenile and adult offenders: A European meta-analytic review. *Psychology, Crime, and Law, 5*(3), 251–278.

Reid, W. J., & Hanrahan, P. (1982). Recent evaluations of social work: Grounds for optimism. *Social Work, 27*(4), 328–340.

Reid, W. J., & Epstein, L. (Eds.). (1977). *Task-centered practice.* New York: Columbia University Press.

Reimer, W. L., & Chatwin, A. (2006). Effectiveness of solution focused therapy for affective and relationship problems in a private practice context. *Journal of Systemic Therapies, 25*(1), 52–67.

Reisch, M. (2000). Social policy and the great society. In J. Midgley, M. B. Tracy, & M. Livermore (Eds.), *The handbook of social policy* (pp. 127–142). Thousand Oaks, CA: Sage.

Reuterlov, H., Lofgren, T., Nordstrom, K., Ternston, A., & Miller, S. D. (2000). What is better? A preliminary investigation of between-session change. *Journal of Systemic Therapies, 19*(1), 111–115.

Reynolds, B. C. (1963). *An uncharted journey*. New York: The Citadel Press.

Richert, A. J. (2003). Living stories, telling stories, changing stories: Experiential use of the relationship in narrative therapy. *Journal of Psychotherapy Integration, 13*(2), 188–210.

Richey, C. A. (1994). Social support skill training. In D. K. Granvold (Ed.), *Cognitive and behavioral treatment: Methods and applications* (pp. 299–338). Pacific Grove, CA: Brooks/Cole.

Richman, J. M., Rosenfeld, L. B., & Hardy, C. J. (1993). The social support survey: A validation study of a clinical measure of the social support process. *Research on Social Work Practice, 3*(3), 288–311.

Richmond, M. (1917). *Social diagnosis*. New York: Sage.

Rigazio-Digilio, S., Ivey, A. I., Grady, L. T., & Kunkler-Peck, K. P. (2005). *Community genograms: Using individual, family, and cultural narratives with clients*. New York: Teachers College Press.

Ritzer, G. (2000). *Modern sociological theory* (5th ed.). Boston: McGraw-Hill.

Robb, M., & Cameron, P. M. (1998). Supervision of termination in psychotherapy. *Canadian Journal of Psychiatry, 43*(4), 397–402.

Roberts, A. R. (2000). An overview of crisis theory and crisis intervention. In A. R. Roberts (Ed.), *Crisis intervention handbook: Assessment, treatment, and research* (2nd ed.) (pp. 3–30). New York: Oxford.

Roberts, N. H. D. (2003). Bowen family systems theory and its place in counseling psychology. *Dissertation Abstracts International, 63*(12-B), 6105.

Robins, C. J. (2002). Dialectical behavior therapy for borderline personality disorder. *Psychiatric Annals, 32*(10), 608–616.

Rodwell, M. K. (1998). *Social work constructivist research*. New York: Garland.

Rogers, G., & McDonald, L. (1993). Thinking critically: An approach to field instructor training. *Journal of Social Work Education, 28*(2), 166–176.

Romanucci-Ross, L., De Vos, G. A., & Tsuda, T. (2006). *Ethnic identity: Problems and prospects for the twenty-first century* (4th ed.). Lanham, MD: Alta Mira Press.

Rooney, R. H. (1992). *Strategies for work with involuntary clients*. New York: Columbia University.

Rosario, H. L. (1998). The descriptive quality of object representation and idealization in a clinical Puerto Rican sample. *Dissertation Abstracts International, 59*(8-A), 3212.

Rose, S., Bisson, J., Churchill, R., & Wessely, S. (2002). Psychological debriefing for preventing post traumatic stress disorder (PTSD). *Cochrane Database of Systematic Reviews, 2*, Art. No.: CD000560.

Rose, S. M. (1990). Advocacy/empowerment: An approach to clinical practice for social work. *Journal of Sociology and Social Welfare, 17*(2), 41–51.

Rosen, A., & Proctor, E. K. (2002). Standards for evidence-based social work practice: The role of replicable and appropriate interventions, outcomes, and practice guidelines. In A. R. Roberts & G. J. Greene (Eds.), *Social workers' desk reference* (pp. 743–747). New York: Oxford.

Rosenthal, R. N. (2004). Overview of evidence-based practice. In A. R. Roberts & K. R. Yeager (Eds.), *Evidence based practice manual: Research and outcome measures in health and human services* (pp. 20–28). New York: Oxford University Press.

Rubin, A. (1992). Case management. In S. M. Rose (Ed.), *Case management and social work practice* (pp. 5–24). New York: Longman.

Ruttenberg, B. A. (1990). A historical perspective on the treatment of neurotic children. In M. H. Etezady (Ed.), *The neurotic child and adolescent* (pp. 349–378). Northvale, NJ: Jason Aronson.

Sadock, B. J., & Sadock, V. A. (2003). *Kaplan and Sadock's synopsis of psychiatry: Behavioral sciences/clinical psychiatry* (9th ed.). Philadelphia: Lippincott Williams & Wilkins.

Safran, J., & McMain, S. (1992). A cognitive interpersonal approach to the treatment of personality disorders. *Journal of Cognitive Psychotherapy, 6*(1), 59–68.

Saleebey, D. (Ed.) (2002). *The strengths perspective in social work practice* (3rd ed.). White Plains, NY: Longman.

Saleebey, D. (Ed.) (1997). *The strengths perspective in social work practice*. White Plains, NY: Longman.

Saleebey, D. (1996). The strengths perspective in social work practice: Extensions and cautions. *Social Work, 41*(3), 296–305.

Sands, R. G. (1984). Crisis intervention and social work practice in hospitals. *Health and Social Work, 8*(4), 253–261.

Santa Ana, E. J., Wulfert, E., & Nietert, P. J. (2007). Efficacy of group motivational interviewing (GMI) for psychiatric inpatients with chemical dependence. *Journal of Consulting and Clinical Psychology, 75*(5), 816–822.

Santisteban, D. A., Coatsworth, J. D., Perez-Vidal, A., Mitrani, V., Jean-Gilles, M., & Szapocznik, J. (1997). Brief structural/strategic family therapy with African American and Hispanic high-risk youth. *Journal of Community Psychology, 25*(5), 453–471.

Santor, D. A., & Kusumakar, V. (2001). Open trial of interpersonal therapy in adolescents with moderate to severe major depression: Effectiveness of novice IPT therapists. *Journal of the American Academy of Child and Adolescent Psychiatry, 40*(2), 236–240.

Sartre, J. P. (1956). *Being and nothingness.* New York: Philosophical Library.

Satir, V. (1964). Conjoint family therapy. Palo Alto, CA: Science and Behaviour Books, Inc.

Sawin, K. J., & Harrigan, M. P. (1995). *Measures of family functioning for research and practice.* New York: Springer.

Scaturo, D. J., Hayes, T., Sagula, D., & Walter, T. (2000). The concept of codependency and its context within family systems theory. *Family Therapy, 27*(2), 63–70.

Schammes, G. (1996). Ego psychology. In J. Berzoff, L. M. Flanagan, & P. Hertz (Eds.), *Inside out and outside in: Psychodynamic clinical theory and practice in contemporary multicultural contexts* (pp. 67–101). Northvale, NJ: Jason Aronson.

Schermer, V. L., & Klein, R. H. (1996). Termination in group psychotherapy from the perspectives of contemporary object relations theory and self psychology. *International Journal of Group Psychotherapy, 46*(1), 99–115.

Schneider, E. L. (1990). The effect of brief psychotherapy on the level of the patient's object relations. *Dissertation Abstracts International, 51*(4-A), 1391.

Schoenwolf, G. (1993). *Counterresistance: The therapist's interference with the therapeutic process.* Northvale, NJ: Jason Aronson.

Schwalbe, C. S., Fraser, M. W., & Day, S. H. (2004). North Carolina Assessment of Risk (NCAR): Reliability and predictive validity with juvenile offenders. *Journal of Offender Rehabilitation, 40*(1-2), 1–22.

Scocco, P., & Frank, E. (2002). Interpersonal psychotherapy (IPT) as augmentation treatment in depressed elderly responding poorly to antidepressant drugs: A case series. *Psycho-therapy and Psychosomatics, 71* (6), 357–361.

Seagram, B. M. C. (1998). The efficacy of solution-focused therapy with young offenders. *Dissertation Abstracts International, 58*(10-B), 5656.

Selekman, M. D. (1993). *Pathways to change: Brief therapy solutions with difficult adolescents.* New York: Guilford.

Serkeitch, W. J., & Dumas, J. E. (1996). The effectiveness of behavioral parent training to modify antisocial behavior in children: A meta-analysis. *Behavior Therapy, 27*(2), 171–186.

Sexton, T. L., & Whiston, S. C. (1994). The status of the counseling relationship: An empirical review, theoretical implications, and research directions. *The Counseling Psychologist, 22*(1), 6–78.

Seyle, H. (1991). History and present status of the stress concept. In A. Monat & R. S. Lazarus (Eds.), *Stress and coping: An anthology* (3rd ed.) (pp. 21–35). New York: Columbia University Press.

Seymour, F. W., & Epston, D. E. (1989). An approach to childhood stealing with evaluation of 45 cases. *Australian and New Zealand Journal of Family Therapy, 10*(3), 137–143.

Shadish, W. R., & Baldwin, S. A. (2005). Effects of behavioral marital therapy: A meta-analysis of randomized controlled trials. *Journal of Counseling and Clinical Psychology, 73*(1), 6–14.

Shapiro, D. A., Rees, A., Barkham, M., & Hardy, G. (1995). Effects of treatment duration and severity of depression on the maintenance of gains after cognitive-behavioral and psychodynamic-interpersonal psychotherapy. *Journal of Consulting & Clinical Psychology, 63*(3), 378–387.

Sharman, J. M. (1998). A brief narrative approach to the treatment of depression in the elderly. *Dissertation Abstracts International, 58*(8-B), 4472.

Shaw, C. M., Margison, F. R., Guthrie, E. A., & Tomenson, B. (2001). Psychodynamic interpersonal therapy by inexperienced therapists in a naturalistic setting: A pilot study. *European Journal of Psychotherapy, Counseling & Health, 4*(1), 87–101.

Sheridan, M. J., & Bullis, R. K. (1991). Practitioners' views on religion and spirituality: A qualitative study. *Spirituality and Social Work Journal, 2,* 2–10.

Sheridan, M. J., Bullis, R. K., Adcock, C. R., Berlin, S. D., & Miller, P. C. (1992). Practitioners' personal and professional attitudes and behaviors toward religion and spirituality: Issues for education and practice. *Journal of Social Work Education, 28,* 190–203.

Shorey, H. S., & Snyder, C. R. (2006). The role of adult attachment styles in psychopathology and psychotherapy outcomes. *Review of General Psychology, 10*(1), 1–20.

Siev, J., & Chambless, D. L. (2007). Specificity of treatment effects: Cognitive therapy and relaxation for generalized anxiety and panic disorders. *Journal of Consulting and Clinical Psychology, 75*(4), 513–522.

Skinner, B. F. (1953). *Science and human behavior.* New York: Macmillan.

Skowron, E. A. (2005). Differentiation of self and child abuse potential in young adulthood. *The Family Journal, 13*(3), 281–290.

Skowron, E. A. (2004). Differentiation of self, personal adjustment, problem solving, and ethnic group belonging among persons of color. *Journal of Counseling & Development, 82*(4), 447–456.

Smith, F. (1990). *To think.* New York: Teachers College Press.

Smith, M. T., Perlis, M. L., Park, A., Smith, M. S., Pennington, J., Giles, D. E., & Buysse, D. J. (2002). Comparative meta-analysis of pharmacotherapy and behavior therapy for persistent insomnia. *American Journal of Psychiatry, 159*(1), 5–10.

Smokowski, P. R., Mann, E. A., Reynolds, A. J., Fraser, M. W. (2004) Childhood risk and protective factors and late adolescent adjustment in inner city minority youth. *Children and Youth Services Review, 26*(1).

Spaulding, E. C. (1999). Unconsciousness-raising: Hidden dimensions of heterosexism in theory and practice with lesbians. In J. Laird (Ed.), *Lesbians and lesbian families* (pp. 11–25). New York: Columbia University Press.

Specht, H., & Courtney, M. (1994). *Unfaithful angels: How social work has abandoned its mission.* New York: Free Press.

Spiegler, M. (1993). *Contemporary behavior therapy* (2nd ed.). Pacific Grove, CA: Brooks/Cole.

Spitalnick, J. S. & McNair, L. D. (2005). Couples therapy with gay and lesbian clients: An analysis of important clinical issues [Electronic version]. *Journal of Sex and Marital Therapy, 31,* 43–56.

Stanton, M., & Todd, T. (1979). Structural family therapy with drug addicts. In E. Kaufman & P. Kaufman (Eds.), *The family therapy of drug and alcohol abuse.* New York: Gardner.

St. Clair, M. (1999). *Object relations and self-psychology: An introduction* (3rd ed.). Pacific Grove, CA: Brooks/Cole.

Steelman, L. C., Powell, B., Werum, R., & Carter, S. (2002). Reconsidering the effects of sibling configuration: Recent advances and challenges. *Annual Review of Sociology, 28,* 243–269.

Steinberg, M. L., Ziedonis, D. M., Krejci, J. A. & Brandon, T. H. (2004). Motivational interviewing with personalized feedback: A brief intervention for motivating smokers with schizophrenia to seek treatment for tobacco dependence. *Journal of Consulting and Clinical Psychology, 72*(4), 723–728.

Stith, S. M., McCollum, E. E., Rosen, K. H., & Locke, L. D. (2003). Multicouple group therapy for domestic violence. In F. W. Kaslow (Ed.), *Comprehensive handbook of psychiatry: Integrative/eclectic,* Volume 4 (pp. 499–520). New York: Wiley.

Strasser, F., & Strasser, A. (1997). *Existential time-limited therapy: The wheel of experience.* New York: Wiley.

Stuart, S. P. (1999). Interpersonal psychotherapy for postpartum depression. In L. J. Miller (Ed.), *Postpartum mood disorders* (pp. 143–162). Washington, DC: American Psychiatric Association.

Stuart, S. P., & O'Hara, M. W. (1995). Treatment of postpartum depression with interpersonal psychotherapy. *Archives of General Psychiatry, 52,* 75–76.

Stuart, S. P., & Robertson, M. (2002). *Interpersonal psychotherapy: A clinician's guide.* London: Edward Arnold, Ltd.

Sullivan, H. S. (1962). *Schizophrenia as a human process.* New York: W. W. Norton.

Suomi, S. J. (2005). Mother-infant attachment, peer relationships, and the development of social networks in rhesus monkeys. *Human Development, 48*(1-2), 67–79.

Swainson, M. & Tasker, F. (2006). Genograms redrawn: lesbian couples define their families. In J. J. Bigner (Ed.), *An Introduction to GLBT Family Studies* (pp. 89–115). New York: Haworth Press.

Szapocznik, J., Arturo, M. E., & Cohen, R. (1989). Structural versus psychodynamic child therapy for problematic Hispanic boys. *Journal of Consulting and Clinical Psychology, 57*(5), 571–578.

Takahashi, T., Lipson, G., & Chazdon, L. (1999). Supportive-expressive group psychotherapy with chronic mental illness, including psychosis. In V. L. Schermer & M. Pines (Eds.), *Group psychotherapy of the psychoses: Concepts, interventions and contexts.* International Library of Group Analysis 2.

Tasca, G., Balfour, L., Ritchie, K., & Bissada, H. (2007). Change in attachment anxiety is associated with improved depression among women with binge eating disorder. *Psychotherapy: Theory, Research, and Practice, 44*(4), 423–433.

Tatrow, K., & Montgomery, G. H. (2006). Cognitive-behavioral therapy techniques for distress and pain in breast cancer patients: A meta-analysis. *Journal of Behavioral Medicine, 29*(1), 17–27.

Taylor, C. (1972). Psychological behaviorism. In P. Edwards (Ed.), *The encyclopedia of philosophy,* Volume 6 (pp. 516–520). New York: Macmillan.

Taylor, S. (1996). Meta-analysis of cognitive-behavioral treatment for social phobia. *Journal of Behavior Therapy and Experimental Psychiatry, 27*(1), 1–9.

Thase, M. E., Buysse, D. J., Frank, E., & Cherry, C. R. (1997). Which depressed patients will respond to interpersonal psychotherapy? The role of abnormal EEG sleep profiles. *American Journal of Psychiatry, 154*(4), 502–509.

Thomas, E. J. (Ed.) (1974). *Behavior modification procedure: A sourcebook.* New Brunswick, NJ: Aldine Transaction.

Thomas, E. J. (1968). Selected sociobehavioral techniques and principles: An approach to interpersonal helping. *Social Work, 13*(1), 12–26.

Thomlinson, R. J. (1984). Something works: Evidence from practice effectiveness studies. *Social Work, 29,* 51–57.

Thorndike, E. L. (1911). *Animal intelligence: Experimental studies.* New York: Hafner.

Thyer, B. A., & Bursinger, P. (1994). Treatment of clients with anxiety disorders. In D. K. Granvold (Ed.), *Cognitive and behavioral treatment: Methods and applications* (pp. 272–284). Pacific Grove, CA: Brooks/Cole.

Thyer, B. A., Wodarski, J. S. (Eds.) (2007) *Social work in mental health: An evidence-based approach.* Hoboken, NJ: Wiley.

Thyer, B. A., & Wodarski, J. S. (Eds.) (1998). *Handbook of empirical social work practice. Volume 1: Mental disorders.* New York: Wiley.

Timmer, S. G., & Veroff, J. (2000). Family ties and the discontinuity of divorce in Black and White newlywed couples. *Journal of Marriage and the Family, 62*(2), 349–361.

Tisdale, T. C., Key, T. L., Edwards, K. J., & Brokaw, B. F. (1997). Impact of treatment on God image and personal adjustment, and correlations of God image to personal adjustment and object relations development. *Journal of Psychology and Theology, 25*(2), 227–239.

Titelman, P. (Ed.) (1998). *Clinical applications of Bowen family systems theory.* New York: Haworth.

Tolman, E. (1948). Cognitive maps in rats and man. *Psychological Review,* 189–208.

Tong, R. T. (1998). *Feminist thought* (2nd ed.). Boulder, CO: Westview Press.

Treasure, J., Katzman, M., Schmidt, U., Troop, N., Todd, G., & de Silva, P. (1999). Engagement and outcome in the treatment of bulimia nervosa: First phase of a sequential design comparing motivation enhancement therapy and cognitive behavioral therapy. *Behaviour Research and Therapy, 37,* 405–418.

Treasure, J., & Ward, W. (1997). A practical guide to the use of motivational interviewing in anorexia nervosa.

European Eating Disorders Review, 5, 102–114.

Tuber, S. (1992). Empirical and clinical assessments of children's object relations and object representations. *Journal of Personality Assessment, 58*(1), 179–197.

Turchiano, T. P. (2000). A meta-analysis of behavioral and cognitive therapies for children and adolescents with attention deficit hyperactivity and/or impulsivity disorders. *Dissertation Abstracts International, 60*(11-B), 5760.

Turner, F. J. (Ed.) (1996). *Social work treatment* (4th ed.). New York: Free Press.

Tzeng, O. C. S., & Jackson, J. W. (1991). Common methodological framework for theory construction and evaluation in the social and behavioral sciences. *Genetic, Social, and General Psychology Monographs, 117*(1), 49–76.

Uhinki, A. (2001). Experiences of therapeutic assessment with couples. *Journal of Projective Psychology & Mental Health, 8*(1), 15–18.

Updegraff, K. A., Madden-Derdich, D. A., Estrada, A. U., Sales, L. J., & Leonard, S. A. (2002). Young adolescents' experiences with parents and friends: Exploring the connections. *Family Relations, 51*(1), 72–80.

U. S. Department of Health and Human Services (2001). *Culture, race, and ethnicity: A supplement to mental health: A report of the surgeon general.* Retrieved 2007, from http://www.surgeongeneral.gov/library/mentalhealth.cre/.

Vaillant, G. E. (1992). *Ego mechanisms of defense: A guide for clinicians and researchers.* Washington, DC: American Psychiatric Association.

Vandiver, V. L. (2002). Step-by-step practice guidelines for using evidence-based practice and expert consensus in mental health settings. In A. R. Roberts & G. J. Greene (Eds.), *Social workers' desk reference* (pp. 731–738). New York: Oxford University Press.

van Minnen, A., Wessel, I., Dijkstra, T., & Roelofs, K. (2002). Changes in PTSD patients' narratives during prolonged exposure therapy: A replication and extension. *Journal of Traumatic Stress, 15*(3), 255–258.

Vaux, A. (1990). An ecological approach to understanding and facilitating social support. *Journal of Social and Personal Relationships, 7,* 507–518.

Vaux, A. (1988). *Social support: Theory, research, and intervention.* New York: Praeger.

Vittengl, J. R., Clark, L. A., & Dunn, T. W. (2007). Reducing relapse and recurrence in unipolar depression: A comparative meta-analysis of cognitive-behavioral therapy's effects. *Journal of Consulting and Clinical Psychology, 75*(3), 475–488.

Von Bertalanffy, L. (1968). *General system theory* (rev. ed.). New York: George Braziller, Inc.

von Held, H. (1987). Supportive group therapy for outpatients with borderline personality disorder. *Praxis der Psychotherapie und Psychosomatik, 30*(5), 236–242.

Von Wyl, A. (2000). What anorexic and bulimic patients have to tell: The analysis of patterns of unconscious conflict expressed in stories about everyday events. *European Journal of Psychotherapy, 3*(3), 375–388.

Wakefield, J. C. (1995). When an irresistible epistemology meets an immovable ontology, *Social Work Research, 19*(1), 9–17.

Walker, M. W. (2007). Differentiation of self and partner violence among individuals in substance abuse treatment. *Dissertation Abstracts International, Section B: The Sciences and Engineering, 67*(12-B), 7393.

Walitzer, K., Dermen, K., & Conners, G. (1999). Strategies for preparing clients for treatment: A review. *Behavior Modification, 23,* 129–151.

Wallerstein, R. S. (2002). The growth and transformation of American ego psychology. *Journal of the American Psychoanalytic Association, 50*(1), 135–169.

Walsh, F. (1998). *Strengthening family resilience*. New York: Guilford Press.

Walsh, F. (Ed.) (2003). *Normal family processes: Growing diversity and complexity*. New York: Guilford.

Walsh, J. (2007). *Endings in clinical practice: Ensuring closure across service settings (2nd ed)*. Chicago: Lyceum.

Walsh, J. E. (2004). Does structural family therapy really chance the family structure? An examination of process variables. *Dissertation Abstracts International: Section B: The Sciences and Engineering, 64*(12-B), 6317.

Walsh, J. (2000). *Clinical case management with persons having mental illness: A relationship-based perspective*. Pacific Grove, CA: Wadsworth-Brooks/Cole.

Walsh, J. (1995). The impact of schizophrenia on the client's religious beliefs: Implications for families. *Families in Society, 76*(9), 551–558.

Walsh, J., & Connelly, P. R. (1996). Supportive behaviors in natural support networks of people with serious mental illness. *Health and Social Work, 21*(4), 296–303.

Walsh, J., & Harrigan, M. P. (2003). The termination stage in Bowen's family systems theory. *Clinical Social Work Journal, 31*(4), 383–394.

Walters, G. D. (2000a). *Beyond behaviorism: Construction of an overarching psychological theory of lifestyles*. Westport, CT: Praeger.

Walters, G. D. (2000b). Behavioral self-control training for problem drinkers: A meta-analysis of randomized control studies. *Behavior Therapy, 31*(1), 135–149.

Watson, J. B. (1924). *Psychology, from the standpoint of a behaviorist*. Philadelphia: J. B. Lippincott.

Weakland, J., & Jordan, L. (1992). Working briefly with reluctant clients: Child protective services as an example. *Journal of Family Therapy, 14*, 231–254.

Webb, S. J., Monk, C. S., & Nelson, C. A. (2001). Mechanisms of postnatal neurobiological development: Implications for human development. *Developmental Neuropsychology, 19*(2), 147.

Webster-Stratton, C. (2001). Incredible years parents and children training series. Available from Incredible Years, Seattle, WA (www.incredibleyears.com).

Weiner, M. L. (1983). Ego activation on the treatment of acutely depressed outpatients. *Journal of the American Academy of Psychoanalysis, 10*(4), 493–513.

Weingarten, K. (1998). The small and the ordinary: The daily practice of post modern narrative therapy. *Family Process, 37*(1), 3–15.

Weissman, M. M. (2006). A brief history of interpersonal psychotherapy. *Psychiatric Annals, 36*(8), 553–557.

Weissman, M. M. (Ed.) (2001). *The treatment of depression: Bridging the 21st century*. Washington, DC: American Psychiatric Press.

Weissman, M. M., Markowitz, J. C., & Klerman, G. L. (2000). *Comprehensive guide to interpersonal psychotherapy*. New York: Basic.

Weissman, M. M., Prusoff, B. A., & DiMascio, A. (1979). The efficacy of drugs and psychotherapy in the treatment of acute depressive episodes. *American Journal of Psychiatry, 136*, 555–558.

Werner, C., & Altman, I. (2000). Humans and nature: Insights from a transactional view. In S. Wapner, J. Demick, T. Yamamoto, & H. Minami (Eds.), *Theoretical perspectives in environment-behavior research: Underlying assumptions, research problems, and methodologies* (pp. 21–37). New York: Kluwer Academic.

Westert, G. P., & Groenewegen, P. P. (1999). Medical practice variations: Changes in the theoretical approach. *Scandinavian Journal of Public Health, 27,* 173–180.

Wetchler, J. L. (2004). A heterosexual therapist's journey toward working with same-sex couples. In J. J. Bigner & J. L. Wetchler (Eds.), *Relationship therapy with same-sex couples* (pp. 137–145). New York: Haworth Press.

Wettersten, K. B., & Lichtenberg, & Mallinckrodt, B. (2005). Associations between working alliance and outcome in Solution-Focused Brief Therapy and interpersonal therapy. *Psychotherapy research, 15*(1-2), 35–43.

Wheeler, J. G., Christensen, A., & Jacobson, N. (2001). Couple distress. In D. Barlow (Ed.), *Clinical handbook of psychological disorders: A step-by-step treatment manual* (3rd ed.). New York: Guilford Press.

White, M., & Epston, D. (1990). *Narrative means to therapeutic ends.* New York: Norton.

White, R. W. (1963). *Ego and reality in psychoanalytic theory: A proposal regarding independent ego entities.* New York: International Universities Press.

Wiener, N. (1948). *Cybernetics.* New York: Wiley.

Wilfley, D. E., Agras, W. S., Telch, C. F., Rossiter, E. M., Schneider, J. A., Cole, A. G., Sifford, L., & Raeburn, S. D. (1993). Group cognitive-behavioral therapy and group interpersonal psychotherapy for the nonpurging bulimic individual: A controlled comparison. *Journal of Consulting and Clinical Psychology, 61,* 296–305.

Wilfley, D. E., Mackenzie, K. R., Welch, R., Ayres, V., & Weissman, M. M. (Eds.) (2000). *Interpersonal psychotherapy for groups.* New York: Basic.

Williams, N. R., & Kurtz, P. D. (2003). Narrative family interventions. In A. C. Kilpatrick & T. P. Holland (Eds.), *Working with families: An integrative model by level of need* (pp. 174–195). Boston: Allyn & Bacon.

Wilson, G. T. (2000). Behavior therapy. In R. J. Corsini & D. Wedding (Eds.), *Current psychotherapies* (6th ed.) (pp. 205–240). Itasca, IL: F. E. Peacock.

Winnicott, D. W. (1975). *Collected papers: From paediatrics to psycho-analysis.* New York: Basic.

Witkin, S., & Gottschalk, S. (1988). Alternative criteria for theory evaluation. *Social Service Review, 62,* 211–214.

Wodarski, J. S., & Bagarozzi, D. A. (1979). *Behavioral social work.* New York: Human Sciences Press.

Wolpe, J. (1958). *Psychotherapy by reciprocal inhibition.* Palo Alto, CA: Stanford University Press.

Wood, S. A. (2000). Object relations, alexithymia, symptoms of psychological distress, and methadone treatment outcomes. *Dissertation Abstracts International, 61*(5-A), 2043.

Woods, M. E., and Hollis, F. H. (2000). *Casework: A psychosocial therapy* (5th ed.). New York: McGraw-Hill.

Wyche, K. F. (1999). Interpreting the life narrative: Race, class, gender, and historical context. *Psychology of Women Quarterly, 23*(2), 323–326.

Yalom, I. D. (1980). *Existential psychotherapy.* New York: Basic Books.

Yeager, K. R., & Gregoire, T. K. (2000). Crisis intervention application of brief solution-focused therapy in addictions. In A. R. Roberts (Ed.), *Crisis intervention handbook: Assessment, treatment, and research* (2nd ed.) (pp. 275–306). New York: Oxford.

Zeigler-Driscoll, G. (1979). The similarities in families of drug dependents and alcoholics. In E. Kaufman &

P. Kaufman (Eds.) *The family therapy of drug and alcohol abuse*. New York: Gardner.

Zimmerman, M. A. (2000). Empowerment theory: Psychological, organizational, and community levels of analysis. In J. Rappaport & E. Seidman (Eds.), *Handbook of community psychology* (pp. 43–65). New York: Kluwer Academic/Plenum.

Zimmerman, M. A., Israel, B. A., Schulz, A., & Checkoway, B. (1992). Further explorations in empowerment theory: An empirical analysis of psychological empowerment. *American Journal of Community Psychology*, *20*(6), 707–727.

Zimmerman, T. S., Jacobsen, R. B., MacIntyre, M., & Watson, C. (1996). Solution-focused parenting groups: An empirical study. *Journal of Systemic Therapies*, *15*(4), 12–25.

Zimmerman, T. S., Prest, L. A., & Wetzel, B. E. (1997). Solution-focused couples therapy groups: An empirical study. *Journal of Family Therapy*, *19*(2), 125–144.

Zlotnick, C., Johnson, S. L., Miller, I. W., Pearlstein, T., & Howard, M. (2001). Postpartum depression in women receiving public assistance: Pilot study of an interpersonal-therapy-oriented group intervention. *American Journal of Psychiatry*, *158*(4), 638–640.

Author Index

A

Abbott, A., 178
Abelson, J., 142
Abikoff, H. B., 141
Ackerson, B. J., 27
Ackloo, E., 323
Adams, C. E., 323
Adams, J. F., 247
Adams, R., 24, 27
Adcock, C. R., 29
Addams, J., 34
Adler, A., 92
Agostinelli, G., 257
Agras, W. S., 194, 195
Ainsworth, M. S., 65
Akhtar, S., 56
Albarracín, D., 142
Aldwin, C. M., 304, 306
Aleman, A., 170
Allen, C., 256, 257, 258
Allen-Meares, P., 143
Altman, I., 21
Aman, L. A., 223
American Psychiatric Association, 75, 304
Anastopoulos, A. D., 223
Anderson, H., 275
Anderson, S., 95
Andreae, D., 231
Andrew, G., 294
Angel, E., 274
Angus, L., 295
Aponte, H. J., 200, 201, 216

Apple, R. F., 194
Applegate, J. S., 86
Appleyard, K., 22
Arean, P. A., 193
Arkowitz, H., 267, 268
Armstrong, M. I., 324
Arnow, B., 195
Arthur, M., 22
Arturo, M. E., 224
Asimakopoulou, K., 268
Avis, J. M., 86
Avnir, Y., 117
Ayres, V., 177
Azim, H. F., 84

B

Bacaltchuk, J., 193
Badger, G. J., 142
Bagarozzi, D. A., 126, 130, 134–135
Baker, A., 267
Baker, L., 223
Baker, M., 13, 14
Baldwin, S. A., 142
Balfour, L., 177, 194
Bandura, A., 125, 128, 147
Banyard, V. L., 306
Bara, B. G., 149
Barber, J. P., 182, 294
Barge, C. T., 215
Barkham, M., 182, 194
Barkley, R. A., 136, 223
Barlow, C. A., 211

Subject Index

Epstein, Seymour, 149–150
Epston, David, 277
Equilibrium pattern in crises, 305
Evidence-based practice, 12–14
Executive authority, 202
Exhaustion stage, 306
Existential crises, 305
Existentialism, 274–275
Exploration intervention, 45
Exposure therapy, 127, 138
External boundaries, 202–203
External interactions, 215
External systems influences on families,
      208–209
Externalization of problem, 236–237,
      282, 283
Externalization of thinking, 102
Extinction, 136–137
Eysenck, Hans, 125

F

Facilitative environment, 72
Fading, 133
False self, 68
Families. *See also* Family emotional systems
      theory; Structural family theory
   aspects, 208–209
   cognitive therapy, 167–168
   crisis intervention, 317–318, 324
   narrative therapy, 293
   solution-focused therapy, 247
   stages, 108, 208, 210
Families of the Slums, 200–201
Family Adaptability and Cohesion
      Scale, 103
Family Assessment Device (FAD), 215
Family emotional systems theory
   assessment, 99–104
   case illustrations, 105–116
   criticisms of, 118
   effectiveness evidence, 116–118
   intervention, 99–104
   major concepts, 94–98
   nature of problems and change, 98–99
   origins and social context, 92–93
   overview, 90–91, 118–119, 120–122
   social justice issues, 104–105
   solution-focused therapy and, 231
   spirituality and, 104
Feedback principle, 93

Feminism, 68–69, 95, 296, 306
Festinger, Leon, 150
Flexibility, 40, 204, 210
Flooding, 138
Formula first-session task, 238
Freud, Sigmund, 34, 42, 92
Frozen crisis pattern, 305
Functional behavior analysis, 130
Functional school, 35
Functionalism, 92
Fusion, 97–98, 207
Future orientation, 40, 235

G

Gender differences, 118
Gender feminism, 68, 69
General adaptation syndrome, 306
General reality adherence, 40–41
General systems theory, 92, 231. *See also*
      Systems theory/thinking
Genograms, 100–101, 103
Gilligan, Carol, 69
Golan, Naomi, 303
Good-enough mothering, 72
Grand theories, 3
Grief, 183, 185
Group therapy case, 82–83
Growth pattern in crises, 305, 307
Guidance intervention, 46
Guilt, 28–29

H

Hamilton, Gordon, 35
Harm as stress, 304
Hierarchical organizations of personal
      constructs, 149–150
High-probability behaviors, 136
HIV/AIDS, 142, 194, 246, 307–308
Holding environment, 72, 75, 78
Hollis, Florence, 35
Hope, 28
Hospice patients, 287–289
Hull, Clark, 125

I

"I" messages/position, 102, 161
Id, 33
Identity, sense of, 38
Impulse control, 38
Independence, 72, 73–74
Individuation, 73